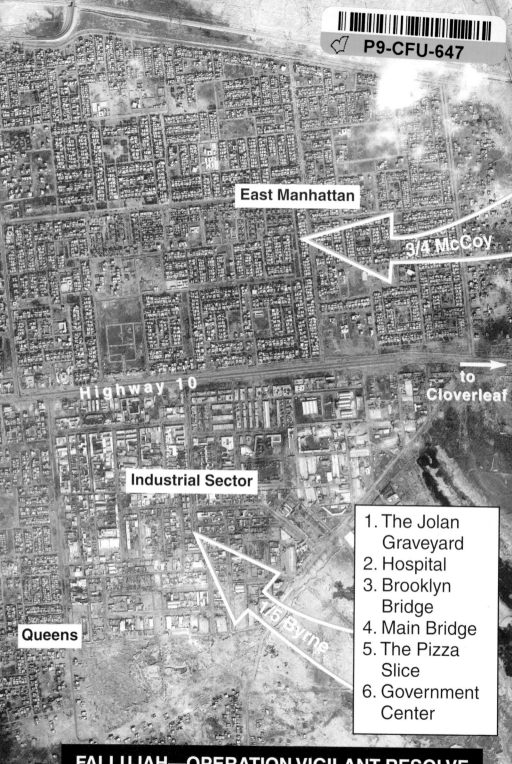

East Manhattan

3/4 McCoy

Highway 10

to **Cloverleaf**

Industrial Sector

1. The Jolan Graveyard
2. Hospital
3. Brooklyn Bridge
4. Main Bridge
5. The Pizza Slice
6. Government Center

1/5 Byrne

Queens

FALLUJAH—OPERATION VIGILANT RESOLVE
(cancelled April 2004 offensive)

Satellite Imagery © DigitalGlobe

NO TRUE GLORY

NO TRUE GLORY

A Frontline Account of the Battle for Fallujah

BING WEST

R A N D O M   H O U S E
LARGE PRINT

The Library of Congress has established a
Cataloging-in-Publication record for this title.

ISBN-13: 978-0-7393-2556-8
ISBN-10: 0-7393-2556-6

www.randomlargeprint.com

FIRST LARGE PRINT EDITION

10 9 8 7 6 5 4 3 2 1

This Large Print edition published in accord
with the standards of the N.A.V.H.

Corporal Daniel Amaya, KIA (Killed In Action)
Corporal Mitch Moorehead,
WIA (Wounded In Action)
Lance Corporal Toby Gray, KIA
Corporal Carlos Perez-Gomez, WIA
Corporal Timothy Connors
Lance Corporal Abraham Simpson, KIA

Corporals are the backbone of the infantry.

Supposing you and I, escaping this battle,
Would be able to live on forever, ageless, immortal,
So neither would I myself go on fighting in the
    foremost
nor would I urge you into the fighting where men
    win glory.
But now, seeing that the spirits of death stand close
    about us
In their thousands, no man can turn aside nor
    escape them,
Let us go on and win glory for ourselves, or yield it
    to others.

HOMER, **The Iliad**

To high officials given glory,
from them much is expected.

CONTENTS

MAJOR CHARACTERS

Abizaid—General (four stars) John P. Abizaid, U.S. Army, commanded CentCom, or Central Command, which included all U.S. forces in Iraq. He reported directly to Secretary of Defense Donald Rumsfeld and spoke directly with President George W. Bush, General Richard Myers, the Chairman of the Joint Chiefs of Staff, and Ambassador Paul Bremer.

Bremer—Ambassador L. Paul Bremer III was the president's envoy to Iraq and director of the Coalition Provisional Authority or CPA. He was responsible for the policies, plans, and budget for the reconstruction of Iraq and its return to sovereignty. Bremer reported to the president through the secretary of defense.

Conway—Lieutenant General (three stars) James T. Conway, USMC, commanded the I MEF or First Marine Expeditionary Force in Iraq. I MEF consisted of an air wing, a logistics command, and a ground command—in this case the 1st Marine Division. Conway reported to Lieutenant General Sanchez, the Joint Task Force commander in Baghdad. Conway also spoke directly with Gen Abizaid. He rarely spoke with Bremer.

Drinkwine—Lieutenant Colonel Brian M. Drinkwine commanded the paratrooper battalion in Fallujah from September through mid-March. He implemented the second extended American strategy for Fallujah.

Janabi—Abdullah Al Janabi was a businessman and a fundamental-ist Sunni cleric who emerged as the central insurgent leader in Fallu-jah. For over a year he also met with American military leaders in Fallujah, including General Mattis.

Sanchez—Lieutenant General (three stars) Ricardo S. Sanchez commanded Joint Task Force 7 (JTF 7) in Baghdad. He directed all American and other Coalition forces in Iraq. Sanchez reported directly to Abizaid.

Suleiman—Lieutenant Colonel Suleiman Al Marawi commanded a poorly trained Iraqi battalion in Fallujah. He was a strong, proud leader who believed Janabi was bringing destruction and death to the city.

Mattis—Major General (two stars) James N. Mattis commanded the twenty-two thousand Marines of the 1st Marine Division. He reported directly to Conway.

Mattis was the ground commander at the April battle for Fallujah. He rarely spoke with Abizaid, Sanchez, or Bremer.

Rumsfeld—Secretary of Defense Donald R. Rumsfeld was responsible for defense policy worldwide and, after approval by the president, for authorizing Gen Abizaid to carry out major operations. Abizaid in turn would authorize Sanchez, who would authorize Conway, who would direct Mattis to take command of the ground battle. Rumsfeld spoke directly with President Bush, Gen Myers, Gen Abizaid, and Ambassador Bremer. He would occasionally talk with Sanchez but rarely with Conway or Mattis.

Toolan—Colonel John Toolan commanded Regimental Combat Team 1, usually numbering four battalions and about six thousand Marines. He was the tactical commander for the April battle of Fallujah and the Marine who met daily with the Iraqis, especially Suleiman. He implemented the third extended American strategy for Fallujah.

Wesley—Lieutenant Colonel Eric Wesley was the executive officer of the 2nd Brigade, 3rd Infantry Division. During the summer of 2003 he assisted in designing and implementing the first extended American strategy for Fallujah.

INTRODUCTION

——

THE OBSCURE, HARDSCRABBLE INDUS-
TRIAL CITY OF Fallujah erupted into the major
battle of the Iraqi insurgency, involving fifteen thousand combatants and claiming 153 American and
thousands of Iraqi lives. Fallujah provides a caution-
ary tale about mixing the combustible ingredients of
battle and politics. This book describes how it came
to do so and why.

The twenty-month struggle for Fallujah had four
phases. The first phase began immediately after
American forces toppled Saddam Hussein from
power in April 2003. That act also toppled the five
million Sunnis who had long dominated the twenty
million Iraqi Shiites and Kurds. In the aftermath
many Sunnis refused to believe they had been
removed from power. These former regime elements
joined forces with radical Islamic fundamentalists to

attack the Americans. Fallujah quickly emerged as a center of the insurgency.

During the summer and fall of 2003, four separate American units in Fallujah applied the classic doctrine for fighting insurgents: namely, they tried to win the hearts and minds of the people who were providing the sea of support in which the insurgents swam. The Americans, though, had little money to spend on economic development; they lacked support from Iraqi leaders; and they responded to attacks with overwhelming firepower, all of which, despite their good intentions, caused resentment.

The second phase began in March 2004, when four American contractors were killed and their bodies mutilated in broad daylight in the heart of the city. The United States Marines were ordered to seize the city, but then, due to international outrage over televised reportage of the assault, were told to stop. For six weeks the Marines engaged in fierce but inconclusive siege warfare.

In the third phase the city was handed over to former Iraqi generals who claimed they could restore order. The Sunnis of Fallujah, the generals explained, were a good people who wanted to be left alone to live under their own leaders. But instead of proclaiming peace, Fallujah promptly began exporting murder. The insurgents who controlled the city ignored the hapless generals, while the arch-terrorist Abu Musab al Zarqawi set up headquarters and dispatched suicide bombers to other cities. Fallujah appeared on nightly news reports to resemble the lair of the monster Grendel, a city of whippings, kidnappings, and beheadings.

In the fourth phase, in the fall of 2004, the Marines were again ordered to seize Fallujah. Hundreds of foreign fighters, drawn to Iraq to fight the infidel invader, awaited them. The Marines—America's shock troops—responded with a full measure of force. The jihadists decided to fight from inside the houses, so once the battle was over, Fallujah's residents returned to a wrecked city.

The extended battle brought to the fore the complex tenacity of the insurgency, the absence of Iraqi leadership, the miscalculations in senior American planning, and the fortitude of the American infantryman.

LYNCHING AT THE BROOKLYN BRIDGE

THE WEDNESDAY-MORNING TRAFFIC IN FALLUJAH was its usual blue-smoke and horn-blaring self. The sidewalks were packed with unemployed men in scruffy **dishdashas** or old work trousers and faded shirts, many smoking and most lounging around, with no money, no job, and no prospects. The assassins drove west down the four-lane highway, cluttered with old cars carelessly double-parked, beeping their horn, waving their AK automatic rifles, and gesturing to other drivers to get out of the way. The truck stopped in the middle of the street, and half a dozen men jumped out, some with **kaffiyehs** wrapped around their faces, others not caring who identified them. One man threw a grenade down the street; the small explosion did not injure anyone but succeeded in driving the onlookers to cover.

"Americans coming!" a man shouted. "Get out of here!"

The gunmen ran to the side of the street and hid in the doorways to the small shops.

————

Around noon **Los Angeles Times** reporter Tony Perry was ambling down the main corridor in the 1st Marine Division headquarters in western Iraq, inquiring about the latest situation reports. The division commander, Major General James N. Mattis—"Mad Dog Mattis" to his grunts—ran a small headquarters staff, all of whom knew one another. It was a slow news day, and Perry was looking for a story.

"There's a garble from a Humvee crew reporting heavy smoke in downtown Fallujah," a lance corporal told him. "Here we go again."

Fallujah lay thirty miles to the east of the division headquarters. Perry didn't want to waste a day pursuing a hunch, so he stepped outside, flipped open his cell phone, and dialed Los Angeles. Maybe the home office had picked up something. An officer walking by overheard Perry describing the situation in Fallujah and called a regiment of Marines stationed a mile outside the city.

"Ed, the lance corporal rumor net has a reporter here spun up about your favorite city," the officer said. "You got anything?"

Fluent in Arabic, Captain Ed Sullivan was the regiment's liaison officer with the city. He had heard nothing. He checked with the operations center next door.

"Is Fallujah acting up again?" he asked.

"Negative. All quiet," the watch officer replied.

Sullivan walked back to his office, where a sergeant at the adjoining desk was pointing at his computer.

"Reuters is running a story that vehicles were hit downtown."

Sullivan went back into the ops center.

"Something's happening. I'll call the mayor and the police chief. Can we get a UAV launched?"

The ops center was showing no Marine vehicles on patrol in the city. An unmanned aerial vehicle could be flying over the city in twenty minutes, quicker than an armored patrol could be assembled and dispatched. Sullivan picked up the phone to reach the mayor.

Back at division headquarters, Perry told the division staff that his L.A. office had confirmed the story on the wire. He immediately asked to go to Fallujah, making a mental note to plug into the lance corporal net wherever he traveled.

At the same time the chief of staff of the division, Colonel Joseph F. Dunford, received a call from the division's higher headquarters, the Marine Expeditionary Force (MEF). "Baghdad has reports of Americans killed in Fallujah," the MEF officer said. "What are you getting?"

Dunford walked from his tiny office into the operations center, where video from a UAV was tracking a mob swarming around two smoking vehicles; the red flames from the burning tires stood out vividly. The UAV circled slowly, its telephoto camera zooming in on a mob beating inert bodies, the sticks repeatedly rising and fall-ing. On an adjoining screen a satellite TV feed showed Iraqi men and boys stomping a body that was charred black and shriveled by the flames.

To Dunford, the scene didn't make sense. No Marine unit was reported in the city. Besides, it was a court-martial offense to travel with fewer than four vehicles. Those twisted corpses couldn't be Americans.

————

Without informing the Marines in advance, four American contractors escorting a supply run had taken a shortcut through Fallujah, the most danger-ous city in Iraq. They were driving in two Mitsubishi Pajero sport utility vehicles on the main thoroughfare, Highway 10. Even in morning traffic it would take only twenty minutes for them to pass through town. The four were members of the North Carolina–based Blackwater Security Consulting company. They were capable men. Scott Helvenston, a former SEAL, had participated in the four-hundred-mile endurance race called the Raid Gaulouise. Jerry Zovko, who was flu-ent in five languages, had served in the 82nd Airborne Division. Michael Teague had won the bronze star in Afghanistan. Wesley Batalona had served both as a paratrooper and as a Ranger.

The contractors crept along in the dense traffic, passing on their right the main police station and the walled compound of the city council, formerly the headquarters for the Baath Party. The Government Center in midtown was the final landmark where the contractors could have turned back, had any Iraqi policeman waved them down. No Iraqi, though, raised a hand to warn them.

Minutes later, emerging from the doorways of shops, insurgents dashed into the street and sprayed both vehicles. (Some claimed an Iraqi police pickup had been leading the SUVs and had sped away at the last minute.) With no armor plating on the vehicles, the four men inside were riddled with bullets. They had had no chance to fire back.

The firing ceased, the shooters drove off, and a crowd of men and boys approached. When an American with bullet wounds in his chest staggered out and fell to the ground, he was kicked, stomped, stabbed, and butchered. A boy ran up with a can of gasoline, doused the SUVs, and struck a match. The black smoke pointed like a finger up into the sky, attracting a swelling crowd.

Egged on by older men, boys dragged the smoldering corpses onto the pavement and beat the charred flesh with their flip-flops to show that Americans were scum under the soles of their shoes. A body was ripped apart, and a leg attached to a rope was tossed over a power line above the highway.

Colonel Dunford reached General Mattis, who was out in the field, by radio. "A mob in Fallujah has killed some American contractors. It looks like a scene from Somalia," Dunford said. "Baghdad wants us to go in."

"What's your take?" Mattis asked.

"The contractors are dead," Dunford said. "If we go in to get their bodies, we'll have to kill hundreds, including kids. Captain Sullivan says the police chief promises to return the bodies. I recommend we stay out."

"Where does the MEF stand?"

"General Conway thinks we should let the mob exhaust itself," Dunford said. General James T. Conway commanded the Marine Expeditionary Force. He was Mattis's direct boss.

"That's it, then," Mattis said. "Rushing in makes no sense."

The macabre carnival in Fallujah continued all day, the crowds spurring on one another, shouting, "Viva mujahedeen! Long live the resistance!" Two of the charred corpses were dragged behind a car through the souk, past rows of small shops and hundreds of cheering men, to the green trestle bridge that the Americans called the Brooklyn Bridge. There the mob hung the bodies from an overhead girder, two black lumps dangling at the end of ropes.

Crowds in the souk and along the highway were swept up in the murderous atmosphere. No police tried to restore order; no fire truck put out the flames smoldering around the SUVs; no ambulance came for the bodies. When two Iraqi nurses tried to take the bodies to a hospital, they were told to leave or be shot. At dusk the remains of three bodies were dumped in a cart pulled by a gray donkey for a final triumphal haul down Highway 10. Men and boys followed the cart yelling **shwaretek,** meaning "Americans, you've lost your nerve."

Technicolor video of the ghoulish scenes, taped by the UAV, was played at the division, at the MEF, at higher headquarters in Baghdad, and at ops centers in Washington. Frustration and anger built hour by hour. In Fallujah crowds proud to show their handiwork greeted Iraqi photographers. Graphic footage was sold to the networks in Baghdad and broadcast worldwide. The next day's front-page photos were stunning: young men smiling and waving as if their soccer team had won a championship match, while behind them dangled the blackened corpses of Americans.

————

From the division's point of view, the lynching was a tragedy, not least because it could have been avoided. The four Americans lost were added to the list of dozens killed in the past year in the Fallujah area. Conway, Mattis, Dunford—all had seen the maimed and the burned. They focused on the issues, not the emotions. War took its capricious daily toll. If you couldn't absorb casualties and keep the mission foremost in your mind, you were in the wrong business. Sending an armored force downtown amid rampaging men and boys would have meant inviting more killing, more agony, and more screams for revenge. There were no lives left to be saved: the war had claimed four more victims.

The Marines had a plan they wanted to stick with. For months American forces had been venturing into

the city only in brief forays in armored vehicles;
meanwhile the opposition had strengthened. Over
the next several months the Marines intended to
move back into Fallujah on foot, district by district,
bringing with them Iraqi forces. The rub for the past
year had been that the Iraqi police and National
Guard had refused to be seen with Americans, yet
they had also failed to control the city. The Marines
intended to coax the Iraqi forces into joint patrols,
regaining control of the city by slipping in "all quiet
like the fog."

Seeing no reason to alter that plan, Dunford sat
down and wrote an e-mail to be used on the evening
news in the States. "We're not going to overreact to
today's violence," he wrote. "We have a methodology
of patient, persistent presence. We will identify who
was responsible, and in cooperation with Iraqi security forces, we will kill them."

———

The Iraqi police returned three bodies the next day,
and the fourth corpse was recovered the following
day. The CIA and military intelligence began to
match the faces of the ringleaders to names and
addresses. More than twenty names were placed on a
list of targets for future raids. Two brothers, for
instance, lived in a wealthy compound that was dotted with date trees on the eastern bank of the
Euphrates. They would be easy to take down.
Another ringleader operated a computer and photo
shop in the center of the city. Reading his e-mails and

samizdat would be revealing. He would be a tough target, though, requiring the expertise of Task Force 6-26. The special operations commandos would need a few weeks to plan and rehearse their raid. If the Marines took it step by step, the ringleaders would be arrested or killed over the course of the next month.

General Conway's senior was Lieutenant General Ricardo S. Sanchez, the Joint Task Force commander in charge of all coalition forces. Sanchez wanted swift, visible retaliation for the lynchings: for instance, bomb the Brooklyn Bridge. Conway rejected that option—he wanted to use the bridge to run convoys. **All right then,** the JTF staff in Baghdad replied, **bomb the computer shop**. No, the Marines replied, we want to read those records, not burn them. Besides, it's an e-mail café, with kids wandering in and out. **Well,** the JTF came back, **bomb the compound on the Euphrates**. No, the MEF replied, families live there, and the ringleaders might not be home when the bombs come calling. When every suggestion for immediate action was rebuffed, JTF headquarters grumbled that the Marines were too reluctant to apply force.

Don't push us, the MEF staff said. Give us a few weeks to pick off the ringleaders when they least expect it. To rush into a city of 280,000 made no strategic sense. Once they occupied the city, what would they do with it? You could do anything with a bayonet except sit on it. The sensible plan was to gain control gradually, leaving Iraqis—not Marines—in charge. **Not the right answer,** the JTF staff replied.

You guys in the field don't grasp the international significance. The mutilation was not a tactical matter; the political symbolism was huge, and the analogy to Somalia was on the lips of television pundits and in newspaper commentaries.

A decade earlier the United States had intervened in Somalia's tribal wars in order to save millions from starvation. But a resentful tribe eventually turned on the military peacekeepers and butchered twenty-four Pakistani soldiers. At the urging of the United Nations, American soldiers set out to arrest the tribe's leader and were trapped in a fierce firefight. When it was over, a vengeful Somali mob dragged the corpse of an American soldier through the streets. American revulsion hardened into determination not to aid such a barbaric country. The mutilation forced a policy review in Washington, resulting in the withdrawal of all American forces from Somalia.

Once again tremors from a mutilation were being felt in official Washington. President George W. Bush was reported to be furious. For a gleeful mob to hang Americans like pieces of charred meat mocked the rationale that the war had liberated grateful Iraqis. The mutilation was both a stinging rebuke and a challenge. National pride and honor were involved. The president's envoy to Iraq, Ambassador L. Paul Bremer III, went on television in Baghdad to denounce the atrocity, vowing that the "deaths will not go unpunished." The spokesman for the JTF, Army Brigadier General Mark Kimmitt, followed up by saying the attack on Fallujah would be "overwhelming." Write an order for the Marines to attack, General Sanchez told his staff, and I don't mean any fucking knock-before-search, touchy-feely stuff.

After six months in the States, the MEF had just returned to Iraq and, the week before, taken responsibility for a province the size of North Carolina, with two million people and thirteen cities. Now Conway was receiving orders, which he believed to be a mistake, about one city. Over the past year Conway had developed a solid rapport with General John P. Abizaid, who was in charge of the Central Command. CentCom commanded all American forces throughout the Middle East. Both Conway and Abizaid had open personalities, and when they issued orders, they explained their reasoning, which won them the loyal support of their staffs. Conway called Abizaid to get some background about what was going on.

"I've discussed this with Secretary Rumsfeld, Jim," Abizaid said. "This one's coming from way up the chain of command. Way up."

To the Marines, Fallujah was notable for having no American base inside the city. Consequently, allowing themselves a few months to move in seemed a prudent tactical matter. But to Abizaid and Rumsfeld, Fallujah was a city, constantly in the news, that had slipped out of control. That situation was unacceptable—tantamount to secession from the new Iraq. Abizaid had visited the province in November to personally threaten Fallujah's leaders, following repeated attacks on Americans, but his warning had no effect. On a second trip in February his convoy had had to pull out of Fallujah under gunfire.

Rumsfeld and Abizaid, with Ambassador Bremer in strong support, had recommended to President Bush that Fallujah be seized immediately. The president ordered the Marines "to go get those responsible," with no waiting, no delay. The president was not told that the Marines disagreed with his order to rush in.

The last time American troops fought street by street had been twenty-six years before in Hue City. That battle had raged for a month, and blocks of houses were leveled. Hundreds of Americans and thousands of Vietnamese had died. The Marines knew that in Fallujah rough stuff lay ahead. They wished others understood that.

On April 2, 2004, the MEF received a written order from the JTF to conduct offensive operations against Fallujah. That settled the matter. The time for talking was over. The Marines had had their say, and General Abizaid had made his decision. If President Bush wanted the city taken, their mission was to take it.

The Marines saluted, turned about smartly, and let slip the dogs of war.

PART I

COUNTERINSURGENCY

April 2003 to March 2004

1

"WHAT KIND OF PEOPLE
LOOT DIRT?"

THROUGHOUT MOST OF IRAQ, the latter days of April 2003 was a time of great joy. Saddam Hussein's murderous regime had collapsed; the shooting and bombing had stopped; and people could go anywhere they pleased and say anything they wanted. In Baghdad, the American forces were greeted with smiles, waves, and shouts of joy. On the eastern bank of the Euphrates near the French embassy, wealthy Sunni suburbanites—anxious to win favor—led American Marines to the estates of Deputy Prime Minister Tariq Aziz and high-level generals. When the giant Stalinesque statue of Saddam, arm raised and mustache bristling, fell in Firdos Square, Americans and Iraqis alike were pulling on the ropes. April 2003 was an interlude of good cheer, reminiscent of the liberation of Paris in 1944—a moment in time when people forgot their wants and their fears and flocked to the streets to cheer the soldiers.

In Fallujah, though, the residents did not cheer when paratroopers from the 82nd Airborne Division drove into the city in late April. In Baghdad, looters as numerous as locusts had stripped every government building, even carting away bricks. In Fallujah, the windows and electric fixtures at the Baath headquarters at the Government Center remained intact. Most looting was confined to the industrial sector, and only the poor people who lived south of Highway 10 greeted the Americans with smiles. Across the Euphrates south of the city, the large estates of prominent Baathists and army officers stood empty but untouched, securely guarded by the curlicue Baathist symbol on the courtyard gates. Saddam's apparatchiks did not consider themselves defeated. They were in temporary hiding and Fallujah was still their bastion, untouched by the war and unbowed by the presence of a few hundred American soldiers.

At dusk on April 28, 2003—Saddam Hussein's birthday—a raucous mob of about a hundred men, women, and children pushed their way into the courtyard of the mayor's office, where the 82nd had set up headquarters. The paratroopers had no warning that an anti-American demonstration was planned and had no idea what the Iraqis were protesting or why. The mob accused the surprised American soldiers of spying on women with night-seeing binoculars and of showing pornography to children. Using translators and loudspeakers, a group of paratroopers warned away the mob. The crowd walked several blocks to another neighborhood, where they harassed another detachment of paratroopers. Several men in the crowd were firing AK-47s into the air, which the veteran paratroopers interpreted not as a threat but as bravado. They told them to move on.

The mob then walked to a schoolhouse to harass another platoon of paratroopers, who were sleeping inside. It was well after nine and dark. The crowd had a new demand: the soldiers had to leave immediately so that the children could go to school the next day. As the mob pressed up to the schoolyard wall, three Iraqis on a nearby roof started shooting their rifles.

Inside the schoolhouse a squad leader, convinced he was under fire, radioed his company commander for permission to return fire. At the same time another sergeant radioed the same request. Believing his men were under attack, the company commander gave the order, and the keyed-up paratroopers unleashed a fusillade of automatic weapons fire. In the next several minutes fifteen men, women, and children were killed and dozens were wounded. None of the paratroopers were injured.

The next day seven major Western news outlets sent reporters from Baghdad to cover the story. Most filed similar stories about a terrible tragedy caused by a sudden flare-up in the dark. Several Iraqis had fired weapons, they reported, but while the Iraqis said they had been shooting in the air, the American soldiers said they had been the targets. The reporters wrote that they did see graffiti written in English on the walls of the school where the soldiers were sleeping, disparaging the Iraqis with slogans like "I love pork" and a drawing of a camel with the words Iraqi Cab Company below it.

The press focused on the human cost of the incident, the clash of cultures, and the bitterness the casualties had caused throughout the city. The shootings, according to the news accounts, would unleash a cycle of retribution: more deaths and more revenge attacks. But they gave no explanation as to why or how Fallujans had mounted an anti-American protest on Saddam's birthday, just days after the regime had collapsed, at a time when most Iraqis were celebrating.

Six months later Jamil Karaba, a Fallujah resident, was arrested after he was overheard bragging about organizing the mob and planting gunmen among the protesters.

Called the "destruction-maker," Karaba was an alcoholic former Baathist with several prior arrests and with ties to the gangster element in town. Provoking an incident was a centuries-old guerrilla stratagem for turning the people against the soldiery. And this time, as so often in the past, it had worked.

The next day a screaming mob carried on its shoulders the mufti Sheikh Jamal—the senior imam who interpreted Islamic laws—to the mayor's office.

"All Americans leave Iraq!" he shouted, as the crowd roared in agreement.

———

Cities acquire caricature, if not character. New York is frenetic and brash; San Francisco is liberal and laid-back; Los Angeles is imbued with glitter and celebrity. Ask Iraqis about Fallujah, and they roll their eyes: Fallujah is strange, sullen, wild-eyed, badass, just plain mean. Fallujans don't like strangers, which includes anyone not homebred. Wear lipstick or Western-style long hair, sip a beer or listen to an American CD, and you risk the whip or a beating.

For centuries the city had traded with—and stolen from—merchants who were headed east to Baghdad. The frontier town bordering an open desert attracted outcasts and criminals. In the early twentieth century European travelers learned not to tarry in Fallujah. After Iraq won its independence in 1959, Fallujah became a source of enforcers for the ruling Sunni-dominated Baath Party. The city's tough reputation continued under Saddam.

Laid out in a square grid of wide boulevards, Fallujah comprised two thousand blocks of courtyard walls, tenements, two-story concrete houses, and squalid alleyways. Half-completed houses, garbage heaps, and wrecks of old cars cluttered every neighborhood. The six lanes of Highway 10 ran straight through the center of the two-mile-long city, from a traffic cloverleaf on the eastern end to the Brooklyn Bridge, over the Euphrates, to the west. South of Highway 10 sprawled the decaying buildings and waste pits of a decrepit industrial zone. On an aerial map the layout of straight streets and dense blocks of houses faintly resembled Manhattan, giving rise to nicknames. Next to the industrial zone was Queens, a poor section of shabby three- and four-room houses. North of Highway 10 were the spacious houses of East Manhattan and Midtown, with its established mosques. The Government Center was in Midtown, while the old souk and marketplace, called the Jolan, were next to the Euphrates to the west. Along the main street were the billboards, restaurants, repair shops, and other struggling efforts of a merchant class. It was a city of monochrome color, without architectural flair.

With forty-seven mosques in its neighborhoods and fifty more in the neighboring villages, Fallujah was called "the city of a hundred mosques." For decades the city had been the repository of the extreme Wahhabi, or Salafi, traditions flowing in from Saudi Arabia. Saddam, distrusting Fallujans' fundamentalism, had restricted their movements and used them as his cat's paw.

Although 60 percent of Iraqis were Shiites, the 20 percent who were Sunnis had held the political power for centuries. When Saddam's army was defeated and thrown out of Kuwait in 1991, the Shiites in southern Iraq, encouraged by ill-conceived American exhortations, had revolted. To crush them, Saddam incited sectarian hatred. The Shiites, he warned the Sunnis, were blasphemers who had to be killed to preserve the true Muslim religion. Imams in Fallujah and other Sunni cities led the faithful in the chant: "Our blood and souls to redeem you, O Islam." Saddam's army, led by Sunni officers, crushed the Shiite uprising.

Just before the Americans drove into Fallujah in April 2003, the mufti Jamal, the senior Sunni cleric in the city, warned the residents that the American invaders would turn Iraq over to the Shiites. The radical clerics were calling President Bush "Hulagu II," a reference to the conquest of ancient Baghdad by the Mongol leader Hulagu, assisted by a Shiite leader who betrayed the ruling caliph. The Americans, the mufti told the citizens, were modern-day Mongols—infidel invaders and occupiers.

––––

Fallujah's pro-Coalition mayor, Taha Bedawi, could not stand up against the anger that the shooting had provoked. He asked the paratroopers to leave the city, explaining that revenge attacks were inevitable. Maintaining peace between tribes depended upon exchanging an eye for an eye, one life for another. If an insult went unavenged, the family and tribe suffered humiliation and were seen as weak, thus encouraging further attacks. While the mayor was talking, a group of men gathered outside under banners that read "US killers we'll kick you out."

The 82nd Airborne units withdrew on schedule in early May and were replaced by a company from the 3rd Armored Cavalry Regiment. In the following weeks, although the American soldiers kept a low profile, repeated firefights erupted. The regiment, assigned to patrol more than a thousand square kilometers, could devote fewer than two hundred mounted soldiers to Fallujah and its environs.

Every day on the dusty brown courtyard walls along Highway 10, more anti-American slogans were scrawled: "God bless the holy fighters of the city of mosques." "Kill the infidel Americans." "USA leave our country."

The JTF decided to make Fallujah the "most occupied city in Iraq," replacing the two hundred soldiers of the 3rd Armored Cavalry Regiment with fifteen hundred soldiers from the 2nd Brigade of the 3rd Infantry Division.

The Fallujah campaign of the 3rd ID had two prongs—the carrot and the stick. The "stick," or force, focused on raids. The 2nd Brigade mounted raids at night on houses that had been identified by informers or by the OGA—Other Government Agency, aka the CIA. During the daytime the 3rd ID conducted large-scale sweeps to search for weapons and arms dealers, locking down whole sections of the city for several hours at a time.

The armored presence of the 3rd ID was intimidating. During the daylight hours things were usually calm, although Iraqi police often turned their backs on the Americans and children were as likely to throw rocks as to laugh and ask for candy. The men rarely smiled. Yet the children were friendly south of Highway 10. The brigade's executive officer, Lieutenant Colonel Eric Wesley, and **New York Times** reporter Michael Gordon felt safe enough to walk into the old Jolan quarter and talk with Iraqis in the crowded souk. **Washington Post** reporter Rajiv Chandrasekaran ate lunch at the Haji Hussein, a popular kebab restaurant.

The raids were getting results, but whenever the wrong house was searched, the entry tactic—smashing down a door in the middle of the night—frightened a family and created more hostile Fallujans. LtCol Wesley called the raid successes "linear," like picking apples in a vast orchard one by one.

The brigade would have preferred to have "exponential" success, which involved the "carrot": winning over Fallujan hearts and minds by infusing jobs, repairing infrastructure, and building relationships with the mayor, the sheikhs, and the clerics. The Americans would provide the city's leaders with money and contracts. They in turn would reach out to the unemployed and disaffected, reducing the appeal of the insurgents and attracting recruits for the local security forces. If the Americans could show that they wanted to help improve the living conditions and would leave intact the city leadership and traditions, the theory went, then most youths would not support the insurgents.

Bargaining went on with the mayor, the sheikhs, and the city elders. The brigade called this a "relational approach"; you do something for me, and I do something for you.

"Let's be reasonable about this," LtCol Wesley told the city elders. "You have a stake in a better future, and we as American soldiers are here only to help you. We have no designs upon this city."

Whenever the nighttime attacks decreased, the curfew was lifted. Amnesty and cash rewards were offered for weapons, albeit with scant results. The Humvee replaced the tank and armored personnel carrier as the routine patrol vehicle, reducing noise and damage to the streets. As long as progress seemed to be made, the brigade would show the velvet glove rather than the iron fist.

Sorting out who among the tens of thousands of males was a committed enemy, though, and gauging the depth of the population's hostility proved vexing. The soldiers spent days with bulldozers and rakes constructing a first-class soccer field downtown. When they finished and returned to base, a mob gathered at the soccer field, ripped down the goalie nets, scraped the dirt from the field, and heaped garbage on the site.

"What kind of people loot dirt?" a soldier asked.

Inside the city were enemies determined to prevent ordinary families from ever seeing that infidel invaders had improved their lives.

In July a massive internal explosion blew out the walls and demolished the roof of the Al Hassan Mosque, killing the imam and several other Iraqis. As a disaster crew removed the bodies, a crowd gathered to blame the Americans. "There is no God but Allah, America is the enemy of God," they chanted, as others screamed that an invisible aircraft had dropped a bomb.

The situation threatened to escalate into a citywide riot. Ra'ad Hussein Abed, a city official who spoke good English and hoped eventually to be appointed mayor by the city elders, approached LtCol Wesley. He arranged a meeting with Sheikh Ghazi, one of the wealthiest and most powerful traders in the city, to try to defuse the tension. Ghazi, a shrewd and urbane businessman, admitted to Wesley that the imam was a radical preacher known to be building improvised explosive devices, or IEDs, to blow up vehicles on the highways outside town. He assured Wesley there would be no riot.

Wesley was convinced that alliances with Ra'ad and like-minded citizens who wanted the city to progress would undercut the appeal of the shadowy insurgents, who were offering fear of the Shiites and hatred of infidels. He believed that there were four types of insurgents: unemployed youths, religious extremists (who benefited by gaining a following), criminals, and former Baathists (the hidden planners and financiers). To pry away from the hard-core insurgents those motivated by revenge, the brigade paid a **solatium**—what Iraqi tribes called blood money—to the relatives of those who had been killed or injured in the April 28 shooting.

The city elders praised the 3rd Brigade for the action and asserted that the Iraqi police were ready to take on more responsibility. The 2nd brigade commander, Colonel Joseph DiSalvo, turned over the twenty-two checkpoints inside the city. But Mayor Taha was worried, fearing that his pro-American stance would leave him isolated. He warned that the opposition was biding its time, not softening its stance.

The brigade contracted with dozens of "companies," sheikhs and loose groupings of unemployed men, to undertake projects like cleaning up the garbage. It purchased fans for the schools, air-conditioning units for the hospital, and a generator for the water-pumping station.

The needs of the city, though, overwhelmed the resources the Americans were able to offer. The brigade disbursed about $150,000 a week, while the city's needs were a thousand times that amount, calculated at $150 million. There were 70,000 unemployed; an industrial park stood idle; and power, sewer, and water plants were decrepit. The farmers were clamoring for seeds, tractors, and gasoline; the schools had no textbooks or lights. Fallujah, like all cities in Iraq, had crumbled into ruin, as Saddam had looted his country. Any accountant would have declared the books hopelessly out of balance. But with their can-do spirit, the American soldiers had set to work.

The occasional sniper, mortar, and RPG round—harassment attacks—was taken in stride by the 3rd ID's combat-hardened soldiers. IEDs, though, were a different matter. In Vietnam hidden land mines were the bane of the infantryman, accounting for 20 percent of the casualties and sapping morale. A grunt never knew when he would be blown up walking down a trail. In the flatlands of Iraq, the highways were the trails. IEDs accounted for 68 percent of all American fatalities. All who traveled the roads feared and loathed them.

IEDs were simple to make—just combine metal (for shrapnel) and an explosive armed with a blasting cap that could be set off by a radio frequency from a garage door opener or cell phone. The triggerman could be on a roof a block away.

The 3rd ID learned to spot IEDs—in the bloated stomach of a dead dog, a barrel tipped at an improbable angle, a cardboard box too heavy to be blown by the wind, a car parked in an odd place. In mid-July, though, one soldier was killed and three wounded when an artillery shell detonated as a convoy drove through western Fallujah. Dozens of local residents had driven around the device, but no one had warned the Americans.

In response, Lieutenant Colonel Eric Schwartz, the U.S. commander in the city, set up a checkpoint to search all cars. "If something like this happens," he said, "we are going to take away one of their basic rights, and that's freedom of movement."

While no major firefights broke out against the enormous firepower of the 3rd ID, an underlying sullenness pervaded the Fallujans. Those who would be seen with the Americans—Taha, Ra'ad, Ghazi—trod carefully. They knew others were watching them, appraising how close they were to the Americans. The town had an edginess, an attitude of simmering resentment. Visiting Fallujah in midsummer, an experienced reporter, Rajiv Chandrasekaran of the **Washington Post,** called it "the most hostile place in Iraq."

It was difficult to single out an enemy who looked like every other civilian. The insurgents wore no uniforms; they operated from their homes, not from military camps; they had no military communications that could be intercepted; and they had no rank structure, yet they all knew one another. Most guerrilla movements, like the Vietcong, had an identifiable hierarchy and a clear chain of command. Not so in Iraq, where in the summer of 2003 hundreds of independent cells operated when the spirit moved them. A rough analogy were the American Indian tribes in the nineteenth century, sharing a hostility toward the settlers while launching raids at different times for different reasons.

Throughout the scorching days of summer—as temperatures reached the 120s and 130s—the 3rd ID persisted with its two-prong approach: responding with force to attacks while working to establish good relations and modestly boost the moribund economy.

In late August the 3rd Infantry Division departed, to return home. LtCol Wesley left believing that the tragic killing of the civilians in April had triggered resentment in a traditional city controlled more by imams and tribes than by former Baathists. He was convinced that a huge influx of money could deflect recruits from the insurgency. The brigade, though, had but a pittance to spend, just enough to convince the residents that the Americans could really make a difference if they wanted to. The sheikhs, quick to criticize while angling for contracts, were unimpressed by the trickle of funds; the 70,000 unemployed remained unemployed; the IEDs persisted; and the soccer field lay looted of its dirt, evidence of a hidden, calculating enemy who could organize the people.

2

A BROKEN CHAIN OF COMMAND

IN THE CITY OF FALLUJAH, AMERICAN battlefield commanders acted as the police, the soldiers, the development planners, the economic administrators, the political advisers, and the court of final appeal. But unlike the colonial powers of Europe that had ruled the Middle East a century earlier, the Americans were filling their military, police, municipal, and political power roles without the assistance of an indigenous army and civil service bureaucracy. In this respect, Fallujah was typical of Iraq in the summer of 2003.

The April attack on Saddam's regime and its headquarters in Baghdad had been overwhelming and the city had fallen more quickly than most had expected. The military leader of the Coalition (mainly American forces, with substantial British forces) was General Tommy Franks, who com-

manded CentCom. Before the war Franks had persuaded Secretary of Defense Donald Rumsfeld that
the development of postwar Iraq should remain
under the control of CentCom.

"Unity of command is an essential principle," he
later wrote in his memoir. "In combat, there had to be
one line of authority."

This approach reflected a lesson learned from Vietnam, where in 1967 the thousand-man American
reconstruction or pacification staff had reported to the
U.S. ambassador. But progress had stalled due to
bureaucratic turf wars and conflicting staff procedures.
By contrast, the U.S. military had a clear chain of command and standardized staff procedures. So a frustrated
President Lyndon B. Johnson had shifted the reconstruction staff and budget from the U.S. ambassador to
the military commander, General Creighton Abrams.
This move pulled together, under one undisputed
authority, all the complex, competing, and often redun-
dant U.S. civil and military pacification programs. It
consolidated both policy and resource decision-making
under a single military commander, charged with the
responsibility for security.

Similarly, Rumsfeld agreed with Gen Franks that
unity of command under military leadership was
appropriate for Iraq. He appointed retired Lieutenant
General Jay Garner as the CentCom deputy for
reconstruction.

Three weeks after Baghdad fell, President Bush signaled that major hostilities had ended in Iraq. "We've

done it," the president declared to rousing cheers on board the aircraft carrier **Abraham Lincoln**.

Although the war seemed over, Iraq was nonetheless convulsed by looting. Television networks nightly showed pictures of friendly but uncontrolled mobs ripping apart government buildings. From the museum of history, artifacts dating back thousands of years were being hauled off in donkey carts. LtGen Garner and his staff appeared unable to get on top of the chaotic situation. President Bush soon decided to change leaders and organizations.

On May 10 he replaced Garner with former Ambassador L. Paul Bremer III, appointing him the president's envoy to Iraq. Bremer would administer a new organization called the Coalition Provisional Authority, or CPA. He would report to the president through the secretary of defense and be vested with the broad policy-making and budgetary authority to build the new Iraq.

In regard to reconstruction, CentCom was thereby sent to the sidelines. The chain of command was broken into two pieces. If the war was over, there was no need for CentCom to remain in charge. Gen Franks, on the verge of retirement, enthusiastically agreed to abolish the post of his deputy CentCom commander for reconstruction. As Franks saw it, Bremer as the president's personal envoy would bring to Iraq more political clout and money from the White House, which was exactly what was needed now that major hostilities had ended.

In early summer, as hostilities persisted, Secretary of Defense Rumsfeld dismissed the attacks as the actions of "dead-enders" who had no chance of prevailing. On 17 July, though, Gen Abizaid reversed Rumsfeld's assessment. The new head of CentCom said the situation had evolved into a "classical guerrilla-type campaign." Far from being over, the Iraqi war was continuing as an insurgency.

With Iraq under wartime conditions, the closest historical analogy to Bremer's post as envoy was that of the British viceroys in India in the late nineteenth century. Back then, though, the British controlled a large indigenous army commanded by British officers, and the viceroy approved all major military operations. Bremer's case was different: he had the responsibility and the money to create Iraqi security forces—police and soldiers—in any model he saw fit, but he had no authority to approve, veto, or even comment on U.S. military operations.

Bremer set up headquarters in a vast, heavily guarded baroque palace in Baghdad called the Green Zone. Gen Abizaid established a forward headquarters in Qatar, four hundred miles south of Baghdad, splitting his time between Qatar and CentCom's other headquarters in Tampa, Florida. Abizaid designated LtGen Sanchez as commander of the Joint Task Force in Baghdad, responsible for operations in Iraq. Sanchez was intense, unaccustomed to political-military geopolitics, and comfortable dealing with the details of military operations. Bremer was intense and intelligent, expert in geopolitics and the ways of Washington, and swift to wield his decision-making authority.

Because Bremer's fledgling CPA was ill-organized and lacked sufficient State Department volunteers to act as provincial advisers, during the summer of 2003 the American and British battalion commanders acted as the de facto mayors of all Iraqi cities, reestablishing primary services and jump-starting governance. Forty battalions scattered across a country the size of California were swamped with demands for back pay, security, sewage, electric power, medical care, fuel, clean water, and the thousand-odd municipal services Americans take for granted. The CPA hadn't either the staff or the funding to be of much practical help; in their frustration, the battalion commanders referred to CPA as Cannot Provide Anything. Across the country personal and organizational relations between the CPA and the JTF became strained.

Among the resources not provided was training and equipment for the Iraqi municipal police departments that under Saddam had investigated petty crimes and indulged in small-time graft. The dreaded intelligence service (Mukhabarat) and the army had dealt swiftly and harshly with the serious criminals. After the Saddam regime disintegrated, the CPA envisioned that a police force of 85,000 countrywide could provide internal security, as did the police in American cities.

As the senior CPA police adviser explained, "It's as simple as, when have you ever seen police lead a coup? If you build a strong police force, you have a republic. If you build a strong military, you have a banana republic."

Whatever its theoretical merits, the CPA security plan was irrelevant to conditions inside Fallujah. The police in Fallujah could expect scant help from the CPA, which did not have any staff in the city and little money to aid in a major way.

In the early fall of 2003, as the 3rd ID was pulling out of the city, Fallujah was not a major topic of discussion at the White House. The president and his advisers, though, were concerned that the Pentagon and the CPA weren't acting as a coordinated team, even as pressures from the Shiites were mounting for immediate elections. So in October a third chain of command was added: the Iraq Stabilization Group, whose purpose was to coordinate Iraqi policy from inside the White House.

In charge of the group were the national security adviser, Dr. Condoleezza Rice, and her experienced deputy, Ambassador Robert Blackwill, who was appointed deputy assistant to the president for Iraq. Bremer and Blackwill were colleagues who had worked together in the State Department.

Thus three powerful and strong-willed personalities—Abizaid, Bremer, and Blackwill—had three separate chains of command and communication channels on Iraqi matters. Abizaid reported to Rumsfeld; Bremer reported to Rumsfeld and, as the president's personal envoy, kept the White House informed; and Blackwill reported to Dr. Rice at the White House.

The priorities and the information sources of the three were vastly different. Bremer faced the most prodigious task—navigating Iraq toward a politically and economically sustainable democracy while relying on a thin staff in the provinces to provide information outside Baghdad. Blackwill was focused on preparing the path for transitioning to an Iraqi government, with eventual elections. Abizaid, working through Sanchez, had the most complete data about security and economic conditions throughout Iraq. While Ambassadors Bremer and Blackwill were concentrating on the Shiites for political stability, Generals Abizaid and Sanchez were concentrating upon the guerrilla war.

In the fall of 2003, in Fallujah and throughout the Sunni Triangle, north and west from Baghdad, there existed no effective local police and no Iraqi army. Approximately 150,000 American soldiers were fighting several thousand insurgents hidden among five million Sunnis, whose leaders were telling them they had all been disenfranchised.

The absence of Iraqi military units and leaders stemmed from two decisions that Ambassador Bremer had made in May. The first was to ban senior members of the Baath Party—a political organization that had served Saddam's regime and provided the entry point for careers such as medicine, teaching, and the military—from government positions. Kurdish and Shiite leaders, who had been oppressed by the Sunni Baathists, acclaimed the ban enthusiastically.

The second decision was to abolish the army. Bremer said he was merely codifying a fact; namely, that the Iraqi Army had dissolved. But on the ground that wasn't quite true. Every American battalion commander was being besieged by Iraqi officers offering to come back to work and bring their soldiers with them. American divisions even had plans designating Iraqi units to be re-formed.

Both the Pentagon and CentCom had the chance to object to Bremer's edict, but neither did so. When Bremer announced his decision in May, the Pentagon, CentCom, and the CPA shared the misimpression that the shooting war was winding down and that consequently there was no need to rush a tainted army back into service. Hearing no serious objection from CentCom, CPA started to develop from scratch an Iraqi army that would protect the country's borders and be excluded from any internal role. Countering an insurgency was not a mission of the new Iraqi Army.

Although Gen Abizaid declared in July that Iraq faced "a classical guerrilla-type campaign," neither CentCom nor the CPA made any major alteration in strategy or budget. This would emerge as a major problem. Reflecting the view that prosperity is the cornerstone of security, in early fall Bremer submitted to the U.S. Congress a budget requesting $18 billion for Iraq, of which 80 percent was allocated for development (electricity, sewage, schools, and the like) and 20 percent for security (police, the army, and border guards). At a time when the insurgency was growing, the policies and the resources of the CPA presupposed an Iraq at peace.

Beginning in late August and running throughout the fall, the deputy secretary of defense, Paul D. Wolfowitz, concerned about the trends, asked the CPA to reallocate funds to develop forty or more National Guard–type Iraqi battalions. One or two battalions would be sent to each Sunni city to back up the beleaguered and outgunned police. Wolfowitz's request resulted in a series of budgetary tussles with Bremer, who joked to his staff about having "to feed the squirrel cages back in the Pentagon" and referred to the "6,000-mile screwdriver from Washington."

Bremer's span of control and the enormity of his duties were staggering. He was responsible for selecting an Interim Governing Council, advising Secretary Rumsfeld and President Bush, informing the United Nations, preparing to return sovereignty, and determining Iraqi economic and security policies and budgets. In light of the onerous restrictions imposed by Congress, readjusting security spending was no easy task.

Nonetheless, Rumsfeld, Wolfowitz, and Abizaid kept the pressure on, and by mid-fall the CPA was reluctantly reallocating money for additional security forces. Once the CPA agreed to Wolfowitz's request, Abizaid directed the U.S. divisions in Iraq to use the money to recruit, train, and pay the new Iraqi National Guard (initially called the Iraqi Civil Defense Corps). Fallujah, though, was near the bottom of the list of cities to receive such a battalion. National Guard soldiers would not arrive there until February 2004.

3

"YOU WORK WITH THE AMERICANS, YOU DIE."

AS THE SUMMER OF 2003 ENDED, the Americans pulled their units into a large base two miles east of Fallujah, sending mounted patrols downtown daily.

At the beginning of September, the 82nd Airborne Division returned. Fallujans were still angry about the tragic killings of April 28, but the JTF had no other division to send. The 1st Battalion of the 505th Parachute Infantry Regiment became the fifth American battalion in five months to enter the city. The battalion, recently returned from Afghanistan, would remain there for seven months.

Lieutenant Colonel Brian M. Drinkwine commanded the battalion. A West Point graduate, he was a quiet leader, comfortable in his command and impressed by the size of the task. The regimental commander, Colonel Jefforey Smith, had called together his six battalion commanders and laid out their missions. The 4,400 paratroopers under Smith's command—spread out over sixteen hundred square kilometers containing one million Iraqis—were to accomplish five tasks: (1) fight and defeat the shadowy insurgents; (2) reestablish local governing councils; (3) defuse the hostility of the Sunni population; (4) aid the Iraqi police; and (5) assist in invigorating the economy. These tasks were similar to what American and British forces were undertaking throughout Iraq. The JTF in Baghdad, however, had provided no master blueprint for rebuilding a nation. Each battalion, Smith explained in his direct, soft-spoken way, was expected to adapt and determine its own priorities.

Drinkwine concentrated on city government during the daytime, driving in town for meetings with administrators, sheikhs, and imams. Every night the rifle companies sent out anti-IED patrols. Six IEDs had gone off the first week the battalion arrived; over the course of the summer the insurgents had become more skilled.

Prime hours for setting in the explosives were just after dark and just before dawn. Knowing the Americans had observation posts, insurgents would ride in two cars, drive toward each other, and stop with their rear bumpers touching, as if one were helping the other change a flat tire. The cars' headlights blinded the American night-vision devices for the few minutes it took to drop the explosive into a pre-dug hole behind a guardrail. A few hours later a man would sneak up and insert a blasting cap, wires, or a radio frequency device. The next day someone hiding in the shrubs would detonate the explosive. As the paratroopers became adept at identifying likely hiding places for IEDs, the insurgents changed locations in a daily hide-and-seek contest.

The battalion's initial patrols were large-scale, with quick reaction forces standing by. Shortly before midnight on September 11, 2003, the 3rd Platoon from Alpha Company left its base at an abandoned amusement park and walked north to stake out a highway. The soldiers settled into an ambush about two hundred meters west of a field hospital that the Jordanian military had established to treat Iraqis.

Around the same time inside the city, somebody in a black BMW fired shots at the mayor's office and then raced out of town, pursued by a police car and two pickups manned by the mayor's militia. With their lights on, the four vehicles raced at high speed down the highway. The American soldiers turned on their flashlights and waved at the cars to halt. When the BMW turned out its lights and sped past the Americans, shots rang out in a confused melee. One police pickup was riddled with bullets and rolled to a halt. The police car and the other pickup skidded to a stop.

A driver hopped out, yelling "Police! Police!" But now the American soldiers were under fire from the roof of the two-story building to the west. Not knowing it was a hospital, they pounded the building with .50 caliber machine-gun fire. Seven policemen and hospital guards died. It was the deadliest friendly-fire incident in the six-month-old American occupation, and it left tremendous bitterness on both sides.

Drinkwine expressed his regret and asked why the police hadn't contacted him by radio or turned on their flashing lights. Because, the police shouted back, you Americans promised us equipment but never delivered. Never. You're all talk. Now you're killing us.

Drinkwine had little to offer the police in the way of equipment. He set up notification procedures to avoid a repeat of the tragedy and purchased some flashing lights. He understood why the police stayed away from his battalion. They lived in the city and surrounding villages; they knew the ex-officers lounging on the street corners, each with an AK at home and a skein of like-minded colleagues. Four American battalions, each offering protection in exchange for information, had come and had gone. But the insurgents were not leaving.

Drinkwine had his hands full. Patrols were finding an average of three IEDs a day. In early October Drinkwine was arriving for a meeting at the Government Center when a man stepped out of a side street, shouted "God is great!" and started firing an AK-47 automatic rifle. The soldiers cut him down, but four bystanders were wounded.

Local residents called the assailant a freedom fighter, and a policeman promised that more would emerge.

"Saddam Hussein is gone. But now we have the same

kind of regime," he said. "Whenever they [the Americans] come inside Fallujah, they will be attacked."

Rather than backing off, Drinkwine increased the pressure. In mid-October, to get to a meeting with the sheikhs at the town hall, Drinkwine walked the two kilometers west down Highway 10 with a platoon from Charlie Company, instead of driving in Bradley fighting vehicles. When they reached the mayor's office, a man in a blue shirt and jeans, hiding behind a silver Oldsmobile, fired point-blank at Specialist John Fox, striking him in the center of his armored vest. The bullet hit a gray smoke grenade strapped to his vest and bounced off. The soldiers shot the man. As he lay dying, he quietly repeated in Arabic, "God is great."

Drinkwine routinely met with the clerics and sheikhs, listening to their complaints and requests for aid and asking in return that they tone down the virulent anti-American sermons. American officials estimated that 43,000 former Baathists and army and intelligence corps veterans lived in and around Fallujah. In every 82nd ops center there were lists, photos, and an organizational skeleton laying out the former regime elements (FREs) suspected of running the resistance. Next to the FRE diagram was a layout of the overt power elite in the city—the sheikhs, imams, and administrators with whom Drinkwine frequently met.

CIA and military intelligence specialists worked together to update the lists. It had taken the CIA six months to persuade the CPA that an Iraqi intelligence service had to be reconstituted, despite the horrors of its predecessor. The formation of a new intelligence service, however, was a year away. In the meantime the U.S. military was developing its own net of suspects, personality profiles, known associates, addresses, informers, and grounds for arrest.

Drinkwine was especially impressed by the skills of special operations Task Forces 6-26 and 1-21. The Special Operations Command could operate in just about any area. Its officers and NCOs were older, more experienced, and low-key. When they showed up, they had a mission and hard intelligence. Drinkwine appreciated how they passed on tips and advice to his paratroopers.

Drinkwine was fortunate in having on his staff Specialist Khaled Dudin, a naturalized American citizen from a prominent Jordanian family that included ambassadors and counselors to the king. Dudin's father had served as a government liaison to the Bedouin tribes across the Arabian Peninsula. As a child, Dudin had traveled with his father, absorbing the nuances of tribal politics. Eventually the family settled in California, and after 9/11 Dudin joined the paratroopers. With his flawless Arabic and an ability to charm an Iraqi audience with tales of sheikhs from long ago, Dudin became Drinkwine's right arm in navigating the politics of the city.

At higher headquarters, meanwhile, the Americans debated whether courting the sheikhs paid actual dividends or merely infused with life a dying totem of feudalism. Although he met with dozens of sheikhs each week, Drinkwine had no way of knowing which ones had real power or where their loyalties lay.

"Think of the Sopranos," Dudin advised him. "For an American to understand Fallujah, think in terms of mob families in a city that's broke after a war their side lost. There's an occupying army in town offering contracts and money, clergy telling you to resist, and former generals hiding out and paying guys to set off IEDs. What would the Sopranos do? They'd play every side, make money, keep their tribe together, and stay out of politics, except when it benefited them. The sheikhs have power in the villages, but only as long as they deliver something. We can horse-trade with the sheikhs, if we give them money.

"Inside Fallujah the imams have more power than the sheikhs. An imam gets power by attracting followers. Most Fallujans are illiterate, and the mosque is the center of the men's social lives. The imam tells them the news and stirs them up. In return he gets donations and a cut of the action. It's hard for an American to horse-trade with an imam. We can give him a little money, but if he loses his following, he's finished. That's not a good trade for him."

Drinkwine thought he understood the basic power structure of Fallujah. The tribal sheikhs had real but limited power. The pro-American mayor, Taha, had been installed by Khamis Hassnawi, the head sheikh of Abu Eisa, the largest tribe. Two younger sheikhs, Ghazi and Barakat, wanted to replace Taha with their candidate, Ra'ad. The 3rd Infantry Division had liked Ra'ad and had appointed him as "city manager," a step below mayor. The old sheikh, Khamis, outfoxed his younger rivals and kept Taha in power. On behalf of their rival patrons, Taha and Ra'ad were vying for the favor of the Americans. At stake were the huge contracts the CPA was promising on Baghdad radio stations.

Sheikh Ghazi ran the top financial family. His compound, across the Brooklyn Bridge on the west bank of the Euphrates, was as large as the hospital next door. His gardens, with red and yellow roses, hibiscus, and trim green hedges, were laid out in the intricate curlicue symbol of the Baath Party. He had a fleet of Mercedes, kept a second wife in a large house downtown, vacationed in seaside Beirut, knew the inner royal family in Saudi Arabia, and met quietly in Jordan with American officials, suggesting he understood the subtleties of wartime diplomacy.

When Drinkwine traced the $2 million the 3rd ID had dispensed during the summer, he found few tangible results. The money spent didn't change attitudes. Textbooks had been distributed to the schools, but the director of education persisted in paranoid rants about evil Shiites. Drinkwine visited the hospital where $200,000 of equipment had been installed, but the director—who was suspected of harboring and treating wounded insurgents—refused to talk with him.

The two hundred or so clerics in town mostly preached the prevailing anti-American sentiment. Drinkwine couldn't distinguish between the city elders who were keeping their mouths shut to stay alive and those who were the true insurgents. The special operations task forces believed the dangerous insurgent leaders rarely showed up in public when American forces were present. Some were in Syria, and those who lived in the city kept a low profile.

Gradually, from wiretaps, intercepts, informers, and the like, the task forces compiled wire diagrams detailing how money moved from former Baathists in hiding through middlemen on the city council and into the hands of the foot soldiers: $50 for a lookout, $100 to dig the hole for an IED, $200 to trigger the device. There was good money to be made if you caught on with one of the right "families."

Sheikh Ghazi, the wealthiest trader, worked through four levels of contractors, leaving no paper trail. Some suspected he was moving funds from Syria to contacts inside the city, with Sheikh Barakat acting as paymaster for local attacks. Barakat's son had bragged about setting off an IED. The senior imam, Jamal, was suspected of hiding insurgents inside his complex and aiding Barakat in payouts after IED attacks. Drinkwine had secured permission from Col Smith to plant listening devices inside Jamal's mosque, risking a riot if the bugs were discovered.

Drinkwine warned the city elders that the Americans were not fools, but the warning produced no change. On October 20 a platoon on the eastern edge of the city (called East Manhattan) noticed that the vendors selling jugs of gasoline to passing motorists were walking away quickly. When a paratrooper stepped on a hidden pressure plate, an oil barrel containing two ninety-pound 155mm shells exploded, sending chunks of red-hot metal in all directions. Sergeant P. J. Johnson was killed and seven paratroopers wounded. Small-arms fire and rocket-propelled grenades hit the platoon from the suburban streets to the northeast. The fighting raged for several hours before Drinkwine could extract his wounded. The pressure plate was the work of a demolitions expert whom the CIA called the "Rocket Man," a local resident.

Furious, Drinkwine turned up the heat on the sheikhs and imams. The special task forces pored over intercepts and captured documents, tying together seven items pointing to the mufti Jamal and Sheikh Barakat. Arresting an imam required gaining special permission. Smith, the regimental commander, listened to a recording of Jamal inciting his followers to kill the Americans and a telephone intercept instructing Jamal to hide a terrorist in his compound. In addition, he had three handwritten letters detailing rebel activities. Smith ordered Jamal and Barakat arrested.

The raid team seized Jamal and found the terrorist— a Yemeni—hiding in a small room in his house. Jamal was brought to Drinkwine's ops center and politely offered tea.

As Jamal was sipping his tea, Specialist Dudin looked at his watch and said, "We have to move you. The party's about to begin."

A perplexed Jamal looked around for partygoers. As they moved across the courtyard, the nightly mortar rounds crashed in nearby. Dudin sheltered Jamal and hurried him inside a bunker. A fifty-eight-year-old man of medium build and scholarly mien, Jamal was shaken by the attack.

"See how dangerous this is?" Dudin asked in his impeccable Arabic.

"Sure, sure," Jamal said.

Badly shaken by the nearby explosions, Jamal wrote a letter confessing that he had been hiding a "fundamentalist" and inciting violence. The next day Drinkwine invited a half-dozen imams to meet privately with Jamal, who again acknowledged what he and Barakat had done. After the two were driven to Abu Ghraib prison, more than seventy sheikhs and imams gathered at city hall to protest the arrests. The head sheikhs, though, showed them Jamal's letters and the protest fizzled out. Drinkwine took this as a positive sign.

————

On the last day of October, a bomb went off inside the Government Center, and a mob gathered, accusing Mayor Taha Bedawi of profiting from American contracts. The protest was a put-up job, soon punctuated by rifle shots that escalated into a full-scale firefight. Drinkwine rushed in two reinforced platoons, covered by armed helicopters. The ensuing firefight raged for thirty hours. When it ended, the town hall was a smoking shell, and Mayor Taha, who had been staunchly pro-American, had fled town.

Ra'ad replaced Taha as mayor, and it looked like Ghazi had out-maneuvered old Sheikh Khamis and set himself up for future contracts. Assured of temporary immunity, a dozen former senior Baathists attended a clandestine meeting hosted by Drinkwine, who wanted to hear their version of the causes of the violence. They asked for a reduced American presence in the city and a return of Baathists to government jobs. They complained that the 82nd was too quick to apply too much firepower. They preferred the approach of the 3rd Infantry Division and the 3rd Armored Cavalry Regiment, which kept its soldiers outside the city and left the day-to-day security duties to the police and local militia.

"They understood us better," Sheikh Khamis said. "They didn't provoke the people like they are doing now. Using more force will not solve the problems here."

The commander of Drinkwine's regiment disagreed with the sheikh.

"Because there was an economy of force early on [during the summer of 2003], former regime loyalists, senior Baathists, and some extremists have created a safe haven," Col Smith said. "What we're seeing is a reaction to our increased activities."

The reaction quickly turned deadly. On November 2 two antiaircraft missiles were fired at a CH-47 Chinook helicopter flying over a cornfield outside Fallujah. In the ensuing crash fifteen Americans died and twenty were wounded. It was the heaviest death toll in a single action since the invasion of Iraq. The news touched off celebrations inside the city, where hatred laced the conversations, children refused candy, and American engineers dared not venture to repair clogged sewer mains and decrepit electric power generators.

The initial reaction from the JTF in Baghdad was to order the 82nd to surround Fallujah and root out the insurgents and their arms caches, block by block. Smith and Drinkwine opposed the planned four-battalion operation, called Dodge City. They argued—in phrases the Marines would echo five months later—that such an attack would drive the youths of the city onto the side of the rebels.

"This is not the way to go," Drinkwine said. "If we overreact, we give legitimacy to what are now gangs."

Gen Abizaid, who flew in for an assessment, agreed. Instead of seizing the city block by block, he met with the sheikhs, demanding that they show leadership and stop the violence. There were as many attacks on the outskirts of Fallujah, where the sheikhs had power, as inside the city, where the clerics dominated. Under the current circumstances, he told them in Arabic, there can be no rebuilding, no contracts, no jobs, no progress toward a better future.

In a separate meeting with the sheikhs Major General Charles H. Swannack, commander of the 82nd, was equally forceful. "I am not going to tolerate these attacks anymore," he said. "I know the sheikhs have the ability to control their tribes."

The sheikhs protested that the 82nd didn't appreciate the limits of their power. Threatening them would do no good. Improvement projects made no difference to the men with the guns. In the eyes of the sheikhs, power had shifted from them to the young clerics in Fallujah preaching that America was waging war against Islam and was bringing in Jews to rule Iraq. That message had inflamed the youth of the city, making it impossible for other clerics to retain a following if they preached moderation. In the mosques, the sermons called for the Americans to be driven out.

"It's a kind of religious belief that they should not accept occupation," said Saadi Muhammad, a schoolteacher in Fallujah.

A few days after the Chinook helicopter was shot down, an American soldier was killed near the city by an IED. In response, aircraft dropped thousand-pound bombs on suspected ambush sites and houses with arms caches. When mortar rounds were fired at 82nd positions, counterbattery radars traced the arc of the rounds to their point of origin, and 155mm howitzers fired in response. The fighting escalated through the fall.

"I expect to get attacked every day—every single day," Drinkwine said. "That may come in the form of a mortar attack, a drive-by shooting at the mayor's office, a vehicle ambush, or a combination of all three."

MajGen Swannack approved a get-tough approach, called Opera-tion Iron Hammer, a series of sweeps for weapons caches and raids to seize insurgent leaders. "This is war," he said. "I am going to use a sledgehammer to crush a walnut."

It was a war the 82nd was fighting alone. Drinkwine's nine-hundred-man battalion was fighting a guerrilla war in a city containing 43,000 potential insurgents. With Sheikh Jamal in jail, the imam who filled the void with the most inflammatory sermons was Abdullah Al Janabi, a saturnine, pinched-faced man in his early fifties. Ra'ad warned Drinkwine that Janabi was a fundamentalist who had fled arrest under Saddam; he was a nervous man, difficult to approach. When Drinkwine asked him to tone things down, Janabi launched into a diatribe about infidels, Shiites, and apostates, meaning anyone who cooperated with the Americans. He seemed to be daring Drinkwine to arrest him and provoke a riot.

Drinkwine drove back to his base by the artificial lake east of the city and wrote Janabi a letter, warning that he would be arrested if he continued with seditious sermons. Knowing his mosque near the Government Center was probably bugged and his apprehension imminent, Janabi temporarily left the city.

The paratroopers didn't know who supported them in the city. During the day they patrolled the outer highways and drove through town in shows of force, searching vehicles at random. At night they conducted raids. It was their favorite tactic: they would drive with night-vision goggles, roar down a street in the pitch black with the lights out, scale a courtyard wall, then rush through the front door and up the steps into the sleeping quarters; sometimes a masked informer would point someone out or shake his head no.

Specialist Dudin said that the people called them the **bou-bous**. "In the States we say watch out for the boogeyman," Dudin said. "In Iraq a mother will say to her kids, 'Stop doing that, or the bou-bou monster will get you.' We were the bou-bous."

In early November, the raid that was most satisfying to the paratroopers occurred when they entered a house and found nothing incriminating. The occupants, however, pointed to a house across the street. Rushing over, the soldiers found a man crouched over a computer monitor in his downstairs study. Open on the screen was a sketch of a sophisticated IED. They arrested Brigadier General Al Mahadaai, Ph.D., aka the Rocket Man, the top trainer and supplier of the IED teams and the man believed responsible for Sgt Johnson's death.

The city elders protested vehemently against the increased use of force, the raids, and the bursts of gunfire whenever an IED exploded, arguing that it was driving the people to the side of the insurgents. Maj-Gen Swannack did release several women, who were being held because they were relatives of insurgents. But that was one of his few concessions. The get-tough policy seemed to be showing results. By mid-November attacks by explosive devices had decreased from two to one per day.

A month later the relentless American campaign to hunt down the top Baathists reached its zenith when television networks broadcast the pictures of a disheveled Saddam Hussein with his mouth open, meekly submitting to a medical exam by his American captors. To many Iraqis, Saddam had been the devil who could not be killed. His capture removed the fear that he would again seize power and wreak revenge on his enemies, as he had after the Gulf War in 1991.

In Fallujah, however, the hope for a dwindling in the insurgent spirit was quickly extinguished. While Baghdad celebrated Saddam's capture, Fallujah rioted. Supporters of the old regime stormed the Government Center, firing AKs in the air and shouting that the fight against the American occupiers would continue. A company of paratroopers in Bradleys and Humvees responded, RPG rockets bounced off several of the vehicles, and one Iraqi was killed.

A few weeks later a visitor to an elementary school in the city asked about American soldiers. "We must resist them!" the children shouted. "We must force them to leave, with bombs, with explosives! I am ready to fight now!"

Inside the insurgent movement the fundamentalist clerics in the city were competing with the former regime elements who had previously dominated them. Saddam's ignominious capture had shifted the balance of power toward the jihadists without weakening the intensity of the insurgency.

As December drew to a close, the minimum force Drinkwine would send into Fallujah was a platoon mounted in six vehicles, and they could not stay in any one place for more than half an hour before the insurgents would sneak up and fire at them. Iraqi National Guardsmen wouldn't be available until midwinter. In the meantime, if the police accompanied the paratroopers, they could warn them about suspicious characters. The police wouldn't have to fight; the paratroopers would take it from there.

The police refused to help.

"We tell them, no, we can't do that," a police captain said. "The mujahedeen would say we are collaborators. You work with the Americans, you die."

4

A BACKWATER PROBLEM

AS THE SEASON OF PRESIDENTIAL POLI-
TICS began, the Democratic Party increased its criticisms of Bush's Iraqi policies. Since the president had
declared major hostilities at an end, 344 Americans
had died in Iraq. With the presidential election ten
months away, two Democratic candidates—retired
general Wesley Clark and Massachusetts senator John
Kerry—were emphasizing their military records to
give weight to their criticisms, while a third, former
governor Howard Dean, was running on an antiwar
platform.

The capture of Saddam in mid-December gave the
president a temporary bump up to a 60 percent
approval rating for his handling of Iraq, but in January 2004 that rating settled back to 50 percent, not a
reassuring number for someone facing reelection.

After the war, when the looting began, essential services failed, and attacks upon Americans grew, the tone of the press reports changed from congratulatory to discontented. The bonds, however, between the journalists in the field and the soldiers remained a constant. IED explosions, like shipwrecks, made news, and the sympathy that the journalists harbored for the American soldiers sharpened the edge to stories describing American sacrifices for Iraqis who did not appear to be grateful or to be fighting for their own liberty. Conversely, the mainstream American press expressed no sympathy for the insurgents' methods or goals, not wanting to see Iraq fall apart and become a breeding ground for terrorists. With the stakes too high for failure, the press focused on how long the fighting would go on and when Iraqi forces would begin to replace Americans.

At the Pentagon, Secretary Rumsfeld was not satisfied with the pace of the Iraqi training or with the clarity of the security assessments. The toughest area was Anbar Province, west of Baghdad and home of Fallujah and other hard Sunni cities. The Euphrates River sliced at a northwest angle across Anbar Province into Syria, 200 miles to the west. Most of Anbar's tribal inhabitants lived in a string of nine cities along the river. Anbar, with two million restive Sunnis and no wealth or political influence, received little attention from the CPA or Iraqi civilian officials in Baghdad. Anbar was Indian Country, best handled by American military.

Despite the obvious insurgency in Anbar, at the beginning of the year General Sanchez was offering an upbeat assessment. "We've made significant progress in Anbar Province. Iraqis have gotten tired of the violence and are cooperating," he said. "They want to get on with living their lives."

Senior officials at the Pentagon weren't so sure about such cooperation, and Wolfowitz was tired of haggling at long distance over minuscule budget matters. A deputy secretary of defense and a lieutenant general on the staff of the Joint Chiefs of Staff should not have to send cables to the CPA asking for money to buy trucks or machine guns for the National Guard, as happened on more than one occasion.

Rumsfeld and Wolfowitz decided to conduct an outside review under CentCom's auspices. In mid-January Major General Karl Eikenberry, an army officer with a reputation for intellectual rigor, arrived in Baghdad with an assessment team. He and his team listened to briefings by the CPA and JTF staffs working in the shambles of the tasteless palace inside Baghdad's heavily protected Green Zone. Each day a thousand Americans left their tiny air-conditioned trailers, lined up for breakfast cafeteria-style, then drifted off to their plywood cubicles to spend a twelve-hour day in front of computer screens. Most never ventured out of the sixty-acre compound, spending tours of three to six months as secure and as isolated as they would have been in any prison in the United States.

The assessment team members visited eighteen American battalions. The battalion commanders were not satisfied with the pace or direction of the training of Iraqi security forces. With the exception of the British down south in Basra, all were disturbed by the fact that the insurgency was growing much faster than the Iraqi security forces.

At the same time, the CPA was structuring an army that was intended to play a very small role inside Iraq's borders. Given the military's depredations during the Saddam era, an army was not to be trusted. The CPA strategy envisioned a peacetime state—starting at an indefinite time two to five years in the future—when the Iraqi police would provide internal stability. It was up to the JTF to bring Iraq to that state of relative normalcy, after which the American forces would pull back to cantonments and the Iraqi security forces would take over.

The Iraqi Army would be based to the north and east, facing mainly toward the Iranian border. Ambassador Bremer had prepared for Congress a budget that allocated $2 billion for the new Iraqi Army to protect the external borders and $75 million for the National Guard to protect the police inside the borders. Per man, the cost was $50,000 for an Iraqi Army soldier for border defense and $3,400 for a National Guard soldier for defeating the insurgents.

This division of labor and resources did not make sense to planners in the Pentagon. "We had the wrong design for that army," Secretary Wolfowitz said.

The CentCom planners had told the study members

that "it is not our desire to use the Iraqi Army internally." The Eikenberry study disagreed, concluding that "we don't have the luxury of an Iraqi Army not involved in defeating the insurgency." The key to the counterinsurgency campaign in Iraq lay "in building up the Iraqis," not in pursuing offensive operations.

The study recommended shifting from the CPA to CentCom control over the budgets and policies of the Iraqi Army and police. Training of the army had already migrated to CentCom, and it made sense to consolidate the various security functions under one manager. The Eikenberry study advocated unity of command, collocating budgetary authority, held by the CPA, with operational responsibility, held by CentCom. After hearing a spirited rejoinder from the CPA about disruptions to existing programs, Rumsfeld worked out an agreement whereby control over the Iraqi Army passed to CentCom, while the CPA retained control over the police.

In Fallujah and elsewhere Iraqi police with scant training and old, thuggish habits struggled on. The CPA wanted to bring in European advisers, as had been done in Bosnia, but few volunteered, and none for Fallujah. The 82nd rated all forty-nine police stations in its area of operations as noneffective. The CPA had provided 92 of the 318 police vehicles requested by the 82nd, 274 of the 1,445 radios, plus sixty pistols and a three-week training course for a thousand officers.

Month after month Gen Swannack asked the CPA for the equipment. Swannack believed his requests were hampered by "bureaucrats" who remained in Iraq only for a few months, leaving before they had made good on their promises. "My comments fell on deaf ears," he said.

The 82nd complained that the CPA retained tight control from Baghdad but failed to deliver. While illustrating the lack of communication between the CPA and the JTF, the charge did not do justice to the thicket of regulations surrounding the CPA. Congress had tied money for Iraqi forces to a labyrinth of peacetime restrictions. Some members of Congress urged the CPA to cut through the bottlenecks, while others blamed Bremer for hasty decisions that seemed to result in waste. Many in the CPA pointed to the layers of congressional restrictions placed upon purchases, slowing expenditures to a dribble.

"Every major project had to go to Washington for a budget review, then over to Congress for authorization. Any change over two per-cent among dozens of programs had to go back to congressional committees for approval," Lieutenant General Jeffrey Oster, the CPA chief of staff, said. "The congressional process for releasing money was a maze."

Rather than have local seamstresses sew uniforms for the Iraqis, competitive bids had to be taken on the American market, causing delays of months. Vehicles purchased for the Iraqi police had to be advertised and competed for in the United States, when a five-hour drive over the border into Jordan yielded trucks at a fraction of the cost (an option several battalion commanders quietly chose).

Inside the administration, friction and backbiting arose about the causes of the slow expenditure of funds. The deputy secretary of state, Richard Armitage, directly blamed the CPA for not spending the authorized money. "We have little complaint about congressional restrictions on [Iraqi] spending," he told a congressional committee. "CPA moved more gingerly than they should have."

Bremer was damned if he rapidly spent the money and damned if he didn't.

———

At the tip of the spear in the most dangerous city in Iraq, LtCol Drinkwine didn't care about the high-level issues of assigning blame or about billion-dollar budgets. His concerns were the lack of equipment for the police, the daily attacks on his troops, and sorting out which city leaders were secretly supporting the insurgents.

Drinkwine began 2004 by coordinating with the special operations forces to search the souk next to the Brooklyn Bridge at the western end of the city, an area the police refused to patrol. The souk consisted of hundreds of one-story boutique shops jammed side by side in a maze of twisting alleyways in the oldest section of the city, called the Jolan District. The insurgents boasted that the Jolan was invulnerable; the tangle of streets provided them with hundreds of back alleys through which to escape and circle back to swarm over any invading force of Americans.

The Special Operations Command came to Drinkwine with an unorthodox solution that he supported enthusiastically. On the morning of January 2 the souk was jammed with people and cars, the smoke from faulty exhaust pipes obscuring the view of the Brooklyn Bridge, a few hundred meters down the street to the west. Drinkwine had two companies poised for a quick raid. Two Delta soldiers were in the souk marking the target shops. None of the hundreds of Iraqi men wandering down the cluttered side streets challenged the crazed man in a filthy dishdasha who hobbled from shop to shop, peering at the weapons for sale and mumbling to himself.

At the edge of the souk he stumbled as he walked around a bread truck. When he angrily slammed a fist against a dented rear fender, the rear doors suddenly opened, he was hauled inside, and the doors slammed shut. The Delta soldier paused a minute to catch his breath in relief. Had an arms dealer challenged him inside the souk, his rudimentary Arabic would have betrayed him. If his partner, fluent in Arabic, couldn't talk their way out, Drinkwine would have had to rush in when the shooting began. Whether he would have arrived in time was another matter.

Safely inside the truck, the Delta operative drew a quick sketch, showing the paratroopers their key targets. Minutes later a company of paratroopers leaped from hiding places as Bradley fighting vehicles roared up to form a cordon. Led by their special forces guides, the paratroopers rushed from alley to alley, arresting fifteen Iraqis and seizing seventeen IEDs. Breaking into back rooms, they found so many explosives and weapons that they had to call for four dump trucks to haul them all away. They withdrew before the insurgents could organize a counterattack.

————

While the raid was a success, it had no wider implications. A few days later insurgents in Fallujah killed two French citizens. The two, working for a U.S. company, had stopped for a quick repair outside Fallujah on Highway 6, the heavily traveled main artery. A passing car had opened fire on the two men. After that no prudent Westerner traveled near Fallujah in a small group.

Travel by air near the city was equally perilous. On January 8 a Blackhawk helicopter, with five huge red crosses on the fuselage, was flying a medevac mission along the Euphrates south of Fallujah when it was downed by a surface-to-air missile, killing nine soldiers and bringing the number of Americans killed to thirty-seven in and around the city. It was the second shoot-down in a week. Of the six helicopters shot down since Baghdad was seized, four had occurred in the Fallujah area.

Informers reported that Khamis Sirhan had sent a surface-to-air missile (SAM) team into the farming district south of the city. A major general under Saddam, Sirhan was the highest-ranking insurgent in the Fallujah area. Before his arrest, Sheikh Barakat had moved money for Sirhan.

Drinkwine set out to find Sirhan, surrounding the farmlands with two companies and searching house to house. The SAM team had left, some said going back to Syria. Sirhan, though, made the mistake of remaining in the city. A woman admitted knowing his cousin, and his cousin gave up an address. At three in the morning of January 11 the house was surrounded and Sirhan was seized without a struggle. He was the eighth high-ranking former officer to be captured in six weeks.

"It had taken us five months to figure it out," Dudin said. "But at last we had a technique. The special ops and intel guys were putting together diagrams of the movers and shakers in the city. Most of them had big houses and big egos. They didn't like living in the boondocks. Sooner or later they came home for a few days. Some nights we'd search their houses and not even wake up their kids. We got that skilled, all quiet like. We missed a lot of times, but we kept coming back."

Believing he had momentum, Drinkwine organized an FPAC, or Fallujah Provisional Authority Council, comprised of sheikhs, business leaders, and imams. Janabi emerged from hiding to claim one of the spots reserved for the imams, and Drinkwine put aside his suspicions in a gesture toward a new beginning. With General Sirhan behind bars, he invited the FPAC to take charge and to work with eleven Fallujah Liaison Teams appointed from his battalion. Bring your requests, Drinkwine said, and we'll try to resolve them.

The mid-January FPAC meeting seemed to go well. A torrent of complaints about American conduct and contracts not delivered poured forth, but there were no threats of violence. Drinkwine noticed that Janabi didn't say a word. The meeting ended with the election of a council president, and a meeting was scheduled for the next month.

Two days later a mob gathered outside the mayor's office at the Government Center to protest the election of the council. When the paratroopers were called to disperse them, a riot ensued and two Iraqis were killed.

"It's great to be nice," Drinkwine said. "But we've found out if you let up for one second against the bad guys, they're right back at your throat."

Drinkwine had tried political suasion and municipal improvement, but in the end it came back to raw military muscle. The battle lines were clear: it was the Americans against the insurgents.

The composition and leadership of the insurgents were changing. As the FREs weakened, Drinkwine received warnings that foreign fighters were infiltrating into the Jolan, including the arch-terrorist Abu Musab al Zarqawi. From Fallujah, Zarqawi sent Osama bin Laden a letter in January asking for help in continuing the guerrilla war. On a night raid two Egyptians were arrested in an apartment with slogans supporting bin Laden scrawled in sheep's blood on a wall. Neighbors told a reporter that foreign fighters were threatening people who played Western music, styled their hair, wore revealing clothes, or even sold wood to contractors working for the Americans.

"Fallujah is controlled by two powers—the Americans and the muja-hedeen," one Fallujan said after the raid. "If we cooperate with the mujahedeen, we get raided. If we cooperate with the Americans, we get killed."

Some groups among the insurgents were becoming bolder, firing RPGs during the daytime from East Manhattan at Bradleys parked at the cloverleaf. More IEDs were being found inside the city than along the highways.

"We heard the Islamic fundamentalists were starting to taunt Saddam's guys, saying the old army guys didn't have the balls to take on the Americans," Dudin said. "We saw changes in tactics."

A Bradley came under fire as it passed an elementary school attended by the daughters of members of the FPAC. The insurgents kept running out from behind the school, firing a few bursts and ducking back again. The soldiers didn't fire back. The next day Drinkwine conducted a two-company sweep from the cloverleaf on the eastern outskirts of the city. Within twenty minutes a white flare went off over the Blue Mosque where Janabi preached, about a kilometer west down Highway 10. Soon pickup trucks were darting out of alleyways, shooting at the paratroopers, and dodging back to cover. When the paratroopers moved forward, the insurgents moved back deeper into the city. Drinkwine declined to follow, seeing no gain in escalating a clash with excitable youths.

Such random fights were constant in Fallujah. Since August his soldiers had engaged in 262 firefights and come under rocket or mortar attack on sixty-one occasions. In addition, 270 IEDs had been detonated or disarmed, and there had been eight serious attacks against helicopters. Faced with such violence, Drinkwine and his brigade commander, Col Smith, preferred the scalpel of the night raid to the broadsword of the daytime sweep.

"The enemy [in Fallujah] is like a cancer," Drinkwine said. "It has had thirty-five years to grow. When you have someone who has cancer, you go and carve out the heart of it. If you just turn away from it, it will continue to grow and it may grow back stronger."

The opposition returned the sentiment, using the same analogy. "The occupation is like a cancer," said Nadhim Khalil, a twenty-five-year-old Sunni cleric suspected of plotting attacks. "It has to be removed."

As January drew to a close, Drinkwine believed the city elders were prevailing over the shrill voices of the Sunni clerics. Preachers like Janabi weren't speaking up in the council meetings. They seemed to be malcontents whose influence could be marginalized by economic improvement. "After you cut out a cancer, you have to rejuvenate the body," he said, elaborating on his cancer analogy. "We're cutting out the FREs. Then the body has to heal. Fallujah needs a healthy economy and hope in the future."

From his perspective, the city elders lived in perpetual fear of political and economic isolation, paranoid about change and the outside world because it had never brought them any good. With their provincial accent, country ways, and enormous rate of illiteracy, they were the butt of jokes among the Baghdad middle class. The bustling eight-lane highway outside the city had devastated their commerce as a waystop between Baghdad and Jordan. Their industry, which had been totally subsidized by Saddam's military machine, had collapsed. Aside from farming, kidnapping, and truck driving, the sources of income in the city were nil. The business leaders had no functioning businesses.

Every family in Iraq was provided with food and electricity, when it was on, for free. This subsistence economy and lack of money gave rise to a belief among the American military that creating jobs was the surest means of combating the insurgency.

Col Smith regularly trekked to Baghdad with a list of the brigade's needs that overwhelmed the resources it received. For Fallujah, he had a total of $200,000 a month to spend. Repairing the sewer and water-purification system alone would cost $20 million. Thirty industries capable of employing tens of thousands of laborers lay idle; the cost of rejuvenating them would be $25 million.

"Baghdad kept too much for itself," Smith said.

Baghdad was the political, economic, and cultural capital of Iraq. Both the CPA and the JTF had their headquarters there. Baghdad had to show progress toward stability and economic growth. The CPA's next priority was taking care of the political aspirations of the Shiites. Then came Kurdish restiveness in Kirkuk and the needs of population centers like Mosul and Basra.

Although Fallujah was at the top of the list in terms of violence, in terms of politics it was a backwater problem.

5

VALENTINE'S DAY MASSACRE

IN FEBRUARY TWO IRAQI NATIONAL GUARD battalions arrived in Fallujah, and on February 12 Gen Abizaid visited one of the battalions at the Government Center. In Abizaid's view, the time had come for Americans to take their hands off the controls and allow the Iraqis to help themselves. "It's their country," Abizaid said. "It's their future."

The Iraqi battalion commander, Lieutenant Colonel Nowar, proudly presented a briefing. When Abizaid asked a question, Nowar began his answer by saying, "Well, we all know Fallujah is a tough town."

No sooner had he spoken than two rocket-propelled grenades exploded in the courtyard.

"See?" Nowar said.

The plan for Abizaid to walk downtown, as American reporters had done the previous summer, was promptly canceled.

The officers of the 82nd were not pleased that the four-star general had been fired upon in Fallujah. The police insisted the attack had been the work of outsiders and criminals. They shrugged off posters promising death to collaborators. There was no insurgency, the police said. If the Americans stayed away, all would be well. With a battalion of National Guard in the city, Drinkwine agreed to remove his soldiers from all fixed checkpoints. The police assured him they could handle the situation.

Two days later, on Valentine's Day, Drinkwine was at his battalion base east of Fallujah when reports came in of a heavy gunfight in the center of the city. Two dozen insurgents, some in National Guard and police uniforms, had launched an assault on the main police station. Shouting "God is great" and "There is no God but Allah," they also attacked the compound housing the National Guard battalion. When the fighting did not let up after half an hour, Col Smith and LtCol Drinkwine decided to send in an armored column, although they hadn't been asked to help.

Before the tanks left the compound, Lieutenant Colonel Suleiman al Marawi drove in, at the head of a half-dozen pickups. A short man with a thick black mustache, Suleiman was in charge of a National Guard battalion stationed on the western peninsula, on the far side of the Brooklyn Bridge. The battalion had been recruited a week earlier and was untrained—it consisted of four hundred former soldiers and unemployed youths, pulled together with the promise that the 82nd would give them three weeks of training, AK rifles, uniforms, and $200 a month. Now Suleiman, summoned by Smith and Drinkwine, had rushed into the American base with a few dozen excited, fresh-faced young men.

Drinkwine had met Suleiman only a few times. Suleiman had gone to high school in Fallujah, then moved to another city before being accepted at the military academy. He had joined the Baath Party, served in the Republican Guard, trained fedayeen insurgents before the invasion, and refused to speak English. He had been the city elders' third choice to lead a column into the city because he was an outsider known as a hardhead, difficult to control. Suleiman told Drinkwine that the Americans had to stay out of the fight. If they charged in with their armor, he said, they would kill the wrong people. He demanded grenades, handheld radios, and ammunition for the operation.

Smith asked where LtCol Nowar was. Gone, Suleiman said. The police chief, Abood, was no help either. Suleiman gestured impatiently. "I need to be the protector," he said to Smith, "not you."

He and his volunteers needed military equipment, not questions. Drinkwine agreed, and the paratroopers piled the pickups full of ammunition. Then Suleiman led his little convoy into the city.

The battle was petering out, and within an hour Suleiman's men were sifting through the wreckage of the shattered police station. The insurgents had freed seventy-five prisoners and killed twenty-three policemen. At most, eight attackers were killed or captured.

When Suleiman called for him to come in, Drink-wine arrived on scene with a company mounted in Bradleys. After his medics extracted thirteen pieces of shrapnel from one insurgent, the dazed guerrilla rattled off the names of his leaders, some of whom had been taken to the hospital.

Drinkwine and Suleiman then drove to the hospital, where the director, Rafi Aieisaw, refused to allow them to see the dead or wounded insurgents, despite blood trails in the main corridor. He relented after Suleiman threatened to kill him. Suleiman identified two of the dead as brothers from a small Luhaibi tribe in eastern Fallujah. One had been a lieutenant and the other a captain in the army. Both were members of a fundamentalist cell working in the city with Zarqawi.

Drinkwine and Suleiman rushed over to the cell's headquarters, an abandoned, battered building that also served as a mosque for a recently arrived imam sponsored by Janabi. According to Suleiman, Janabi, who was nowhere to be found, had been a business-man for most of his life and had taken up preaching as a lucrative side business. The paratroopers moved on to search four small "mosques"—shabby, half-built buildings—set up by Janabi in the same neighbor-hood. All contained weapons and explosives.

The next day Drinkwine fired the police chief when he refused to wear his uniform. LtCol Nowar, having failed to fight, stepped down in disgrace. Many in the police and the city hierarchy had known the attack was coming and had left town for the day. The mayor, Ra'ad Hussein Abed, had been mysteriously absent during the attack and was uncooperative in answering questions the next day. He was arrested on charges of conspiracy and withholding information. Ra'ad protested that many people had heard of a possible attack. His enemies were setting him up so they would get the American contracts. Call the 3rd ID back in Texas, he said; their commanders would vouch for him. His entreaties were to no avail, and he was sent to prison.

The following night, despite threats from the insurgents, a thousand people turned out to elect representatives to the Anbar Provincial Council. Safe inside the Government Center, the sheikhs condemned the killings and threatened tribal revenge. In previous attacks insurgents had assassinated translators and contractors who picked up the garbage at the 82nd base. This was the first attack against fellow townsmen who had refused to cooperate with the Americans.

Drinkwine hoped the sheikhs would retaliate. After a few days he concluded they would mutter and fulminate but not take up arms. The sheikhs had been cowed. The traditional system of tribal retaliation no longer protected anyone in the city. As the American-mounted patrols had daily rolled past the mosques and suburbs, the roots of the rebellion had grown stronger.

While Gen Abizaid's principle was to "take American hands off the controls," if that happened in Fallujah, the insurgents would grab the controls. BrigGen Kimmitt, the deputy director for operations at JTF headquarters in Baghdad, acknowledged this point when asked to comment on the fight at the police station. "The fact remains," he said, "that places like Fallujah are not ready for local control."

Working together, the jihadists and the former soldiers had killed the policemen they had grown up with, eaten with, and prayed with. No longer was it enough in Fallujah to be a local who minded his own business and was careful in his dealings with the Americans.

The twenty-three deaths by small-arms fire were the highest number in any firefight in the Iraqi war. The size of the attack and the exuberance with which neighbors killed neighbors showed a depth of military opposition not previously encountered by the 82nd. The cultural system of clans encouraged submissiveness to a few alpha males; the attack signaled the rise of a new group of alphas. Fallujah had lurched into a new phase of warfare.

Reaction to the police slayings focused on arrests and investigations of traitors rather than an assessment of the event's significance. The CIA had only a few agents at the 82nd base camp, and there was no functioning intelligence service inside the Iraqi government. Janabi was not redlined for special attention by Task Force 6-26, and the two fundamentalist cells implicated in the attack received no further attention.

The Valentine's Day Massacre was a watershed event, underplayed because the American forces were in a period of transition. Drinkwine's battalion was preparing to pull out of Fallujah and return to the States, leaving a city where the outcome was in doubt.

The destruction of the police station brought Fallujah to the front pages of American newspapers for a few days. The city's notoriety, however, was soon eclipsed by massive car bombings across Iraq. On March 3, 143 Shiites on religious holiday in Karbala were blown to bits; most likely it was the work of Zarqawi, as he tried to provoke a civil war between the Shiites and the Sunnis. The following week 192 people were killed in Spain when al Qaeda terrorists blew up a train. Five days later Spain elected a prime minister who pledged to pull all Spanish troops out of Iraq.

Despite these setbacks Drinkwine saw some signs of hope. Due to the intelligence task forces, he was having success with raids. LtCol Suleiman had emerged as a determined leader, unafraid of his fellow Baathists. In the Valentine's Day Massacre in Chicago in 1929, mobsters posing as police had gunned down seven other criminals; a revolted citizenry then rose up and took back their city. Drinkwine was hoping the sheikhs would support Suleiman as their modern-day Eliot Ness.

In late February the Fallujah Provisional Authority Commission met to appoint a new mayor, a man who had served in that post under the Saddam regime. The sheikhs then joined the new mayor in berating the Americans for arresting men suspected of participating in the massacre. Suleiman, some murmured, had violated Islamic law by searching the dead martyrs at the hospital.

Drinkwine's battalion was nearing the end of its seven-month deployment. With the city elders showing no backbone, Drinkwine revised his expectations about the future as he prepared to turn the city over to the Marines, who would replace his paratroopers. "None of this [armed resistance] was here when we got here," he told a reporter in March. "And six months from now, when the Marines leave, they will have created much more. They will have captured and killed more of the enemy. But there will still be more out there that will pick up a gun and attack."

———

Handing Fallujah off to the Marines was not like handing the baton from one runner to the next. Each division brought its own style and ways of doing things. A year earlier the 1st Marine Division had feinted and slashed through six Iraqi divisions and, ignoring orders to slow down, had seized the eastern half of Baghdad weeks ahead of plan. The Marines had then spent several months restoring municipal services in a dozen relatively peaceful Shiite cities before returning to the States.

In March that same Marine team was back in Iraq. Well seasoned after leading the 66,000 Marines from Kuwait to Baghdad in 2003, Lieutenant General James T. Conway commanded the 1st Marine Expeditionary Force, comprised of an air wing, a logistics support group, and an infantry division. Under Conway the 1st Marine Division was commanded by MajGen Mattis, who had a reputation for boldness and who constantly visited the frontlines to sense the rhythm of the battlefield. Like the 82nd, the 1st Marine Division would be spread across the sixteen thousand square kilometers of Anbar Province.

Back at Camp Pendleton, Conway and Mattis had considered two courses of action for their return to Iraq. The first emphasized offensive operations— sweeps and raids. That approach could be successful— there was no lack of targets—and it would provide rewarding feedback to the troops. Over 50 percent of the eighteen thousand Marines in the division were veterans of the march up to Baghdad—they could handle combat. But there were hundreds of thousands of potential recruits for the insurgents in Anbar Province. Americans by themselves couldn't win an insurgency.

The second course of action, which they chose, emphasized showing respect for the population and training Iraqi soldiers. Retired Marines from the Combined Action Platoon (CAP) program in Vietnam were invited to Pendleton to share lessons learned about how to live with indigenous soldiers. In 113 Vietnamese villages individual Marine squads had lived for a year with the farmers, training them to fight as local militias. The CAPs had been singularly successful, liked both by the villagers and by the American squads.

Mattis invited Arab experts to address his commanders, while the troops studied Arabic phrases and learned how to avoid giving offense. The Marine Corps Small Wars Manual, which describes how to quell an insurrection, was required reading. Legendary figures such as Chesty Puller and Smedley Butler, who had earned their reputations as leaders of local troops in remote barrios, were held up as examples. Frisbees, soccer balls, and teddy bears were packed in crates alongside combat gear.

Journalists had passed along stories of rough treatment by American soldiers stationed in Ramadi and Fallujah—doors smashed in, cars banged aside by Bradleys, an us-versus-them attitude.

"The enemy will try to manipulate you into hating all Iraqis," Mattis wrote to his troops. "Do not allow the enemy that victory. With strong discipline, solid faith, unwavering alertness, and undiminished chivalry to the innocent, we will carry out this mission. Remember, I have added 'First, Do No Harm' to our passwords of 'No Better Friend, No Worse Enemy.' "

The Marines would knock on doors, Mattis said, not kick the door down and put a boot on a man's neck. There would be no bulldozing of houses or arrests of the relatives of insurgents. If shot at, no fusillade would be loosed in response. Mattis emphasized marksmanship—one shot, one kill. The hope was that restraint in attitude and firepower would lead to more toleration of U.S. troops and less toleration of the armed resistance. Arab newspaper accounts of the new training circulated in Anbar Province. Insurgent leaflets nicknamed the new troops **awat**, a sugary, soft cake that crumbles easily.

In the States, press articles suggested that the Marines were implicitly criticizing army tactics, a charge both

Conway and Mattis denied. "We are learning from what the army has done," Conway said. "We will achieve the level of fire superiority necessary to take care of each situation. But we need to be discerning in our fires to make sure we don't create enemies in the process."

Despite the efforts to deny it, Army and Marines did have different approaches. The Marines operated on lean budgets with less equipment, emphasizing marksmanship and aggressive small-unit leadership. Because they constantly deployed from ships onto foreign shores, they instinctively sought out the local leaders to work out the ground rules. They intended to interact as amicably with the Sunnis as they had with the Shiites.

Every new unit thinks it can do a better job than the one before. Many of the departing paratroopers believed the Marines were too optimistic, while many of the Marines believed the paratroopers had been too quick to shoot. The Sunnis weren't the Shiites, however, and Fallujah wasn't Karbala, where a year earlier the Shiite city council had tried to elect the Marine battalion commander as mayor. The 82nd hadn't found the Sunnis willing to bond. The paratroopers had had a grueling tour, greeted by scowls, explosive devices, and Fallujans who complained of random return fire when an American was fired upon, but remained silent when insurgents killed their fellow Iraqis.

The commander of the 82nd held a press conference as the division's tour came to an end. Unlike

Drinkwine's soldiers, he believed the war against the insurgents was largely won. The Marines, in his judgment, would face only low-level opposition.

"I'm discounting a very serious insurgency ongoing here [in Anbar Province] right now," MajGen Charles Swannack told reporters, "because of these factors—successfully taking away the leaders of the insurgency, the funding and the facilitation of the insurgency. Now it's more low-level individuals who still have a gripe against coalition forces that attack us."

The CPA senior diplomat in Anbar, Keith Mines, was also leaving in March. In contrast to the general, his final report was stinging.

"Development of the security forces is a failure difficult to comprehend," he wrote. "Ten months into the operation there is not a single properly trained and equipped Iraqi security officer in the entire Al Anbar province. There are over 10,000 police and civil defense officers on the rolls, but none have received anything more than ad hoc training and rudimentary equipment."

In his view, the province was too vast to be controlled by one division, either the 82nd or the Marines. Worse, Mines wrote, not a single Iraqi police officer in Anbar had had more than three weeks of training, and the National Guard units were completely ineffective. Security depended entirely on the American soldiers; yet their presence inflamed Sunni nationalism.

After seven months in the city, LtCol Drinkwine too was reserved. His battalion had suffered ninety-four killed and wounded in seven months. He saw in the Valentine's Day Massacre a "marriage of convenience" between the clever Baathist leadership and the religious extremists. The people listened more to the imams than to the sheikhs, and his list of radical clerics was growing. At the top he placed Janabi and three others, but he had not apprehended a single one of them. The insurgents had begun to kill their fellow townspeople, who weren't fighting back.

The Marines thought they could work with the Iraqi soldiers, but Drinkwine had found only one leader with gumption—Suleiman—and he stayed in his compound on the peninsula. Drinkwine doubted that the Marines could stop the IEDs and random gunfights. They were the work of the footsoldiers in the insurgency, and Fallujah could produce thousands of them.

"I think the Marines will enjoy working in Fallujah," he said. "But they'll be bloodied."

PART II

SIEGE

March to May 2004

6

"THEY CAN'T DO THAT TO AMERICANS."

THE 82ND WAS TURNING ANBAR PROV-INCE over to the Marines in the last week in March 2004. Prior to that the commanders spent several days together. The 2nd Battalion of the 1st Marine Regiment, or Battalion 2/1, was assigned to Fallujah. The commander, Lieutenant Colonel Gregg Olson, was a tall, bespectacled man known, like Drinkwine, for being thoughtful and analytical.

On March 18, Drinkwine and Olson drove to the Government Center to meet with the city elders. While the officers palavered with the sheikhs, paratroopers and Marines kept guard on the roof. At midday Army First Sergeant Roger Parker sent up fresh troops to change the watch.

In the midst of the turnover, no one heard the faint **plunk!** of a mortar round leaving the tube. The shell hit dead center on the roof, spraying the backs and legs of dozens of paratroopers and Marines. It was the first round fired from a makeshift location—a one-in-a-thousand shot.

Captain Doug Zembiec, commanding Echo Company of Battalion 2/1, was kneeling on the roof when he heard a sharp **crack!** and turned to see a cloud of black smoke and dust, with soldiers and Marines screaming. In the courtyard 1/Sgt Parker heard the yelling: "We got wounded up here!"

Parker radioed for the four-vehicle evacuation team on the edge of town to come forward. Marines and soldiers were running up the stairs. Four more shells exploded harmlessly inside the perimeter. Two rocket-propelled grenades sailed over the compound, killing two Iraqi civilians standing on a side street. Small-arms fire broke out and quickly escalated. Everybody seemed to be shooting wildly.

"Cease fire!" Zembiec screamed. "Cease fire! I don't want to hear one goddamn round unless you have eyes on target!"

The shooting stopped as abruptly as it had started, and everyone turned to helping the wounded down the stairs. Parker was supervising the triage, making sure the most serious wounds were treated first. He saw Private First Class Dimitry Todeleski carry down one paratrooper, then go back for another. When he turned to climb up the stairs a third time, his legs buckled, and he sat down heavily.

"I'm tired, First Sergeant," Todeleski said. "I feel wore out."

Parker looked at the blood seeping into the cement around the PFC.

"You're not tired, Todeleski," Parker said. "Stay there and let the medics patch you up. You've done enough for the day."

One shell had peppered eighteen paratroopers and seventeen Marines. No one was killed, but four soldiers required evacuation to the States. One hundred and eleven pieces of shrapnel were pulled out of one soldier. As the paratroopers withdrew, the Marines formed an honor guard, a gesture Drinkwine's paratroopers appreciated.

"That was a wild first day," Zembiec said, "I mean, what kind of a town tries to kill the town council?"

On March 24, the 82nd formally handed over authority to the MEF; the ceremony outside Fallujah was briefly interrupted as helicopters evacuated two Marines wounded near the city. That night a special operations squad returning from a mission was attacked on Highway 10 in eastern Fallujah, with two wounded. The next day a convoy was ambushed at the same place and a Marine was killed, bringing to twenty-six the number of attacks in March in Fallujah.

That ended Conway's patience. "I ordered my division commander to take action," he said. "I wanted the route through the city made safe for military traffic."

Two rifle companies from Battalion 2/1 got the job. Zembiec, a bundle of energy who had been a wrestler at the Naval Academy, led Echo Company. On his right flank Captain Kyle Stoddard, whose shaved head and cut physique made him look like Mr. Clean, led Fox Company. With six Humvees with .50 caliber machine guns and Mark 19s that fired streams of small 40mm grenades, Stoddard and Zembiec led their Marines north from Highway 10 into East Manhattan where many former army officers lived. The Marines moved cautiously through the upscale neighborhood—straight paved roads lined with walled courtyards holding imposing cement houses and scraggly palm trees. Not accustomed to seeing Americans on foot, Iraqis left their houses to gawk. At each burst of firing, they fluttered away, then flocked forward again, curiosity overcoming common sense.

Confined to the long narrow streets, the Marines passed boys on bikes, men standing on street corners with cell phones in their hands, taxis scurrying by, and black kites flying over distant intersections. The people began slamming shut the gates to their compounds and retreating indoors. The Marines started taking intermittent fire, one or two men stepping into the street a few hundred meters away, shooting from the hip and quickly dodging behind cover. The insurgents were poor shots, firing wildly and hoping to get lucky.

Seeing a man crouched on a roof talking on a cell phone, a Marine sniper shot him. A crowd quickly gathered, screaming that the man had meant no harm. The man's brother sat on a curbside, sobbing. Iraqis grabbed the Marines by their sleeves, gesturing they should leave as a crowd gathered to carry the body to a mosque. The Marines left, and a few blocks farther on insurgents fired a volley of RPGs at them. An Iraqi cameraman poked his head around the corner to see the reaction of the Marines. He died when a bullet struck him in the head.

All day the company probed the northeastern sector, encountering sporadic opposition, a burst of fire here, an RPG rocket there, then a lull of fifteen minutes, then another burst of fire. In midafternoon a dozen bullets ricocheted off the wall next to Stoddard. When he looked around, he had no idea where his attacker was.

The insurgents ran in and out of courtyards, hoping to get off a shot before they were seen. A car would screech across the street several blocks away, men leaning out the windows and firing wildly. The Marines controlled only the street they stood on, while on the next street a gang lurked in ambush.

At dusk the mortar rounds started dropping and the firing increased. It was dark when Zembiec and Stoddard withdrew their two companies, having lost one Marine. They hoped the residents would say to the insurgents, We don't want trouble—start a fight somewhere else.

Initial reports, however, suggested the opposite. Radio intercepts indicated several wounded fighters were taken to the hospital. Iraqi medical workers warned Western journalists to stay away from the hospitals because the grieving families were armed and seeking revenge. The response to the sweep was not resentment of the insurgents. Instead, it was defiance of the Americans.

———

For the next few days, to avoid inflaming the situation, the Marines concentrated on patrolling the edges of the city, while opening negotiations with LtCol Suleiman to conduct joint operations. But on March 31, less than a week later, the four American contractors from Blackwater Security drove down Highway 10 and were ambushed in the heart of the town. Watching TV in a mess hall outside Fallujah, Capt Zembiec said, "They can't do that to Americans!"

Over 2,500 years ago in **The Iliad,** Homer laid down the basic rule of war. Achilles knew that it was wrong to drag behind his chariot the body of his arch-enemy Hector. Mutilation would have signaled that the vanquished deserved no dignity and that the victor was bound by no rules. To dismember Hector would have been to treat all Trojans as animals, without rights, and someday another tribe would treat Greeks in that manner. Unless soldiers abided by rules, Homer told us, civilization could not progress.

But no matter what the moral proscription was, murderous mobs would commit outrages, as witness the lynchings in the United States at the turn of the 20th century. LtGen Conway regretted the deaths of the four errant American contractors. The MEF had the photos, names, and addresses of the perpetrators and was determined to arrest or kill them. The Marines, though, planned nothing dramatic or sudden. In Fallujah they had seven months to gain control of two miles of homes, apartment buildings, storefronts, boulevards, and alleys. After a week of skirmishes, the division had adjusted its expectations, taking into account the depth of the xenophobia, the influence of the extremist clerics, and the smoldering resentments of American firepower.

"The best we can hope for in Fallujah is not to lose. Not to have an emotional jihad uprising because of something we do or to let it foster as an insurgent base," said Col Dunford, the division's chief of staff. "Americans will never be welcome there."

The division wanted to reduce the insurgency to a tolerable level of violence, install capable Iraqi security forces, and restore Fallujah to its rightful place as an obscure backwater far from the headlines. After that, the local police and soldiers could fight it out with the extremists for the next decade.

Washington, however, thought that was the wrong approach. The mutilation was no longer a battlefield crime but a symbol of America's humiliation and a challenge to the American occupation.

"What makes you come here, Bush, and mess with the people of Fallujah?" the mob had chanted as they dragged the bodies through the streets.

Under a headline reading "Reminder of Mogadishu: Acts of Hatred, Hints of Doubt," the **New York Times** correspondent in Baghdad wrote that "there are hints that American generals are not as sure as they were only weeks ago that they have turned the corner in the conflict." When Somali tribesmen in 1993 dragged the body of an American soldier through the streets of Mogadishu, President Clinton had withdrawn the U.S. forces. In 2004 the stakes were too high for the Americans to pull out of Iraq. President Bush believed that American soldiers had liberated the Iraqi people.

"Where is Bush?" a boy had yelled, pointing at a charred corpse. "Let him come here and see this!"

President Bush did see the mutilation. The response to the sickening images was emotional and aggressive. Defense Secretary Rumsfeld and Gen Abizaid decided that the Marine plan to respond in measured steps ignored the international impact of the event. A city could not be allowed to lurch out of control.

That sentiment was shared by Ambassador Bremer. Seeing the pictures on television, Bremer called General Sanchez into his office.

"I encourage a vigorous attack," Bremer said. Sanchez agreed. He too was dissatisfied with the tempered Marine approach.

The Marines at the tip of the spear didn't understand why they were being ordered to launch—without careful thought—an attack on a city of 280,000 people. Those who incited the mob had been passersby, not insurgent leaders. In any case, before they attacked, key Iraqi officials and allies had to be informed and brought on board. And once the Marines seized the city, someone had to administer municipal services—electricity, water, traffic movement. That meant insuring Iraqis supported the attack. The strategic groundwork hadn't been prepared.

The CPA diplomats in the province aligned with the

Marines, sending e-mails to Baghdad urging a focused approach. Let the special operations forces deal with the ringleaders, they urged. They received back an e-mail note saying "the cat was out of the bag."

BrigGen Kimmitt, the deputy director of operations for the JTF and the spokesman for the Coalition's military, spoke to the press on April 1. "U.S. troops will go in," he promised. "It's going to be deliberate; it will be precise: and it will be overwhelming."

Fallujah, the heart of the insurgency and the symbol of resistance in Iraq, was about to feel the overwhelming force of America.

———

On April 2 the MEF ordered checkpoints and a cordon set up around the city. Only food and medical supplies were allowed in, and the only military-age males allowed out were those accompanying families. Bulldozers began throwing up a berm of dirt around the city, which measured roughly five kilometers on a side. LtCol Olson met with the city council, thanking them for returning the bodies and asking for a written denunciation of the lynching. Show the world where you stand, he urged; do not align with murderers. The sheikhs and imams rejected Olson's request, issuing instead a bland statement that opposed mutilation but not the killing of Americans.

On April 3 the MEF sent the division the JTF-written order directing offensive operations against the city of Fallujah. The CPA had prepared a public affairs plan in support of the offensive, although it didn't address the Arab press. Bremer and Sanchez shared the plan with the CPA diplomats in Anbar, who agreed it seemed reasonable.

General Conway directed his MEF staff to lay out the overall concept and specify the key tasks to be performed by the air wing, the logistics support team, and the division. As the ground commander, Mattis would direct the battle.

Officers of all services are trained how to compile and coordinate an operational plan for battle, specifying the mission, forces, and tasks. Op plans run for dozens of pages and include numerous appendices spelling out who, what, when, where, and why. An op plan is a regimented document that provides a specific blueprint for combat.

In Washington, however, there was no comparable strategic plan for Fallujah. The JTF order didn't specify what the seizure of the city was intended to accomplish. There was no strategic document laying out the mission as set forth by Gen Abizaid, its intent as articulated by Secretary Rumsfeld, the CIA's projection of opposition at the strategic level, the CPA's consultations with the Iraqi Governing Council, or the State Department's coordination with allies. The anticipated phases and timelines of the strategic campaign—warning the population, consulting with allies, gaining Iraqi agreement, preparing the press, briefing the Congress, marshaling the forces, timelines for seizing the city, reestablishing a city government—were not laid out.

On April 4, Fallujah was dominating international headlines because all major news outlets had rushed reporters and video crews there after the administration's vow of an overwhelming response. But the fighting was threatening to sweep far beyond Fallujah.

A week earlier Ambassador Bremer had shut down the incendiary newspaper **Hawza,** controlled by the radical Shiite cleric Moqtada al Sadr. For a year Sadr, the twenty-eight-year-old son of a revered imam killed in 1993 on Saddam's orders, had been preaching sedition in the slums of Sadr City on the east side of Baghdad. He railed against the Americans as infidel invaders and branded as traitors all Iraqis who were cooperating with the Coalition.

After an Iraqi court secretly indicted Sadr for the murder of a rival cleric, the CPA wanted to arrest him but could not act without the power of the JTF. The JTF refused, agreeing instead with the Shiite clerics who argued that an arrest would provoke violence. The Shiite clerics claimed they could marginalize Sadr. But left unchecked for a year and funded by Iran, he had gained control over an ever-growing militia of impoverished Shiite youths throughout the south. His populist movement had spread from Sadr City to the poorest sections of major Shiite cities.

After shutting down Sadr's newspaper on April 2, Bremer ordered the arrest of Sadr's top aide, Mustafa al Yaccoubi. The next day Sadr called for rebellion. His militia, called the Mahdi Army, took to the streets.

"Terrorize your enemy!" Sadr shouted on Al Jazeera television.

Thousands of excited, impoverished Shiite youths armed with AKs and RPGs poured into the streets in Kufa, Karbala, Najaf, Nasariya, Kut, and Basra. The Iraqi police in the Shiite cities, like the police in the Sunni cities, fled to their homes. The multinational division assigned by the JTF to the normally peaceful Shiite cities fell apart. The Bulgarian battalion in Karbala took shelter in its base and called for American soldiers. The Ukranian battalion in the city of Kut came under siege and cracked. The Spanish soldiers in Najaf abandoned the streets. Sadr's militia—street gangs, actually—was taking over city after city without a serious battle.

The speed, breadth, and depth of the rebellion took American officials by surprise. The fall of Saddam's regime had removed the yoke of oppression from the necks of the majority Shiites; yet the Shiite leaders had tolerated the rise of a demagogue who urged attacks on the Americans who had brought them freedom. If the Americans withdrew, the Sunnis would easily dominate the Shiites; yet when Sadr's armed mobs rampaged through the streets, no Shiite leaders emerged to restore order. Instead they wrung their hands, called for dialogue, and left the fighting to the Americans.

The consequence of having broken the chain of command in two was that each half exercised its authority to launch a major action. On April 1, General Abizaid moved against the Sunni city of Fallujah.

On April 2, Ambassador Bremer moved against the Shiite supporters of Sadr. Within a day, these two separate operations provoked a chain reaction of Sunni and Shiite rebellions across western and southern Iraq.

———

Sadr's uprising in eastern Baghdad and in the Shiite cities to the south did not seem connected to the Sunni city of Fallujah to the west. The JTF sent no order to hold off against Fallujah. So on April 4, the Marines proceeded to marshal their forces and cut off the city, knowing full well that urban combat would be a mess for all concerned. Conway was convinced that the forthcoming assault would further inflame an already embittered population and fuel support for the insurgents. Mattis knew that once his Marines had fought their way down Fallujah's long streets, neither they, nor the surviving insurgents, nor the innocent civilians would be in a forgiving mood. Taking Fallujah by raw force meant subduing a hostile city and declaring terms of obedience. Given his mission, Mattis crafted four objectives: arrest the perpetrators, clean out the foreign fighters, remove all heavy weapons from the city, and reopen Highway 10 for military traffic.

The MEF sent the JTF order to the division, which sent it to Regimental Combat Team 1, commanded by Colonel John Toolan. Raised in Brooklyn, Toolan had a stern, angular face and an air of calm reserve. An informal man with the Irish gift of gab, if he found a conversation interesting, he'd pursue it. When he ran behind schedule, his staff would say, "We're on Toolan time." He was also an experienced tactician, having commanded the regiment on the march to Baghdad.

The plan worked out by the division, called Operation Vigilant Resolve, was simple and direct. The 1st Recon Battalion would act as a screening force to the south, while Battalion 2/1 pushed in from the northwest and Battalion 1/5 moved up from the southeast.

It would take a day for Toolan to get those forces into position. He used that time to demand that the city elders turn over the ring-leaders of the mob. For a year the elders had complained for hours at a stretch about American misconduct, poor crops, neglect from Baghdad, the high price of seeds, Shiite plots, poor water, contracts not delivered, erratic electric power, favoritism toward the wrong tribes—issuing great rivers of words. The final message was always the same: send money and stay out of town; "outsiders" were causing all the trouble.

Well, Toolan told Mattis, the sheikhs couldn't blame the mutilation on "outsiders." As the city elders listened to the bulldozers and tanks clanking around the outskirts of the city, maybe they would take the sensible route and deliver the criminals.

Hunkered down in the city was a hard core of about twenty insurgent leaders. A mixture of former Baathists, army officers, criminals, jihadists, and terrorists, these hard men believed that causing American casualties would have the same results as in Vietnam and Somalia. They controlled about six hundred tough fighters, plus a thousand part-timers who would grab a weapon to defend the city or Islam or whatever someone told an impoverished, impressionable teenager to defend.

The two chief weapons of the insurgents were the AK-47 automatic rifle and the rocket-propelled grenade. There were literally millions of AKs in Iraq; the Russian rifle was brilliant in the simplicity of its design, with a short barrel and a jam-resistant mechanism, firing the sturdy 7.62 cartridge in lethal bursts. Even a child could pick up a light AK and in seconds figure out how to load, clean, and fire it. Saddam's factories had churned out AKs as if they were cigarettes. You could rub mud, dirt, or sand all over an AK, dip it into a muddy puddle, shake it a time or two, and still blaze away. Saddam's workers were sloppy in filling powder into cartridges, and often the rifle would misfire. But with good bullets, the AK was a deadly weapon.

The RPG was just as simple but even more destructive: a slim tube with a grenade attached to the end of the barrel, a simple trigger mechanism, open iron sights, and a short stock. Any teenager could shoot the weapon without training or thinking. You could point it in the air and lob it like a mortar, or you could aim directly at a vehicle or a person. When the grenade hit a building, chips of cement flew like darts in all directions.

With sound weapons, a vast pool of recruits, and a rallying cry of defending the city against the infidel invaders, the insurgent leaders in Fallujah were in a strong position. As Toolan and Mattis expected, the city elders did not stand up to them. No mob leaders were delivered on April 4 as the Marines worked long into a cold, dust-filled night to string concertina wire, set in barricades, direct streams of fleeing civilians into tents, and move the rifle companies into position.

7

MUTINY

ON THE EVENING OF APRIL 4, LtCol Olson led a column of trucks, amphibious vehicles, and Humvees toward an apartment complex on the northwestern outskirts of Fallujah. The undefended complex would provide Battalion 2/1 with a launch point to probe the defenses of the Jolan District.

"People are holding rifles and rocket-propelled grenades, and they are prepared to use them if Americans enter their neighborhoods," said Qais Halawi, a local sheikh.

As Olson pulled up with his lead unit, he was astonished to see a dozen men, most of them unarmed, pushing a trailer truck across the highway to block the Marines, while other insurgents opened fire from the flanks. To Olson, it seemed senseless. The Marines made short work of the flimsy ambush and proceeded to the apartment complex.

Accompanying 2/1 was a company from the 36th Iraqi Battalion from Baghdad. Most were Kurdish soldiers who wasted no time in ordering the apartment residents to pack and get out, giving each family $200. Olson sent Golf Company to hold the peninsula at the western end of the Brooklyn Bridge. Echo and Fox spread out along the trash heaps north of the city. A train station with loading platforms, low-slung buildings, and abandoned rolling stock sat about three hundred meters north of the city. As Fox was crossing the rail tracks, insurgents from inside the city launched a barrage of automatic fire and RPGs, killing Corporal Tyler Fey. The battle for Fallujah had begun.

On the morning of April 5, Stoddard led Fox Company past a mosque and cemetery on the edge of town and down narrow streets lined with three-story houses and apartment buildings. At first swarms of children ran out, gesturing as though holding pistols in their tiny fingers, shouting **bang! bang!** The streets quickly emptied, and from alleys and roofs AKs started chattering. The insurgents moved in gangs of five to ten men, rushing forward and firing wildly before dodging down alleys. Empty buses and cars blocked intersections to stop the tanks that advanced with the infantry. Mortar shells were exploding, some disconcertingly close, others distant echoes. It was hard, tiresome work for the Marines in their heavy body armor, and after a few hours Olson sent Capt Zembiec and Echo forward to pitch in. All day the battle seesawed up and down streets of the Jolan District.

When LtCol Olson discussed sending Zembiec a kilometer to the east to conduct a frontal attack parallel to Fox, Zembiec and Stoddard demurred. The insurgents were showing too much moxie. Every few hours a group of five to ten young Iraqis ran forward, eager to close on the Marines, who killed them on every charge. Zembiec didn't understand why they persisted in running to their deaths. He was sure, though, that if he advanced with Echo on a separate axis, his Marines would be swarmed from all sides.

Instead of continuing into the tangle of buildings in the Jolan, Stoddard cleared a block of two-story houses that fronted on a cemetery, providing an unobstructed field of fire to the east. Zembiec pulled in on Stoddard's north flank, and the two companies began fortifying the roofs.

At dusk on April 5, as the dogs began their nightly howling, rockets landed in the complex where Olson had set up the battalion ops center, about three hundred meters behind Echo Company. Around ten o'clock bands of insurgents began slipping forward, staying in the shadows of the buildings, groping for the Marine lines. Circling over the city was Slayer, an Air Force C-130 loaded with infrared scopes, two 20mm Gatling guns, and a 105mm howitzer firing fifty-pound shells. The four engines of the powerful aircraft sounded like a thousand hammers beating on steel pots, and what became routine nightly radio chats began.

"Oprah, this is Slayer One. About one hundred meters south of your strobe I see a group of about twenty in a courtyard. Want me to take them out?" The Air Force officers in the AC-130 were informal and low-key.

"Slayer One, this is Oprah," Captain Michael Martino, a forward air controller with Echo, replied. "We'd appreciate it."

The ensuing burst of 20mm fire had a low, ripping sound, like a chain saw cutting through hard wood.

"This is Slayer One. Scratch that group. We'll make another pass over your sector. If we don't see anyone else, we'll swing over to War Hammer."

Three kilometers to the south Battalion 1/5—call sign War Hammer—was conducting a night attack. Col Toolan wanted to squeeze the insurgents between 2/1 in the northwest and 1/5 advancing from the southeast. To clear the southeast industrial sector, Lieutenant Colonel Brennan T. Byrne had taken advantage of night-vision goggles to move his battalion forward at three in the morning. The Marines picked their way among rows of shabby repair shops, heaps of broken pipes and junked cars. While the command group set up in a four-story soft drink factory, Bravo and Alpha Companies pushed up to the south side of Highway 10, directly across from where Zembiec had fought a few days earlier in East Manhattan.

In the predawn Col Toolan drove up in a Humvee, attracting a brace of rocket-propelled grenades. While the Marines assaulted the attackers, Toolan compared notes with Byrne, who was convinced the insurgents slept in their houses north of the industrial zone, got up, had breakfast, met their buddies, and hailed a cab to the battlefield.

Sure enough, Bravo and Alpha spent the day of April 5 shooting at insurgents clustered at a mosque on the north side of Highway 10. The insurgents were firing mortars and RPGs, scampering in and out of courtyards to let loose bursts of AK fire, knowing enough not to bunch up. As Zembiec had noticed a few days before, some of the civilians treated war as a spectator sport, standing on street corners to watch the Marines. Sergeant Tim Cyparski saw a man with an RPG standing amid several families; the children were laughing and the women were hiding their faces in their veils, peeking out at the action. The insurgent hastily fired the RPG, scattering the crowd and hitting a nearby house. A minute later the crowd gathered around the inept gunner, treating him like a rock star. Unable to take a shot, the Marines ran toward the man, who nimbly dodged among some parked cars and disappeared. The Marines walked on, waving at the small crowds to get off the street. As if in response, the insurgents too waved at the women and children to get back inside.

While the fighting was going on, LtCol Byrne had Weapons Company systematically clearing the filthy industrial buildings, knocking down false walls and hauling out dozens of machine guns, RPG launchers, and rockets welded from scrap piping. The soldiers found over a ton of TNT and black powder for IEDs. Major Peter Farnum, 1/5's operations officer, estimated that there were enough weapons and ammunition for a battalion.

By the afternoon of April 6, Toolan concluded he had exchanged enough jabs with the insurgents to understand their fighting style. They had no formal, hierarchical military structure with a commander and subcommanders. Rather, they were gangs organized around mosques, neighborhoods, and local leaders. Knowing the streets and alleys, they were fighting a running battle, instead of setting up a fixed defense inside a row of houses.

Toolan didn't need massive firepower—he needed more infantry. Byrne had momentum. By adding a battalion on Byrne's right flank, Toolan could push the insurgents northwest into the Jolan and crush them against Olson's lines. He spoke with Gen Mattis, who said he had two battalions moving in, one American and one Iraqi.

———

All the American generals—Abizaid, Sanchez, Conway, and Mattis—wanted to put an Iraqi face on the fight at Fallujah. The Iraqis with Battalion 2/1 were commandos, but they couldn't stay in the city for the long term. So the 2nd Iraqi Battalion of the new Iraqi Army, based north of Baghdad, was ordered to proceed to Fallujah.

After graduating from boot camp in October, the seven hundred soldiers in the battalion had received some additional training from the 1st Armored Division. But when a team of American advisers arrived in

March, they found that the Iraqi soldiers had decided political freedom meant the end of discipline. When Staff Sergeant Andrew Garcia, one of the new advisers, told an Iraqi soldier to clean up the barracks, the man replied, "I refuse to pick up trash. I am now free."

Garcia was speechless. Nothing had prepared him for a pompous private. A few weeks earlier the husky sergeant had been serving as a drill instructor at Parris Island. In SSgt Garcia's universe, dogs didn't talk, and neither did privates. The advisers held an emergency meeting and agreed it was time to reestablish the natural order of the military world.

"We treated them like recruits, green as June grass," Garcia said. "We rolled them out at zero five hundred for physical training, then spent the day drilling in infantry basics. We got in their faces, we screamed, the usual routine, gave them back their self-respect a little at a time. They learned to pick up trash."

When Mattis requested Iraqi troops, the advisers believed the 2nd Battalion was ready. The senior adviser, Major David Lane, flew by helicopter to Toolan's headquarters. Lane assured the regimental staff that his Iraqis could perform simple duties like traffic control and organizing the thousands of civilians fleeing the city. While Lane coordinated with the regiment, the 2nd Battalion packed up. On April 5, the Iraqi soldiers and nine American advisers set out on the five-hour drive south, escorted by four U.S. Army Humvees.

After leaving camp, the convoy initially made good time because few civilian cars were on the highways. Fighting was flaring up everywhere. Sunni insurgents were battling in Fallujah, while in the slums of Baghdad the Shiite militia loyal to Sadr were rioting. Television stations were showing skirmishes and mobs in a dozen cities and villages. As thousands of unemployed men gathered in marketplaces and murmured to one another, the general atmosphere of unrest and tension spread.

On the northern outskirts of Baghdad, the highway narrowed to four lanes. Cars were parked haphazardly, forcing the military vehicles to proceed at a crawl in single file. The scruffy shops and two-story storefronts on both sides of the road were crowded with men who stared unsmilingly at the Iraqi soldiers. The Iraqi officers acted nervous, yelling at the restive onlookers to get out of the way and let the convoy pass.

To the unease of the American advisers, who were sitting in pairs in separate trucks, the convoy stopped while the driver of the lead Humvee shouted at a trucker to stop blocking the way. Men started running into the street, rolling out barrels and rocks. In the fourth truck back in line, Garcia yelled over his handheld radio, "Go around that truck! Drive up the median! Let's get the hell out of here!"

It was too late. Rifle fire crackled from the rooftops of the stores, and the crowd broke and ran, ducking behind the shops and darting down alleys. Acting without orders, several Iraqi troops leaped down from their open-back trucks and fired wildly. More soldiers joined them. More firing. Garcia saw small groups of men gathering at the ends of the alleys, AKs and RPGs in hand. Soon the insurgents crawled forward on the flat rooftops and stuck their rifle muzzles over the edge, firing wild bursts. The Iraqi soldiers were equally undisciplined, spraying bullets every which way. There were no apparent leaders on either side, only clusters of young men blazing away. Crowds were swarming in, like hordes of mosquitoes.

Garcia thought the situation absurd yet deadly. "Cease fire! Get back in the trucks!" he yelled. "Cease fire! Move, move!"

Strung out over a mile of road and entangled with civilian traffic, the convoy broke down. The company-grade Iraqi officers were looking around helplessly, unable to take action, awaiting orders from above. Up and down the line Marine NCOs were yelling at the soldiers, pulling them back to the trucks, screaming at everyone to mount up and get the hell out of there.

The senior adviser, Major Chris Davis, was riding in the sixth truck in line. When all movement stalled and the firing began to pick up, Davis ran forward to the first truck. There he found the Iraqi battalion commander, the nephew of a powerful sheikh, arguing with a gathering crowd. **This is crazy, Davis thought—you never stop a convoy in a kill zone, let alone debate with the natives.** The battalion interpreters had fled, but it took only a few seconds for Davis to understand from the gestures and rants that the crowd wanted the American advisers handed over. The battalion commander was shaking his head no, vigorously debating the point.

Davis grabbed his shoulder: "Let's go, let's go!"

The battalion commander looked around as if seeing the wild scene for the first time. While he was arguing with one group, only a few hundred meters down the street a gun battle was raging. When he hopped into his Humvee, the Iraqi soldiers climbed back into the trucks and the convoy moved slowly forward.

When the firing had started, the driver of Garcia's truck had leaped down and run away. Garcia saw the other trucks leaving. The cracks of the AK rounds were getting closer to his truck. Ejected shells jingled on the pavement around him as Iraqis on the roof above his head fired blindly. Garcia saw Staff Sergeant Johnny McKnight a block away, trying to organize a base of fire.

"Get up there!" Garcia yelled, pointing at the abandoned truck. "You drive! The hajis will get back in when they see we're leaving. We're not staying here!"

McKnight ran to the Hyundai truck, which was still idling. As Garcia predicted, the Iraqi soldiers followed, clambering into the truck bed, spraying bullets in every direction. The truck jerked and bucked forward, McKnight making no effort to change gears. Sitting next to McKnight, Garcia could see rifles poking out of windows and along rooftops. The store owners had joined in. Down the alleys he saw crowds of men running, trying to get into firing positions in front of the truck. A U.S. Army Humvee with a .50 caliber whizzed by, followed by another, heading for the rear of the convoy. The gunner gestured to McKnight to accelerate.

McKnight didn't have to be encouraged. To his right,

bearded men were rolling barrels into the road. Some boys were throwing rocks, while others crouched in the roadside ditch, pitching objects under the truck's tires. McKnight's scalp tingled as he imagined grenades going off. Then he saw they were flipping small stones, playing some sort of game.

A pickup truck skidded out of an alley and jerked to a stop in front of him. McKnight swerved to the left, bounced off two parked cars, then regained control and headed down the dirt median strip. Men were throwing rocks, concrete blocks, and pieces of metal onto the highway. Others were shooting.

A bullet smashed the driver's mirror next to McKnight's shoulder. Another went through the windshield. McKnight was praying. In front of him a large blue farm truck—the kind used to haul cattle to market—blocked two lanes. The rear half was on fire, thick black smoke pouring into the air. As McKnight trundled by, several men were throwing a bucket of gasoline onto the truck, more interested in their private bonfire than the escaping convoy.

The scene was not a military action; it was madness. Some Shiite militia supporters of Sadr were shooting at the Americans; others were firing at the Iraqi soldiers, half of whom were Shiites; some shop owners were screaming about the damage to their stores; others had grabbed their AKs and were shooting at nothing; cars and trucks were dented, smashed, and lit afire; boys were laughing, throwing rocks, and scampering about as if at a carnival. McKnight was driving for his life, taking in the bizarre sights, including one man running toward the truck, AK in hand, waving and smiling. McKnight couldn't tell whether the man wanted to help him or kill him.

It took an hour for the convoy to zigzag out of the congestion and bedlam. Like steel balls in a pinball machine, the trucks banged off cars and median railings and bumped over rocks and chunks of concrete. Men in old work shirts and baggy trousers were running out of the alleys, firing AKs from the hip, then ducking away. The Marines saw none of the organized fedayeen in their black ninja outfits or black kafkas, only ordinary unemployed Iraqi men swept up in a frenzy not one of them could explain. Garcia saw one man standing in an alley, with a pistol in each hand, shooting straight up at the air.

As the convoy threatened to be overwhelmed by sheer numbers, two Apache helicopters swooped in, and the mob raced for the safety of the buildings. The battalion finally broke clear of the street of little horrors, drove a few miles along a stretch of deserted highway, then pulled into a wide defensive circle to regroup.

"I ruined the engine driving in second gear. There was no way I was going to shift and risk stalling out," McKnight said. "I'll never joke about a Hyundai again."

For all the chaos, damage was light. A U.S. Army retriever truck had been hit by an RPG, disabled, and left behind to be burned by the mob. Two wounded Iraqi soldiers needed helicopter evacuation. An American soldier had been shot in the face and killed protecting the convoy. Garcia admired the bravery of the American soldiers from the 1st Battalion of the 36th Infantry in the four Humvees. Throughout the fight they had driven up and down the gauntlet, ensuring no one was left behind.

Once the trucks had circled in a solid defense, more than a dozen Iraqi soldiers changed into civilian clothes and ran away at high speed. The Marine advisers were dumbfounded. The Iraqi officers, who had resolutely refused to surrender the Americans to the mob, shrugged. The soldiers lived in the area, they explained, so they wouldn't be harmed.

When the officers showed no leadership, the advisers took charge, setting the Iraqis on line, sighting in fields of fire for the machine guns, insisting that two-man fighting holes be dug around the perimeter. The Iraqi officers stood and watched. The Marines were angry that an undisciplined, chaotic mob—a wild surge of mankind without any coordination or unified purpose—had flummoxed the 2nd Battalion and forced it into pell-mell retreat.

"We were embarrassed. We expected the battalion to behave better. They should have easily controlled that mob," Davis said.

Chagrined, Davis called Maj Lane in Fallujah, explaining that the battalion had to return to base to regroup. They would pick up more ammunition and fly out by helicopter that night. As they piled back onto the trucks, the Marines took muster: two Iraqis were wounded and twenty-eight were "missing in action," having deserted.

During the ride back there was excited jabbering in the trucks, and when they arrived at the airfield, dozens of Iraqi soldiers approached Lane, proffering their ID cards. We quit, they said. We won't die in Fallujah. It was an American plot for Shiites to attack Sunnis, they said—the Americans had led them into an ambush. The Americans could have sent tanks to crush the mob; instead they wanted the Iraqi soldiers to be massacred.

Other Iraqi soldiers pressed forward, chanting at the mutineers, "Cowards! Cowards!" The Iraqi officers stood off to the side. Fallujah was an American problem, they said; it was wrong for Iraqi soldiers to fight there.

Maj Davis ordered the Marines to take the weapons of one hundred agitators, who were placed in a gymnasium under guard. They would be stricken from the payrolls and dismissed the next day, along with the battalion and company commanders. Davis took the roll call again. Of 695 soldiers, eight were wounded, 106 had deserted, and 104 had mutinied. Thirty percent of the battalion had evaporated.

Davis called Lane. "We've had a mutiny," he said. "We're not coming to Fallujah."

8

THE TIPPING POINT

WHILE THE MARINES WERE ASSESSING THEIR next steps in Fallujah, the insurgents were preparing a major offensive against another city. On April 5, electronic intercepts and agent reports vaguely suggested trouble might be brewing in the provincial capital of Ramadi, thirty miles west of Fallujah. With 400,000 people, Ramadi was larger than Fallujah, with narrower streets and smaller houses, and the same dingy, crowded atmosphere. The largest and most vibrant city in Anbar, Ramadi was the seat of the senior Sunni mufti and the only Anbar city with a smidgen of influence in Baghdad. Ramadi was the tipping point, the pivotal city that signified whether the insurgents or the government controlled Anbar Province. The vague warnings of an insurgent offensive did not signal any grave danger, though; the city had been relatively peaceful for a year.

In mid-March the Marines had relieved an Army National Guard unit, the 1st Battalion of the 124th Infantry Regiment, in Ramadi. Stretched thin, the battalion had mixed nighttime raids with daytime mounted patrols, primarily along the main avenues. The battalion commander, Lieutenant Colonel Hector Mirable, had tried to persuade the tribes to patrol their own sectors. He spread $700,000 in contracts among the sheikhs, but few projects were completed. "The sheikhs claimed to be the power brokers. But they hoarded the money for their own families and the others got little," Mirable said. "The sooner the sheikh system goes away, the better."

The new battalion commander, Lieutenant Colonel Paul Kennedy, had decided to concentrate on military tactics and avoid Iraqi politics. Mirable had kept a lid on the violence, guarding the heart of the city, but Kennedy set a more ambitious goal: control of the whole city. A former instructor in infantry tactics, Kennedy told Battalion 2/4 that they would concentrate upon foot patrols. "Let's work for the reputation that we're everywhere," Kennedy told his company commanders. "There's no place we won't go, night or day. We're going to own this city."

The governor of the province, Kareem Burgis, invited the battalion staff to dinner and endorsed the concept. Kennedy had received a glowing report about Burgis from Keith Mines, the senior CPA adviser who was leaving the city as Kennedy arrived. A special forces major in the reserves who had spent years in the jungles of Latin America, Mines was a diplomat who understood insurgencies. He referred to Burgis as "my key Iraqi partner and the unifier of the region's various factions." Mines, who believed Ramadi was coming along nicely, talked Burgis up in Baghdad, calling the governor "a man of vision and moderation who shares our goals."

With the support of the governor, the Marines spread out across the city. Kennedy set up headquarters on Hurricane Point at the western end of Ramadi, a small peninsula jutting out into the Euphrates. He kept with him Weapons Company as the battalion's Quick Reaction Force. From a nearby base, Fox Company patrolled daily. The eastern end was covered by Echo and Golf Companies, based three kilometers down Route Michigan, the main highway that ran through the middle of the city, in a walled compound called the Combat Outpost.

Eight-hour foot patrols became the routine. For the first few days, traffic in the city slowed as drivers stared in disbelief at the small groups of Americans, most escorted by packs of shouting children. Downtown Ramadi was eight kilometers long and five kilometers wide, containing 45,000 buildings. The Marines walked into neighborhoods miles away from main avenues and poked around courtyards where the dogs had never smelled an American. By the end of March, shin splints and bone bruises were common and even the fittest in the battalion were fatigued.

The patrols were wearing, too, on the insurgents, who resented Americans walking around wherever they pleased. One morning outside Hurricane Point the Marines found a scraggly gray donkey with "Bush" painted on one flank and "American forces" on the other. After washing off the paint, two corporals kept it as a pet until its smell and braying led to its banishment. A few days later the donkey came back looking for another meal, again with mocking graffiti on its flanks. Still, the insurgents hadn't done anything to make it clear that they, and not these new Americans, owned the streets. It wasn't clear who was **awat,** or soft cake—the Marines or the insurgents.

On April 5, when electronic intercepts picked up unusual chatter, Kennedy sought out Governor Burgis, who said he, too, had heard that something was brewing. The police chief, Muhammad Jaddan, warned Kennedy that the **irahabin** (or criminals, an Iraqi term for the insurgents) were bragging that they would kill many Americans. Every Iraqi policeman seemed to know the irahabin, yet not one had been arrested.

A voluble, outgoing man with nicotine-stained teeth, Police Chief Jaddan had a mixed reputation. When spot checks had turned up ghost names on police payrolls, Jaddan had claimed the real records had been destroyed in a fire. Still, he seemed a likable rogue and had worked amicably with the previous American unit.

A few days earlier, Kennedy and Sergeant Major James Booker were driving back from dinner with the police chief when a volley of four rockets ripped out of a side alley. The Humvees skidded to a stop, and the Marines hopped out and attacked down the alley. The insurgents fled under the cover of an RPK machine gun, but one stopped in the shadows to fire another rocket-propelled grenade. Booker got off two snapshots with his rifle. The man fell, got up, and ran away. Using a flashlight, the Marines followed the blood trail, so thick at first that they mistook it for a pool of spilled oil. They found the man bled out under a car inside a courtyard.

The next day an aide to the police chief yelled at SgtMaj Booker, complaining that he had killed his cousin. The aide was a thug, part of a Mafia-type element Jaddan kept on his staff. Rumors persisted that some of Jaddan's aides had been "long away," returning after Saddam had released all hardened criminals from prison a year ago.

Booker let the man rant for a few minutes before replying.

"I apologize for my shooting. I fired twice," he said. "I should have killed that son of a bitch with my first shot."

On April 4, Iraqi police, health, and education officials did not show up for scheduled meetings and morning traffic was unusually light. Police Chief Jaddan advised bringing tanks into the city, as if he were a sympathetic fan at a sporting event. Kennedy asked the CIA for help. He wanted to launch a preemptive attack before he was hit. The CIA came up with a list of suspected insurgent leaders and their home addresses. Digital overhead photos showed in detail every street, alley, and house. In a city with thousands of buildings, sixteen were pinpointed for search in Operation Wild Bunch. At one in the morning of April 6, Marines were banging on doors.

Captain Rob Weiler, commanding Weapons Company, drew a house in the southeast sector. After a Humvee broke down the gate to the compound, Weiler, a large, imposing man, strode up to the front door and banged on it with his M16. A mild-mannered man invited him in, offering tea. Speaking through Weiler's interpreter, he said he had recently been released from Abu Ghraib prison, showing papers with American signatures. Weiler thought the papers were in order, but the interpreter said he was pronouncing his name in a peculiar fashion. The Marines were looking for two brothers. Ah, said the man, his brother had been killed in the war against Iran. Yes, it's true, said his mother.

The interpreter asked who lived next door. No one knew. That's strange, the interpreter murmured to Weiler. The two knocked on the door next door, and a smiling man let them in and politely led them through each room. Everything was in order but his papers, and there was no weapon in either house. He seemed too accommodating.

Weiler brought both men back to Hurricane Point. After four hours of questioning, their cover stories fell apart. Operation Wild Bunch had netted two insurgent commanders—the Farhan brothers, Adnan and Majeed.

Both denied knowing anything about an attack. The brigade reported intercepts of increased telephone conversations. But intercepts were unreliable, since the insurgents routinely bragged to each other about battles that had never developed. So Kennedy continued with business as usual on April 6.

It was standard procedure to begin each day's patrols when the city was stirring. The more people saw the Marines walking around, the better. It was after nine when Second Lieutenant John Hessner led the 3rd Platoon of Golf Company out the sandbagged gate of the Combat Outpost and walked west along Route Michigan. The destination was the Government Center, three kilometers away.

Each of the three squads headed down a separate street, several blocks apart. The technique, called "satellite patrolling," was employed by British troops in Northern Ireland to quickly surround any sniper who shot at a passing patrol. The Marines stayed in touch by radio. Hessner checked with his first squad, call sign Joker 3-1, which was near a soccer stadium, several blocks south of Route Michigan.

Joker 3-1 reported that the residents were going about their morning chores, scurrying back and forth on the narrow, garbage-strewn side streets.

"We got one asshole tagging behind us," Staff Sergeant Dameon Rodriguez, the platoon sergeant, reported. "That's all."

The morning traffic was light, with most cars heading west, out of town. Just as Hessner noticed that the police and National Guard troops were not at their usual posts, he bumped into a wave of insurgents slipping up on the Government Center. The initial exchanges of fire were intermittent, a burst from an

AK followed by answering shots from an M16, a rocket-propelled grenade fired blindly down a street, a pause, then a few more shots. Within half an hour the desultory firing had swelled to a roar, as the two separate squads bumped into gang after gang of fleeing shooters.

The third squad was battling in a large cemetery adjacent to Route Michigan, a kilometer east of the Government Center. Hessner and the second squad ran two blocks and linked up among the gravestones. The insurgents were running among the crypts, firing wildly. The Marines were staying under cover, using the grave markers as resting points for their rifles, trying to hit anyone standing still for more than a few seconds.

Lance Corporal Jeremiah Letterman was struck in the stomach, a serious but not grievous wound. Hessner called his company commander, Captain Chris Bronzi, requesting a medevac.

"I have a solid defense here," Hessner radioed to Bronzi. "But I'll need a lot more troops to push through, and Joker three-one's a click south near the soccer stadium."

"Hold where you are," Bronzi said. "I'll pick up Joker three-one and come to your pos."

The enemy were out in force that morning. Fearing the Farhan brothers would talk, the imam who served as their second-in-command had ordered the attack to seize the Government Center a day ahead of schedule. Hundreds of insurgents had moved in from the Sofia District to the east, driving in civilian vehicles and slipping on foot down the back alleys. These were gangs rather than regular military units, small and medium-sized clusters of armed, excited youths, each with its own leader. Some were tough former military, trained in tactics and accustomed to being obeyed and feared. Others were unemployed, uneducated young men eager for adventure and comradeship. Some had been recruited weeks earlier by the Farhan brothers, while others at home merely saw the fighters running past, grabbed their rifles, and followed.

The hard-core insurgents wore black shirts and trousers, with knock-off Adidas sneakers. Some wrapped their faces in red-and-white-checked kaffiyehs, while others were bareheaded. Most carried AK-47s, and many hefted RPGs along with a fair sprinkling of RPKs, a machine gun popular throughout Eastern Europe.

While the battalion ops center dispatched a Mobile Assault Platoon to pick up the wounded Marine, Bronzi left the Combat Outpost with three squads and eight Humvees. Kennedy had driven from Hurricane Point to the Government Center, where two Marine squads were spread out on the upper floors and on the roof, looking for targets. Bullets and an occasional RPG round were striking the walls of the center. But the attack lacked heft, and the Marines were pouring out much more fire than they were taking. With Hessner holding his own at the cemetery, Kennedy sensed the main insurgent forces were massing to the east. He hopped in a Humvee equipped with two radios—grandiosely called a Jump CP (Command Post)—and drove toward the soccer stadium to link up with Bronzi.

———

A kilometer southeast of the cemetery, Joker 3-1 had monitored Hessner's call for a medevac. The eleven Marines in the squad could hear the shooting, but no one had taken them under fire. With one insurgent still trailing behind them, they crossed a highway west of the soccer stadium, heading to the cemetery. As they trotted across the four-lane road, homeowners shut their courtyard gates and ducked inside without a glance at the passing Americans. When they reached the next cross street, there was not a person to be seen.

"Time to watch our asses," SSgt Rodriguez said.

Seconds later firing erupted from four sides. To Rodriguez, everything suddenly became so bright that he thought he had stepped onto a Broadway stage. He could see no one, but all around him bullets were zinging off courtyard walls. The noise was deafening. Somehow he was down flat on his chest, his M16 firing up at a rooftop. He knew that's where they were because he could see empty shells hitting the ground in front of him. Unable to hear above the din, he glanced around and saw that the other Marines were lying prone, too, firing madly. After ripping through a few magazines, the Marines paused, looking for targets.

Sergeant Allen Holt, the squad leader, saw a head duck back on a roof. He straightened the cotter pin on a grenade, gathered himself with one knee on the ground, pulled the pin, yelled "Frag out!" and pitched it onto the roof. The explosion was accompanied by a scream of pain, and the firing momentarily slackened. Before the Marines could collect themselves, the firing resumed from another direction.

Rodriguez called Capt Bronzi. "Joker six, this is three-one. Need some help here," he said. "Platoon-sized element, all around us."

"We're on our way," the Golf Company commander replied. "We'll close in fifteen mikes."

Fifteen minutes seemed reasonable enough. Bronzi thought Joker 3-1 was east of the soccer stadium. Actually, the squad was west of the stadium.

The Marines formed a hasty perimeter, taking pot-shots at rooftops with their M203 grenade launchers. After they had lobbed a few rounds, Rodriguez watched a man suddenly pop up on a roof, leap down to the top of a courtyard wall, hop down to the street, and sprint around a corner.

"Did you see that dude?" Rodriguez yelled. "He was wearing flip-flops. How'd he do that?"

"Motivated!" Holt yelled back.

Rodriguez wondered if he had overreacted in asking for help. This didn't seem too bad. Then the incoming fire started to swell again. The insurgents had been finding new positions, not running away. The squad was taking steady fire from behind a parked car down the street to the east. As Lance Corporal James Gentile moved forward, an insurgent ran out, got behind the wheel, and drove in reverse down the street. When Gentile opened up with his SAW, or squad automatic weapon, the driver leaped out and ran away.

Rodriguez saw a man in a white T-shirt step onto the street and then step back out of sight. Rodriguez sighted in on the spot. A minute later the same man, holding an AK, darted back out. Rodriguez shot him in the chest, and he fell into the street. Five minutes later an ambulance drove up; two men got out, placed the body in the back, and drove off.

The eleven Marines had spread out on both sides of the street, protecting both ends, so the insurgents would have to cross an open area to close on them. So far the defense had worked. Time and again the squad leader, Sgt Holt, saw cars—battered four-door Caprices, sedans with no windows, shabby little orange and white taxis—stop for a few seconds in alley entrances. The passengers would fire and the cars would dart back under cover.

They were half an hour into the fight now, and still no Quick Reaction Force. The noise was deafening— the banging sounds of the M16s and SAWs reverberated off the cement—and after a while the ringing in the Marines' ears wouldn't stop. Rodriguez, shouting into his radio handset, was hearing no response.

The insurgents were sneaking in closer, and rounds were ricocheting off the cement walls. Gentile was hit in the neck, the bullet passing out the side of his face. He dropped his SAW and staggered to Rodriguez and Holt, who carried him into the shelter of a courtyard. Gentile's eye socket was fractured, and he was bleeding profusely from the neck wound, breathing hoarsely. As Holt wrapped him in a pressure bandage, Gentile asked him to take his picture. He thought it would look cool.

Corporal Joseph Hayes and four Marines stayed out in the street. Hayes had just fired a 40mm grenade at an Iraqi in a window and thought he had nailed him. But the man popped back up firing just as Private First Class Deryk Hallal, a big man at six foot seven, was running across the street. Hallal was struck in the leg and went down. The sound of the hit, a large **smack!**, caused Holt to spin around.

"Get Hallal!" he yelled.

Lance Corporal Tapia ran out and was bandaging Hallal's leg when a car spun out of an alley, with men firing out the windows. Hallal was hit in the back of the head as the car disappeared. Hallal kept opening his mouth, trying to breathe, while the Marines gave him a shot of morphine and said a prayer. After a few minutes, Holt called Rodriguez over the radio.

"Hallal's dead."

Tapia didn't want to leave the body of his close friend, but they were under heavy fire. Hayes pulled the three Marines crouched near him behind a courtyard wall. A grenade landed in the courtyard. They ducked. Dud. Another grenade. **Bang!** Two more Marines went down, their hands riddled with shrapnel. Hayes and Tapia crouched by the wall, shooting at the rooftops.

Several houses farther down the block, Rodriguez signaled to the remaining Marines to get inside the house where he had put Gentile. Private First Class Moises Langhorst flopped down just outside the courtyard wall, signaling to the others to duck inside while he covered them. Langhorst tore through a drum of ammunition, the SAW screeching for several seconds before falling silent. Rodriguez crawled out to help Langhorst change barrels and found the SAW gunner dead.

The squad was split into two groups, each at the far end of a separate block, unable to provide supporting fire for the other. Two Marines were dead. Rodriguez had one Marine seriously wounded and four who could shoot. Hayes had two wounded and two who could shoot. With the insurgents putting steady grazing fire down the street, Rodriguez couldn't carry Gentile to link up with Hayes. Transmissions between the two groups on the handheld radios were spotty.

"I can't reach Joker six," Rodriguez radioed. "Can you?"

"Negative," Hayes replied.

Both groups bunkered in to wait, each rotating a guard on the roof and another near the courtyard gate. Rodriguez propped Gentile up against a wall, and the Iraqi who owned the house wrapped him in blankets. When the blood soaked through, the Iraqi brought fresh blankets. Each group had about three dozen magazines, enough to hold out for about an hour.

It was only a matter of time before the insurgents found a roof high enough for them to fire rocket-propelled grenades down into the courtyards or before they packed explosives into a satchel charge. Explosives were the way to finish defenders lodged behind cement.

———

Joker 3-1 hadn't been forgotten, but it had been misplaced. The location plotted in the company ops center showed the squad near the soccer stadium, a kilometer east of its actual location. Bronzi had dismounted at the stadium with fifty Marines. Bronzi couldn't raise Joker 3-1 on the radio, but he could hear the shooting and knew he was at the wrong spot. He wasn't sure, though, how long it would take to reach the squad.

The moment his Marines poked their heads around the western end of the stadium, they had been hit by a heavy burst of fire. RPG rockets were whizzing by, bullets cracked overhead, and machine guns were chattering, reminding Bronzi of **Phase Line Green,** a book about a platoon in Hue that had fought for three days to cross one street. With Joker 3-1 ten blocks away, Bronzi called for another platoon from the Combat Outpost.

Having four Humvees with mounted .50 calibers and Mark 19s behind them as fire support, Bronzi's force headed northwest on foot, moving by bounds. The insurgents were staying under cover, firing from street corners and upper-story windows. The sharp sounds of battle echoed off the buildings, making it difficult to know what fire was coming from what building. The squads advanced in a triangle formation, watching their flanks. Wherever the Marines massed their fire, the insurgents scattered and fell back.

Iraqi men were rushing around, running to their homes to grab their AKs and dashing out into the streets to join up with the neighborhood gang. With a tinge of irony, the Marines called them "Minutemen." These spontaneous volunteers had swollen the ranks of the insurgents who had set out hours earlier to seize the Government Center, and their presence changed the focus of the battle. Whatever coordinated movement the insurgents had planned, it had collapsed into a swirling melee. Wherever the Marines turned, someone was there to shoot at them.

LtCol Kennedy had left the Government Center with eleven Marines and two Humvees, all afoot as riflemen except for two drivers and two machine-gunners. Listening to the radio, Kennedy thought the fighting resembled a fur ball, a dozen cats kicking and clawing in the dust. His plan was simple. He would join Bronzi, link up with Joker 3-1, and proceed to the cemetery. Along the way a Mobile Assault Platoon would join them. Major Dave Harrill guarded the rear.

It was taking Kennedy longer than he liked to get to Bronzi. The command element would walk safely down one block, then in the next insurgents would pop out on roofs only twenty meters away, blazing away for a few seconds with AKs before ducking back. Others would drive across the intersection in beat-up old cars, firing out the windows. Some got away and some didn't.

Possessed of more firepower, the battalion Quick Reaction Force made better time. Gunnery Sergeant Anthony Crutcher, commanding Mobile Assault Platoon 3, headed toward the cemetery with thirty Marines in five Humvees. MAP 3 found 1/Lt Hessner's troops crouched among the headstones, busy racking up kills. The cemetery was several blocks long, and Hessner was moving methodically, making sure he didn't leave any insurgents to his rear.

After supplying Hessner's Marines with ammunition and carefully loading the wounded Marine into a Humvee, Crutcher continued south to join Bronzi. Less than a block from the cemetery, Sergeant Deverson Lochard spotted a man in a long-sleeved shirt and red-and-white checkered **aqal** standing alone on a street corner as if waiting for a bus, an AK slung over his shoulder and an RPG dangling at his side.

"Can I take him out?" Lochard radioed.

"Sure," Crutcher replied.

The vehicles stopped, and Lochard got out and shot the man just as an orange-colored pickup came around the corner. A burst from the Mark 19 sent the pickup crashing into a wall. The Marines were thinking the hunting was easy when RPGs and small-arms fire hit them from the east.

Crutcher called for instructions. "Continue south," Kennedy radioed. "Guide on the heavy firing."

The insurgents had dropped some palm trees across

the streets, but the Humvees bumped around them, with the Marines moving in front of the vehicles, spraying the edges of the rooftops. Crutcher had no difficulty distinguishing the heavy banging of Bronzi's .50 calibers over the cracks of the AKs and M16s. As Crutcher's Mobile Assault Platoon gingerly reached Bronzi, the platoon from the Combat Outpost was linking up to cover Bronzi's east flank.

With more than 120 Marines and nine mounted .50 calibers and Mark 19s, Bronzi picked up the pace, anxious to close with Joker 3-1. The terrain was dictating the nature of the battle. The Marines were fighting in the heart of the residential area, densely packed two- and three-story cement houses, laid out in a square grid, each block on average fifty meters wide and one hundred meters long, containing about thirty houses linked by cement walls as tall as a man. Each block was a small fortress, offering the insurgents two shooting opportunities—from the flat rooftops bordered by small retaining walls, and from the alleys outside the courtyard walls.

The Marines wanted to move up the long north-south axis of the city blocks, where they encountered less crossfire from the alleys and could employ the heavy weapons mounted on the Humvees. Both the .50 cal and the Mark 19 were fearsome weapons, yet neither could penetrate walls two feet thick. Still, the shock of the shells abrading the concrete, throwing up clouds of dust and sparks, unnerved most of the inexperienced insurgents and sent them scampering away.

The Mark 19 was the favorite weapon for dusting off the roofs.

Corporal Jared McKenzie, a squad leader in MAP 3, estimated that insurgents on the roofs were popping up only fifty meters away, while those on the street, seeing the approaching vehicles, stayed several hundred meters away, darting out of alleys, firing from the hip. Sergeant Kenneth Conde, walking in front of McKenzie, suddenly spun around and dropped, blood spurting from his shoulder.

"Shit, you're shot," McKenzie said.

Conde stood up, fired down the street, and fell back down. As McKenzie ran up, Conde staggered back to his feet.

"Let's get you out of here, man," McKenzie said.

"I didn't come here to get evaced," Conde said. "It stings, that's all."

McKenzie sat Conde down beside an overstuffed Dumpster, while a corpsman bandaged his shoulder. They started on again, trailing the rest of the squad. When they crossed the next alley, three men with AKs were sneaking out and bumped into them. The first stopped and stared. McKenzie shot him in the face. The second backpedaled, hands held out in supplication. McKenzie shot him in the chest. The third turned and ran. McKenzie shot him in the back.

Gunny Crutcher walked by a house where a pile of shell casings had fallen from the roof onto the ground. He broke down the door and in the center of the room found an RPG on the floor and a man hiding behind a couch. In a bag the man had half a million dinars, about eight thousand dollars. Crutcher flex-cuffed the man and placed him in a Humvee along-side an Iraqi policeman who had been captured while firing at the Marines.

Sergeant Michael Williams saw an insurgent with an AK duck behind a new model car parked on Easy Street. Williams fired, the man fired back, and Williams sighted in, waiting for him to reappear. Instead, a woman in a black burka with a child clutching her hand walked out of an alley next to the car. Both Williams and the man behind the car yelled at her, and she stood still. The little girl tugged at her hand and led her back down the alley. The insurgent ran away, keeping the car between him and Williams.

Corporal McKenzie walked by a Marine squad peeking out of an alleyway, shortly after a flurry of RPG rockets had whizzed past.

"Let's keep it moving," McKenzie said.

Shaken by the near miss, the Marines didn't respond, refusing to move. McKenzie shrugged and moved on. The Marines weren't from his unit, so he wasn't going to get on their case. They'd get it back together soon enough.

The MAP squads had become used to the noise and confusion, the snaps and cracks of the bullets, the dull pops of the RPGs, followed by the explosions and showers of sparks. When they hit a rough spot, they called up a Mark 19 or .50 caliber to soften things up.

After fighting for about thirty minutes, Bronzi had

moved about eight blocks and the M16 fire from Joker 3-1 was sounding only a few streets away. Behind him, he heard the growling of tracs. Colonel Buck Connor, Kennedy's brigade commander, had been listening to the fight in his Tactical Operations Center, three kilometers outside town. He had radioed Kennedy, asking if he needed armored ambulances. Told yes, Connor grabbed two ambulances and two Bradleys and drove over to lend a hand. The twenty-ton Bradley, with a 25mm Bushmaster chain gun, could scrape down alleys too narrow for the Abrams tank. With the added firepower of the Bradleys, Bronzi hastened forward to find Joker 3-1.

————

For the past half-hour, in their two separate houses, the riflemen of Joker 3-1 had held off several rushes. Rodriguez had posted Private First Class Peter Flom inside the courtyard gate. Twice an Iraqi had run up to the gate, and twice Flom had shot at point-blank range. Both men had hobbled away. Flom couldn't believe it. Men were supposed to be blown away when a burst was fired into them, not wander away like they'd had too much to drink.

Insurgents kept popping up at different spots, plinking from roofs or darting out from around corners. They knew they had the two sections of the squad trapped and isolated from each other. Yet they didn't close to finish the fight. They brought up an RPK machine gun and used it to pepper the courtyard wall where Hayes was holed up. The Marines were worried the machine-gunner would cover the dash forward of a suicide bomber strapped with explosives.

Hayes was down to the last of his nine magazines when he heard the whine of powerful engines and the unmistakable grinding sound of metal treads.

"Goddamn, that's the sweetest sound I've ever heard," he radioed to Rodriguez, farther up the block.

Seeing the armored column advancing toward them, the insurgents fell back and the firing ceased. Hayes ran out into the street, where Bronzi greeted him. Together they retrieved Hallal's body. While the medics attended to the three wounded Marines, Bronzi reported to Kennedy, who had just arrived.

Seeing Col Connor and LtCol Kennedy conferring with Capt Bronzi, Gunny Crutcher was struck by how many officers were clustered around half a squad. "I think the commandant's just around the corner," he said.

Rodriguez was a block away, on the other side of an alley too narrow for the Bradleys. Bronzi sent McKenzie's squad to aid Rodriguez. Colonel Connor dismounted and followed behind with the Brigade Command sergeant major, Ronald T. Riling, followed by his command humvee with a mounted .50 caliber machine gun. The insurgents had pulled back, and the firing had stopped.

From the corner house, Rodriguez waved at them, and soon the wounded were being taken care of. They retrieved the body of Langhorst outside the wall on the northwest corner. His SAW was gone, and he was covered with a blanket.

Joker 3-1 had lost two Marines.

"Hallal wasn't locked on in garrison, but he loved the field. He was into sports. Wanted to be a broadcaster," Rodriguez said. "Langhorst was bright, religious, saw God's will in things. He ate a lot, too. He stayed at his post when I was getting the wounded inside, covering us. He was a Marine."

After seeing to the evacuation of the casualties, at two in the afternoon Kennedy paused for a quick update. The ops center was roiling with activity. Over the past hour the ops officer, Major David Harrill, had tracked ten separate firefights, dispatched three medevacs, monitored the calls of the battalion and brigade commanders from the battlefield, and traced the movements of seven units. He had also directed five to knock out an RPK machine gun.

"My ops map looked like a kindergarten painting," Harrill said, "lines zigzagging everywhere."

Back at battalion headquarters, the word had spread that "the streets were on fire," as black smoke poured from tires set ablaze up and down Route Michigan. The troops were clamoring to go to rescue, and the battalion executive officer, Major Mike Wylie, had to continuously clear the ops center of eager volunteers.

"Get the hell out of here!" Wylie said more than once. "Get back where you belong, goddammit. If I need you, I'll call for you."

The fight raged up and down the streets. Bronzi had

with him fourteen squads from Golf and Weapons
Companies, each supported by a Humvee with a
heavy gun. Sometimes the insurgents were in front of
them, often on their flanks, and sometimes in their
rear. They had hidden caches of weapons and munitions, running swiftly to a house or mosque, shooting,
and running on.

Bronzi worked out a grid, assigning about one
block per squad, and they moved east using cross
streets as boundaries, careful to keep on line. The
insurgents had been fighting since ten in the morning, and they lacked the conditioning of the Marines.
Despite cases of bottled water in the Humvees,
twenty-one Marines were treated for heat exhaustion
by Dr. Kenneth Son, the battalion staff physician.
The fig-ure was probably far higher among the insurgents. By early afternoon, Kennedy and Bronzi sensed
they had the insurgents beaten in the downtown area.
It was a matter of keeping up the pressure, encouraging their tired Marines to sweep block after block and
search house after house, not letting up.

Harrill radioed Kennedy that Echo Company was
heavily engaged east of the city, with Weapons Company sending reinforcements. The battle was like a
forest fire that seems to be contained, only to have the
flames arc across the trees and set off another blaze. At
the peak of the fighting the dispersed Marine units—
three hundred riflemen in all—were engaging hundreds of insurgents in ten separate firefights.

Around two in the afternoon, Col Dunford had
called to say that CIA sources were reporting that a

hundred insurgents had massed south of the Government Center and that three mosques were calling for jihad. Kennedy called back, wryly commenting that he had confirmed the CIA sources. Dunford wished Kennedy good luck and turned his attention to Fallujah.

Kennedy focused on Echo Company in the suburbs east of Ramadi, where the battle was suddenly escalating.

9

FAINT ECHOES OF TET

THE FIGHTING ERUPTING ACROSS IRAQ ON April 6 threatened to become politically explosive back in the United States. When the multinational force proved incapable of coping with Sadr's militia south of Baghdad, the Joint Task Force had to employ the 1st Armored Division, which had been packing up to return to the States. With no uncommitted reserves left in Iraq, American newspapers were speculating about the need for additional troops. Sending more troops from the States would touch off a divisive political debate and evoke scathing criticism from the Democratic presidential contenders. There were faint echoes of Vietnam. After the Tet Offensive in 1968, President Lyndon Johnson's reelection hopes had imploded when the military asked for additional troops to be sent to Vietnam.

It was well known in military circles that the 82nd

Airborne Division had been stretched too thin across Anbar Province. Now the 1st Marine Division, having concentrated four battalions against Fallujah, was covering the same area with fewer forces. Across the breadth of Anbar, the rash of attacks was spreading, with Ramadi suddenly at the epicenter.

To the south, the 1st Armored Division had sent one task force to Najaf on April 4 to pry the holy city loose from Sadr's militia. "We will attack to destroy the Mahdi Army," BrigGen Kimmitt said.

But there was never a consensus, then or later, among the CPA, JTF, and Iraqi officials to finish off Sadr and his "army." In contradiction of Kimmitt, Pentagon officials were telling the press that military commanders would move "gingerly" against Sadr to marginalize him. The CPA's intent was to whittle down Sadr's power base without making him a martyr. Ambassador Bremer had urged the JTF to undertake "Lincoln's anaconda strategy," a reference to the multiyear strategy to squeeze the Confederacy by slow attrition. Similarly, the Mahdi Army would be driven from city after city and slowly whittled down.

To drive out Sadr's militia, the JTF had extended Major General Martin E. Dempsey's 1st Armored Division for another ninety days. Half the division's vehicles and helicopters were already in Kuwait; redeploying them required the largest cargo airlift of the war, an effort compared to the Red Ball Express in World War II. Dempsey's lines of communication—roughly, the road networks used daily—had expanded from 500 to 25,000 square miles, a fifty-fold increase that required ten new forward operating bases, while his track vehicles were averaging a hundred miles per day. Commanders told the press they might send more forces to Iraq if the situation worsened. Another task force from the division was moving to take back the city of Kut, where the CPA staff had pulled out under fire.

While the CPA in the field appreciated Dempsey's soldiers, there was scant cooperation or even civility between the military and the CPA planners in Baghdad. In an effort to bring the CPA and JTF staffs closer together, LtGen Sanchez and Ambassador Bremer shared a briefing room inside the palace in the Green Zone. Usually, though, Bremer's staff was briefed at seven in the morning and Sanchez's staff half an hour later.

With the CPA team driven out of Kut by Sadr's gangs and in desperate shape elsewhere, Bremer's chief of staff, Jeffrey Oster, asked for a briefing from the JTF about its next steps.

"That's military business," a colonel told Oster, "not to be shared with the CPA. LtGen Sanchez doesn't work for the ambassador."

Oster, a retired Marine lieutenant general, was outraged by such bureaucratic folderol. He went to Sanchez's chief of staff, Major General Joseph Weber, who readily agreed to share information in the future. The incident, though, indicated how difficult it was for the CPA and the JTF to form a common strategy in the midst of battle.

The CPA civilians and all Iraqis were relying on the

press to inform them about the military situation. Reports about the fighting came from two major sources—Western journalists, principally American, and the Arab press. The two dominant Arab satellite networks were Al Arabiya, based in Dubai, and Al Jazeera, based in Qatar. In addition to reaching hundreds of millions of Arabs, their reportage was more trusted by Iraqis than was the U.S.-funded channel called Al Iraqiya, based in Baghdad. About 25 percent of Iraqis—the more wealthy and influential—had access to satellite reception, and by a five-to-one margin they preferred Jazeera to Iraqiya. Jazeera was financed by the emir of Qatar and Arabiya by a Saudi sheikh.

Both networks had learned not to bite the hands that fed them. Criticism of the autocracies in Egypt, Syria, and elsewhere had resulted in the closure of offices and the withdrawal of advertising revenues. Diatribes about the Israeli occupation of Palestine and the American occupation of Iraq were the two staples of their coverage that received wide approval among Arab governments.

In September both networks had been barred from reporting in Iraq for two weeks because they were tipped to attacks on convoys and filmed the events without warning authorities. In November, when Arabiya aired a taped message from Saddam Hussein urging attacks upon Americans, Bremer responded by approving another temporary suspension of the network. A few days later Secretary Rumsfeld accused both Arabiya and Jazeera of cooperating with insurgents by continuing to videotape attacks on American

troops. The complaints did not change the tone of
Jazeera's reportage.

In April the insurgents invited a reporter from Al
Jazeera, Ahmed Mansour, and his crew into Fallujah,
where they filmed scenes from the hospital. Hour
after hour, day after day in the first week in April, the
airwaves were filled with pictures of the dead, the
bleeding, and the maimed. The Arab media were calling the resistance an intifada, linking the insurgent
fighting against the Americans to the Palestinian
uprising against the Israelis. The sound bites featured
the wails of the mourners, the sobs and screams of
mothers, and the frenzied shouts and harried faces of
blood-bespotted doctors and nurses. No one with a
breath of compassion could watch Arab TV and not
feel anguish. Most poignant were the pictures Jazeera
ran of babies, one after another after another, all calm,
frail, and pitiful in the repose of death. Where, how,
or when they died was not attributed. The viewer
assumed all the infants were killed by the Marines in
Fallujah. The baby pictures would bring tears from a
rock.

In Baghdad mullahs in Shiite mosques called on the
faithful to donate blood and food for Fallujah, while
residents in Sunni neighborhoods lauded the radical
Shiite cleric Moqtada al Sadr for rebelling. The clerics
in Baghdad urged protests in the streets as calls for
jihad rippled across the city.

Fallujah became the rallying point for anti-Coalition
anger. Among Iraqis, vehement shouts of support for
besieged Fallujah released simmering resentments

about power outages, day-long lines for propane and gasoline, drive-by shootings, and random, dreaded suicide car bombings. Pent-up anger burst forth about foreign occupiers who shot at cars at vehicle checkpoints, rammed their armored vehicles through thick traffic, and ransacked homes at three in the morning. Iraqi men from all walks of life—students, laborers, doctors, policemen, shop owners—flocked to the mosques to exchange passionate denunciations of the infidel occupiers.

Al Jazeera and Al Arabiya were unrelenting in broadcasting the plight of the civilians in Fallujah, while the Internet amplified the message of Marine callousness and sped protests around the world on a minute-by-minute basis. On the Google search engine, during the month of April, the word **Fallujah** leaped from 700 to 175,000 stories, many highly critical of the Marines. Quantity had a spurious quality of its own, resulting in an erroneous certitude based on the sheer volume of repetition.

The reports filed by Western journalists embedded with the Marines did not support the allegations of widespread, indiscriminate carnage. Senior U.S. government officials, though, didn't have the time to peruse tactical reporting. Instead, in their offices they turned on cable news, where video clips from Fallujah were shown over and over again. The images, obtained from a pool that included the Jazeera cameramen inside the city, affected viewers in Iraq, in Washington, and in Crawford, Texas.

In January 1968 overly optimistic reports about

progress in the Vietnam War had been shattered by a wave of countrywide attacks called the Tet Offensive. The press reported in vivid detail the fighting and the destruction in dozens of towns and cities. The Vietcong gained an unexpected strategic victory in the States, where support for the war plummeted. Years later, analysts concluded that Tet had been an operational disaster for the guerrillas, resulting in devastating losses.

Peter Braestrup, in his award-winning book on how the 1968 Tet Offensive was miscast as a Vietcong victory, wrote that "most space and play went to the Tet story early, when the least solid information was available. There was no institutional system within the media for keeping track of what the public had been told, no internal priority on updating initial impressions."

Similarly, the initial impression, created by Al Jazeera, of massive civilian casualties became the accepted storyline about Fallujah. Because entering the city meant capture and beheading, the Western TV networks pooled video shot in Fallujah by Arab cameramen who were approved for entry by the insurgents. Predictably, the pictures stressed destruction and death, although the Western networks could not corroborate the scale of the damage. Lacking any other source, most major U.S. newspaper and television outlets worldwide repeated the estimates cited in the Arab press based on the allegations of Iraqi and Jordanian doctors in Fallujah, arriving at an unsubstantiated consensus figure of more than six hundred dead and a thousand wounded.

"Al Jazeera is lying," said Brigadier General John Kelly, the assistant division commander.

Nothing was done about his complaint. In the face of this press onslaught, the White House, the Pentagon, the CPA, and CentCom were passive. Partially this was a military reflex to avoid any comparison to the "body count" debacle of Vietnam. None of those at the top of the chains of command, though, requested from the Marine units in daily contact any systematic estimates that distinguished between civilian and enemy casualties. Given the video recorded by the unmanned aerial vehicles and the imagery required of every air strike and AC-130 gun run, records of the damage would have been easy enough to collect and verify had anyone thought of doing so.

In the absence of countervailing visual evidence presented by authoritative sources, Al Jazeera shaped the world's understanding of Fallujah without having to counter the scrutiny of informed skeptics. The resulting political pressures constrained military actions both against Fallujah and against Sadr.

10

FARMERS OR SHOOTERS?

ON APRIL 6, THE PRESS WAS FOCUSED on the fighting in Fallujah, while the real battle was raging in Ramadi. By noon, Bronzi and Gulf Company had the situation under control downtown. In the afternoon, the fighting shifted from downtown to the suburbs to the east, where Echo Company had the mission all infantrymen hate—sweeping for IEDs.

Every day an IED exploded somewhere along the thirty kilometers of roads that Echo Company tried to sweep. The IED attacks were wearing on the company, but they didn't complain. They knew that a sister battalion at Qaim on the Syrian border was sweeping 170 kilometers of roads—a staggering responsibility.

The Marine Humvees weren't properly armored to withstand the increasing power of the IED explosives. The insurgents were adapting more quickly than the

American procurement system could improve the soldiers' equipment. The men and their commanders shared the risks equally. MajGen Mattis was hit on three occasions, and both his regimental commanders were wounded by IEDs. In the States, the secretary of the navy was demanding a daily tally of new armor shipped to Anbar. But until production stateside caught up with the needs of the battlefield, the Marines would continue sweeping and varying their techniques. Snipers were one means of keeping the insurgents with IEDs off balance.

The night before, a sniper team called Head Hunter 2 drew the duty. Head Hunter 2 was an unlikely-looking team of snipers. Sergeant Romeo Santiago, originally from the Philippines, had been a Marine for six years and had received his citizenship papers only six months before now. A sniper for four years, he smiled constantly, not at all the cold-eyed type. Corporals Ted Stanton and Cameron Ferguson, like Santiago, were easygoing and quick to joke. Not one of the three weighed over 150 pounds, and all looked ludicrously small when burdened down with their sniper gear.

The fourth team member, Corporal Richard Staysal, was big and muscular. "Staysal's our California surfer dude," Stanton said with a smile. "He's our token minority, so we'd give him all the shit details, except he's so frigging big, he'd pound us."

Echo Company covered the Sofia District to the east of Ramadi; thirty-five square kilometers of farmland, expensive houses, palm trees, and irrigation ditches. There were few main roads. Sofia's longtime residents included smugglers, wealthy Baathists, and former army officers. The snipers knew the terrain and had good communications, so Captain Kelly Royer sent them out for an overnight stakeout on Route Nova, a main road into Sofia that looped along the bank of the Euphrates north of Echo Company's base.

The four-man sniper team slipped out of the Combat Outpost after dark, walking north through the noisy suburbs. It was after curfew and no cars were moving, but the dogs were yapping and every so often the cows would join in, mooing at the strange-smelling Marines. The snipers crossed Nova at the Tank Graveyard, a field littered with the hulks of shattered Iraqi tanks. On the north side of Nova a few pumping stations sucked water from the Euphrates and emptied it into a maze of ditches. The team sat on top of a cement station, out of the dirt, and took turns watching an empty road through their night-vision goggles. During the night they saw no Iraqis sneaking up to set in IEDs.

On the morning of April 6, they walked a hundred meters north to the edge of the river and sat in the shade of some scrub growth. The radio transmissions and the steady rumble of distant gunfire made it sound as if every squad in Golf and Weapons Companies were in a battle. Everyone seemed to be in action except them: no traffic was moving on Nova.

"Maybe someone will call us to send our ammo," Staysal muttered.

Not wanting to listen to constant complaints about being left out of the fight, Santiago walked across the field to take a closer look down Nova, which was built up about two feet above the paddies to avoid flooding. When he climbed up onto the road, he surprised a dozen men crouching on the other side, most of them dressed in green Iraqi Army uniforms. Not hesitating a second, Santiago sprinted for his life back across the field, yelling, "Hajis! Hajis!"

Behind him, an Iraqi in a red-and-black-checked kaffiyeh poked his head up, looked quizzically at the startled Marines, ducked down, and popped his head up a few minutes later for a second look. The Marines responded by firing their grenade launchers, lobbing two shells to fall among the insurgents, who were now shooting furiously. As RPGs burst in the trees, two Iraqis hopped over the road, spraying AK fire from the hip, and ran toward the river north of the team. Once they were above the Marines, they intended to push in from the flank, using the shrubs as concealment. The Marines had only two M16s with M203 grenade launchers attached, and two M40 bolt-action sniper rifles with telescopic sights—not much good against enemy crawling forward in hip-high grass and ducking behind scrub trees. The Marines were carrying only nine magazines each and had already ripped through half of them.

"Keep dusting off the road," Santiago said. "If they rush us, we'll have to swim for it."

"You're crazy," Staysal said.

Santiago was calling for a Quick Reaction Force, but with the sounds of the firing, his message at first was garbled at the company ops center.

"No, I'm not asking for permission to fire!" he yelled. "You can hear us firing. We need help."

Another garble.

"No, I'm not dead!" he yelled. "How could I be screaming at you for the QRF if I'm dead?"

It was shortly after noon, and north of Head Hunter, Echo's 1st Platoon was conducting a road sweep. They had found an artillery shell with wires leading into the shrubbery, where they came across a small clearing marked by cigarette butts and flies buzzing over a pile of human feces. They cut the wires, called for engineers to detonate the shell, and walked on. A few hundred meters farther on they came across two more shells wired to a remote control device. They withdrew a safe distance to wait for the engineers and were sitting under some palm trees when their platoon commander, First Lieutenant Vincent Valdez, heard Santiago's call for help over the radio. Valdez loaded ten Marines into an open-backed Humvee and sped down the road. Five minutes later Santiago saw the Humvee approaching at high speed. Staysal popped a white smoke to mark their location and warn them that they were driving into a firefight.

It was too late. The Humvee drove smack into the insurgents, who had gathered to rush across the road and were lying in the weeds among the tank hulks. The unarmored Humvee, with eight Marines sitting in back, was riddled. Rounds ricocheted off the barrel-release latch of the 240 Golf machine gun, putting the gun temporarily out of action. Private First Class Brandon Lund had a round go through his hand, and as he wrapped it with a pressure bandage, he thought, **I don't believe it. I'm shot and I don't see anybody.**

Private First Class Benjamin Carmen pitched forward, blood spurting from his right arm. Lieutenant Valdez grabbed the machine gun, slammed down the release latch, and sprayed the area to the left side of the Humvee, while the corpsman, Hospitalman 3rd Class Tyronne Dennis, worked on Carmen. Dennis saw that a high-velocity bullet had gone through a gap in the plates of Carmen's armored vest, plowed through his arm and chest, and exited his back. There was nothing Dennis could do. Carmen turned white, then pale blue, blood coming from his nose.

"We've lost him," Valdez said. "This Hummer's a magnet. Get out! Get out!"

If caught in an ambush, the immediate action drill was to counter-attack, not to remain inside the kill zone. Even as Valdez was arranging his men in a skirmish line to push toward the Tank Graveyard, mortar shells were landing around them. With the first explosion, the squad leader, Corporal Hurtado Barron, felt he had been punched in the stomach. He leaned over, gasping for breath and patting the front of his armored vest. None of the hot slivers had sliced through the front plate. He grabbed his rifle and ran to catch up with his squad.

Seeing Valdez pushing east into the Graveyard, Santiago and his sniper team crossed the road to protect the southern flank, firing as they dog-trotted along. Staysal was snapping off shots, and to his delight an Iraqi dodging around a tree a few hundred meters away went down and didn't get back up. Staysal started shouting like a madman.

"I got that mother! I nailed him! Oorah!"

I wish Staysal would shut up, Santiago thought. His four-man team was moving forward two hundred meters south of the Marines with Valdez. The two groups could plainly see each other and communicate by yelling and hand signals. Santiago didn't want to get out in front and have his team attract all the fire. When the sniper team reached the tank hulks, Staysal yelled that some insurgents were running up behind them.

Corporal Stanton felt a hammer had hit him in the back, knocking him to his knees. He lay down and yelled for help. Ferguson trotted over, tugged at the back plate of Stanton's armored vest, and saw a hole about the size of a dime, oozing blood. He didn't know what to do about it, unsure whether a compression bandage could stop the bleeding.

"Piece of shrapnel. No blood," Ferguson said. "Forget it. Get up and fight."

No blood? Bullshit no blood, Stanton thought, feeling the sticky wetness. He got to his feet and started forward. Rounds were snapping around them, closer now, making that distinct **crack!** that means someone is aiming at you, not shooting wildly.

"The fucker's hiding behind there!" Staysal was

yelling, pointing at a tank. "He's over there, I tell you, over there!"

Then a bullet hit Staysal in his shoulder, and he screamed and went down. Santiago froze, standing erect, rifle in the classic offhand position, sweeping back and forth with both eyes wide open, waiting for a movement. He saw a man leaning over the engine compartment of a tank to steady his rifle, less than a hundred meters to their rear. Santiago put a round into his left chest. The man slid sideways and fell clear of the tank. Santiago shot him twice more in the chest and moved forward to make sure he was dead. He reached the body—a clean-shaven man with no mustache, dressed in a dark gray dress and sandals—and picked up a Russian Dragunov SVD sniper rifle with a scope.

Staysal lay on the ground screaming for Stanton, who was still concerned about his own wound. As Stanton cut away Staysal's armored vest, he forgot about his own worries. The Iraqi sniper's bullet had broken Staysal's collarbone, plunged downward into his chest, and exited his back, leaving a large hole pouring blood.

"How bad is it?" Staysal asked. "Don't lie to me. It's bad, isn't it? My mom's going to be pissed."

Time and again wounded Marines mention their wives or mothers, concerned that someone is going to be upset or sad because somehow they've screwed up. Stanton felt he was going to throw up. He clumsily wrapped a pressure bandage around Staysal's chest, waited for a lull in the firing, and yelled across the open field to Corporal Pedro Contreras, the nearest Marine in Valdez's skirmish line: "Corpsman up! Corpsman up!"

Hearing the call, HM3 Dennis dropped out of the line and trotted toward Stanton.

"Take the grenade out of my pocket. It hurts lying on it," Staysal said to Stanton. "Hey, pull the pin and throw it. Let's see what it looks like."

"Fuck you and your stupid-ass ideas."

Stanton rummaged through Staysal's daypack for more bandages, finding only a crumpled-up poncho liner.

"Son of a bitch!" Stanton shouted. You should've carried extra ammo."

One field over, the squad with Valdez continued to engage. Lance Corporal Marcos Cherry eagerly shouted to Cpl Barron, his squad leader.

"I got one!" Cherry yelled.

Then a machine gun opened up, killing Cherry instantly. Barron took Cherry's wallet and ID and hurried to rejoin the skirmish line. Valdez was pushing east in the tall grass, following drag marks, intent on finishing off any insurgents lurking around. Santiago and Ferguson, too, headed on.

Dennis and Stanton stayed behind to tend to Staysal, as mortar shells dropped randomly in the fields. They were two hundred meters in from Route Nova, wondering about their next move, when two army Bradleys pulled up on the road. The Marines waved wildly, and the soldiers gestured back, signaling that the trac vehicles couldn't cut across the ditches. The Marines would have to make it to the road.

"Can you walk?" Stanton asked Staysal.

"No, goddammit."

Staysal would have been a load to carry, and Stanton and Dennis, both small men, were already exhausted.

"Well, that's too fucking bad for you, because you're too heavy to carry," Stanton said. "We'll leave you a vest to keep off the mortars."

"Fuck you, stand me up."

With Stanton and Dennis propping him up, Staysal limped and hobbled across the lumpy fields, breathing hoarsely through a punctured lung, blood pouring from his shoulder and back.

Colonel Connor was standing beside the Bradleys. He had monitored the fight on the radio, and as he had done with Joker 3-1, had brought forward a doctor and an armored ambulance. Staysal was properly bandaged and the medics moved on to tend to two other wounded.

With Staysal attended to, Stanton was eager to rejoin the fight. It was approaching two in the afternoon. In the past two hours, the sniper team had seen more than a dozen insurgents ducking and dodging over the course of the four-hour engagement. They had shot perhaps three or four. The Iraqi fighters weren't bent on suicide; they were employing sound hit-and-run guerrilla tactics.

Seeing the two about to strike out on their own to find the other Marines, Connor offered help. "You're

a little short-handed," he said. "Want a few more
shooters?"

"I'd appreciate it, sir," Stanton said.

Connor walked to his command vehicle, radioed
the 1st Battalion of the 34th Infantry to block the
roads leading out of Sofia, and told the three soldiers
in the back of the Bradley to join Stanton.

His command sergeant major, Riling, shook his
head. "They're raw green, sir," he said.

"So?"

"We should go along."

The sergeant major and the colonel told the recruits
to follow them and got on line next to Stanton. They
advanced cautiously, killing one Iraqi before coming
under sniper fire from some distant houses. They
moved by bounds to close on the houses, and by then
the firing had ceased. Stanton led the stack into the
first house and found nothing. It was the soldiers'
turn at the next house.

"Go in as a three-stack," Connor said.

The three soldiers looked blankly at him. Fresh out
of infantry school, it was their first day in country.

"You want me to show you how?"

"Yes, sir. If you would."

Connor guessed the young private would quickly
make corporal. The colonel went in first, followed by
the sergeant major. As usual, no armed insurgent was
in the house and the occupants knew nothing. When
Stanton pointed to blood in the dirt of the courtyard
behind the house, the occupants repeated that they
had seen nothing.

Head Hunter 2's fight at the Tank Graveyard had come to an end. The insurgents had melted away, becoming unarmed civilians in a suburb filled with civilians.

———

Upon hearing that Head Hunter 2 was engaged, LtCol Kennedy had ordered Weapons Company to assist. The company commander, Capt Weiler, assembled Mobile Assault Platoon 3, commanded by First Lieutenant John Stephens, and set out from Hurricane Point. In six vehicles the thirty Marines drove pell-mell east up a narrow road lined with one-story shops and an occasional parked car or truck. Rocks the size of soccer balls were scattered across the road, but the Humvees easily dodged among them. With Iraqi men wandering in and out of shops along the road, 1/Lt Stephens didn't think the flimsy rock barricades were meant to trigger an ambush.

Then they were hit by a sustained burst of fire from a field about 150 meters to their right. The bullets passed high overhead but could easily have killed the men in the shops, who had known the ambushers were lying in wait and hadn't taken cover. The Marines wheeled their Humvees left and right off the road in a herringbone pattern and jumped out, looking for targets. A moment before there had been a dozen vehicles on the road. Now most traffic had stopped. Off to the right a bongo truck was bouncing over the ruts in the field. The Marines let it go, giving the driver the benefit of the doubt that he had not dropped off the insurgents who were firing at them.

Stephens watched as a ten-year-old boy with a lighted torch ran by him, shoved the flames into a pool of black fuel, and proudly ran back inside a shop. The fuel burned with a low flame, throwing off stifling black smoke. A man in a black dishdasha and red-checked kaffiyeh ran out of an alley with an RPG on his shoulder and fired a rocket that went skipping down the street. In a minute it was raining RPG rockets. Some were arcing in like mortars, exploding in the maze of overhead telephone wires. Others were skidding and sizzling through the dirt as though someone were skipping rocks. One bounced up and caught in the cattle catcher of an open-back Humvee just as another burst alongside in a swirl of black smoke. Shaken but unhurt, the driver pulled up closer to the next Humvee in line.

Stephens, deciding the stones in the road and the smoky fire were target reference points for the RPGs and machine guns, moved his platoon farther up the road and watched as the insurgents continued to fire into the smoke. The road was a mess of burning oil slicks, black smoke, and Humvees snarled amid civilian cars. Shadowy gunmen and bulky Marines were firing in all directions. Staff Sergeant Patrick Coleman burst into a house and found five men with AKs hiding under the stairs with women and children. Unsure whether they were insurgents or homeowners, he flexcuffed the men. As he herded them toward a Humvee, he skirted around a pool of blood, where a severed foot protruded from a sandal.

Rounds were snapping steadily, and taxis and motorcycles were dropping off more fighters. Stephens watched as two ambulances slowed down and men hopped out and ran down an alley. He was fairly certain they were insurgents catching a ride to the battle, but he chose not to shoot the ambulances.

Captain Weiler didn't want the Marines to become so engaged that they couldn't get to Head Hunter. Trying to gauge the extent of the ambush, Weiler kicked in the door to a house and dashed up to the roof to gain an overview and figure out how to get out of the area.

Corporal Luis Perez, his radio operator, followed Weiler and handed him the handset to talk with Kennedy. "Head Hunter's been reinforced," Kennedy said. "Your mission is to kick the shit out of any enemy encountered. Keep pushing east. This one's big, very big."

Weiler called back for another platoon to come forward, while 1/Lt Stephens pushed forward. The Marines, catching only passing glimpses of the shooters, were attacking by fire team rushes in the direction of the heaviest fire. They ran by an old woman baking bread in an outdoor oven, oblivious to the chaos, and broke into the courtyard of a mosque where there was a stack of wooden coffins. A dark blue BMW had pulled to a halt up the road, and four men, without weapons, hopped out and ran into an alley. Within seconds, rounds were coming from the alley. Minutes later a white and orange taxi pulled up. A Marine fired an AT-4 rocket that rocked the small car, sending thick smoke billowing from the hood. A passenger stumbled out a rear door, spilling ammunition onto the road. A man on a motorcycle sped out of an alley behind the smoking car, firing an AK with one hand. He was greeted by a fusillade, dropped his weapon, kept his balance, and swerved down the street, the bike on fire.

"That's so cool," Sergeant Shane Nylin said.

RPG rockets were whizzing across the road, hitting telephone poles and shaking loose hot wires that snapped and danced in showers of sparks among the parked cars. A man in a running suit dashed across the street and tripped over a live wire. He rolled and thrashed about, sparks sizzling around him, then got up and staggered away. The Marines broke into several houses, confronting silent women, crying children, and grim-faced men who said they knew nothing. It was like fighting a swarm of mosquitoes. Within an hour the Marines had flex-cuffed sixty men and Weiler knew they'd soon have hundreds, with no proof any had fired a weapon. The Marines lacked chemical test kits for determining the residue of gunpowder.

"Cut 'em loose unless you catch 'em with a weapon," Weiler said.

Lieutenant David Dobb—call sign Rainmaker—and his platoon drove up and joined the fight. There were now sixty Marines scrambling to engage the elusive enemy. A taxicab emerged from a side street, the occupants firing out the windows. In seconds the car was riddled; one man escaped and staggered off. A man popped out from behind a truck firing an AK-47. He was hit, dropped his rifle, and ducked back. Two men with AKs ran across the road and tried to climb over a wall—neither made it. The Marines pumped steady fire into a field next to the road where they had pinned down two men in black dishdashas. Suddenly both leaped up and, exhibiting world-class speed, ran away unharmed.

The insurgents didn't seem to care where they were shooting, as long as they were firing their weapons. The machine-gun fire was too high, and there was no pattern to the RPG rockets. Staff Sergeant Coleman, a huge man, was hit in the face with light shrapnel. Like a ferocious pirate, he rushed around, blood dripping down his chin, roaring at his Marines to "kill any fucker who shoots at you." His Marines laughed and urged him on.

A near miss forced Weiler to duck inside a courtyard, where he found four Iraqi police in their blue shirts hiding behind a wall. They invited him to hide with them; he invited them to join the fight. They didn't appear to have weapons, but as he stepped back out into the street, he wondered whose side they were on.

Several rockets were fired from the courtyard of a small mosque with a graceful blue-hued dome. A Marine on a nearby roof said he was positive there was a man in the minaret, shouting down instructions to the RPG crews. Weiler wasn't authorized to take down the minaret, but the wall surrounding the minaret was fair game. Dobb called up a Humvee with an antitank TOW missile and blew out a section of the wall, sending body parts high into the air.

Under sporadic fire, Stephens directed a rush over the front wall of an attractive, well-kept house with expensive windows and fragile dome-shaped arches. Inside the courtyard a blond camel was calmly nibbling at the grass. An old man introduced himself as a sheikh. Stephens flex-cuffed him and led him away as several women rushed down the driveway shrieking and screaming, certain he was going to be killed.

The fight went on for two hours. Nylin saw about fifteen insurgents, one here and two there. No other Marine saw more than six in total. The insurgents knew how to find concealment along the roads, in the palm groves, and among the houses and alleys. When they were in the open, the Marines had to be quick to get off a shot, and most snapshots missed. Sergeant Jeremiah Randle fired at a man in a gray dishdasha about a hundred meters away who ran into the middle of the street with his AK, danced a little jig mocking Randle, and then ran back to cover. A few minutes later the man repeated his dance act, and again Randle missed. When two more tried their luck, Randle found the range with his grenade launcher and knocked one of them down.

As the fight petered out, Weiler hopped up onto a small wall, raised his rifle, and began yelling, "Come on, you bastards! We're here, we're here! Is that all you got?"

Thereafter Weiler was stuck with hearing his men

murmur **We're here, we're here** whenever he called a staff meeting.

When MAP 3 reached Head Hunter 2, it was midafternoon. First Lieutenant Valdez and Col Connor had the situation under control, and the battle had shifted to the east.

———

When the Head Hunter fight broke out, Capt Royer had sent out patrols to cover the flanks. Shortly after noon a squad came under fire to the east near "the arches," an Iraqi National Guard barracks that had been mortared and blown up before it was completed. Royer set out for the arches with two platoons, commanded by Second Lieutenant John Wroblewski and Second Lieutenant Tom Cogan. Three kilometers down the road, they linked up with the patrol that had taken light fire and spread out to search dozens of houses. Cogan led a squad on foot across a series of irrigation ditches to check out the sound of firing to the north. A few hundred meters away another squad with Royer had also moved off the road.

Cogan's unit was coming under fire from rooftops several hundred meters away, and he found the fight frustrating. The Marines would advance by bounds. When they closed on a house, men in dishdashas or long pants would come out of nowhere and walk away. They had no weapons or military clothing. A few minutes later bullets would fly overhead from another house or palm grove hundreds of meters away.

Half a kilometer away Royer and a separate squad

were finding the same pattern. They would take fire, advance by bounds, and search a house where frightened children cried and unarmed, sullen men denied knowing anything. They would emerge from the house and take fire from another location.

When Royer's radioman told him that another patrol from Echo Company was in a heavy firefight several clicks to the north, Royer decided to pull all the squads together, get back in the vehicles, and move north.

The original plan had been for 2/Lt Wroblewski to move all the vehicles forward to a checkpoint, a kilometer northeast. Marines on foot with Royer and Cogan would cut across the fields and meet the vehicles there. Wroblewski had just started the vehicles rolling to the checkpoint when Royer radioed and waved to him to stop. Cogan did the same thing. As he went around a corner and out of Royer's sight, Wroblewski slowed down, trying to listen to the radio over the noise of the engine. While most of the other vehicles stopped behind him, two highbacks—Humvees with benches for troops to sit in the rear—swung around Wroblewski and kept going toward the checkpoint.

In front of the two highbacks the road sloped upward and joined another road at a right angle. The two roads formed a T, and the Marines proceeded up the long stem. At the top a row of dingy single-story shops crowded each side of the road; lying flat on the roofs behind low cement walls were a dozen or more insurgents. A grove of palm trees and shrubs to the side concealed a heavy machine gun.

The lead highback had a mounted machine gun but no armor. The insurgents waited until the highback was almost on top of the hidden machine gun before opening up from three sides, catching the vehicle in a fusillade of plunging fire. The windshield and tires were peppered; the driver died immediately and the truck rolled to a stop. For a few seconds the Marines futilely returned fire, with Private First Class Ryan Jerabek swinging the machine gun in all directions and cutting down two Iraqis before being killed.

The tailgate was down, and Lance Corporal Deshon Otey rolled out and sprinted behind a low wall. Lance Corporal Travis Layfield and the corpsman Hospitalman 3rd Class Fernando Mendezaceves also flopped out and ran into the nearest shop, while the attackers on the roof above them fired down. Mendezaceves was killed inside the shop. Layfield staggered out the back door and succumbed to his wounds. The other Marines never got out of the truck. Their attackers were too close, firing point-blank on them from the roofs and sides, while the machine gun to the front shredded the cab of the Humvee. Big, muscular Staff Sergeant Allan Walker and four other Marines quickly died.

While the ambushers were pouring their fire into Walker's vehicle, the Humvee behind Walker jerked to a stop and the Marines piled out and dashed into a small storehouse. In seconds, bullets were chipping at the thick cement walls. The building was set back from the road, unattached to the row of shops occupied by the ambushers. The seven Marines inside were trapped, but the insurgents weren't about to close on them across open ground.

Seeing his chance, Otey leaped up and sprinted for the open door as the Marines shouted "Run! Run!" Otey dove through the door and lay panting on the dirt floor, patting himself on his armored vest, amazed that not one of the bullets zipping by him had even grazed him. The Marines, led by Corporal Marcus Waechter, slammed shut the door, took up posts on either side of the one tiny window, and waited for the ground assault.

When the ambush was sprung, Walker's truck and Waechter's Humvee were about three hundred meters in front of Wroblewski. The insurgents on the roofs could see Wroblewski's Humvee, and soon a machine gun was hammering away and rocket-propelled grenades were ricocheting off irrigation ditches. While his crew sought cover in the ditches, Wroblewski knelt beside the passenger door, calling on the radio. A bullet smashed into the side of his face, and he went down. Firing from a dozen roofs the insurgents raked the edges of the ditches where Wroblewski's crew had taken cover. Corporal Ken Smith, the acting platoon sergeant, lay facedown, watching the bullets churn up the dust on the road.

"Get some fire down range!" he yelled to the Marines scattered behind him. "Suppress! Suppress!"

One by one the Marines began squeezing off bursts, short ones at first, then longer ones. Soon the ambush turned into a firefight—as many rounds were going out as coming in. No one could stand erect on that bullet-swept road and live. Smith listened to the rounds cracking and snapping past. At eye level he was looking into Wroblewski's bloody face, ten meters away. The lieutenant was holding the handset, still trying to talk on the radio.

"Ah, shit," Smith said. "Fuck it, I'm going out. Fire, you sons of bitches, give me fire!"

The Marines ripped through magazines in long bursts as Smith gathered himself and dashed out, bullets kicking up dirt around him. In a few frantic strides he reached Wroblewski, gathered him up like a sack of clothes, and pulled him back to the safety of the ditch. A corpsman crawled to the lieutenant and applied pressure bandages to his neck and jaw. Two army Bradley fighting vehicles, their hatches closed, came up behind the beleaguered Marines and drove straight on toward Walker's shattered Humvee, their tracs kicking up clouds of dust. A few minutes later one returned, and the driver stuck his head out of the hatch.

"You've got wounded up ahead around the bend!" he yelled at Smith. "We've gotta haul ass to another mission."

With that, he closed the hatch and drove back up the road, firing the 25mm chain gun in short spurts. Corporal Smith was on his own. With 2/Lt Wroblewski down, the next senior person was SSgt Walker, and he was up ahead where the Bradley driver said there were wounded Marines. Smith knew he had to get this mess straightened out. He shouted orders for the squad leaders to spread their men out. Then, drawing a deep breath, he rushed out a second time to scoop up the radio so that he could contact his company commander. Again bullets struck the road around him. Smith sprawled back into the ditch and pressed the handset.

"Lieutenant Ski's down hard," he told Royer. "I'm sending him back. The Bradley said we have wounded up ahead. Do you want me to push up?"

Royer was as much in the dark as Smith. He had seen the Bradleys rush past and assumed they were part of the brigade's QRF. But he hadn't been able to raise them on his radio, and no one had told him anything about wounded Marines to the front.

"Go, go, get on up there," Royer said. "I'll cover your north flank. Don't wait on me."

Smith called forward a Humvee and gently placed Wroblewski inside. The Humvee raced back to the casualty collection point at the Combat Outpost, a ten-minute drive. At the outpost Dr. Kenneth Son and the corpsmen had already been busy. Earlier two Abrams tanks had come screaming in, with no advance warning, throwing up vast clouds of dust and severing the electric cables running to the main generator, cutting off all power.

"They're dying, they're dying!" screamed a soldier standing upright in the turret of the first tank, pointing to the other tank.

The navy corpsmen swarmed on board the second tank and from the blood-soaked compartment pulled out one soldier with his right hand and wrist missing and another with his jaw dislocated and his right leg dangling at the knee by a few tendons, blood gushing everywhere. While the Blackhawk medical helicopters were en route, the medical crew applied tourniquets, transfusions, and oxygen bags. On the way to the makeshift helipad, the medics shielded the two wounded from the dust raised by the blades of the medevac birds. Inside fifteen minutes they were on their way to a hospital.

When Wroblewski was brought in, the medical crew was ready. He was conscious, and though his pulse was weak and his blood pressure low, they thought he was going to make it when they put him on the Black-hawk, but Wroblewski succumbed on the way to the hospital.

Back in the field near the ambush site, 2/Lt Cogan knew Wroblewski had been taken to the rear, but he didn't know how badly his platoon sergeant, Walker, and the others had been hit. Cogan was in his own fight, pinned down by a machine gun firing from a house only fifty meters off the road.

"I need suppressing fire," Cogan radioed to Smith. "I'll mark target. Watch my tracers."

Seeing Cogan's tracers bouncing off a nearby house, Smith directed a seven-ton truck to pull up and fire its Mark 19. The rounds punched some holes but didn't do much damage.

"Never mind," Cogan radioed to Smith. "I'll take care of it. You punch up to Walker's pos."

The Bradley crew had indicated that the wounded Marines were to the northeast. But Smith's force was being hit by machine-gun fire from the east. The twenty-year-old corporal wasn't going to advance with his flank exposed. Within shouting range he had eighteen men from Weapons, 2nd and 3rd Platoons. It didn't matter what unit they were from; as the acting platoon sergeant, he had the authority and Royer had given him the mission.

Smith led them east, moving by bounds, pinching in on a house about four hundred meters away thought to be the source of the automatic fire. But it was hard to tell. The weapon was set back inside a window, not showing any muzzle flashes, and the noise of outgoing and incoming fire was constant. Smith's men ran from one low wall to another, skirting open fields, searching each house they passed so as not to leave an enemy in their rear.

Not that they had any idea who the enemy were. Everyone was in civilian clothes. Some of the dead bodies they passed had on two sets of civilian clothes, dirty shirts and pants, some in flip-flops, most in sneakers. Inside the houses some women said **ali babas** had come that morning and told them to stay inside, promising that many Americans were going to die. These **ali babas** were "outsiders" with kaffiyehs wrapped around their faces.

As Smith moved his riflemen forward, cars and taxis were coming and going. In the flat terrain, the Marines could see men several hundred meters away hopping in and out of vehicles. With all the shooting, a sensible civilian did not stroll or drive around. Still, they couldn't shoot every man they saw outdoors. The Marines felt they were chasing ghosts.

With his flank secure, Smith headed toward the T near Checkpoint 338, where SSgt Walker had driven an hour before. The Marines who had taken cover in the shed heard shouts in English, and the volume of fire pelting the shed petered out. When an Iraqi ran by the window, a Marine leaned out and shot him in the side of the head. Otey and the others then tumbled out the door, flopped down along a wall, and began shooting up at the roofs.

The ambushers were fleeing. Cars were driving up behind the line of shops, and doors were slamming. Corporal Waechter's squad cautiously advanced, joined by Smith. They saw Walker's Humvee up ahead, all four tires deflated, its machine gun canted skyward.

Waechter reached the vehicle first. "They're all dead!" he shouted.

Smith walked forward at the center of a line of skirmishers. He saw three Marine bodies lying in the back of the Humvee amid besotted sandbags and the brown plastic of MREs. Nearby an Iraqi in a blue shirt and a green camouflage-cloth armored vest lay facedown in his own blood, his head half blown off. Several meters from the Humvee another Iraqi lay on his back, barefoot, his flip-flops a few feet away, a white strip of pudgy belly showing between his blood-soaked blue shirt and brown trousers. A hand grenade lay near his outstretched arm, and he groaned as the skirmish line approached. The Marines killed him, put the grenade in a ditch, and moved on, prodding two bodies sprawled next to an orange and white taxi with shredded tires.

The battleground was eerily clean. The weapons and armored vests of the dead Marines had been taken, and no AKs or RPGs were lying around. On the rooftops even the brass of the ejected rounds had been collected and removed. All that remained were hundreds of cigarette stubs. Smith thought the ambushers must have lain there for hours, obeying a commander who had carefully picked his spot and patiently waited.

Smith set up a defensive perimeter and called forward a Humvee and a seven-ton truck. When the Combat Outpost was alerted that seven dead and five wounded were coming in, back in the rear Staff Sergeant Jeffrey Craig and Sergeant Damien Coan yelled for reinforcements, although they had received no orders to do so. "Saddle up! Echo, grab your gear!" Coan shouted. "We're going out!"

The Combat Outpost was little more than a large warehouse with a cement floor and a large center bay for parking vehicles indoors. With the electricity out and dusk nearing, to catch the light the medical team had set up in the doorway at the northern end, nearest the helipad. After the seven-ton pulled in and the bodies were respectfully unloaded, the floor became slippery with blood. Marines in full battle gear were sliding and pushing at each other as they clambered to board the truck. In the deepening shadows, it took Coan a few seconds to make out what the commotion was all about. A fight was under way for the seats in the back of the seven-ton. There was room for only ten additional riflemen, and there were too many volunteers. Coan had to leave some back. When Craig and Coan drove out, having "forgotten" to inform anyone that they were joining the fight, they left behind a dozen bitter faces.

Coan's seven-ton reached the ambush site shortly after Royer and Cogan, having fought their way across the irrigated fields, arrived. Cogan had approached from the west, warily circling around a few grenades booby-trapped on trees and finding Layfield's body behind the row of stores along the side of the road. Cogan picked up an abandoned RPK machine gun and waited while his men followed blood trails that led nowhere, indicating cars had picked up the insurgent wounded and dead.

Iraqis civilians swarmed outside moments after the firing ceased and set about their daily routine tasks. Eight Marines had died at the T and the ambushers had disappeared, replaced by men walking or driving by, not in itself unusual in a crowded suburb. Royer thought, **Are they farmers or shooters?** Smoldering with anger, he set about consolidating his men.

It was after dusk before the last vehicles left the Sofia. The insurgents, who rarely fought at night, had dispersed. In eight hours the fight had rolled across twelve kilometers of roads and fields. Colonel Connor and his Bradleys returned to brigade headquarters. Kennedy was out on his feet. The exhausted Marines went back to Hurricane Point and the Combat Outpost to clean weapons, resupply, and sleep. In the ops center Maj Harrill, past trying to make sense of the firefights scrawled like spaghetti across his map, sent a terse sum-

mary to division. The NCOs attended to the administration and casualty reports, while the officers visited
the wounded and planned the next day's operations.

The insurgents had planned the offensive and
brought in fighters to respond to Battalion 2/4's ever-
expanding foot patrols. No Arab and few Western
reporters were present. Had the Government Center
been overrun, as the police station in Fallujah had
been in February, or had 2/4 pulled back, the political
consequences would have been dire. As it was, Kennedy had swung back with both fists, and the insurgents had pulled back. As in Tet of 1968, the initial
press stories focused on the American casualties. "12
Marines Killed" was the headline policy-makers and
politicians read on the morning of April 7. The press
coverage of the Ramadi battle repeated the number of
American lives lost, not that the insurgents had failed
in their planned offensive.

11

AVOIDING THE PERFECT STORM

WHILE THE INTENSE FIGHTING IN RAMADI on April 6 was going on, Battalion 1/5 had consolidated its lines in southern Fallujah. Bravo and Alpha Companies had pushed west two kilometers to Phase Line Violet, a four-lane avenue running north-south. To the north of Alpha, Weapons Company was holding the south side of Highway 10, having hauled .50 cals and Mark 19s to the roofs and backed their Humvees inside walled courtyards to avoid the ever-present RPGs. Battalion 1/5 had seized the industrial quadrant of Fallujah—about 25 percent of the city's geography.

The insurgents held the north side of Highway 10 and the west side of Violet. Most wore kaffiyehs, T-shirts or long-sleeved shirts, trousers, and flip-flops or running shoes. Some were dressed in black ninja outfits, and a few were wearing the blue shirts of police officers or the brown utilities of the Iraqi National Guard. Phase Line Violet (later called Phase Line Henry) marked the main line resistance of the insurgents. Once LtCol Byrne was given the signal, the two companies would surge across the avenue, break the defense, and turn north into the Jolan.

On April 7 LtGen Conway and MajGen Mattis drove west from the industrial section with their guest, General Michael Hagee, the Commandant of the Marine Corps, who was visiting from Washington. The Marines called these visits "windshield tours" and paid them no heed. Senior officers were expected to be forward. If someone took a bullet through the windshield, that was considered part of the job. It was important to Conway that the commandant get a first-hand understanding of the messy fighting.

As the ground commander, Mattis had no illusions about the possibility of defeating the insurgents by attacking through the city. Without Iraqi forces to take over, many of the insurgents would simply pose as civilians and bide their time. The best outcome of the attack upon Fallujah was to duplicate the outcome at Ramadi, where LtCol Kennedy held the main highway, protected the Government Center, and patrolled wherever he wished.

After pulling over at an intersection, standing near Gen Hagee, Mattis watched as one insurgent group after another fired a few AK rounds and then ducked into the Al Kubaysi Mosque south of High-way 10. Exasperated, he turned to Maj Farnum and said, "If those assholes keep it up, put a TOW [antitank missile] through the front door."

The insurgents persisted in firing from inside the mosque's courtyard, so the Marines put a Hellfire missile and a five-hundred-pound laser-guided bomb into the wall. When they went forward a half-hour later, they found no bodies, the Iraqis having carried off the casualties. At least four journalists embedded with the battalion accurately reported the story in their respective papers. All reported that the Marines had taken continuous fire from the mosque. The clear video shots of the air attacks, of course, made good television footage in the States. Al Jazeera reported twenty-six civilians had died. The lead press story on April 7 was that a mosque had been struck.

At division headquarters outside Ramadi, Dunford was conferring with the CPA diplomats, who warned that images of the fighting were causing political chaos in Baghdad. Dunford said the MEF had been alerted that the attack might be stopped. The CPA diplomats sent an e-mail to Bremer urging that the attack continue.

On April 7, President Bush was at his ranch in Crawford, Texas, having left Washington for a long Easter weekend. The news was somber for the commander-in-chief. The headlines led with the Marine losses at Ramadi, the most costly ground engagement in a single day since the fall of Baghdad, followed by an air strike against a mosque in Fallujah. Fights were raging in Ramadi, Fallujah, Baghdad, Kut, and Najaf, where American soldiers were attacking Sadr's militia. The tone of the stories was apprehensive, lending an air of "what's going to happen next?" with U.S. forces in Iraq stretched thin.

In Washington, a policy fight under the klieg lights of the television networks was brewing: a parade of witnesses were testifying before the 9/11 Commission that was aggressively investigating whether the administration had ignored warnings about the terrorist attack on the Twin Towers and Pentagon.

The president began a round of calls with his national security advisers and foreign leaders. On the international front, Bush won renewed pledges of support from Italy, El Salvador, and Poland. But Spain had already declared its troops were pulling out, and the Ukrainian troops, who had been driven out of Kut on April 6, had shaky support from a citizenry back home that was fed up with a corrupt government.

The president spoke with Prime Minister Tony Blair against a background of reports that the departing British envoy in Baghdad, Sir Jeremy Greenstock, had objected to Bremer's decision-making style and general approach to the Iraqis. The tension went both ways, with Sanchez disturbed by British military high-handedness in Basra and the CPA concerned about separate British channels of communication with Iran.

The British leaders believed the attack on Fallujah was creating more insurgents among the residents of the city. "The lid of the pressure cooker has come off," British Foreign Secretary Jack Straw told BBC radio a few days later. "It is plainly the fact today that there are larger numbers of people, and they are people on the ground, Iraqis, not foreign fighters, who are engaged in this insurgency."

A decade earlier, as political pressures mounted against throwing Saddam out of Kuwait by force, Prime Minister Margaret Thatcher had famously advised President George H. W. Bush, "Don't go wobbly on me, George." This time the advice from the British was to halt the attack.

Unlike the British, pundits writing in major American newspapers on April 7 argued for continuing with the attack in Fallujah. "There has to be a strong response or else this will encourage more of this," said Andrew Krepinevich, the director of a Washington think tank.

"This is a turning point. We have been challenged," retired Lieutenant General Bernard Trainor, a noted military author, said. "If we back off on this thing, we are sending a strong signal that the Americans will not be able to control the situation. Most of the Iraqis are sitting on the fence waiting to see which side is going to win. If the tide starts to turn, you will get a mob reaction."

––––

The president spent part of the day gauging the reactions and soliciting judgments about Fallujah, including a televideo briefing from Bremer. Usually the national security adviser, Dr. Condoleezza Rice, collected inputs about Iraq from three sources—her deputy for Iraq, Ambassador Blackwill; Ambassador

Bremer; and Secretary Rumsfeld. It wasn't always that neatly divided, though. The secure video teleconference, or "sivits," had emerged as a twenty-first-century staple of senior government officials, permitting advisers thousands of miles apart to pop up on different quadrants of a video screen to discuss important matters. The sivits had the advantage of immediate, corporeal interaction and the disadvantage of shaping decisions without coordinated staff papers.

Rice was in Washington preparing to testify before the 9/11 Commission. Richard Clarke, a civil servant who had coordinated counterterrorism activities at the NSC, had endorsed Senator Kerry for president and charged that Dr. Rice had ignored his pre-9/11 warnings about a terrorist attack. Clarke had testified a week earlier before the 9/11 Commission, and reporters had portrayed him as a twenty-first-century Paul Revere, the bureaucrat who valiantly tried to awaken a somnambulant administration. Rice was due to testify the next day, and the press was building up the event as round two of a momentous intellectual boxing match. The 9/11 commissioners were an impressive group of former government officials and politicians, knowledgeable and aggressive. The stakes for Dr. Rice were high—her reputation, her career, and the administration's credibility. The next day's hearing demanded her careful preparation.

By dealing directly via sivits with Abizaid and Bremer, the president was hearing first-hand the judgments of the two separate and coequal chains of command he had established. The battle for Fallujah had become equally a military matter and a political matter.

Both Bremer and the president's deputy assistant for Iraq, Ambassador Blackwill, were under intense pressure in Baghdad. Blackwill was pulling together an interim government to take power when Iraq regained sovereignty in June. He was also dealing with the Algerian diplomat Lakhdar Brahimi, who had been sent by the UN to help in the transition to sovereignty. Brahimi hadn't established an easy rapport with the Ayatollah Sistani, the reclusive Shiite religious leader, and an old photo of Brahimi smoking a cigar with a beaming Saddam had circulated over the Internet, further complicating his dealings with the Shiites. Brahimi's daughter was engaged to the son of King Abdullah of Jordan. Both men were prominent Sunnis—eighteen of the twenty-one Arab countries in the Middle East were ruled by Sunni leaders—who objected strongly to the attack on the Sunni city of Fallujah. Brahimi insisted that a compromise had to be negotiated in Fallujah.

At the same time Bremer was trying to assure the Sunnis of equitable treatment while balancing the demands of a Shiite majority aroused and confused by Sadr's rebellion. Hourly television depictions of American forces destroying Fallujah and cutting down Sadr's Shiite militia in Najaf and East Baghdad were rallying widespread sympathy and forging common bonds among Shiites and Sunnis.

The Iraqi Governing Council was comprised of

twenty-four Iraqis who had opposed Saddam. None were military men; they had no experience or yard-stick to put the fighting in perspective. In response to the attack on Fallujah, one member of the council had suspended his membership, and four others threat-ened to quit. Bremer faced a revolt inside the very Iraqi Governing Council that he had hand-picked.

One misstep, and the ambassadors would find them-selves in the perfect political storm, defied by the Iraqi Governing Council, by the UN representative, and by Sunnis and Shiites alike. On April 7 Bremer and Black-will, the two top diplomats in Iraq, saw the situation the same way. "If the top [of the Governing Councils] blows off," a senior diplomat said, "that is a huge polit-ical defeat for the Coalition and for what we're trying to do in Iraq. Advancing the sovereignty of Iraq is the key, not seizing one city."

The Fallujah battle as portrayed on Arab TV threat-ened to collapse months of sensitive negotiations and leave America ruling Iraq without Iraqi partners. The diplomats were under the impression that it would take ten days to seize the city. They did not know Mattis was moving a third battalion into position to finish the fight in a few days. The message via sivits to the White House was succinct and to the point:

"Sir, we have a growing political problem," Bremer told the president.

———

While the president was mulling the political situa-tion, at the fighting level Col Toolan was aligning his final pieces on the Fallujah chessboard. A year earlier the American military had charged up two narrow corridors and pounced on Saddam's headquarters in Baghdad. That strategy, called Maneuver Warfare, employed speed and maneuver to strike the enemy's "center of gravity" (Baghdad) and deliver a quick knockout rather than to slog forward relying on firepower and attrition. There were theories for applying Maneuver Warfare to urban combat: for instance, conducting raids against the houses of known insurgent leaders, or sending a column of tanks directly into the Jolan District to break the center of resistance. Toolan rejected these theories as quick fixes sure to fizzle.

Given the JTF order, the regiment intended to attack block by block, demolishing strong points, blowing up arms caches, and killing all who stood and fought. To aid in the fight, Mattis had ordered a third battalion, 3/4, to pull out of a city to the north and report to Toolan. Battalion 3/4 was a seasoned combat unit; most of the officers and over 60 percent of the troops had fought together a year earlier. It was 3/4 that had hauled down Saddam's statue in Firdos Square, signaling the fall of Baghdad.

On April 8, while 3/4 was moving into position to the east, Battalion 1/5 was receiving fire from the Al Samarri Mosque, north of Highway 10. Lieutenant Josh Glover led a platoon to the mosque's gate, blew the lock, and charged in. The insurgents fled out the back, leaving behind three hundred RPGs and 122mm rocket rounds, as well as suicide vests.

As they cleared through the junkyards, the Marines advanced cautiously. Thousands of civilians were fleeing through their lines; insurgents sometimes hid behind groups of women and children. The door of a car or taxi amid hundreds of slowly moving vehicles would open and ammunition would be dropped off. Eventually the residents were allowed to leave only on foot, as concern about suicide bombers increased with the amount of explosives discovered.

In Battalion 2/1's zone, in the northwestern corner above the Jolan District, civilians weren't a problem; they had all fled the houses and apartments. The insurgents fired rockets and mortars that fell with no particular pattern or time interval. Like 1/5, Battalion 2/1 absorbed successive assaults by small gangs on April 7 and 8. Three or four times a day, a dozen or so insurgents would run forward; some would be cut down, and others would retreat. Whenever the insurgents persisted in firing from a particular building, the Marines called in fixed-wing bomb strikes and Cobra rocket attacks.

On the afternoon of April 8, Col Toolan visited Echo Company of 2/1, which was holding a line of buildings along the edge of a cemetery. In his usual state of high energy, Capt Zembiec let it be known that he favored a tank-supported assault into the Jolan. Toolan counseled patience. Battalion 3/4, he told Zembiec, was setting into position to the east. He wanted to catch the insurgents in a net and finish them, not let them scatter out of the way of a single-axis attack and regroup later.

By the evening of the eighth, Toolan was set to take back the streets of Fallujah. He told MajGen Mattis all he needed was the go-ahead signal. Mattis estimated it would take forty-eight to seventy-two hours to finish the fight.

———

It would be an American rather than an Iraqi force, though. The 36th Iraqi National Guard Battalion, with its four hundred men and seventeen U.S. special forces advisers, was on the lines with 2/1 and fighting well. But it was showing signs of fraying at the edges and couldn't continue much longer as a frontline unit. The JTF had found no other reliable Iraqi force to join the attack. In the past several days a wave of Iraqi desertions and no-shows had swept throughout central and southern Iraq. In Baghdad, as MajGen Dempsey aligned his 1st Armored Division against Sadr's militia, he ruefully watched Iraqi police and National Guard units that he had nurtured for months abandon their posts. To the Shiite south, the Coalition's Multinational Division, comprised of Poles, Bulgarians, and the like, offered scant resistance to Sadr's bands of thugs, while the Iraqi police and National Guard melted away. In the rebellious Sunni Anbar Province, to the west, the Marine Expeditionary Force staff was ticking off the desertions of one Iraqi unit after another. Over 80 percent of the police and National Guard had deserted.

General Abizaid later concluded that the problem lay in the lack of a functioning Iraqi chain of command. The separate Iraqi forces—police in one city, a National Guard battalion in another—had no organizational structure or set of higher allegiances. If the battalion commander folded, as happened in the case of the 2nd Battalion, or if a police chief felt he was overmatched and left his police station, his men followed. By running away, the police and National Guardsmen had saved their own lives. No higher chain of command had intervened, and no senior officers rushed to the scene to take over or to impose discipline for desertion in combat. While three- and four-star American generals regularly visited their troops on the front lines, Iraqi senior officers did not have that leadership tradition.

The insurgents, too, lacked a command structure and possessed only basic arms. Yet they fought enthusiastically against the Americans and routed the Iraqi security forces. Al Jazeera and Al Arabiya provided a scorecard as they reported heroic resistance spreading from Fallujah to Ramadi to Quaim, Hilla, Karbala, and Najaf. Not a single member of the Iraqi Governing Council, ensconced in Baghdad, left the capital to rally the Iraqi security forces or to urge a single unit to fight back. In city after city the insurgents held the streets.

———

In Baghdad Ambassadors Bremer and Blackwill were fending off a torrent of complaints. Just as President Bush had reacted a week earlier to the images of the mutilated bodies of four American contractors, so too were Iraqis reacting viscerally to the images from Fallujah. After two more members of the Iraqi Governing Council quit and five others threatened to follow suit, Bremer agreed to an evening meeting on the eighth. Attending were three members of the council. Sheikh Ghazi Yawar represented the old, established power base of Sunni sheikhs. Hachim Hassani led a Sunni group called the Iraqi Islamic Party. Energetic and smooth, Hassani had lived for sixteen years in California and had embraced Fallujah as his special cause. The third member was eighty-year-old Adnan Pachachi, a polished former diplomat and a favorite of the State Department. Like the other two, Pachachi was railing about Fallujah, holding daily press conferences to denounce "an act of vengeance" and going on Arabiya television to complain that "it was not right to punish all the people of Fallujah. We consider these operations unacceptable and illegal."

Generals Abizaid and Sanchez agreed to participate in the evening meeting. Sanchez called Conway to warn him there might be a delay before "the big push."

Conway was not happy. "We control thirty percent of that city," he told Sanchez. "The ACF [anti-Coalition forces] are short of ammo. We have a battalion tearing up their ammo dumps in the industrial sector. This isn't the time to stop. We need just a few days to finish this. That's all—days."

The senior diplomats in Baghdad, where CPA relations with the JTF were frayed, had been shown no written ops plans or estimates of the time it would take to seize Fallujah. Based on verbal discussions, they were under the impression that the Marines needed a week to ten more days—a timeframe fraught with political risk.

The CPA diplomats who were in the field agreed with the Marines that the fight should continue. Nate Jensen, a CPA diplomat, was talking with Toolan in regimental headquarters next door to the MEF when they heard that Baghdad might stop the attack. He called Stu Jones, an experienced foreign service officer, at Camp Blue Diamond, and Jones sent an immediate message to Bremer, arguing that a delay would strengthen the insurgents and accomplish no useful purpose. Ambassador Michael Gfoeller, the senior adviser in the province to the south of Anbar, sent a forceful dissenting message to Bremer, stating that any delay would be seen as weakness by the Sunni insurgents and would encourage Sadr in his rebellion as well.

Sanchez and Abizaid attended the evening meeting at Bremer's office. The interim Iraqi defense minister, who favored continuing the attack, was not there. The three Sunni Iraqis from the Governing Council presented a powerful case against the attack, warning of massive street protests and mass resignations. The director of the Fallujah hospital had reported on Al Jazeera that six hundred civilians had died and a thousand had been seriously wounded. The Iraqi officials were passionate and convincing. Hassani showed that he was a skilled debater, deflecting Abizaid's requests for several days to finish the fight. Hassani retorted that soon Iraq would be one big Fallujah.

Threatened resignations might be a bluff, but Fallujah did provide a means for the appointed Sunni officials to gain popular legitimacy. The IGC, heavily comprised of expatriates who had returned after Saddam was toppled, had gained only shallow support among their fellow Iraqis. Now the appointed leadership of the fledgling Iraqi democracy was rushing to the rescue of insurgents dedicated to killing them.

Abizaid agreed with Bremer that the attack on Fallujah was jeopardizing the political stability of Iraq. At the conclusion of the meeting, Abizaid ordered the Marines to suspend offensive operations. "I know major military action could implode the political situation," he said, according to one official quoted in the **Los Angeles Times.**

Sanchez informed Conway of Abizaid's decision, stressing that the threats of the Iraqi Governing Council to resign could not be ignored. Conway had a different perspective: "Once in, we're committed," he said. "Stand by it."

The halt would be temporary, Sanchez assured Conway. The purpose was to bring medical supplies to Fallujah's two hospitals and to permit a delegation from the Governing Council to talk with the city elders. What that was intended to accomplish was not clear. Conway relayed the news to Mattis, who discussed it with Col Dunford. Mattis reacted by quoting Napoleon.

"First we're ordered in, and now we're ordered out," Mattis said. "If you're going to take Vienna, then by God, sir, take it."

On April 9 the American press was focused on analyzing the testimony of Dr. Condoleezza Rice before the 9/11 Commission. The hearing had provided high drama, with Rice calmly refuting allegations of past administration failures and refusing to be baited into making any impolitic statements or showing any anger. The CPA announcement that U.S. forces in Fallujah "had initiated a unilateral suspension of offensive operations" received little play.

Sanchez met with reporters to stress that JTF resolve had not weakened. "We have got Fallujah under siege at this point," he said, "and we will continue our deliberate operations in the city until we've accomplished our objectives."

To assuage the glum Marines, Gen Abizaid visited Camp Fallujah. The MEF staff began the meeting with a briefing on Marine forces in contact. The thrust of the briefing was clear: the Marines were engaged while the politicians were talking about cease-fires. The briefing ended with the statement that the battalions were ready to continue the attack. Abizaid said the plan was to cease pushing forward for twenty-four hours and then assess. He said the insurgents inside the city thought they had beaten first the army (the 82nd) and now the Marines. They would make exaggerated claims to the press that should be ignored. Arabs had done that before, as in the 1967 war against Israel, when they declared victory knowing they had been defeated.

"But we haven't defeated them in Fallujah," a Marine observed.

"We're dealing with the nastiest people here," Conway said, making it clear he believed the attack should continue.

"The IGC has threatened to resign," Abizaid replied. "That would be a terrible optic. We need time to get it politically right."

Mattis arrived late to the meeting. His small command convoy was racing down the highway from Ramadi when two Humvees flagged them down. On patrol from Battalion 3/11, the Marines had been hit by machine-gun fire from a house about four-hundred meters to the north. Not wanting to leave the ambushers in place, Mattis added the firepower of his two LAVs to the patrol from 3/11.

"The general flanked the hajis from the south," his crew chief, Gunnery Sergeant David Beall, said. "He sent me in on the north flank. We caught them in a crossfire. Then the general called in two Cobras and that ended it. We pulled out two or three dead Iraqis and one machine gun and took off down the road. He was running real late."

When Mattis arrived at the MEF, he apologized for his delay.

"I was late getting here, General," he said, "but give us twenty minutes and we'll be ready to jump off."

Battalion 3/4 was closing on the cloverleaf east of the city. Mattis was ready to squeeze the city from the east, south, and west.

"No," Abizaid said. "Not for at least twenty-four hours. Then we'll reassess."

The four-star general flew out, leaving behind a group of smoldering Marines. When Mattis returned to his LAV, he said nothing to his crew or to the few embedded reporters who had been with the division for a month. This was highly unusual. It was his habit to explain to them what he had been doing in a meeting, make a few tactical observations, and take questions. The crew always gathered around. They were family and liked knowing what their leader was thinking. On the ninth, though, Mattis kept his distance. He was the general, keeping counsel only with himself.

The next day, April 10, the written order from the JTF to halt offensive operations reached Toolan's regiment. Offensive operations were suspended, but deliberate operations could continue, meaning that the Marines could move forward reasonable distances to strengthen defensive positions. Sanchez was trying to give them as much maneuver space as possible.

In the States, President Bush delivered his weekly Saturday radio talk to the nation. "In Fallujah, Marines of Operation Vigilant Resolve are taking control of the city, block by block," he said. "Our offensive will continue in the weeks ahead."

The Marine commanders tried to understand the contradictory verbal and written orders they were receiving. How an offensive could take control of the city block by block when it had been ordered to halt was mystifying. As far as they could understand it, Sanchez believed the pause would continue for only a day. After that pause, the offensive could resume, as the president indicated on the radio. They cherished the hope that it would.

There hadn't been a mutual cease-fire on April 9. The insurgents had opened fire whenever they had the advantage. Battalion 3/4 had taken mortar and rocket fire all night and on the morning of the tenth had edged into the first set of buildings on the northeastern side of Fallujah, while Battalions 2/1 and 1/5 remained in place. The Iraqi officials Hassani and Yawar—drove in from Baghdad, met with some Iraqis at the Government Center, and later held a press conference at the MEF headquarters outside the city. They told the press that the city was "devastated" and that the doctors who had accompanied them were "aghast" at the conditions.

"We want to put the good people of Fallujah in control of their city," said Saif Rahman, a member of the negotiating team from the Governing Council.

The officials then hastily left for Baghdad, where council member Adnan Pachachi went on Arab and American television to deliver the lines he would repeat for the next two weeks.

"We consider the action carried out by U.S. forces as illegal and totally unacceptable," he said. "It is a form of mass punishment."

12

MANY DIE, THEY ARE GONE

WHILE NEGOTIATIONS AND POSTURING ENSUED AT Fallujah, thirty miles to the west in Ramadi fighting raged for several days. On April 6, twelve Marines died battling the insurgents across the city and in the suburbs. The fighting had continued the next day, when the brigade staff ordered a psychological operations team into the city. On top of their Humvees the psyops crew had loudspeakers instead of machine guns, so LtCol Kennedy told Weapons Company to provide cover for the mission.

Linking up with the two psyops Humvees, a platoon commanded by First Lieutenant Lucas Wells walked slowly into the marketplace, with the speakers blaring in singsong Arabic, **"Thank you for pointing out the insurgents. Do not let them cause you fear."** The Marines walked on both sides of the vehicles as hundreds of incredulous Iraqi men gathered about, hooting and shouting insults and making slicing gestures across their throats, showing the soles of their flip-flops and saluting with their middle fingers. Nearby minarets blared an appeal for blood for the jihad, drowning out the psyops message. The Marines handed out pamphlets that the Iraqis ripped up or rubbed across their asses and flung back. A few stones were thrown, then a few more. The Marines, as angry as the jeering mob, swung their rifles back and forth, daring someone to challenge them.

"This is not a success," 1/Lt Wells radioed back to Capt Weiler.

"Okay, go north a click," Weiler said. "That way it doesn't look like we're being run out of town. Let some cows hear the message, then come home."

Walking north, the Marines bumped into a procession of unarmed men, many in white dishdashas, carrying a wooden coffin. The Marines stood to the side to let them pass. Hard stares were exchanged, neither side saying a word. When they reached the open stretch of road where the Head Hunter sniper team had fought on April 6, they knew they were in for it. No one was outside, and most of the livestock had been herded into the walled courtyards. They scanned the open fields, the pine trees, and the set-back houses, waiting for the attack. As usual, it began with scattered RPG rockets and AK and machine-gun fire, followed by an IED detonated too far away to do damage.

Wells called for a skirmish line to advance on the nearest large house, where they found only a frightened woman and three children hiding on the roof. In a nearby palm grove, a Marine saw movement at the top of a tree and let loose a burst from his Mark 19. Two men with AKs fell twenty feet to the ground. In the shrubs the Marines captured two other Iraqis wearing tree-climbing harnesses. As he walked back to the waiting Humvees, Lance Corporal Marshall Cummings was shot in the back, the bullet puncturing his lung. A man knelt up in the tall grass to see if he had hit anyone. The Marines put several Mark 19 slugs into his chest, placed Cummings in a Humvee, and drove back to base at breakneck speed through the thick downtown traffic, bumping cars out of the way. At the base Dr. Son stabilized Cummings, and a Blackhawk evacuated him.

Kennedy didn't like concentrating patrols on the inner city; it left the initiative in the suburbs with the insurgents. In the attack on April 6, the core of the insurgents had come from outside the city. Historically, insurgents hid in the countryside and squeezed the government forces that were holding the cities. The flat land of Iraq provided no jungles or forests to hide in. Instead, the excellent road system enabled insurgents to live in safe areas, hide caches of arms inside a city, drive to assembly points, pick up the weapons, attack, and drive away. Sofia was the assembly area for the attacks inside Ramadi.

At the strategic level, the Marines couldn't control Ramadi by a strategy of attrition; only Iraqi government forces could reclaim Ramadi from the insurgents, and that, Kennedy believed, was a long-term proposition. There were more than thirty thousand young, disaffected Sunni males in the city. The police and National Guard had disappeared. The Marines had seen the police vehicles zipping around, driven by insurgents. Most police stations had been stripped of their equipment.

To regain immediate control of Ramadi, the Americans would have to fight alone. As the flames of rebellion spread across the province, Kennedy was determined to put an end to the five-day uprising. On April 10, he moved to finish the fight, attacking into Sofia, three kilometers east of downtown where Echo Company had suffered serious losses. Working with the CIA and Special Forces, Kennedy had pinpointed ten upscale houses to be hit in a raid. In the pale light of dawn, Echo Company spread out and advanced on foot toward the houses.

Sergeant Santiago's sniper team was moving with Lt Valdez and the 1st Platoon across the open fields when a cow charged Corporal Chris Ferguson, who shot the unfortunate animal. Stanton and Santiago were laughing when rounds started snapping around them. They barged into the nearest building, an outhouse littered with piles of human feces around one small drainage hole. On the verge of vomiting, the two snipers tumbled back out, bullets zipping between them, and ran into the nearest house.

Once inside, Santiago demanded that the fearful owner hand over the weapon every homeowner was allowed to keep. His own sniper rifle fired only one round at a time, but with the borrowed AK Santiago fired off a full magazine in the general direction of the nearest palm trees. The distinct snapping sound of the AK attracted return fire from half a dozen Marines in other houses. As bullets peppered the farmhouse, the farmer jumped in front of his children and yelled at Santiago to get out before he got them killed. After giving the children some candy, Santiago followed a hooting Stanton out the back door.

Outside they rejoined Ferguson, who was firing at a man hiding behind a palm tree 150 meters away. Santiago told Ferguson and Stanton to bound forward fifty meters to the next berm while he provided covering fire. When they broke from cover, the Iraqi opened fire. Santiago sighted in—and his rifle jammed. The Iraqi missed, and in seconds an alarmed Stanton was lying behind the far berm.

"You son of a bitch!" Stanton yelled. "You did that on purpose!"

The three Marines then enveloped the lone Iraqi, who hadn't budged, and let loose a barrage that mortally wounded the man and set the tree on fire.

Farther to the west, Capt Royer was directing his platoons when his command group was taken under machine-gun fire from the south and the northeast. Caught by interlocking fires in a flat, open field, the Marines survived the first bursts by diving into a ditch. When Royer glanced up, a bullet hit his helmet, leaving him dazed but unharmed. Sergeant Kenneth Hassel dashed toward the nearest house, hoping to call mortars on the gun positions. Two streams of tracers seemed to converge on him, and he leaped back into the ditch, breaking his leg in two places. Wrapping Hassel's leg in palm branches, the Marines dragged him along the ditch, as rounds bounced off the dirt inches above their heads.

The ditch served as the local commode, and when the Marines slithered out from behind the protection of the large berm, their uniforms were black and they were gagging from the stink. They pulled Hassel across a canal in mud and water up to their waists and crawled into the courtyard of a farmhouse held by a squad from 2nd Platoon. Hassel refused morphine and kept his rifle, insisting he could fight.

Around them were palm groves with clusters of two or three houses separated by small open fields and gardens. The Humvees were unable to cross the ditches, so the Marines were separated from their supporting fires. The insurgents, familiar with the neighborhood, were swarming in from all directions. There were Cobras overhead, but Royer didn't want to call them in until he was sure where his Marines were, and most had gone to ground in different houses, fighting in squad-sized groups.

The insurgents would dash forward until they were fifty or sixty meters away from a house, then apply aimed fire. They weren't closing to finish the fight. Two snipers in Royer's house, Lance Corporal Patrick Ashby and Corporal Samuel Topara, were on the roof, taking a steady toll of the insurgents who were darting through the palm groves in groups of four to six.

When the firing began, Ashby had broken into a house and run to the roof. The family had rushed up after him, showing him religious pictures and a cross, fumbling with words to say that the insurgents would execute them as Christian traitors if he didn't leave. So Ashby had run over to Royer's house.

Each time Ashby poked his head above the low wall on the roof, he heard snapping noises like the cracking of a whip. With Royer acting as spotter, he put a 203 round through the window of the nearest house, silencing fire from there. Then he resumed sighting in with his rifle, selecting an individual target, taking an aimed shot, ducking back down, wriggling along the roof, waiting a few minutes, and popping up to shoot again from a different place. Ashby noticed that many of his targets were dressed in black and were employing sound tactics. There had been talk about an Iraqi special forces unit in the area. Earlier that morning he had shot a man and recovered a German Mauser rifle with a telescopic scope. Whoever these insurgents were, they had had military training.

Fifty meters southwest of Royer an Iraqi machine gun was firing, the gun set back inside a window and not affected by M16 rounds. The Marines fired an AT-4 rocket from inside their house—the reverberations shook the foundation—then rushed into the next house. From there they crawled forward, threw grenades into the next house, and stormed inside. They repeated this three times before destroying the machine gun. It took ninety minutes to move seventy meters and clear five houses in one small palm grove.

A hundred meters to the south of Royer, the same sort of close-in fight was raging. Lance Corporal Sims and another sniper, Corporal Jose Ramirez, were on the roof, engaging small groups of insurgents who were lying down in the ditches about a hundred meters away. Whenever an Iraqi was hit, a woman would come out of a nearby house and drag him inside.

Then the Iraqis started rushing forward, two and four at a time, not throwing grenades but trying to get close enough to aim in. An Iraqi would appear from behind a wall or on the top of a ditch, sight in, fire a burst, then duck down. Ramirez noticed that some Marines, seeing the Iraqis closing in, were firing wildly, a few not even bothering to aim, just sticking a rifle barrel over the wall and pulling the trigger.

Trained as a sniper, Ramirez stayed low and sighted in wherever he had last seen an Iraqi shooter. Then he waited. Time and again a shooter reappeared at the same place—in the center of his sight picture. Despite his fear and his dry mouth, Ramirez was beginning to feel comfortable.

He and Sims had a rhythm going. First one and then the other would fire an aimed burst, crawl to a different spot, and wait for another opening. Then Sims knelt up at the wrong moment, and a bullet hit him in the shoulder, penetrated his chest, and lodged in his back. Ramirez helped to carry him downstairs, where HM3 Sergio Guitterez tried to slow the internal bleeding.

Corporal Jeffrey Andrade radioed to Royer. "We need a bird for Sims right now, goddammit, right now!"

Listening to the reports of the close-in fighting, the

ops center refused to allow a helicopter to land for a
medevac for either Sims or Hassel, who were about a
hundred meters apart. Colonel Connor, as in prior
fights, came forward with the armored 113s. They
couldn't cross the irrigation canal, but they added
heavy firepower. With Andrade screaming at everyone
to help, four Marines carried Sims across the muddy
ditch to the ambulance, where his pulse faded out.
After fifteen minutes of CPR his pulse revived faintly.
But the internal bleeding and the shock had taken too
heavy a toll, and he eventually succumbed to his
wounds.

The four-hour fight that had swirled around Echo
Company was like a thunderstorm that came without
warning and ended as suddenly as it began. The insurgents didn't retreat gradually, leaving behind a rear
guard; one moment they were there and the next they
were gone, with children again out playing in the
yards, cars driving by, taxis stopping, women hanging
laundry, dogs barking, and cows and sheep being
herded back into the fields. Corporal Stosh Modrow,
a sniper, looked at the pastoral scene that minutes
before had been a battlefield and shook his head in
astonishment.

Over the course of the fight, the four snipers
attached to Echo Company from Battalion 2/7, all
employing M-16s because the range was short and
they wanted to fire bursts instead of single shots, had
accounted for fifteen insurgents. In addition to the
snipers, Echo Company had shot twenty or thirty
others. Modrow knew that inside every house in sight

were dead bodies, rolled in rugs or blankets, mourners waiting for the Marines to leave so they could bury the fallen. Iraqis attended to their dead immediately and with respect. A body left unattended offended their religious beliefs.

————

While Echo was fighting, Mobile Assault Platoon 1 led by Lieutenant Dan Crawford set up on the main road. A few minutes later three Bradleys pulled up alongside Crawford's Humvees and opened fire with their 25mm chain guns. Several hundred meters out in the fields, a dozen women and children cowered in a courtyard as bands of red tracers streamed by them. The children were clinging to the women, some of whom were holding their hands to their ears, as if blocking out the sound would stop the shooting.

With no radio communication to the vehicles, Crawford popped a red star flare and the Bradleys stopped firing. Sgt Santiago led a fire team across the field and shooed the petrified women and children inside. Seeing Americans in the open, two men with AKs rushed out of a clump of palm trees and were cut down by a Mark 19 gunner. Santiago searched the house behind the dead men and flex-cuffed six men hiding in a back room. The fire team found a rifle, shotgun shells, two bayonets, four pairs of binoculars, four cell phones, a stun stick, and a videotape labeled in English, **Killing in a Small Town**. Crawford chewed out the embarrassed Bradley crews and positioned them on his flank. By then the fight had turned farther east and they saw no action for the rest of the day.

———

Having heard Echo's repeated demands for an urgent medevac, Kennedy had driven forward to determine why a helicopter couldn't land. When he arrived, he saw that Capt Royer had the situation well in hand.

Accompanied by Capt Weiler and Lt Dobb's platoon in seven Humvees, Kennedy continued northeast a kilometer hoping to cut off the fleeing insurgents. As they drove forward, an occasional Iraqi would shoot a few rounds from a palm grove or pop out from behind a wall, fire, and disappear among the houses. Weiler thought that, unlike the combatants on April 6, this group was professional, with no part-timers pitching in.

Kennedy headed north, walking with Weiler behind Dobb's platoon, which had fanned out to search the houses alongside the road. The insurgents could pop up anywhere. Only a kilometer back, Sgt McKnight had seen three men in black dishdashas hiding in the shrubs, aiming in with AKs. The bullets barely missed the driver, and the Humvee skidded to a stop. The shooters fled, and McKnight led six Marines on line across the field in pursuit. The Iraqis threw their weapons away and broke into a full sprint. Weighted down with their armor and gear, the Marines fell far behind but plodded after them. About ten minutes later they came to a house in the middle of a field and closed on it by bounds, receiving no fire. Inside were three men, two in white dishdashas and one sweating in a tan jogging suit, muddy at the knees. They flex-cuffed the three and led them outside, where they saw an unarmed man running across the next field. They chased him for over a kilometer before giving up and returning to their Humvee with their three prisoners.

With Weiler behind him, Dobb had moved up the street barely a hundred meters when an RPG rocket wobbled by him so slowly that it looked like someone had thrown it. Weiler guessed the shooter would try another shot and told SSgt Garcia to aim in at the next corner. When the rocketeer stepped out a second time, Garcia shot him in the chest. He dropped the RPG and stumbled away.

Garcia ran to the rocket launcher, which was smoking and making a hissing sound. The rocket had misfired, sticking to the muzzle. Garcia gingerly placed the launcher in a ditch and looked around for the shooter. Following a blood trail, he entered a house and found a man wrapped in a blanket, pretending to be asleep, blood dripping from his chest. He was flex-cuffed and put in a highback Humvee holding seven other detainees. He later died of his wounds.

Dobb deployed a squad on each side of the road to search the houses as they walked northeast toward the Euphrates, a kilometer away. There was a short firefight about every hundred meters, two or three insurgents letting loose a burst of AK fire, then running north, dodging among the houses along the road. The Marines found a few dead and several wounded; the 5.56mm bullets from the M16s left small holes in the torsos. Those still alive were put in the highback humvee and attended to by HM Contreras, who injected morphine into the four most grievously wounded. Several of the wounded gestured at Contreras to kill them.

Accompanying the platoon was an army detachment of female soldiers, assigned to deal with Iraqi women in case any needed to be searched. With one brief fight after another breaking out, Weiler grew concerned they would be hit. "There's some Bradleys down the road," he told them. "Maybe it's better if I call one forward, and you can ride buttoned up with them."

"No thank you, sir," came the reply from the soldiers. "This is the shit!"

Taking this as a compliment, Weiler told them to continue on with Dobb's platoon. The rows of houses petered out near the river, giving way to grain fields occasionally washed by floods. Amid the waist-high wheat stalks and grass, Sergeant Joseph Lagdon flushed four insurgents, who leaped to their feet and fled. Lagdon shot down three and rushed forward, Weiler at his heels. Lying on his stomach, a dying Iraqi emptied his full thirty-round magazine into the dirt, sending Weiler diving over a pile of rocks.

Picking himself up, Weiler saw they had come to the bank of the Euphrates. One isolated house stood on the bank. Inside the Marines found boxes of medical supplies, many of them labeled UNICEF. The owner of the house said he was a nurse, and the occupants, three men and seven women, said they hadn't seen any insurgents. One had a gunshot wound in his arm, the result, he said, of a stray bullet.

It was after four in the afternoon. They had reached the river, the firing had stopped, and to their south Echo's fight was over. Weiler had seventeen detainees and eight dead bodies. Weiler marveled at how quickly the citizens of Ramadi swept clean the battlefields. Fighters, passersby, and neighborhood women alike repeatedly risked their lives in the midst of battle to carry off the dead. Spent brass was plucked from the dirt, round by round; Weiler figured there must be a market for it somewhere. When the firing stopped, shattered vehicles were scavenged and pushed off into the fields, while the blood was washed from the road.

To Weiler it seemed odd. Every empty lot overflowed with heaps of garbage; human feces filled the ditches; green plastic grocery bags flapped from trees across the landscape. The scattered detritus in most neighborhoods reflected communal neglect. Yet the people instinctively tidied up after the insurgents as if they were their own rather than intimidating outsiders.

Knowing the bodies would be properly attended, Weiler left them by the side of the road and sent the detainees back to brigade headquarters. With the Marines were three local interpreters, two of whom never suggested that anybody was an insurgent. Weiler believed they assured their neighbors they weren't really helping the Americans. They wanted to keep their jobs and stay alive—if they were lucky. When the third translator thought someone was an insurgent, he would whisper to a Marine when they were alone.

April 10 was the first time Weiler had seen the three translators offer a joint opinion. "Many, many die," they said, "they are gone. They don't want to fight you anymore."

———

The Iraqis who fought in the five-day battle for Ramadi were a mixture of committed insurgents, semi-believers, or "Minutemen," and the emotional tagalongs who grabbed a weapon, ran alongside the Marines from the safe distance of a block, then exuberantly trotted home. Not all fired a weapon; most rushed around, yelling to one another, brandishing weapons, returning to their homes sweaty and excited, later in coffeehouses and on street corners feverishly exchanging stories of near-misses with death.

However ill trained and foolish many of them were, there were thousands on that battlefield, and history is replete with instances of armed rebellions that swelled like a tidal wave and swept all before it, as happened in Tehran in 1978 and in Baghdad in 1959. The Marines' successful battle for Ramadi prevented a serious setback in public perception. Had Kennedy's battalion backed off or been forced into negotiations, Ramadi—the twin sister of Fallujah—would have whirled out of control.

The fight ended on the evening of April 10. Battalion 2/4 had suffered sixteen killed and more than one hundred wounded. After the five-day battle, the local hospitals were filled and the graveyards were extended. The insurgents' spirit had been broken in the Sofia District that day, when they had had to leave behind their dead and the swift-moving Marines had collected the bodies, dumped them by the roadside, and rolled on, looking for the next fight. The insurgents could draw comfort from the refusal of the Iraqi police and National Guard to join in. But Al Jazeera hadn't been on scene, and no Iraqis had hastened forth from Baghdad to threaten the dissolution of the new republic if the Americans continued to attack.

Challenging the Americans to a stand-up fight for control of the provincial capital had been a disaster.

13

EASTER WITH THE DARK SIDE

ON APRIL 11, 2004, THE CITY of Ramadi returned to its normal restive self. The marketplace was packed with sullen men. Bradleys controlled the highways, and Battalion 2/4 resumed its daily patrols inside the city. By force of arms, the Americans had imposed an uneasy quiet.

Not so in the sister city of Fallujah. On the third day of the "cease-fire," the insurgents were probing the Marine lines and firing whenever they saw an opportunity. On the Coalition side, negotiating channels were proliferating. The MEF was working with Ambassador Richard H. Jones, a seasoned diplomat reporting directly to Bremer. Another ambassador from the CPA, Ronald L. Schlicher was conducting separate talks. Catherine Dale, political adviser to the JTF, was exploring options for LtGen Sanchez. Even the translators for the American generals were palavering with Iraqis claiming to know one insurgent gang or another. Everyone, it seemed, was negotiating with someone else.

Most bizarre of all, that morning several trucks loaded with food and young Iraqis pulled up to the cloverleaf east of Fallujah. The excited men—Shiite militia from Sadr's Mahdi Army and Sunnis recruited from mosques in Baghdad—claimed that an American lieutenant colonel had authorized them to bring aid to their suffering brothers there. A flabbergasted Col Toolan called the lieutenant colonel in Baghdad. The colonel, working at CPA headquarters, explained that he had sent the men to help. Armed Marines turned the trucks around before the men could join the insurgents. Toolan told the colonel to send no more such help.

On the Iraqi side, the alliances swirling among a dozen different teams of negotiators were equally confusing. Hassani emerged as a favorite of the Marines, but it wasn't clear how much influence he—or any other negotiator—had with the insurgents, who were operating through layers of middlemen.

On the insurgent side, Janabi was back in town. He had fled in November, tipped off that Drinkwine was about to raid his mosque. When some sheikhs plotted revenge for the Valentine's Day Massacre, he quickly disappeared again. On his first trip into Fallujah on April 10, Hassani met with Janabi's representative, but the conversation went nowhere. The next day, an IGC negotiator from an upper-class, old-school Sunni clan assured Major Dave Bellon, the intelligence officer for

Regimental Combat Team 1, that he knew how to deal with his brother Sunnis. The Iraqi drove into the city for his first meeting, where he was knocked down, spat upon, kicked in the ass, and thrown back into his car. Before he sped off to Baghdad, he complained to Bellon about the "wild element" in town. Bellon, who had reports that the insurgents were mocking the negotiators behind their backs, told him he was lucky to escape with his life.

The role of the Marines during the cease-fire negotiations was not spelled out in writing. Once Abizaid and Bremer had jointly agreed to negotiate, it wasn't clear what was military or CPA responsibility. On the eleventh, Conway invited the CPA representative for Fallujah, Nate Jensen, to a meeting where the MEF staff was discussing the creation of a local military force led by former senior army officers. Jensen advised against it, saying their loyalties could not be trusted.

"You're a civilian," Colonel J. C. Coleman, the MEF chief of staff, said. "Let me explain something to you. When you plant the flag, those in the military rally to the colors."

Affronted, Jensen pointed to the American flag behind Coleman's desk. "Those are my colors, goddammit," Jensen said. "And I know what I'm talking about."

After Conway defused the confrontation, Jensen dismissed the idea of enlisting senior Iraqi officers as a trial balloon that had burst. Obviously, bringing back Baathists would be a momentous policy decision that required CPA and White House leadership. In the absence of a single viceroy for Fallujah, though, it was easy to confuse military and political responsibilities in negotiations.

———

While the MEF was conducting the negotiations for the Marines, Mattis as the ground commander was preparing to seize Fallujah as soon as the cease-fire lifted. Toolan, as regimental commander, was the battlefield commander for the battalions on the lines. But since the regiment's headquarters was next door to the MEF ops center just outside Fallujah, Toolan was frequently pulled into the negotiations. That didn't deflect him, though, from keeping first things first.

The JTF instruction called for a suspension of offensive operations, verbally amplified by Abizaid to mean twenty-four or so hours. That timeframe had expired, and Battalion 3/4 was being hit by mortars at the cloverleaf east of the city. Conway, Mattis, and Toolan agreed that 3/4 shouldn't sit out in the open and get pounded, and the JTF didn't object to strengthening 3/4's position.

On Easter Sunday morning, April 11, Battalion 3/4 resumed the attack. Kilo Company moved forward into East Manhattan, a neighborhood used as a launching pad for attacks along Highway 10. With three platoons on line, Kilo began searching the rows of sandcolored houses.

There were about twenty to thirty houses on each block, most enclosed by courtyard walls. One or two squads took each block, posting a four-man fire team for outside security, while another team used a loop of det-cord to blow the locks on the gates. A half-dozen Marines with the assault element would rush inside a courtyard and stack themselves against the wall of the house. If there was no shooting, they broke down the door and swarmed in, covering each other as they searched the rooms for weapons. If there were outside stairs or if they could jump from roof to roof, they would clear down floor by floor. In about every fifth house, the Marines found a family, generally huddled together in the center room. The Marines warned them to stay inside and moved on.

It took about twenty minutes to clear each cluster of houses. After two hours, the company had advanced no more than two blocks inside the city when the insurgents started to drive up, jammed four to six to a car, AKs and RPGs sticking out the windows. Lieu-tenant Colonel Bryan P. McCoy had posted snipers on the roofs, but they caught only glimpses of the cars scooting down the back alleys. Video from the UAVs overhead showed vehicles speeding east toward 3/4 and south toward 1/5, indicating the insurgents thought 3/4 might be feinting.

As in Ramadi, the Marines were quickly engaged by gangs of insurgents who knew the back streets and fell back before they were trapped. The insurgents darted into houses and fired from open windows, staying well back so the muzzle flashes would not be seen. Many wore black warm-up suits with AK-47 maga-zine chest pouches, sneakers, and red-and-white-checked kaffiyehs. From alleys several blocks away, rocket-propelled grenades arced in and exploded randomly. The insurgents fired from one row of houses for a few seconds, then ran out the back to another position, never pausing for long or getting too close to the advancing Marines.

The battalion gunner, Chief Warrant Officer Gene Coughlin, was angered at seeing so many fleeing targets escape. "Shoot faster, with both eyes open, damn it!" Coughlin yelled.

The insurgents seemed to be using the same old "shoot and scoot" tactic, but then a squad from the 3rd Platoon approached a house at the end of a narrow alley. After the Marines kicked in the gate, a burst of fire from an AK drove them back. Using the wall as cover, they sneaked up and pitched grenades, dashing forward after the blasts. An AK burst cut down Corporal Smith as he stepped into the courtyard. He was dragged back and evacuated by a Humvee.

Corporal Daniel R. Amaya regrouped his squad. A veteran of the march up to Baghdad, he had extended his time in the battalion because he didn't want his squad returning without him. The risible Amaya entertained his squad by improvising lyrics to wacky pop tunes like "Stacy's Mom." Crouched outside the courtyard, Amaya called for a shoulder-launched multipurpose assault weapon, or SMAW. The SMAW looked like a World War II bazooka and fired a thirty-pound thermobaric rocket that created a tremendous overpressure to crumble rooms from the inside. The rocket zipped through the window and detonated in a cloud of dust. For good measure, two more grenades were pitched into the room.

The Marines poised to rush inside. Amaya saw that the Marine in the lead didn't have a flashlight attached to the barrel of his M16.

"You can't see in a dark room, man!" Amaya said. "Move back. I'll go in first."

With that he swung inside, followed by his men. The front room where the SMAW round had detonated was empty. M16 at the ready, Amaya eased down a narrow corridor to the rear of the house, the other Marines in single file behind him. He stepped into a small room at the rear and flashed the light attached to his rifle around the room.

"Shit, shit, shit!" he yelled. "It's a trap. Out! Out!"

There was a long burst of AK and M16 fire, all mixed up, and Amaya staggered out and collapsed, fatally shot in the neck.

The Marines dragged him outside and around the courtyard wall. The company commander, Captain Tim Walker, came forward with a tank that fired six 120mm shells point-blank into the house. But even after absorbing repeated hits, the house didn't collapse. Every few minutes the **pop! pop! pop!** of AKs challenged the Marines.

Deciding there had to be an underground bunker, Walker called for a D-9 monster bulldozer to crush the house, but no dozer was available. On the roof of the house was a cistern of fuel for heating and cooking. The Marines shot a hole in the cistern and waited until the fuel poured down and collected in a large pool in the corridor where Amaya had been shot. They then pitched in incendiary grenades and burned the defenders to death, listening impassively to the screams.

While Kilo was reducing the hard point, Lima Company was advancing six blocks to the north, joined by the 36th Iraqi National Guard Battalion. With U.S. Army Special Forces advisers encouraging them, the Iraqi soldiers were kicking in doors, rushing inside, hastily clearing, and holding their own alongside the Marines. Glad to see Marines all around them, the Iraqis offered to go first and search each mosque as they advanced.

McCoy was pushing east with two rifle companies abreast, the pace quickening as the Marines found their battle rhythm. McCoy sent India Company and gun trucks from Weapons Company east through the garbage dumps outside the northern edge of the city. They had an easy time of it at first, advancing west for over a kilometer and getting far out in front of the companies in the city. The Humvees with their .50 calibers and ten-power optical sights leapfrogged along the wide avenues that ran north-south, cutting down insurgents as they fell back into the city.

When India Company reached the train station outside the city, resistance stiffened, and RPG, machine-gun, and AK fire erupted from the city streets three hundred meters to the south. The first unit to reach the railhead was a pair of gun trucks commanded by Sergeant Winston Molina. As he maneuvered forward

among the thousands of people fleeing the city, he saw
a group of men milling around outside a small compound belonging to the 505th Iraqi National Guard
Battalion. Approaching cautiously, he saw that they
had stacked more than a hundred AK rifles neatly
along the wall. Some soldiers were hastily changing
from their National Guard uniforms into civilian
clothes. The soldiers explained that their officers had
fled and they too were leaving.

Molina was flummoxed. The men had a good defensive position and were well armed. Yet they were
deserting under fire. He angrily leveled his .50 cal at
the men, placed them on the ground, and flex-cuffed
them, about fifty in all. Seeing the commotion,
an interpreter hastened over and questioned the men.
He then explained that the soldiers refused to fight
"against their Fallujah brothers" but didn't want their
"brothers" to steal their weapons. It was an American
fight. All they wanted to do was go home.

Molina radioed for instructions, reporting that the
505th Iraqi Battalion had disintegrated. The Iraqi
police and National Guard were to be ignored, he was
told; they weren't hostile. LtCol Suleiman still had
some of his 506th Iraqi Battalion in his compound
west of the city. But he too was staying out of the
fight. Inside the city, the police had folded.

Exasperated, Molina ordered the men cut loose and
turned his attention back to the battle. The firing had
increased as India Company took up positions along
the railroad tracks. Molina yelled at several Marines to

aim in rather than poke their rifles over a wall and spray the area without looking.

Lining the approaches to the station were several searchlight towers, easily fifty feet in the air. Lance Corporal Toby Gray and Lance Corporal Stone were ordered to climb a tower and take out any snipers. Rifles over their shoulders, they climbed awkwardly up the rungs, which looked like giant staples welded onto the pole. Stone and Gray hadn't been on the searchlight platform five minutes when machine-gun bullets began ricocheting off the steel pole. Gray yelled down for supporting fires, and Marines fired frantically. Molina, using a monocular to try to spot the machine gun, yelled, "Calm down! Calm down!"

But they all knew the situation was dire. Up on the tower platform there was no place to hide. A bullet struck Stone's armored vest like a closed fist, and he staggered back. He was bleeding from a cut on his cheek. "We gotta get off here, man!" he yelled. "We gotta get down."

Gray grabbed Stone and threw him down on the platform, lying on top of him, pinning him down. "Stay down. We're too exposed!" Gray shouted. "Stay down, damn it!"

Stone struggled for a few seconds as bullets zinged off the platform, then felt a wetness in his face. Gray was lying on him, still now, blood gushing from his neck. Stone screamed and yelled. At the base of the tower, Molina and twenty other Marines redoubled their fire. The Iraqi machine gun went silent, and the

Marines talked Stone down. When he reached the ground, he was trembling and covered with blood. They gave him a shot of morphine, noting that he had an ugly welt on his left tricep and a bruise over his heart where the armored vest had saved his life.

Above them, high up on the platform, Gray lay facedown, his blood dripping down into the dust. Molina took a bodybag from his Humvee and joined two other Marines for the climb. Once they were exposed on the pole, the Iraqis started shooting again; the **pings** and **whangs** against the steel made Molina wince. They tugged and hauled at Gray's body and began the slow, awkward descent. Several times a rifle or a helmet or the body got hung up on the climbing rungs. Each time a Marine grabbed tight to a rung with one hand and worked free the jam, hoping the Iraqis would continue to miss.

No one was hit during the ten-minute descent. When they got off the pole, an amtrac was waiting to transport Stone and the body of LCpl Gray to the medical aid station at the cloverleaf. From there a Humvee drove Stone to the battalion rear, where he sat in cammies soaked with Gray's blood, mumbling through the morphine that Gray had saved him but he hadn't saved Gray.

Corporal Graham Golden, the tough machine-gunner on McCoy's personal crew, walked over to him.

"Here, put these on. I stink too much to use them," he said, handing over his second pair of cammies. "Throw those away and get back to your platoon. That's what Gray would want."

Gray had been a favorite of LtCol McCoy, one of "my baby-wipe killers," as he referred to Marines too young to be served in a bar. At the Marine Corps Ball in Las Vegas the previous November, eighteen-year-old Gray had received the piece of cake given to the youngest Marine.

A few feet away, inside the plywood building where 3/4 had a few laptops and military telephones to keep track of personnel and logistics, Major Andrew Petrucci, the battalion's executive officer, was recording yet another fatality. Battalion 3/4 had rushed to Fallujah, leaving First Lieutenant Oscar Jimenez to organize a field train and follow with all their gear. Jimenez, a family man, had made the march up to Baghdad with the battalion, and Petrucci had full confidence that he would handle the seventy-kilometer logistics move on Easter Sunday without a hiccup. But after one wrong turn on a back road and a sudden ambush, Jimenez was now dead.

Easter Sunday was proving costly for 3/4, but the unit had momentum. From the northwestern corner of Fallujah, Capt Zembiec and the Marines of Battalion 2/1 could see Sgt Molina's gun trucks under the searchlight towers at the railroad station. Battalion 3/4 had a gun truck pointed down every main street, and each time the insurgents tried to cross a street, a machine gun or Mark 19 opened fire. Lima Company could attack from the station and block the center of the city. Byrne had Battalion 1/5 ready to pounce on the insurgents south of Highway 10, while McCoy had Kilo and India, with 36th Iraqi National Guard units, moving through East Manhattan.

India was in the lead now, several blocks inside the city, heading west with Lieutenant Drew Lee's platoon out in front. Lee was finding it hard to keep two squads abreast of each other. Inside the thick-walled houses, the handheld radios of the Marines worked only intermittently, and the squads were picking up the pace on their own, sensing the insurgents were falling back. As Lee approached a line of houses separated by a field from a large mosque, bullets rattled off the concrete. Lance Corporal Robert Villalobos dodged around Lee and led his fire team to a roof to see where the firing was coming from. Not able to see anything, he took a running start and leaped the three feet onto the next roof, followed by his men.

Down on the street, Lee thought they were going to break their necks.

"Goddammit, knock that shit off!" he yelled.

Villalobos pretended not to hear his lieutenant. His team had reached the roof of the outside building, with a clear field of fire toward the mosque. A brick wall ran down the center of the roof, and they had to stand on tiptoe to see over it. They could hear bullets occasionally chipping at the other side of the wall. Lance Corporal Ricardo Hernandez heaved his bulk at the wall, and it tumbled down.

Their squad leader, Sergeant Timothy Funke, was down on the street with Lee. At the sound of the tumbling bricks, he looked up.

"Get down, you idiots!" Funke yelled. "Get the hell

down! You're under fire. What the hell's the matter with you? Use your weapons!"

On the roof, Villalobos's excited fire team now had a commanding view of the nearby streets, the garbage-strewn field, and the mosque on the far side. They were the battalion's point, the fire team farthest into the city. On a roof about two hundred meters away, three insurgents were firing an RPK machine gun, the barrel resting on a low retaining wall. Villalobos and his men lay down behind their own retaining wall, aimed in, and fired back. One Iraqi staggered as if hit, and the other two picked up the machine gun and followed him off the roof.

Villalobos poked his head up and glanced around. On the far side of the field, a blue car had swung around the corner and was speeding toward them, the driver having no idea the Marines were on the roof. Villalobos couldn't believe his luck.

When the car was almost below them, the three Marines popped up, firing down at point-blank range. The car's windshield shattered, and the hood sprang open as the car hit the side of the house. Iraqis with AKs strapped to their bodies tumbled over each other to get out. Four sank to the ground within several feet of the smoking car. A fifth didn't make it out. The driver, a large man wearing Adidas sneakers, leaped out and sprinted several meters into the field as Villalobos shot him in the back.

No sooner had the Marines changed magazines than a dusty white car swerved around the same far corner and barreled toward them. The Marines looked at each other—a twofer. Suddenly the driver saw them, and the car skidded to a halt. The driver sprinted away, running too fast for the Marines to shoot him and leaving his companions to their fate. A man with an AK stepped out of the rear door and shouted after the driver. Villalobos rested his M16 on the low wall and shot him. Two more Iraqis popped out of the car and ran away before the Marines could aim in. In less than a minute the three Marines had killed eight men.

A block to the rear McCoy was moving up with the command group, monitoring the various radio nets. An electronic intelligence team was providing a running commentary on the Iraqi cell phones they were intercepting.

"They don't know which way to go," the intelligence section chief said. "They're saying, 'They're all over the place!' They're having trouble in all sectors. Sounds like one-five's opened up with tanks. They're panicking. They're losing it."

The insurgents were feeling the vise closing.

Major Kevin Norton, the 3/4 operations officer, told McCoy that the cell phone intercepts suggested a breakdown in command.

"The muj are saying the Marines are attacking from all directions," he said. "They're panicking. We can roll them up."

"Is that just your judgment?" McCoy asked.

"Negative," Norton said. "Solid progress in every sector."

McCoy's company commanders sensed they had

momentum. There is a rhythm to battle, and the squads knew how the insurgents were fighting. The fight resembled the one in Ramadi. The insurgents were falling back, running into the fires of the gun trucks facing down the north-south boulevards.

Every house could be turned into a pillbox—Cpl Amaya had died at such a hard point. But the insurgents weren't systematically defending that way. The Marines didn't have to clear every house; it was more important to keep abreast and sweep every alley and courtyard. If other hard points lay ahead, the Marines would call up tanks. If their main guns didn't level a house, it could be marked and bypassed.

As far as McCoy was concerned, Fallujah was about to be brought to heel. McCoy called Lieutenant Colonel Sparky Renforth, the regimental operations officer.

"Sparky," he said, "we've reached the eighty-nine Easting. We are prepared to continue the attack. I'll have the Hidra mosque inside an hour."

The insurgents were jabbering over their cell phones, aimlessly dodging around the back streets of the Jolan in trucks and taxis, unsure whether to head south to meet Byrne and 1/5, or to head east to defend against McCoy. India Company had two vehicles and a half-dozen bodies strewn in front of them, clear fields of observation, and mutually reinforcing fires. All they had to do was advance the infantry with tanks westward, while on their right flank the gun trucks leapfrogged along, covering the streets that ran north-south.

McCoy believed the Jolan could be squeezed and popped like a pus head.

"B.P., that is a negative," Col Renforth said. "The division does not have permission to advance. You will hold firm at the eight-nine easting."

―――

On Easter Sunday, after Daniel Amaya, Toby Gray, and Oscar Jimenez had died, Hassani appeared on Al Jazeera to make an announcement.

"If it [the cease-fire] sticks," he said, implying he had the authority to speak for the U.S. military, "there will be a phased withdrawal from the city."

14

"YOU WANNA SHOOT AT ME? THIS AIN'T NO PICNIC!"

AS THE UNILATERAL CEASE-FIRE DRAGGED on, Mattis was concerned that the vacillation at high levels was encouraging the fighting to spread at the tactical level. Each day the cease-fire was extended another day. Hassani was forever on the brink of making a real breakthrough with mysterious agents of the insurgency. And every day the Arab press pointed to the grisly siege of Fallujah. Between April 6 and 13, the CPA documented thirty-four stories on Al Jazeera that hyped, misreported, or distorted battlefield events. Rumsfeld called the TV reports "vicious, inaccurate, and inexcusable."

For the insurgents, the strategic propaganda, fueled by sermons in the Sunni mosques, was effective. Men and boys with AKs were climbing into pickups in every village and hamlet around Fallujah and driving out to the main highways, there to join gangs from other tribes. Former officers came forward, suggesting rudimentary tactics and good spots for ambush. Humvee and tractor trailers were hit, and Iraqis rushed out onto the highway to set the crippled vehicles on fire.

"It's an emotional uprising," Col Dunford said. "Call it a jihad if you want. It's a spirit, a feeling. It's emotion-based, so it doesn't have staying power. We have to get after it and not let it grow."

Mattis set out to break that spirit. Since 3/4 was forbidden to advance farther into Fallujah, the division commander gave them another quick mission. The town of Karma, six miles northeast of Fallujah, had fallen to the insurgents. The police and the National Guard had abandoned the town, and the insurgents were blocking Route Chicago, which ran toward Baghdad. McCoy was told to reconnoiter in force.

He left with Kilo Company at four in the morning of April 13, hoping to be inside the town before the insurgents got up for breakfast. On the outskirts of town, however, the insurgents had blocked the highway with a dozen cement Jersey barriers. Kilo Company was stuck, not knowing how to get around them.

Slayer, the Air Force AC-130 gunship, was circling overhead in the dark.

"Need a burn?" the pilot asked Captain Vincent Delpidio, Kilo's forward air control officer.

"We could use some help."

"Follow the dancing ball," the pilot said, turning on the plane's massive infrared searchlight.

On the ground, the drivers of the light armored vehicles leading Kilo Company adjusted their night-vision goggles and focused in on the searchlight. Behind them a dozen Humvees fell in line. As the circle of light moved off the blocked highway and through the back alleys, twisting and turning among repair shops, hulks of old cars, and stunted palm trees, the drivers followed it. Some of the turns were so tight, the LAVs scraped against the walls of shops.

They emerged on the other side of the barricade shortly before dawn and drove slowly up the empty road. With the first smudges of light, the LAVs started taking small-arms fire from a grove of palm trees on the other side of a narrow bridge. McCoy deployed his force on both sides of the highway, and the Marines fanned out, searching through the palm trees and tall grass for some deep irrigation ditch or cow path not covered by fire. They found none. Whenever a Marine stood or ran to a new position, half a dozen AKs unloaded at him.

A kilometer up the road on the right was a mosque with a minaret that provided a clear view of the advancing Marines. Soon Iraqi men were pouring out of the town on the far side of the mosque. Some wore black ninja outfits, others dishdashas, most civilian trousers and long-sleeved shirts. Only a few were wearing kaffiyehs. Soon there were more than a hundred of them, dodging about in groups of five to ten, hanging back a respectful distance of four to five hundred meters from the Marine weapons, firing AKs and RPKs in long bursts and lofting volleys of RPG rockets.

The LAVs with their 25mm chain guns and ten-power optics were providing most of the return fire.

But the insurgents were crouching low alongside a row of cement houses with the usual high courtyard walls. The LAVs weren't doing much damage, and with mortar rounds crunching in, they had to shift positions constantly. The result was an enormous volume of fire exchanged with few casualties inflicted. Neither side was offering an easy target.

On the left side of the road a few hundred meters to the north was a water-pumping station with the usual assortment of jutting pipelines, holding tanks, and low-slung buildings. On the right side a long wall enclosed an abandoned military post, with the mosque on the far side. It took the Marines two hours to gain sufficient fire superiority to reach the pumping station and the post. Once they did, their fields of fire opened up. Squads shot at the various houses half a kilometer away; thousands of bullets chipped the cement walls and raised small columns of dust.

The insurgents weren't backing off. They knew the LAVs, now firing short bursts to conserve their dwindling ammunition, were the heaviest firepower the Marines had, and that was not enough to dislodge them. Taxis and cars were making their usual drop-off runs, the drivers careful to keep a wall or a house between themselves and the LAVs.

McCoy was striding about, exhorting and correcting, trying to find the key to breaking the resistance, ignoring the bullets snapping around. A few steps away Sergeant Major David Howell was glaring at him and muttering, "Goddammit, sir." Howell had cautioned McCoy before, and the battalion commander had agreed that he had to be careful. Now he was doing it again. Sooner or later he was going to get clipped.

A jump-qualified recon Marine, Howell was happiest in the field, competing in ultramarathons and backcountry alpine skiing races. Twice divorced, the Marine Corps was his life. Behind his back his crew called him "Uncle Dave," an oxymoron that reflected deeper feelings. When angered, Howell looked like a mean bulldog.

McCoy didn't want to be the brunt of that scowl. "See what you can do to relieve pressure on the left flank," he told his sergeant major.

Howell drove cautiously over to the pumping station, where Marines were lying behind palm trees and piles of loose pipes, exchanging fire with insurgents among the cement houses to the north. Through his binoculars Howell could make out the fresh dirt of a trench line behind a row of toppled palm trees. The Marines were staying flat, warning him about a sniper and pointing at a two-story house with a balcony leading back to an open alcove. The sniper, tucked back somewhere inside the alcove, had already hit one Marine in the shoulder.

"They're hard to kill!" Private Jason Bruseno yelled. "Like hunting cockroaches in the day."

"Goddamned Groundhog Day. Diyala all over again," Howell muttered, referring to a fight the battalion had waged a year ago almost to the day.

Howell eased his unarmored Humvee forward, trying to keep behind the trees, and pointed out the house to his Mark 19 gunner, Lance Corporal Ryan Kennelly.

"Kennelly, can you hit that?" Howell asked.

Kennelly squinted through a pair of binoculars called Viper, which gave the azimuth and a laser read of the distance to a target.

"Five hundred and fifty meters," he said. "I'm on it, Sergeant Major."

The gunner placed fifty rounds of 40mm explosive shells into the small alcove, and that was the last the Marines heard from that sniper. Howell nodded.

Over on the right flank, McCoy's crew was engaged. The radio operator in McCoy's unarmored Humvee, Corporal Brian Hemmelgarn, was responsible for five radios and the Blue Force Tracker, a GPS-equipped computer that tracked the location of all similarly equipped vehicles. Taking care of his radios came first, and when two bullets struck the Humvee's hood, Hemmelgarn had pulled in to defilade in a culvert.

"No way we're ducking down, man," said Cpl Golden, the machine-gunner standing on a small platform behind the driver. "Get me back up there."

Golden's grandfather had been a machine-gunner with 3/4 in Korea, and his father had been a machine-gunner with 3/4 in Vietnam, where he was twice wounded. A linebacker with a 3.5 GPA at the University of Arkansas, Golden had dropped out of college and enlisted after 9/11. On the machine-gun range he had scored 94 out of 100, the high score in the battalion, and now he had a chance to live up to the family tradition. The driver, Corporal Tom Conroy, wasn't about to argue with the huge corporal, so he reversed and pulled up slope enough for Golden bring his machine gun to bear. Over the next few hours, Golden put three thousand rounds downrange, a fair day's shooting.

By noon the Obstacles Clearing Detachment had shoved the massive Jersey barriers off the highway, allowing two tanks to come forward to join the battle. In the next few hours the tanks burned through thousands of rounds, while RPGs burst around them and occasionally bounced off them.

The din of the battle was a constant roar, and McCoy was thinking it would never subside when "Jason," a senior special forces NCO, came up to him. Jason was advising a platoon from the 36th National Guard Battalion, attached to 3/4. The Iraqi platoon had just cleared two buildings and captured an insurgent who had talked immediately.

"No rough stuff, the guy started jabbering on his own!" Jason shouted in McCoy's ear. "The muj headquarters is that mosque to your front. The imam is on our bad guy list."

All morning the Marines had seen armed Iraqis dodging in and out of the wall surrounding the mosque.

"I'm taking it down," McCoy said.

McCoy turned the target over to Capt Delpidio and the FAC talked to an F-16 loitering overhead. Delpidio marked the friendly lines with flares and had the pilot make a practice run from southwest to northeast. When that went well, the pilot swung around and made a second pass. With eyes on the F-16 and sure of its alignment, Delpidio said, "Cleared hot," and the pilot dropped two five-hundred-pound bombs, knocking down the minaret and collapsing half of the main building.

After the usual several moments of shock that follow a successful bomb run, the insurgents resumed firing. McCoy wasn't sure what effect the strike on the mosque had had on their leadership. Running low on ammunition, he pulled his Marines back, and the insurgents made no effort to follow. McCoy radioed to Col Toolan that he estimated about a hundred insurgents had been killed or wounded, and more still held the town of Karma.

Toolan told 3/4 to return to the lines in northeastern Fallujah. He had heard enough to recommend to Mattis that the surrounding suburbs, to include Karma, be swept by another regiment. Toolan's regiment needed to focus on Fallujah.

———

Battalion 3/4 wasn't the only unit heavily engaged on April 13. At about one in the morning, a special operations CH-53 "Pave Low" helicopter on a secret mission was hit on the outskirts of Fallujah and went down in a controlled crash, landing southeast of 1/5's lines. LtCol Byrne had organized his Weapons Company into mounted Mobile Assault Platoons to respond to emergencies. Byrne tapped a MAP commanded by 1/Lt Josh Glover to go to the aid of the downed helicopter. Glover had an easy rapport with his Marines and an instinct for navigation, a useful talent for a

Quick Reaction Force. Glover—radio call sign Red Cloud—headed out with fifty-five Marines packed into nine Humvees.

After driving ten kilometers, the Hummers turned off the paved road and cut across farm fields, guided by the infrared spotlight from a circling AC-130. They reached the crash site after another special operations helicopter had evacuated the downed crew. The CH-53 lay crumbled in a wheat field, the front canopy smashed, the nose of a rocket-propelled grenade stuck through the windshield. The left pilot seat was smeared with blood. The Marines recovered some sensitive items—crypto gear, a tan knapsack, and a transmitter—and settled into a defensive perimeter for the night, with the AC-130 hovering above them.

In the morning mortar rounds started dropping in while many of the Marines were still sleeping. With shells bursting around them, the platoon drove hastily away with three wounded. In the sandy soil of wheat fields in spring blossom, the wheels of the Humvees were spinning out. To avoid bogging down, the drivers chose to speed along the tops of the irrigation ditches, where cows and water buffalo had packed down the mud.

As they jounced along, they were easy targets and began taking small-arms fire from the fields. A burst struck the radio in Sgt Cyparski's lead gun truck, and not knowing which way to go, he turned south instead of west. Under fire from both sides, the column headed in the wrong direction, braking to a halt at a small pond. Glover got them turned around, handing Cyparski a Garmin GPS showing the route to get out.

Cyparski led them back through the gauntlet a second time. The insurgents had gathered by the dozens during the night, drawn like a magnet to the downed helicopter, the symbol of a triumph over America. This was the fourth chopper to have been brought down in the Fallujah area. As the vehicles drove past them, the insurgents fired, some standing up and spraying from the hip, some shooting RPGs, others staying hidden in the wheat fields, firing at the sound of the trucks.

Cyparski, in the lead with the .50 caliber on his truck, pounded through seven hundred rounds. Behind him the next gun truck in line ripped off a thousand rounds of 7.62mm machine-gun bullets. Then came the five highback Humvees, with Marines sitting on center benches facing outboard and firing their M16s. Two gun trucks brought up the rear. When the Mark 19 jammed in the last gun truck, Corporal Christopher Moss-Warrington and his crew unhooked the gun and replaced it with a .50 cal in under thirty seconds. The gun was barely operational when Moss saw two Iraqis firing at him from behind a dumptruck. He put thirty shells through the cab, hitting both men crouched on the other side.

"Die, bitches!" he yelled. "You wanna shoot at me? This ain't no picnic!"

Hunched over the steering wheel, Lance Corporal Victor Didra was laughing at Moss when a man hopped out of the weeds, aiming an RPG directly at him. There was an immediate explosion and a cloud of dust—and Didra breathed again, thinking the insurgent had blown himself up. Then he glanced to his left and saw smoke where the grenade had burst. The man had missed from ten feet away.

Bouncing along at high speed, the Marines were shooting frantically in all directions. No one could hear over the whine of the engines and the roar of the guns. The Marines saw RPGs zipping past, felt concussions from near misses, sensed some hits, and dimly heard some grunts and screams. All were praying that no one fell out and no vehicle rolled over. Practically every tire had been hit, and strips of rubber were peeling off. If one Hummer stopped, they all stopped, and then it would be the Little Big Horn. It was a melee, both sides blazing away for ten minutes.

At one point Lance Corporal Charles Williams, shooting from Glover's Humvee, counted nine RPG gunners out in the fields. The speeding Humvees were proving hard to hit. Not all of the excited RPG gunners missed, though. Private First Class Noah L. Boye, shooting from a highback, was hit by an RPG in his upper leg, ripping open a huge hole too large for pressure bandages. As the highback bounced along, the Marines frantically tried to stanch the flow of blood with a poncho liner. The platoon sergeant, Staff Sergeant Daniel Santiago, had told Boye more than once to stop playing his guitar at three in the morning, imitating Mötley Crüe and the Temptations, improvising weird lyrics, and enticing other Marines to join in. Life wasn't, the platoon sergeant said, one long party. Boye would grin and tone it down—for about a week.

Once they hit the paved highway, Santiago screamed over the radio at the drivers to push faster on the bare rims. They had to get Boye to surgical. But no one could stanch the blood flowing from the terrible hole, and Boye died before they reached the aid station at the cloverleaf.

Nate Jensen, the foreign service officer assigned by the CPA to be on scene at Fallujah, was at the cloverleaf when Glover's vehicles skidded in. The diplomat had driven to the aid station to collect evidence about foreign fighters and terrorists inside the city. Battalion 1/5 had found suicide vests, stashes of money, and foreign passports. A wounded Marine had a sniper's bullet embedded in his armored vest. If it was foreign made, Jensen intended to show it to the Iraqi negotiators.

The Marines were smoldering at the costs of the "cease-fire" and resented the presence of a civilian who was part of the negotiations. Jensen understood their feelings and stayed off to one side as they pitched handfuls of spent brass and sopping bandages out of the vehicles.

Of the fifty-five Marines who went out, twenty-one were wounded. Seven had to be hospitalized. Lance Corporal Merado Alcaraz was wearing shatterproof glasses that saved his eyes when an RPG had exploded overhead, peppering his face. Shrapnel had grazed Glover's face and scratched up his glasses, but his eyes too were fine. Glover sent to the rear three highbacks slippery with blood that needed to be washed down, along with several Marines who had to change out of their sticky cammies before the blood dried like a coat of paint.

While Glover was sorting things out, two amtracs were delivering supplies to a sniper position forward of Bravo Company's lines, near the center of town. They took a wrong turn and bumped into a company-sized group of insurgents of all ages, from their teens to their fifties. The surprised insurgents reacted quickly, firing RPG rockets as the amtracs spun on their treads and raced east. A rocket punched through the armor of the rear trac, ripping a chunk out of the leg of the platoon commander, Lieutenant Christopher Ayers. The white-hot shell lodged in the engine, which burst into flames, trapping the crew chief, Corporal Kevin T. Kolm, a third-generation Marine. Kolm's grandfather had fought on the island of Peleliu in World War II, and his father had fought in Vietnam.

The smoke-filled amtrac turned the wrong way, heading down what the Marines called Shithead Alley, a cluttered street leading west, deeper into the city. As the Marines desperately tried to extinguish the blaze and free Kolm, the crippled trac faltered to a halt. With the blaze spreading and dozens of insurgents running down the street to finish them off, the Marines on board poured out of the trac before its ammunition cooked off. They heard Kolm scream, but his hatch was locked, the flames were searing, and they had no way of prying the hot metal open.

Lieutenant Ayers pulled himself halfway out of the

top hatch, only to have his armored vest snag, pinning him to the burning chassis. Staff Sergeant Ismail Sagredo and Lance Corporal Abraham McCarver grabbed Ayers by the vest and pulled with all their might, ripping the Velcro strip from the vest and spilling Ayers into their arms. Propping him up between them, they hobbled into a nearby house and set up a hasty defense, with snipers on the roof and Marines peering out the windows on all sides.

Close behind, the insurgents didn't stop to make a plan. They rushed toward the house, and Sagredo shot the first man who ran into the courtyard, hitting him in the head. Marine snipers on the roof shot down two more in the street. The other Iraqis fell back, ducking into alleys and running around the back of the house, searching for an uncovered approach. Although seven of the sixteen Marines were wounded, Ayers and Sagredo had set up a strong defense. Radio communications were sketchy, but they knew the battalion wouldn't leave them out there for long.

The fire inside the amtrac continued to blaze, the flames feeding on the electric wiring, the aluminum sides melting slowly from the top. Occasionally the insurgents fired another RPG rocket into the trac, an instinctive gesture, saying, **See what I've done.** It pained Sagredo to think of Kolm's body being pummeled, but there was nothing he could do until help arrived.

Back at Battalion 1/5's ops center, 1/Lt Glover's Quick Reaction platoon had guzzled down bottles of Gatorade, stocked up on ammo, and patched the bullet holes in the radiators and hydraulic lines. Glover had six vehicles and thirty-seven Marines ready to go when Maj Farnum told him to mount up and find the missing amtrac.

Supported by four tanks, Glover's platoon cut west to where the fight had been reported. No one was there, no Marines, no insurgents, and no civilians— only a cluttered, empty street and courtyards with shuttered and locked gates. Upon climbing to a roof-top, a Marine sniper team saw a column of thick black smoke about a kilometer to the southwest. The Marines hopped back into their vehicles and headed that way.

At the next block the street narrowed and the column continued in single file, Marines walking beside every vehicle, Glover's Humvee in the lead. Within a minute he saw two men in tracksuits with RPGs run out of an alley thirty meters away and fire. Both rockets missed. The Marines shot the men and dragged the bodies out of the way of the tank treads. The tankers buttoned up their hatches, and within seconds the street erupted, men leaning out windows and peeking around walls to shoot for two seconds, then duck away.

"I know you can hear me," Glover yelled over his radio, set to the frequency of the tank commanders. "I can't hear a word with all this shooting going on. I'll guide you. We're all around you, so don't fire your main guns."

It was shortly after six in the evening, and the buildings cast long shadows across the dirty street, making it difficult to spot the insurgents. The Marines were shooting in all directions, the tanks joining in with their coaxial machine guns.

Behind Glover, Cyparski was following in his gun truck. An RPG rocket skidded along the ground and lodged in a rear tire without exploding. The radiator and the gear hub each took two bullets, fragments from the side mirror grazed Cyparski's face, a case of MREs in the rear compartment was shredded, and the exhaust pipe was peppered. The windshield was not even scratched. Sitting in the front passenger seat with the .50 cal hammering away above his head, Cyparski began to feel he was immune to the bullets cracking by.

Glover's Humvee was wheezing, having taken two bullets in the windshield and four in the radiator. While the driver, LCpl Williams, popped the hood to inspect the damage, Glover called Sgt Cyparski over to check their position. With bullets snapping by, Williams was stanching leaks in the radiator and Glover was poring over his map. Cyparski doubted the middle of the fire-swept street was the proper place to meet.

"Don't worry," Williams said as he slammed down the hood. "It'll make it."

While they were stopped, LCpl Didra drove his gun truck forward to resupply Glover with four cans of ammo. Not wanting his truck to be riddled, Didra then reversed at high speed. The rear door flung open, and Sergeant Louie Osborne was catapulted into the street, his helmet, rifle, ammunition, pack, and everything else in the backseat tumbling all over the macadam. The firing ceased momentarily as the insurgents as well as the Marines watched the furious sergeant grab for his rifle and Kevlar, screaming at Didra to come back. The firing resumed as Osborne hopped back in.

Old oil barrels filled with junk stood at the corners of some alleys, and when the tanks rolled by, the insurgents loosed volleys of RPG rockets, using the barrels as their reference markers. The rocket-propelled grenades had no effect on the tanks, which kept rolling despite taking repeated hits. The tanks were knocking down small palm trees and power lines, and the Marines kept a wary eye out for hot wires as they jogged along.

Two blocks to the east, Maj Farnum, the ops officer for 1/5, stood on a roof with the forward air controller, who directed two Air Force F-15s—call sign RO-MO—to make repeated gun runs several blocks to the west. As Glover radioed back the coordinates of his lead trace, Farnum relayed the data to the FAC, who adjusted the next gun run.

It took Glover twenty minutes to reach the intersection where the amtrac was blazing. Sagredo's Marines, down to two magazines per man, waved them forward, and Glover distributed boxes of ammunition. Sagredo was furious about the repeated RPG hits on the burning trac. Glover called up the tanks, deploying them in a wagon wheel at the intersection. Most of the RPG shots were coming from a gray stone house on the far side of the intersection. Floor by floor, room by room, the main guns of the tanks demolished the house.

After the first dozen tank rounds, the battlefield quieted as the insurgents dispersed. The wounded were placed in the Humvees, and the Marines walked slowly back to their lines, a tank towing the smoldering amtrac and the body of Kevin T. Kolm, a third-generation corporal of Marines.

———

As if to confirm that the offensive was about to resume, that night the special operations forces showed up at the regimental ops center, buoying the Marines' hopes. The spec ops could roam where they wished in country, so when they came to visit, it meant they had heard something was about to break.

Computers had replaced the banks of radios in ops centers, greatly reducing the squawking and hissing noises that gave ulcers to past generations of staff officers. Major Dave Bellon, the intelligence officer for Regimental Combat Team 1, was hunched over his computer screen squinting when someone tapped him on the shoulder. He looked up at a tall soldier in a gray jumpsuit, flanked by a stocky younger man.

"My name is Jamie, and this is Will," the soldier said politely, with a southern drawl. "The way we see it, there's going to be a lot of killing soon in that city. We'd like to help organize that."

Bellon knew "Jamie" was a lieutenant colonel and "Will" was a captain who had played on the West Point football team—they were the leaders of the "Z Squad" that had hunted down Saddam. Now they were after fresh prey, the terrorist Zarqawi. Will inserted his flash stick into the computer and showed Bellon pictures of a street near city hall, then zoomed in on a house with a walled patio and proceeded to walk Bellon through the front door, down a hallway, and into a large room with banks of electrical panels on the walls. There, Will said, is where we need to insert "certain" devices.

"We can't install your gizmos, Colonel," Bellon said. "That requires too much finesse. Marines think a hammer is high tech. We'll electrocute ourselves."

"Okay, we'll install them. Just get us in there."

"I can lay on a diversion and insert you," Bellon said. "But l have to check with Colonel Toolan about getting you out."

"Why?"

"Because it'll take three battalions," Bellon said.

Bellon didn't like sounding negative in front of such professionals, but hundreds of armed young Iraqi men would rush forward to engage any raid force. The insurgents had taken casualties but not enough to dampen their enthusiasm for a common cause tinged with adventure and danger. Whatever the fissures among the foreign terrorists, the Wahhabi clerics, the Baathist politicians, and the former generals and colonels, they were all determined to resist the Americans. Fallujah was as unified as Berlin in 1944 and Hanoi in 1968. Sending in the Z Squad meant alerting the entire regiment to stand by for a donnybrook.

"We'll never get permission from higher, sir," Bellon said. "Once you're in, we'd have to take the city to get you out."

"Well, we're here with our people," Jamie said. "Mind if we give you a hand?"

Bellon readily agreed. The Z Squad was the military equivalent of the NFL pro-bowl team. Bellon gave Jamie a seat next to him to work out how the Task Force 6-26 snipers, breachers, and assault teams would be spread among the Marine companies.

"We'll support whatever raid you want," Bellon assured Jamie, "as soon as the cease-fire is lifted."

15

FALLUJAH: A SYMPTOM OF SUCCESS

IN THE FIVE DAYS SINCE GENERAL Abizaid and Ambassador Bremer had declared the unilateral "cease-fire," the battles along the lines in Fallujah had continued. The fighting had settled into a pattern of skirmishes, flare-ups, and rest periods.

The Coalition had lost the initiative in the fighting as well as in the negotiating. Each day at the Fallujah Liaison Center, two kilometers east of the city, the Iraqis and Americans crowded into a small, bare conference room and sat around a long wooden table, sipping cold bottled water and eating oranges. The Iraqis never tired of talking, issuing long litanies of complaints, making passionate promises of stability, and stoutly denying the presence of foreign fighters. The Fallujans were good people, fighting to protect their city. If the Americans would stop firing and pull out, all would be well. It was never clear, though, who spoke for the fighters. Those with the power of the guns remained shadowy figures, never mentioned by name.

Day after day different groups of negotiators met. Sometimes Ambassador Richard H. Jones represented the CPA. Other times the meetings were at a lower level between Stu Jones and the current mayor of Fallujah, Ibrahim al Juraissey. Flocked by somber sheikhs in fulsome beards and flowing robes, Juraissey, Fallujah's third mayor in ten months, was full of assurances that all Iraqis wanted peace, and laments over the destruction done by the Marines. MajGen Weber on occasion represented the JTF at the negotiating table. LtGen Conway sometimes attended and often sent a deputy. When he did attend, he chaired the meeting.

At the same time, one hundred kilometers to the southeast, MajGen Dempsey and the 1st Armored Division had trapped the radical cleric Moqtada al Sadr and his followers inside the Shiite holy city of Najaf. Frantic negotiations were under way on that front as well. The Sunni rebels trapped in Fallujah and the Shiite rebels trapped in Najaf desperately needed negotiations to prevent their destruction.

MajGen Mattis usually didn't attend the interminable meetings. Each day he was out with his troops, stopping here and there for a few minutes, keeping his finger on the pulse of morale and fighting conditions. He knew what the troops were saying: **Let us finish the job.**

Marines were dying, and the terrorists in Fallujah had beheaded an Italian and were holding hostage five

Japanese, three Turks, and an American named Nicholas Berg. The Marines were frozen in place while the insurgents consolidated their position inside the city and escalated their tactics of defiance.

On April 14 Mattis stopped by Battalion 3/4's lines, telling McCoy to expect an order to resume the attack within a day or two. "I don't forecast this stalemate will go on for long," he said.

That they would be permitted to finish the fight was the prevailing belief throughout the division. The battalions, caught up in fighting and dying each day, assumed the senior leadership saw the world the way they did. If you played patty-cake with the insurgents, they would cut your hand off. Seize the city first, then talk to them when they were supplicants.

At the Pentagon, Rumsfeld and Wolfowitz had grown increasingly uneasy about the "temporary" cease-fire that dragged on without a cutoff date. The longer the delay, the more the political pressures were building to call off the attack altogether. In their view, getting on with the attack was imperative.

The power of a secretary of defense resided in shaping the longer-term direction of the military, not in directing ongoing operations. In 1993, Secretary of Defense Les Aspin overrode a request for tanks submitted by the commander of U.S. forces in Somalia. Later, an American raid force was trapped in a vicious firefight without tank support and took heavy casualties. Aspin was fired for having imposed his judgment over that of the operational commander.

Concerning Fallujah, Rumsfeld urged Abizaid to

take action, but issuing a direct order would be imprudent. Bremer and Abizaid were the field commanders calling the shots. As long they agreed with one another to continue the "cease-fire" and the negotiations, that would be the course pursued.

"John [Abizaid] stressed to the president the need to be firm about Fallujah. At the same time, he pointed out that seizing the city would cause turmoil. He understood both points of view," a senior aide in the White House said. "He consistently made three points—Fallujah was a difficult situation, we were going to prevail, and the morale of the troops was terrific."

General Richard Myers, the Chairman of the Joint Chiefs of Staff, had arrived unexpectedly in Baghdad on the fourteenth. He would bring back to the Pentagon a fresh perspective to supplement the reports from Gen Abizaid. The Marines hoped that Myers would be properly briefed in Baghdad. The sallies by McCoy into Karma and Red Cloud into the center of the city weren't exceptions; the insurgents were surging forward whenever they sensed an opportunity.

On the fifteenth, Gen Myers held a press conference in Baghdad. He described the attacks throughout the Sunni province of Anbar and Sadr's revolt as "a symptom of the success that we're having here in Iraq."

Concerning Fallujah, he issued an anodyne warning. "We have to be prepared and prepare ourselves that there may be further military action in Fallujah," he said. "It's a situation where you clearly have some for-

eign fighters, former regime element members who—
again, while the cease-fire is ongoing—are attacking
our Marines."

While not a clarion call to arms, his remarks signaled
that the chairman had doubts about the negotiations.
Later that day Conway and Weber met at the MEF
headquarters with Ambassadors Jones and Schlicher to
review the situation. Colonel Coleman, the MEF chief
of staff, said the time had come to attack. Irfan Siddiq,
the diplomat representing the British, responded that
an attack was out of the question. He urged a negotiated solution that would provide a "dignified exit" for
all parties. Ambassador Jones did not take either side.
Instead he pointed out that Abizaid had briefed
POTUS on the fourteenth. The president had rejected
both launching a full-scale attack and continuing the
status quo. Jones said the president was meeting with
Prime Minister Blair on the sixteenth and was not
about to tell him the Marines were in the assault as
they spoke.

"I want other options," President Bush had said.
While expressing confidence in the Marines, the president asked for the development of other alternatives
rather than an attack through the city. E-mails immediately flew among staffs far removed from Fallujah.

"How the fuck," said a senior American general
emerging from one televideo conference, "can they
make operational decisions back in Washington?"

Conway suggested that perhaps some Iraqi generals
could be pulled together to take charge of the city,
though that would take two to three weeks. Jensen, the

foreign service officer, said that with all due respect, that was a fantasy. Baathists, Jensen said, wouldn't fight the insurgents, most of whose leaders were also Baathists.

Conway's suggestion wasn't a fantasy, though. The CIA, which in Iraq was under the operational control of the JTF, was developing a new Iraqi intelligence service headed by General Muhammad Shawany. Several days earlier two CIA operatives working at the MEF had mentioned to Conway that some former Iraqi generals recommended by Shawany could help out in Fallujah. The generals could create a military unit in Fallujah comprised of former soldiers and insurgents. Conway was intrigued. After the meeting broke up, a diplomat from the CPA followed the operatives to their small house trailer.

"You don't flip out half-baked ideas to a three-star," the diplomat said. He stalked off, thinking he had persuaded them to drop the idea. Instead, Conway had quietly pulled together a military team to discuss terms with the Iraqi generals. Talks with the Iraqi generals were proceeding in an MEF channel not disclosed to the civilian diplomats.

On the fifteenth, the meeting at the MEF with the ambassadors from the CPA concluded with no new plan of action. After weeks of wrangling, it appeared that if four or six senior American officials discussed Fallujah, the conclusion would be four or six nuanced positions.

When Prime Minister Tony Blair visited the White House on April 16, he was under serious pressure to persuade President Bush to call off the attack in Fallujah. Robin Cook, the former British foreign secretary, urged Blair to warn Bush about "heavy-handed tactics" in Fallujah, citing "1,000 civilians dead." Fifty-two former senior British diplomats were signing on to an open letter accusing the Marines of applying "weapons unsuited to the task . . . the number killed in Fallujah is several hundred, including many women and children." Dana Allin of the prestigious London-based Institute for Strategic Studies described "a sense in the British Foreign Office and the British military that the U.S. tactics have been too heavy-handed."

British diplomats and senior officers believed in an approach to the insurgency that mixed diplomacy and contracts, playing off the various tribes while coaxing them into compliance. Blair had received a memo from his Foreign Office severely criticizing the siege of Fallujah. "We need to redouble our efforts to ensure a sensible and sensitive U.S. approach to military operations," the memo read. "The message seems to be accepted at the highest levels but not always implemented lower down the command chain." Concerns about Iraqi civilian casualties had rippled from Iraq across the greater Middle East to London, where many officials believed they understood Iraqi politics better than did their American cousins.

The chief of the British general staff, General Sir Michael Jackson, weighed in as well. In 1999 Jackson, then commanding British troops in Bosnia, had refused a direct order from General Wesley Clark because he believed it was strategically imprudent.

Now Jackson didn't mince words about Fallujah, either. "We must be able to fight with the Americans," he told **The Times**. "That does not mean we must be able to fight as the Americans. That the British approach to post-conflict is doctrinally different to the U.S. is a fact of life."

Yet British officers were not present in Fallujah to make firsthand judgments about the Marine tactics. Regardless of how the British military had reached its conclusions, Prime Minister Blair warned President Bush that an assault on Fallujah imperiled the solidarity of the coalition.

In their joint press conference, the president heaped praise upon UN representative Brahimi. "We're grateful that Mr. Brahimi will soon return to Iraq," he said, "to continue his important work." It was Brahimi who had publicly threatened to withdraw his support if Fallujah were attacked. The president's statement sent a strong signal that no such attack would take place.

16

TWO-FACED SHEIKHS AND IMAMS

BY APRIL 16, HIJACKINGS AND ATTACKS ON convoys had spread across Anbar Province. As on most battlefields, the moral was to the physical as four to one. The longer the Americans temporized, the more they invited attack. Inside a semicircle extending about one hundred kilometers out from Baghdad, roving gangs in pickup trucks and dilapidated cars were randomly shooting at trailer trucks and setting up roadblocks.

The cumulative effects of the constant random attacks were serious. By mid-April, military supply convoys from Jordan and Kuwait had slowed to a trickle. Stocks of military fuel dropped as low as two days' supply. The ordinary good fare of food at bases was cut back and in some cases replaced by MREs. Logisticians at the 1st Marine Division were con-

cerned lest a few bridges or unguarded highway over-
passes be dropped, isolating Baghdad.

Inflamed by rumor and Arab television, Sunni
youths were flocking to their villages and local mosques
to listen to imams who urged them to revolt. The division's intelligence officer, Lieutenant Colonel Mike
Groen, had analyzed the enemy in a score of battles
during Operation Iraqi Freedom I. He hadn't seen anything like this uprising. "The mujahedeen are on an
emotional high," he told Mattis. "This fight isn't controlled from the top. Instead, it's hopping from mosque
to mosque. It's a jihad wave sweeping east."

Colonel Dunford saw cunning behind the spon-
taneity. In Fallujah and Ramadi, sheikhs and former
Baathists enriched under Saddam encouraged the
imams to call for jihad, insisting it was the duty of
every Muslim to take up arms against the infidel
invaders. The American occupation had shoved from
power both the Sunni clerics and the Baathist officials. Now Sunni nationalism and religious extremism
had converged, resulting in calls from the mosques to
kill the infidels.

The justification was a jumble of accusations and
imprecations. Israel had assassinated Sheikh Ahmad
Yassin, the spiritual leader of the Hamas party. The ally
of Israel, America, was destroying Fallujah, demolishing mosques and raping women. Stolen Iraqi oil was
being shipped to America and Israel. The Governing
Council in Baghdad were traitors and apostates. On
and on went the sermons, the vitriol unchecked by any

Iraqi official. Anbar Province was on the verge of slipping out of control.

Mattis was determined to stamp out the insurgent fires before they reached inferno stage. Baghdad was the critical center. If the highways were seized, Sunni gangs in orange and white taxis and Nissan pickup trucks would converge on the capital, making an alliance with Sadr's Shiite militia. The stage would be set for a replay of Tehran in 1978, when mobs swelled so large they could not be fired upon and the regime fell.

To prevent that development, Mattis decided to apply such overwhelming force along the main lines of communication that no gang could move toward the capital. The exuberance at firing a few RPGs at lumbering American convoys before darting away had to be replaced by the fear of being hunted down and killed, with crushed bodies left in shattered pickups for some stranger to bury.

Mattis called on Colonel Craig Tucker to pull together most of his Regimental Combat Team 7, or RCT 7, and sweep the area south and east of Fallujah. The task Mattis had given him demanded balancing risks. With four battalions Tucker was responsible for a huge area, including a thousand kilometers of border with Saudi Arabia, Jordan, and Syria. One of Tucker's battalions had been sent to Fallujah, and another was engaged in daily fights along the Syrian border. Tucker gambled that he could pull together his light armored reconnaissance (LAR) battalion and Battalion 2/7, move eighty kilometers south, scrub five hundred square kilometers of suburbs, and quell the attacks on convoys. This would set back security across the province, but there was no alternative.

Tucker's force came down from the north as subtly as a bulldozer, a column of 168 LAVs, Humvees, and seven-ton trucks, with amtracs and Abrams tanks in support. As intended, Task Force Ripper presented an imposing sight as it rolled down the deserted highways: kilometer after kilometer of armored vehicles, gun barrels pointed outboard, moved and stopped in unison.

Mattis drove out from division headquarters to meet Tucker. The general traveled light, with three or four Humvees and a command LAV outfitted with six radios. The vehicles moved constantly at high speed. The LAV driver, Lance Corporal Andrew Wike, scarcely slowed down when making turns, and more than once Mattis was almost thrown out. The men enjoyed moving with Mattis. They saw the countryside, and they saw action.

They were hit three times by IEDs and fought off two ambushes, losing one Marine and having three others injured. Some on the staff believed the insurgents were targeting Mattis, who shrugged off the warnings. In an LAV he could move around, stopping wherever he wanted without covering everyone in dust from the backwash of a helicopter. Mattis never mentioned the attacks.

The meeting with Tucker was brief. "We're getting mortared from south of the city, so start there," Mattis said, pointing to a map. "Move decisively. Everywhere you go, act like you're staying, like you're going to homestead and become their new best friend, whether they like it or not. Were going to break this jihad."

As he spoke, Mattis's hand swept across the dozens of black grid squares on the map. Each square measured one kilometer by one kilometer and contained hundreds of houses, each surrounded by a cement wall; some were shaded by palm trees, while others were open to the blistering sun and frequent winds. At a glance, the area held more than a hundred thousand people and ten thousand houses. Tucker's task force would clear south and east of Fallujah along the southern side of the Euphrates, relying on about nine hundred dismounted Marines to search the houses. In physical terms, it was impossible to conduct a thorough search. Instead, the intent was psychological. Rumor and emotion had fueled the jihad; Mattis was counting on emotion to spread the rumor that the Marines were everywhere in force, searching in every house for the insurgents.

Too many teenagers treated opposing the American soldiers as a game, an adrenaline rush, the thing to do after listening to the impassioned imam in the village mosque. A young man ran home, grabbed an AK, embraced a fearful mother, received a blessing from a father, and drove off in high spirits, waving his rifle in the air, promising to free Fallujah, protect Islam, and kill an infidel American. A day later at some dusty crossroad, the youth would crouch with his friends behind a house listening to the clipped voices of an approaching Marine patrol. Eyes wide, he would nod vigorously to his friends and run out in the street, AK at his waist, pulling the trigger as he ran. A Marine would raise his rifle, center the front aiming post in the rear reticule—as he had done a thousand times on a half-dozen different rifle ranges—and squeeze off a three-round burst. Mattis called it "senseless killing" and reserved his special scorn for the Sunni clerics who encouraged it.

To feel enthusiastic for martyrdom among the like-minded inside the local mosque was one thing; it was quite another to be at home with the family, isolated and alone, when the American war machine rumbled by, shaking the walls. Then young men had second thoughts about joining the resistance.

To create the largest visible impact, Col Tucker spread out his force. A dozen rifle platoons formed the nucleus of the search teams. Lieutenant Bill Vesterman of 2nd Platoon, Fox Company, Battalion 2/7, drew a six-kilometer sector on the west side of the highway leading north to Fallujah. Vesterman had quit his job in investment banking and enlisted after 9/11.

Vesterman's sector was the same as the others—long stretches of dirt covered by dust inches thick, clusters of tan-colored brick and cement houses, each with a courtyard enclosed by a cinder block wall, most with rough-barked palm trees topped with dark branches providing shade and casting a touch of green to the monotonous ochre color of the countryside. Vesterman's platoon hopped down from their seven-ton trucks and trotted in a skirmish line toward the nearest line of houses. As they moved forward, four LAVs slowly kept pace on the highway, the 25mm guns ready to provide covering fire.

Each of the three squads selected a house. One fire team would provide outside cover while the other two rushed into the house. Within minutes Iraqi men and boys were herded outside and forced to lie facedown, while the women and children huddled against the walls. A fire team went back into the house for a quick search, starting with the **diwan**, or living room—with worn rugs covering rough cement floors, scattered cushions, an overstuffed chair or two—then on to the bedrooms and closets stuffed with blankets and more cushions, and through the meager kitchen with a dripping faucet and one or two burners fueled by a small propane bottle. A desultory peek at the bathroom with its hand shower and hole in the cement completed the search. The squads were finished in minutes, emerging with AKs with plastic stocks and a few bolt-action rifles, relics from a bygone war.

"Whose are these?" a fire team leader, holding an AK, yelled at the men lying on the ground. "You have papers? Papers?"

The Iraqis looked at the dirt in front of their faces.

"Get some interpreters up here," Vesterman said.

Two Marine sergeants from the HET, or Human Exploitation Team, joined the platoon. One sergeant, with a slender build, was of Lebanese descent and spoke Arabic; the other, a huge African American with a West African accent, spoke no Arabic. The two moved among the Iraqis, tugging up sleeves and examining the soles of feet for the telltale acid burns that form after handling explosives.

The slender sergeant asked questions in soft Arabic, while the huge sergeant roared at the startled Iraqis: "Where Ali Baba? Where Ali Baba?"

At Vesterman's request, an Iraqi interpreter named Abdul Mehlik had joined the platoon. A Shiite from Najaf, Mehlik did not hide his dislike of Sunnis from Fallujah. But he stood off to one side shaking his head as the HET team yelled at the men. At one point Mehlik told Vesterman that it was "bad" to force the Iraqi men to lie down in the dirt.

Vesterman shook his head in disagreement.

"Can't take a chance. They stay down," he said. "One hidden grenade and I'd lose a Marine."

Mehlik said no more, standing aside and tagging along, attached to but not part of the platoon.

As the platoon continued up the west side of the road, the size of the houses and the palm trees increased and the fields held more cows, sheep, and donkeys. As the platoon crossed a field dotted with palm trees, they heard the sharp **crack! crack!** of AK bullets passing overhead. They dispersed, took cover, and bounded ahead. But the shooter was gone, hidden somewhere among the acres and acres of fields and palm groves.

A kilometer in from the highway, Vesterman's platoon was walking through farmlands where no Americans had ever patrolled. The villagers and farmers looked at the Marines with curiosity, showing neither hostility nor friendliness. They simply stared as the Marines trudged across the open fields. Farther on the platoon searched some houses large enough to be called estates, devoid of rugs and personal items but with expensive doors, windows, and dust-laden electrical fixtures still intact. The owners had packed up and left, yet such was their aura of power that in the year since the regime had fallen, no one had dared loot the empty houses of prominent Baathists.

In late afternoon, after walking six kilometers across the fields and randomly searching between one and two hundred houses, the platoon came to a small mosque. The Marines pounded on the door, and about thirty men of all ages filed out, followed by a young imam with sandy hair and a neat beard, wearing a spotless white dishdasha. Vesterman politely asked the imam for permission to search his mosque.

With the air of a neutral translator, the policeman, Mehlik, explained to the imam that the search was inevitable, not a request. The Marines were in and out in less than two minutes. The Iraqi men stood in a row at a distance, all their mustachioed faces showing anger. Several asked permission to go home to be with their wives and families before the Americans swept through the neighborhood.

At dusk the sweaty Marines stopped, ate their MREs, and slept in the dust in a rocky, furrowed field. They awakened at four to begin another sweep and decided to start with the largest house in the neighborhood, a tasteful brick edifice with wrap-around balconies and black marble on either side of the doorway. As they drove up, the platoon sergeant, Staff Sergeant Lirette, spotted a man running out the back.

Corporal Carroll, Vesterman's third squad leader, ran around the house and came back, holding by the elbow a large bearded man in a mud-speckled white dishdasha. Within seconds, screaming women and crying children streamed out of the house and ran to his side. Complaining volubly, the man handed a laminated ID card to the interpreter, Mehlik.

"He is a sheikh," Mehlik said. "The head man. Very rich."

"I don't care," Lirette said. "He ran when he saw us. He's hiding something. He's busted."

"He ran because he was afraid," Mehlik said. "You should let him go. His card is signed by an American colonel."

Cpl Carroll and his squad stood watching the encounter, waiting for orders.

"You don't tell me nothing. This is my decision," Lirette said to Mehlik. "This dude's going back, and that's the end of it."

Prior to joining the platoon, Lirette had been a drill instructor. While 2/Lt Vesterman was the tactical leader of the platoon, Lirette, a man of firm views, was the disciplinarian and the voice of enlisted authority. He wasn't about to have his leadership questioned. Vesterman backed up his platoon sergeant.

The sheikh was flex-cuffed and pulled into a truck, leaving behind the shrieking women. SSgt Lirette and Mehlik walked to the idling Humvees, neither looking at the other.

The platoon moved on to the next neighborhood, which was a slum, with no indoor plumbing, puddles of sewage on the streets, ramshackle huts, and goats and pigs wandering among the run-down houses. In a pile of soiled hay next to a pigsty, the Marines found a long wooden ammunition box stamped in English with a lot number and the date, 1991. A fire team leader said it proved insurgents lived there.

"All it proves is that this farmer is a pack rat," Lirette said. "I've seen lots of them in the States, too."

Lirette stood in the center of a rubbish-strewn dirt street, directing the squads. A bearded old man wearing a red kaffiyeh and a soiled brown dishdasha hesitantly approached him. They tried to communicate in pantomime, the old man gesturing as if he were giving orders. Exasperated, Lirette shook his head.

Overcoming his pique, Mehlik stepped forward. The old man, he explained, was the local sheikh. He was asking if Lirette would please go through him if he wanted to search. This time Mehlik didn't tell the staff sergeant what to do. He stated the request and, like the indigent sheikh, waited for a response.

"Carroll, get your squad over here!" Lirette yelled. "Listen up!"

The Marines gathered around, and the sheikh, pleased with the chance to show off, began a long, rambling discourse. At first Mehlik tried to translate every sentence for Lirette, but he soon gave up and ticked off the main points.

"He says the bad people are in Fallujah. Everyone knows that. Maybe a car or two came through here, but that was days ago. The Americans are rich, but Baghdad is keeping all the money. His people are poor. Look at the water. He wants to know when you fix things."

Warm pita bread was served. Lirette smiled, chewed, listened, and nodded while Vesterman sat in his Humvee tending to the radio. When the sheikh offered to share a chicken meal, Lirette politely declined, a large smile on his face.

"Make up some nice excuse. Tell him we have to go," he told Mehlik. "We're not eating their food. They're poor enough as it is. Thank him for us." Lirette couldn't help adding, "See, I'm not so bad at this diplomatic stuff."

Mehlik shook his head and offered a wry smile.

As the Marines were climbing into the trucks, the HET team drove by, returning the wealthy sheikh to his house, his hands free of the plastic handcuffs.

———

Colonel Tucker next set his sights on an apartment complex called the Two Towers, twenty kilometers to the east. The towers were home to more than a thousand families of Republican Guard officers—whitewashed three-story apartments with air-conditioning, balconies, windows, satellite TVs, medical care, playgrounds, a beautiful mosque, a park, private schools, and a swimming pool. On the roofs were a maze of radio and television antennas and small satellite dishes. Dominating the skyline were a narrow, graceful blue-domed minaret and a huge, saucer-shaped cement water tower. The Two Towers was a minicity, an enclave of privilege.

The Republican Guard made sure the Two Towers had no military target that would tempt the Americans to strike. During the coalition's attack in March–April of 2003, not one tank or artillery piece had been permitted inside the compound, not one communications building or headquarters. No incidents occurred near the housing complex, no shootings, no abductions, no IEDs.

Tucker heard from agent reports and communications intercepts that a hundred or more former soldiers knew his task force was on the move and were talking about making a stand at the towers. Tucker doubted they would actually stay and fight, but he deployed prudently.

He sent his light armored vehicles ahead to cut off the roads leading into the towers. Then in a night move Vesterman's platoon joined the rest of Fox Company in setting up a picket line around the towers. With Carroll's squad at point, the company snaked its way through farmlands a few hundred meters outside the walls of the towers, listening to music from the apartments and shielding their eyes from the bright streetlights. At four in the morning, Vesterman's Marines lay shivering in the filthy straw of a farmyard where the thick mud had been churned up by the hooves of water buffalo and pigs. Inside the farmhouse a dog was barking furiously.

While Fox Company kept guard around the towers,

Col Tucker met with Lieutenant Colonel Phil Skuta, who commanded Battalion 2/7, for a final adjustment of plans. Tucker ran an efficient, Spartan command post consisting of a few open-sided tents and multiple communications feeds. Through a new marvel called Smart-T, Lieutenant Colonel Nick Vuckovich, the regimental operations officer, had data and voice links with the ops officers at 2/7 and the LAR battalion. They routinely exchanged briefs, intelligence summaries, orders, and map overlays, calling back and forth to iron out details.

Not a shot had been fired from the towers, and enemy chatter over cell phones had ceased. Emissaries were telling Tucker that the Iraqi National Guard were waiting to escort the Marines through town, as though on inspection. It appeared there would be no fight.

"Okay, Phil," Tucker said. "If there's not going to be any shooting, let's adjust."

Once they modified their plan, Tucker and Skuta drove into the Two Towers. To enter the town, Captain John Kelly, the Echo Company commander, was assigned point. He walked up the clean main street leading to the mosque, looking relaxed and nonbelligerent. Behind him strode hundreds of wary Marines. Small groups of boys and young men gathered on the sidewalks to stare, some of the little ones smiling, the rest showing no emotion. Kelly stopped at the National Guard headquarters next to the large mosque and asked the commander if he had seen any insurgents.

"No terrorists come here," Lieutenant Razeed Zouad Kadem said. "If they do, we kill them."

"Where are your records?" Kelly asked.

"No records. We kill the terrorists. We don't turn them over to anyone."

Kelly cocked an eyebrow. "You have no weapons."

"Marines took them. We need them back to kill the terrorists."

Kelly shook his head. With the National Guard deserting across Anbar, the Marines had seized armories before the weapons disappeared. Tired of the lies, Kelly walked on.

The battalion translator, Abu Yusef, remained behind to chat. Abu Yusef was a common Iraqi name, like John Smith. Yusef's real name was Gilbert Jacob, and he was fifty-seven, from Modesto, California. For the first twenty-seven years of his life he had lived in Iraq. With his distinct Baghdad accent, mustache, stubble beard, and scruffy kaffiyeh, he was plain old Yusef, translating for the stupid Americans for good pay.

"Isn't it great what the brave martyrs are doing in Fallujah?" Lt Kadem said.

Gilbert agreed and excused himself. He walked over to the hospital to meet LtCol Skuta, passing by a banner that read, "The committee receives the brave heroes of Fallujah." Skuta was inspecting the clean hospital, which had only a few patients.

"Where are the patients?" Skuta asked.

"Not many get sick here," a doctor said.

"They moved the wounded **irahibeen** before we got

here," Gilbert murmured. "They forgot to take down the Welcome Home banner outside."

Skuta and Gilbert left the hospital and walked to the mosque to meet the imam. Gilbert occasionally translated the graffiti sprayed on the sides of buildings: "That one says 'Death to Americans.' The larger one says 'Yes to Saddam,' with Saddam scratched out, so now it reads 'Yes to Islam.' "

As they walked, Gilbert listened to the imam on a loudspeaker urging the people to turn their backs on the Americans. Gilbert thought the man was stupid or arrogant or both. The imam, in black turban and full beard, met them in the courtyard and launched into a diatribe. Skuta knew that the imam, Sheikh Shawket, could at any moment call thousands of women and children into the streets for a bloody riot. He wasn't about to provoke chaos. Instead, he asked the imam to point out what needed fixing in town. The imam agreed, and they strolled along the street, each accomplishing his purpose. The imam was showing that the Americans had to come to him, and Skuta was avoiding a messy confrontation. As the imam stated his demands, Skuta took notes.

Confiding in Abu Yusef, the imam said, "Even if this man gives us equipment, I won't shake his hand."

Gilbert heard the hate in his voice and smiled, nodding his head in agreement.

Skuta was adding up the imam's demands. "This is a lot of stuff," he said. "I can't order generators for every apartment building. The sheikh will have to meet with the big colonel. I'll call and see if he's available."

After calling Col Tucker, Skuta escorted the imam to a waiting helicopter. There his hands were flex-cuffed behind his back. The imam Sheikh Shawket was the top name on the high-value target list for Two Towers. For weeks he had urged his followers to join their brothers fighting in Fallujah. The CIA had his sermons, dozens of hours of rants, on tape. Gilbert took satisfaction in watching the trembling imam placed on the helicopter. After ten months in Anbar Province, he was tired of what he called "two-faced sheikhs and imams."

"The sheikhs know who is attacking us, and they won't tell us," he said. "To deceive us makes them heroes. Self-interest can put some Baathists on our side, but not extremists like Shawket. Wahhabis want to kill Americans. It's that simple. As long as we Americans are alone fighting this war, the Iraqi people will slowly turn against us. Iraq needs a strong Iraqi leader, not an American."

Tucker told Skuta to pull his battalion out before the population could organize a protest against the imam's arrest. As Skuta's battalion left, civilian traffic began moving on the main highway for the first time in weeks, a sure sign the insurgents had pulled back.

———

There were four major battles in April. The first was Ramadi, provoked by the insurgents. The second was Fallujah. The third was the defeat of Sadr's militia down south in Najaf. And the fourth was the sweep by Task Force Ripper that clamped a lid on the uprising sweeping like a prairie fire toward Baghdad.

Moving constantly for a week, Tucker's LAVs and dismounted platoons had swept hundreds of kilometers of highways, roads, and farm fields and searched thousands of houses. It was one thing for four or five young men to jam themselves into an old rattling Datsun, RPGs and AKs akimbo, and drive parallel to a major highway, looking to shoot at a supply truck. The excitement fizzled when they saw Tucker's juggernaut rolling forward.

17

LALAFALLUJAH

ON APRIL 9 GEN ABIZAID AND Ambassador Bremer had declared a unilateral twenty-four-hour cease-fire inside Fallujah. Two days later—Easter Sunday—Battalions 1/5 and 3/4, buffeting the insurgents from two directions, sensed they could break the resistance, only to be ordered to halt. When Gen Myers visited Iraq on April 15, the Marines had expected the green light, but again nothing had happened. Every few days the rifle companies were told to get ready to go. Each time the alert proved to be a wishful rumor.

By the third week in April, the three battalions (2/1, 1/5, and 3/4) had settled into the routine of trench warfare, confined to cement houses instead of dirt trenches. Each platoon occupied a house, using the ground floor for storing supplies. The second door was for sleeping; the Marines lay side by side, each with his rucksack at the head of his tiny space, the floors strewn with blankets, comforters, and sleeping bags. They carefully stacked the belongings in the houses in corners, often covering them with sheets to keep off the dust. After First Sergeant William Skiles of Golf Company yelled at one squad when incoming rounds broke some dishes, the china in some houses was stacked out of the line of fire. When not on duty, the Marines lay propped up on their sleeping bags, reading **Playboy, Men's Journal, Sports Illustrated,** and **Motor Trend.** Meals were MREs, with an occasional run to Camp Fallujah to pick up vats of hot meals. The third floor leading to the roof housed the unit leaders, radio operators, and ops center. On the open roof sandbags stacked atop the low walls provided protection for the snipers and machine-gunners.

During the day the Marines moved cautiously. The insurgents had some decent snipers hiding among the maze of rooftops, waiting hour after hour, shooting once or twice a day. Mortar attacks were common, day and night. Sometimes the shells dropped in with disturbing accuracy; other times they missed by a city block. Whenever a Cobra gunship flew over the city, it attracted a fusillade of machine-gun fire and RPG rockets, a few detonating in the air, most exploding on roofs and streets. Every Cobra returned to base with numerous bullet holes.

Fallujah after dark was a cacophony of sounds: dogs yapping and howling, explosions near and far, bursts of small-arms fire, the annoying whine of the Predator

UAV and the rumble of Slayer overhead, and high-pitched calls from the minarets to evening prayers. Each night the translators attached to every rifle company—Iraqi Kurds, Sunnis, Shiites, and Iraqi Americans—climbed to the roofs and listened to the imams preaching over loudspeakers. The same message was broadcast from most minarets: **America is bringing in Jews from Israel and stealing Iraq's oil. Women, take your children into the streets to aid the holy warriors. Bring them food, water, and weapons. Do not fear death. It is your duty to protect Islam.** After a few nights, when asked what the imams were yelling, the translators, bored by the repetition, simply said, "Stealing oil, bringing in Jews, protect Islam. The usual stuff. Same old, same old."

It was old, and all the more powerful for its historical roots. Islamic Holy Law, or sharia, stressed that the community or state and the religion were inseparable from each other. The religion conferred legitimacy upon the community, while the community protected the religion. In Fallujah the power of the imams was impressive as they nightly exhorted the people, and the longer the siege dragged on, the more the resistance became a community obligation.

LtCol Olson and Capt Zembiec watched through binoculars as boys about ten years old lugged mortar shells across a road. On the roof with them were a Delta Force sniper with a .50 caliber rifle and a Marine corporal with the standard .308 sniper rifle. They sat in separate sandbagged shelters, peering out through mouse holes. Zembiec called them "cooperative carnivores." They waited all day, hoping that a grown-up insurgent would grow impatient and walk out to take one of the mortar shells from a boy. None did.

From Zembiec's roof, through his ten-power sniper scope Corporal Ethan Place could see for a thousand meters down a wide street leading into the Jolan District. Place had been an accomplished hunter before qualifying as a sniper.

"I've popped a few at four and five hundred yards, but it's at six hundred that they get stubborn," he said. "They look up the street and don't see anyone. They can't believe I can see them."

Place had used a laser range-finder to select aim points on either side of the street at six and eight hundred yards from his position. When a man with a rifle sprinted across the street, he fired at an aim point and the insurgent ran into the bullet. In three weeks Place had shot thirty men.

There was a sniper team on every fourth house held by the Marines, and each day they killed ten or twenty insurgents. Working to the east with Battalion 3/4, Sergeant Sean Crane did not have one long avenue to fire down, as did Cpl Place. Instead, he employed traditional sniper tactics and shifted from spot to spot. The day after Cpl Amaya was killed, Crane staked out the house where the defenders had been burned to death and in the late afternoon saw three Iraqis with AKs sneak around a corner. From three hundred yards away he squeezed off four rounds in fifteen seconds, hitting all three. The next day, as refugees continued to pour out of the city, he noticed insurgents in groups of two and three crossing the streets behind the women and children. They walked casually, AKs close to their sides, trying to blend in. Over the course of six hours Crane shot five before the others learned to sprint, not walk, across streets.

To Crane, sniping was like fishing, requiring long hours of patience. The targets were a quarry, like fish. He tried not to think of them as men. One day at dusk he took fire from a house about three hundred yards away. The next day he watched the house for seven hours. In late afternoon an old man, assisted by a tall young man, slowly shuffled next door and returned with a loaf of bread. At the courtyard gate the old man continued inside while the young man paused to glance toward the house where Crane sat hidden behind sandbags. A few minutes later, as the shadows lengthened, the gate opened and the young man slipped out, AK in hand, and ducked behind a burnt-out car. Crane placed the reticule of his scope on the car. When the man peeked out, Crane fired. The man slipped forward into the street and lay still. A scream of pain or grief came from inside the house.

Crane waited. A few minutes later the old man walked out, holding himself stiffly erect. Knowing he was in the line of fire but refusing to look toward Crane's position, the old man shuffled to the body, grasped the dead man under the armpits, and step by step tugged the body back inside the gate. Crane watched and waited. A few minutes later the old man stepped into the open courtyard with a shovel and dug a grave.

Of the ten men he had hit, Crane had not seen one knocked off his feet, as happened in the movies. When hit in the chest, most men flinched and staggered on for a few steps before sitting down and slouching over, or lying down and bleeding out. He had hit one man in the arm, then in the foot, and still he hobbled away. He shot him again in the jaw and the man stayed upright with three bullets in him, disappearing around a corner.

Day by day the Marine snipers took a steady toll of the armed insurgents. At the Fallujah Liaison Center the city elders complained bitterly to sympathetic listeners from the Iraqi Governing Council. Both the city elders and the Baghdad delegation agreed that the American snipers were inhumane and must stop shooting.

LtGen Conway, presiding over the U.S. delegation, disagreed. "I find it strange," he said to one group, "that you object to our most discriminate weapon—a Marine firing three ounces of lead at a precise target. A sniper is any Marine with a rifle. I reject your demand, and I wonder who asked you to make it."

About one Marine in four had an M16 with a three-power scope, which increased kills at three and four hundred yards. The M40 sniper rifles with ten-power scopes reached out half a mile during the day. Inside the city were European as well as Arab aid workers and journalists sympathetic to the insurgents. Describing the fighting from the other side, a British journalist in Fallujah wrote that "it is the snipers the people of Fallujah fear more than anything else."

At night the 7.62mm machine gun with a thermal scope took over for the sniper rifle. The thermal was clunky, temperamental, and gobbled up batteries. It also was excellent at detecting a heat source a quarter of a mile away, meaning that no infiltrator could sneak close enough to pitch a grenade. Mangy packs of wild dogs scavenged in the dark, wriggling through the concertina wire and setting off trip flares. The Marines called them "sapper dogs." The thermals picked them up easily, thus avoiding shooting at phantom attackers. When Iraqis did try to probe, they stood out clearly as black "hot spots." When hit by a burst of bullets, a hot spot would gradually dim and fade out, at which time the machine-gunner would report another kill on the lines.

Every day Red Crescent ambulances drove up to the lines to remove the corpses. During the first week in April, Marines shot the drivers of two ambulances carrying armed fighters. After that the ambulances stayed out of the fight and conducted only humanitarian missions, tending to the wounded and the dead, distributing food to the stubborn families living in no-man's-land between the two sides.

At a few places they left the dead where they had fallen. When Cpl Villalobos of Battalion 3/4 had shot up cars careening toward his position, one of the drivers lay out in the field where he had been shot, unattended. The body, black with flies, had swelled and split apart, the stink of rotting death wafting into the house where Villalobos and his squad lived. They doused the body with gasoline and tried to burn it, which only increased the mess—a dog carried off a roasted thigh.

At a meeting at regiment, Captain Shannon Johnson, the company commander, requested flamethrowers. "That way, sir," he explained to Col Toolan, "we clean up the mess in front of our lines and torch the hard points once the cease-fire is lifted."

Corporal Amaya had been one of Johnson's squad leaders. If jihadists were going to barricade themselves in houses to kill Americans before dying, better to burn them out than send in a Marine.

"You know I can't make that kind of decision," Toolan said.

There was no reprimand in his tone. Strong requests were not unusual from aggressive fighters. The translators said the Iraqis called McCoy's battalion the "Black Plague." The Marines liked the image that they were one of the Four Horsemen of the Apocalypse, but the Iraqis were referring to their fear of disease from the blackened corpses in front of the battalion lines. Before jumping off in the attack, McCoy had the habit of gathering his troops and playing at full blast "Let the Bodies Hit the Floor." In 1804 Andrew Jackson's musketeers had advanced to drum rolls composed by Beethoven; in 2004 Marines attacked under the blare of hard rock composed by Eminem.

Each battalion had its idiosyncrasies. Byrne's Battalion 2/1—more partial to blasting Jimi Hendrix at 110 decibels—had been the first to persuade the U.S. Army Psychological Warfare teams to initiate scatological warfare. Platoons in 1/5 competed to dream up the filthiest insults for the translators to scream over the loudspeakers. When enraged Iraqis rushed from a mosque blindly firing their AKs, the Marines shot them down.

The tactic of insult-and-shoot spread along the lines. Soon the Marines were mocking the city as "Lalafallujah" (after the popular stateside concert Lollapalooza) and cranking out "Welcome to the Jungle" by Guns 'n' Roses and "Hell's Bells" by AC/DC. Not to be outdone, the mullahs responded with loudspeakers hooked to generators, trying to drown out Eminem with prayers, chants of **Allahu akbar,** and Arabic music. Every night discordant sound washed over the lines.

———

And every night images of civilian casualties were transmitted worldwide via satellite and across the Internet. Western TV networks pooled video from Fallujah, including film from the Arab cameramen with the insurgents. Predictably, the pictures stressed destruction. Al Jazeera was unrelenting in depicting the deaths of civilians.

In three weeks of fighting, eighty-two buildings and two mosques had been bombed. The average number of air strikes per day was four. Massive civilian casualties, however, became the accepted storyline. The Coalition made no institutional effort to rebut each false report or to conduct systematic assessments. Given the imagery from the UAVs and from every air strike, records were certainly available to inform the press. In the absence of such data, however, Al Jazeera shaped the story.

————

During the third week in April, Ambassador Richard H. Jones, Bremer's experienced deputy at the CPA, chaired four sessions at the Fallujah Liaison Center to resolve the siege. Every day Iraqis in civilian clothes, robes, and kaffiyehs thronged into the FLC to meet with American diplomats and generals. Every day the Iraqis promised to curtail the violence. Every day rusted and broken weapons were turned in as symbols of progress while the violence continued. As for expelling the terrorists, the negotiators denied they existed. Foreign fighters, they said, were a myth and an excuse to punish the city. At one point Nate Jensen counted thirteen negotiating groups—five American and eight Iraqi teams. Rarely did the meetings have a written agenda.

Having survived by cunning under Saddam, the Iraqis were shrewd at sorting out which American colonels reported to which generals and which verbal assurances sounded most promising. Determined to prevent a Marine attack, the Iraqis pushed for concessions and argued the insurgents' case with the doggedness of top-flight defense lawyers. Conway, a genial and courteous man, became so angry in one meeting that he pounded the table. In another session, a front man for Janabi insisted that Mattis agree to forty-five written demands. Mattis responded by walking out.

"The Iraqis have never won a battle," Mattis quipped to Jensen, "or lost a negotiation."

Whenever the Americans appeared at the end of their tether, Hassani, in the role of interlocutor, called a halt for the day, assuring both sides that tomorrow would be better. Hassani's pleasing personality and laid-back California style were soothing, but the basis for such assurances was opaque. No insurgent leader sat at the negotiating table. Hoping they would play a mediating role, Bremer agreed to release from prison Sheikh Barakat and the imam mufti Sheikh Jamal, whom Drinkwine had arrested for sedition in November. Once freed, however, Barakat disappeared and Jamal played no significant role in the negotiations.

On the American side, there were too many negotiators with authority. Ambassadors Jones, Bremer, and Blackwill were well-seasoned diplomats, trained to advance America's interests by outwitting foreign leaders. The three leading generals—Abizaid, Sanchez, and Conway—were managers of violence. Each had a distinct personality. Abizaid was thoughtful and even-handed in his deliberations; Sanchez focused on operations, preferring to leave political-military matters to others; Conway was courteous and fair. Despite their different styles, however, the three generals shared the trait of leadership. Everything they did was based on teamwork and on achieving the objective at the least cost to their men.

If diplomats played poker, generals played bridge. A diplomat can zig and zag to outwit or win over his opponent; a general must calculate each move to fit the capabilities and concerns of his troops. Where a diplomat might urge a nimble strategy of fight and talk, a general would think long and hard before he started his men down one track and then switched to another. Jones and Blackwill had years of experience in negotiations in the Middle East, but the area of operations belonged to the military and the MEF. Without a clear written agenda, goals, and deadlines, the roles of the diplomats and generals in the negotiations became confused.

The ambiguity about negotiating roles reflected the diverse chains of command and communication channels. Conway made the decisions for the Marines, with Mattis in an off-again/on-again supporting role. Mattis's headquarters was outside Ramadi, and Conway was outside Fallujah. Abizaid was operating from Qatar and Tampa. Bremer and Sanchez were in Baghdad. Abizaid was talking to Rumsfeld and Rice; Bremer was talking to Rumsfeld and Rice; and Blackwill was talking to Rice.

At the same time Conway was secretly meeting with former Iraqi generals. Their titular head was Muhammad Latif, a colonel in the intelligence branch who had been imprisoned for seven years by Saddam. Only the MEF staff knew the details of this negotiating channel. The American diplomats were not informed. The Sunni generals claimed they could exert authority over most of the fighters in Fallujah and restore order—provided the Americans turned control of the city over to them. Conway was intrigued by the proposal and impressed by their sincerity.

The Iraqi Governing Council had achieved nothing in its negotiations. On April 19, Hassani grandly announced to the press that the insurgents were turning in their heavy weapons. Calling the weapons "junk," Mattis met the next day with Conway, arguing strongly for permission to attack.

"My civilian masters in Baghdad believe I'm a dumb, bloodthirsty grunt," Mattis said. "But I know what l have to do, and l sleep well at night."

Openly dismissive of the credentials of the negotiators, Rumsfeld was urging Abizaid to resume the attack. On April 21 a frustrated Conway told the press that an attack was "days, not weeks, away." MEF staff officers added that they "desperately wanted to avoid a bloody urban siege." After speaking with Abizaid on April 21, Rumsfeld and Wolfowitz believed the attack was scheduled to commence in a few days. Abizaid had pushed back hard, though, arguing with Rumsfeld on several occasions that massive force at this late juncture would inflame the Sunni region and should be considered only as a last resort.

On April 23, Bremer warned that "if these [insurgent] bands do not surrender their military weapons and instead continue to use them against Iraqi and Coalition forces, major hostilities could resume on short notice." That afternoon, as JTF commander, Sanchez sent the MEF a warning order to be prepared to resume offensive operations.

At the same time, all parties were aware that the president wanted options, not a full-scale attack. So they agreed to meet at the MEF on the twenty-fourth to discuss the situation.

————

The twenty-fourth was a typically hot April day, moderated by a steady wind. On the street outside the walled compound of the MEF, parking was crowded as diplomats, generals, and Iraqis from the Governing Council convened to discuss the next steps.

When Bremer came to the meeting, he was managing two crises: Sadr in the south and Fallujah in the west. The 1st Armored Division had trapped Sadr in Najaf. In return for pulling back his followers, Sadr was working out terms that permitted himself to go free. The Sadr crisis looked to be about over, with a messy but not disastrous ending.

That left Fallujah. Bremer believed the mood in the White House was not to take the city, and he felt he had allies for this point of view. Abizaid had sided with Rumsfeld in recommending a full-scale attack at the beginning of April; by the third week in April, Bremer believed Abizaid agreed that to recommence the attack would be a political blunder. The president of the Iraqi Governing Council, Massoud Barzani, was publicly complaining that the United States "has only itself for blame for the military deadlock in Najaf and Fallujah because it allowed its troops to change from an army of liberation to an army of occupation." Feeding on its own negativity and reinforced by daily press attention, the Iraqi Governing Council was continuing its complaints about the American military while remaining silent about Sadr's militia and the Sunni insurgents.

The Americans lacked support for an attack from both the Iraqis and the British. Although LtGen Sanchez preferred employing massive force, he had been warning Conway that White House support was slipping away. Conway understood: a full-scale attack would not be authorized.

The diplomats and generals were walking a fine line, in trying to reach agreement with the Iraqi negotiators to bring stability to Fallujah, using the threat of an attack as leverage, while knowing it was an empty threat.

———

One hundred feet away from the generals and diplomats, in the regimental ops center, Col Toolan was planning the final attack. Early that morning the buzz had zipped through the battalions: the JTF and the MEF, fed up with weeks of lies, had reauthorized the offensive.

From around the periphery of the city the Marine battalion staffs arrived in small clusters of Humvees and LAVs, dismounting outside the walls of the MEF, striding in tight groups through the makeshift plywood door into the alcove of the stone mansion that served as the regimental HQ, draping their ceramic armor vests and Kevlar helmets over the wooden racks that lined the wall outside the conference room. Sev-

eral carried M4 carbines or M16s, while others wore
pistols on their hips or in shoulder holsters. It was like
a meeting of knights in the fifteenth century—large,
purposeful men neatly arraying their armor before sitting down at the banquet table to discuss the business
of making war.

The mood was upbeat, with many smiles exchanged.
The dickering was over. It was time to finish the task.
They stood talking until Col Toolan strode in; then
they took seats around a long, square table with a huge
photomap of Fallujah on the wall.

"Gentlemen," Toolan said, "the commanding general is planning a division attack against Fallujah. RCT
7 will block and clear around the outskirts. RCT 1 as
the Main Effort will take the city."

The regimental intelligence officer, Maj Bellon, gave
the first briefing. ODA had identified seventeen
enemy groups in the city, he said, with grandiose
names like Allah's Army and Battalion of God. A "battalion" numbered twenty to forty fighters. All together
there were about five hundred hard-core fighters and a
thousand part-timers. Some were assigned to city
blocks, while others scooted around in small, orange-
striped Nissan pickups. The insurgents didn't employ
standard infantry tactics such as interlocking fields of
fire along fixed defensive lines. Instead, they tended to
swarm forward.

Once the blood started flowing, Bellon believed
many of the part-timers would stash their weapons
and melt away. The hard core not killed on the streets
would retreat to the safe houses where they ate and

slept. There might be twenty to forty fortified houses like the one where Cpl Amaya was killed. Each house was an isolated pillbox, vulnerable to a tank gun or a laser-guided bomb. The danger came when those inside held their fire until the Marines were inside.

Toolan turned next to his ops officer, LtCol Renforth, for the scheme of maneuver. Square and stocky with a shaven head, Renforth looked imposing, like a wrestler or a bodyguard. The battalions appreciated that Renforth didn't demand nitpicking reports. Renforth had started his career by enlisting as a sailor and was surprised when chosen to go to the navy prep school in Newport, Rhode Island.

Back in the early 1980s, he had seen himself as a rough-and-ready good old boy from Arkansas. At prep school he proved his rough manners by throwing a chair and a fellow student out a dorm window. His section leader gave him a scathing dressing-down for embarrassing his parents and disgracing himself. The section leader wasn't going to foist him off on someone else and send him back to a ship. Instead, Renforth spent every Saturday and Sunday for the next twelve weeks in "special study," meaning he was confined to base for three months. He grew to love the discipline of mathematics, graduated from the Naval Academy, and earned a commission in the Marine Corps. The name of the section leader: Jim Mattis.

In the ops center an electronic map tracked the positions of all friendly units. Below the map each new situation report was displayed in large type, with space for comments to be entered. Forty laptops tied together the staff sections. For a month Renforth had been studying the photomap and watching patterns develop from the sitreps and from visiting the battalions on the line.

For the attack Renforth had to plot the geometry of fires. In flat terrain rounds would travel for a thousand meters down straight streets. Battalion 2/1, under Olson, would provide the anvil, holding the rooftops in the northwest quadrant above the Jolan market in the old city. But which battalion would swing the hammer? To avoid friendly fire, they couldn't all charge forward at once.

Three kilometers due south of 2/1, Lieutenant Colonel Gyles Kyser had moved into position with his battalion, 2/2. To Kyser's right lay the section of houses called Queens. Byrne and 1/5 held the industrial quadrant east of Queens. He would swing west, flush out Queens, and join up with Kyser. The two battalions would then be set to drive straight north into the Jolan and crush the defenders against 2/1. At the same time 3/4 would push in from the east. The two forces would be at right angles. At some point Renforth would have to halt one battalion before they fired into each other.

Each battalion wanted to seize the Jolan. For three weeks they had lain on the rooftops absorbing mortar attacks and exchanging sniper fire and taunts with the insurgents. Wounded Marines had left the field hospitals and returned to their companies to finish the job.

The four battalion commanders were good friends. Olson had been McCoy's best man at his wedding, and Kyser, a hard-charging recon type, had served as

McCoy's executive officer in a rifle company years earlier. Byrne and McCoy had attended command and staff school together.

Each battalion commander knew that his Marines wanted to be in the fight and that they were relying on him to give them that chance. Byrne looked at Queens on the photomap. To him, it was a matter of jujitsu, pushing the insurgents off balance and letting their own confusion trip them up. He liked using the darkness to move forward a kilometer, then backsweeping when light came, catching the insurgents off guard.

McCoy planned to have Kilo and India Companies press forward, followed by Lima Company. When a strongpoint was hit, the lead company would mark it for Lima to destroy.

Kyser and Olsen each had six tanks in support. Renforth gave McCoy two and held six in reserve. McCoy considered this an injustice, arguing mightily for eight tanks.

"Do you think I'm crazy?" Renforth replied. "With eight tanks, Bryan, you'd be on the Euphrates in a day and I'd be stuck cleaning up the mess in the rear. Unh-unh, buddy. I'm keeping you on a leash. Two tanks, that's it."

"Too much back-clearing could slow us down," Bellon said, coming to McCoy's defense.

Back-clearing, the tedious searching of the thousands of houses behind the front lines of the advancing Marine troops, could bog down the speed of the offensive, allowing thousands of civilians to gather before the accommodating cameras of Al Jazeera. Bellon's concern was massive civilian protests filling the streets in front of the onrushing Marines.

"Maybe Bellon's got a point about too much back-clearing," Renforth said to McCoy. "We'll see about getting you more tanks once the attack gets rolling."

Renforth sat smiling like the cat that ate the canary. He wasn't about to let McCoy set too fast a pace. He might give McCoy and the "Black Plague" battalion more tanks—it depended on how the division attack developed.

"Satisfied I'm not screwing you?" Renforth asked with a smile.

He wanted to give 2/2 and 1/5 to the south enough time to straighten their lines. That way, as the battle unfolded, Toolan would have a choice of seizing the Jolan from the east (McCoy) or the south (Byrne and Kyser).

"No. Let me explain again why I need more tanks," McCoy replied.

While the two argued back and forth, Toolan stepped out to take a phone call. He was gone for less than fifteen minutes. When he returned, he looked grim.

"The attack has been called off," he said. "Instead, each battalion is to begin joint patrols with the Iraqis. We're to meet with the Iraqis tomorrow."

18

STRATEGIC CONFUSION

"IN WAR, YOU SUPPORT THE TROOPS," President Bush said. "It's not complicated. You give them support."

In Fallujah, supporting the troops had become complicated. On April 23, President Bush said that "most of Fallujah is returning to normal," an assessment that threw into question who was providing him with information. Continuing the unilateral cease-fire was causing American casualties and increasing the morale of the insurgents. Thirty-two soldiers and Marines had died in the fighting west of Baghdad—thirteen inside Fallujah itself—in the past three weeks.

The president prided himself on making firm decisions, showing no tolerance for hand-wringing. But the longer he uncharacteristically agreed to incremental extensions of the cease-fire, the more the political pressures were building to call off the attack altogether. On April 24 the president conferred with his advisers about whether to risk the "potentially disastrous public relations impact" of an American assault on the city.

Although Bremer had delivered a tough speech warning that hostilities could resume shortly, he had repeatedly cautioned that widespread uprisings would be a consequence of an attack and he did not want that to happen. Rumsfeld was pushing Abizaid to get on with the attack, and Abizaid was pushing right back, arguing that the Sunnis had to be given a chance to determine their own futures. From Bremer's perspective, he and Abizaid were in agreement that taking the city would be a disaster. Instead, both wanted to see moderate Iraqis step forward as leaders rather than have Americans thrust themselves into the lead.

"We must in all things be modest," Gen Abizaid had said. "We [Americans] are an antibody in their culture."

The president's pro-consul to Iraq (Bremer), the president's representative (Blackwill), and the theater commander (Abizaid) all offered judgments to the White House. But despite the ease of worldwide communication, the military's rigid hierarchical system prevented those with the battlefield knowledge from giving the president advice. Mattis talked to Conway, Conway to Sanchez, Sanchez to Abizaid, and Abizaid to Washington. Mattis insisted that his battalions were poised to attack, but Mattis wasn't even at the meeting at the MEF.

31 March 2004. Mutilation at
"Brooklyn Bridge" infuriated America.
AP/World Wide Photos

All photos by author unless otherwise noted.

Downtown Fallujah looking toward
Brooklyn Bridge to the west.

Lieutenant Colonel B. P. McCoy and Major
General James N. Mattis confer in east Fallujah.

Typical reaction as American soldiers
drive through Fallujah.

Lieutenant Drew Lee under fire on the rooftops in east Fallujah.

Iraqi family protected by Lieutenant Lee during fighting in east Fallujah.

Snipers—the weapon insurgent leaders feared the most. Bodies collected and left for local burial.

Skeptical Iraqi
listens to
Major Mark
DeVito in
Fallujah
suburbs.

National Guard officer professes his loyalty to a skeptical Captain John Kelly.

Marines on patrol in east Fallujah.

Private 1st Class Eric Ayon removes Sergeant Walker's humvee from the ambush site in east Ramadi. He's killed in action three days later in the same area.

Private 1st Class Ryan Jerabek's bloody glasses at the ambush site in east Ramadi.
PHILADELPHIA INQUIRER / DAVID SWANSON

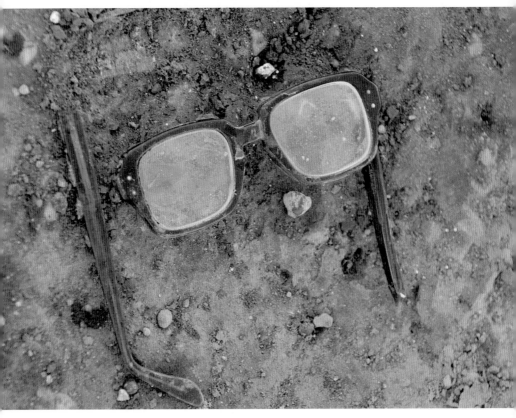

House to house fight in the Jolan. Lieutenant Wagner's house at right; insurgent house at left.

The Jolan Fight—memorial to Lance Corporal Austin.

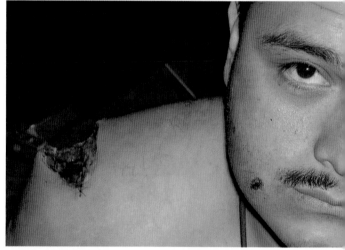

Despite his wound, Lance Corporal Carlos Gomez-Perez continued to fight in the Jolan graveyard.

Dr. Covey, USN

0331 Aarron Cole Austin GUNS UP
"A Friend, A Brother, A Marine"
Till We Meet Again
April 26, 2004
Texas
Stands Proud

Natural enemies? Major General Saleh shaking hands with Colonel Toolan. AP/World Wide Photos

Colonel Toolan (below, at left) appraises the Fallujah Brigade, April 26, 2004.

Marines guard Iraqis while searching
houses, Fallujah suburbs.

Lieutenant William Vesterman asks imam
for permission to search mosque,
Fallujah suburbs.

...owntown Fallujah as Marines ...dvance during Operation ...hantom Fury.
...S. MARINE CORPS

...orporal Timothy Connors ...utside house that held the ...hadist family, south Fallujah.

Battalion 3/5 approaching Brooklyn Bridge (in background), west Fallujah.

Under fire, 1st Sergeant Bradley Kasal exits the house from hell, south Fallujah.

Merry-go-round in Jolan Park next to the torture house.

Arab victim in torture house at Jolan Park.

Brooklyn Bridge: "This is for the Americans that were murdered here in 2004. Semper Fidelis"

Had they been asked by the White House, Conway and Mattis would have said that taking the city would require two to four days—after eighteen days of waiting on the lines. But they were not asked. The MEF and division commanders were like the general manager and the coach of a football team, sometimes included in discussions about the game being played and sometimes not.

The mood at the White House was not to take the city. The president had expressed serious reservations about both American and civilian casualties as well as damage to the city, shown to be extensive by Arab TV crews.

Lacking any other source, the press worldwide repeated Al Jazeera's estimate of over six hundred dead and a thousand wounded civilians in the city. Based on the sheer volume of repetition, the allegations acquired plausibility.

Stu Jones sensed that all the negotiators—Marines, American diplomats, and Iraqis from Baghdad—were affected by the incessant reports of mass civilian casualties.

"The Iraqis were so excited," Jones said. "Incessant complaints about Marine snipers. I thought at least a thousand civilians had died. Only later did I learn it was under three hundred."

The president had asked for options.

At the MEF on April 24, Bremer explained to the generals that two negotiating tracks were under way. First, the Governing Council negotiators, led by Hassani. They were waiting in Conway's bedroom with

Jensen, Stu Jones, and MajGen Weber. Second—unbeknownst to the Hassani group—Ayad Allawi, soon to be named prime minister, was holding secret negotiations with Janabi.

Conway did not tell Bremer that the MEF was pursuing a third negotiating track via CIA contacts with former Iraqi generals.

To those gathered at the MEF, one option now seemed viable. The Iraqis at the MEF recommended that the Marines patrol with the National Guard who had deserted two weeks earlier. The delegation from Fallujah nominated a new commander to be placed above LtCol Suleiman. He was LtCol Jassim Hatim, a trim, neat man who spoke some English and presented a distinct military bearing. Details about where he came from and his past were hazy, but the city elders pushed him in front of Suleiman, who was considered an outsider because he was born in a different town.

The MEF staff and Conway believed joint patrols were a reasonable request. They told Bremer they needed a few days to work out the details. On the afternoon of April 24, Abizaid, Bremer, Sanchez, and Conway agreed to extend the cease-fire for another three days so the Marines could patrol jointly with the Iraqis. Bremer flew back to Baghdad for a sivits teleconference with Washington, satisfied that the Marines' idea of conducting joint patrols was sound.

———

On April 24, the battalion commanders left the meeting with Toolan not understanding why the game plan had been changed at the line of scrimmage. Mattis had his troops psychologically motivated to attack. There were four battalions on the line, a ten-minute drive from one to the next. Mattis knew every sergeant major and battalion commander; Toolan knew every gunnery sergeant and platoon commander. From Col Toolan to McCoy to Cpl Amaya's squad, those fighting and dying on the lines were a small, tight-knit group. After weeks of the nightly taunting, the sharp **crack!** of the sniper's bullet, the metallic **thunk** of a mortar shell leaving the tube, and the boots and rifle ceremony for another dead comrade, every Marine entrenched around the city wanted to finish the fight, not walk away from it. The Marines understood that if they stopped, the insurgents would believe they had won, grow stronger, and be harder to defeat the next time.

By the evening of the twenty-fourth, as each Marine battalion planned in detail, the concept of joint patrols appeared to ensure victory in another guise. Each patrol assumed it would be attacked, so each had requested a Quick Reaction Force to stand by with tanks. The odds were overwhelming that heavy fights would erupt within hours. Battalion 3/4, for example, was planning that Kilo would lead with a patrol to Janabi's mosque, with Lima and tanks standing by. A fierce fight was guaranteed. The same was true when Byrne advanced toward the government center, when Kyser turned up the Yellow Brick Road, and when Olson headed down toward the Jolan.

Once the patrols began, the insurgents would fight

back, the "cease-fire" would be shattered, and the Blue Diamond would be back on the offensive. At the tactical level, the Marines believed that the Iraqi security forces were a token gesture that provided political cover without altering the military strategy. The joint patrols were a brilliant negotiating ploy. The generals and ambassadors had set a trap. All that was needed were a few Iraqi soldiers to lend a joint flavor, and the battle was on.

———

The next morning, Toolan and his battalion commanders met at the Fallujah Liaison Building with the Iraqi National Guard officers. Over the course of the previous week 350 Iraqi soldiers had returned to their barracks, more than enough for joint patrols. With the air-conditioning turned on full blast, a dozen Iraqis and Marines sat uncomfortably around the table, notebooks open. No one was smiling.

Toolan got right to the point. "The Fallujah council agreed yesterday that we are going to patrol together," he said. "The council nominated Colonel Hatim to be the Iraqi brigade commander."

As a Marine interpreter rapidly translated, Toolan leaned forward to look directly at a stern-faced LtCol Hatim in a white shirt and pressed chinos. Originally from Fallujah, the former army officer had returned to his hometown a few days earlier. The story was that he had accused a National Guard unit somewhere to the north of fraud and had to flee for his life. Toolan had authorized Hatim to use a confiscated black

BMW, but Hatim refused, saying that he couldn't be seen working for the Americans. Now Hatim was being offered the senior command.

When Hatim didn't respond one way or the other, Toolan turned to LtCol Suleiman, commanding the 506th Battalion. The mutilation at the trestle bridge happened on March 31, a week after the Marines had taken over from LtCol Drinkwine. The Marines knew Drinkwine admired Suleiman, a solidly-built man with a bristling mustache. But since Fallujah had erupted, Suleiman had stayed in his compound with his few remaining soldiers. Toolan knew him slightly.

"I need leaders from Fallujah to stand up," Toolan said to Suleiman. "We'll equip your men. We need them to live with our Marines twenty-four hours a day for the next few weeks. We'll pay them good money and take care of them."

"They won't do it," Suleiman said, shaking his head.

Toolan looked at a pinched-faced Iraqi sitting next to Suleiman. Lieutenant Colonel Jabar, who commanded the 505th Battalion and took his cues from Suleiman, refused to say anything. The 505th had collapsed at the railroad station on April 13, when LCpl Gray was killed in the searchlight tower.

"You're asking too much," Suleiman said, answering for Jabar. "We cannot do this."

Toolan turned to the police chief, an overweight man who was drinking a second bottle of cold water.

"My police have lost everything," the chief said. "No cars, no equipment. We can do nothing."

"I'll provide cars," Toolan said. "Bring ten or fifteen

of your men tomorrow. I'll have a hundred Marines walking with them, with tanks."

"No walking. We should drive to the city hall [Government Center] together," the chief said. "Marines on the street make the people nervous. It's better to drive to city hall, then leave."

"That's the old way and it didn't work. I was with the 82nd when we drove to city hall in March. We were shot at and the police disappeared," Toolan said. "If someone shoots at us, we are shooting back this time until it is over. We walk, and we choose where we walk."

The Iraqi leaders shook their heads and looked down at their notebooks.

"The people refuse joint patrols," Hatim said. "You can destroy the city, like Hiroshima. I believe in dialogue, not force."

LtCol Olson tried his hand. "Colonel Suleiman, we must build trust together," he said. "Show the people we work together. We won't enter a single house unless we are shot at. Like any city in the world, we must have feet on the ground to know what is going on."

Suleiman shook his head no and looked away.

Hatim, becoming more agitated, ignored Suleiman and leaned across to speak to Toolan. "All is like the war last year. No electricity, no water," he said. "The Americans before you didn't have respect for the people. Drove where they pleased. Many mistakes. I had eighteen years in the army all over Iraq. This is a good city. This fighting is America's fault."

"The city is not safe now, Colonel," Toolan said.

"Together we'll bring safety, and I'll bring money. Forty million dollars. I'm here until October. By then the city will have electricity, clean water, many jobs."

Hatim shrugged and looked down at his hands.

LtCol Byrne tried a different tack. "Colonel Hatim," he said, "can we agree that we share the same goals? We both want the heavy weapons and the foreign fighters removed from the city, do we not?"

"That is an American story. There are no foreign fighters," Hatim said. "Anyone attacking my house, I fight. You are fighting everyone. There is no trust of you. We take care of security by ourselves. If you are not here, there is no problem."

Toolan looked again at Suleiman, who had withdrawn from the conversation. It was impossible to tell whether he was distancing himself from Hatim's remarks or was miffed that the Fallujah council had offered Hatim a position above him.

"My boss," Toolan said to Suleiman, "wants joint patrols."

Suleiman shook his head.

"My soldiers will not come," he said. "They are afraid to be seen with Americans. Their families are afraid. We will not go into Fallujah with you."

———

When the Iraqis left, Toolan told his commanders to stay behind and beckoned to an army staff sergeant sitting in the corner. Staff Sergeant Rashed Qawasimi walked forward and sat next to Toolan.

"Well?" Toolan asked.

Qawasimi, a Palestinian by birth, had the linguist's gift for mimicking local dialects. An intelligence operative, he had worked for Mattis and Toolan a year earlier. He wanted to remain undercover as long as possible, listening but not speaking Arabic.

"Colonel, they won't come around, no matter how many meetings you hold," SSgt Qawasimi said. "Joint patrols are dead. Anyone seen with us ends up with a cut throat."

"What's going on between Hatim and Suleiman?"

"Suleiman's genuinely pissed. You said you were placing Hatim on top of him. His pride is hurt."

"I said the council wanted to do that," Toolan said.

"You're the man, Colonel," Qawasimi said. "You provide the payroll. Council's got squat."

"The Council goes along to get along," Toolan said. "They want Hatim. That means Hatim's acceptable to the other side, and Suleiman's not. I'm not anointing Hatim just yet."

"They're both staying away from us, sir," Qawasimi said. "Joint patrols will never happen."

———

While Toolan was meeting with the Iraqis, Mattis was driving back to division headquarters outside Ramadi. Toolan called Col Dunford to say the joint patrols looked like a nonstarter. Back at the Blue Diamond, Dunford pulled together a dozen officers to assess the alternatives. When Mattis arrived, Dunford began the meeting by saying that the only written guidance was the JTF Warning Order of April 22, advising the division to be prepared to resume offensive operations. The concept of joint patrols had been passed verbally to the division. Now that idea was dead. **We've lost weeks,** Dunford concluded, **and we're back at square one. The division is ready to execute, but the staff doesn't know what's going on at higher levels.**

"If you're not confused," Mattis said, addressing everyone in the room, "then you don't know how confusing the situation is. Now, what's our take on what's going on inside Fallujah?"

The G-2 intelligence staff section and the "G-X" section, specializing in Iraqi personalities and culture, jointly answered. Inside the G-X staff section were several senior Arab Americans born in Arab countries and hired through an American corporation. The real leaders in Iraq weren't the city council, they said; the real leaders were anti-Coalition imams, sheikhs, and former Baathists, many of them thugs, gangsters, and shakedown artists. With the electric power turned off, the sources of news were the mosques, and in most cases the news was stridently anti-American and anti-Baghdad. Petty crime was rampant throughout the city.

Kidnapping was the new growth industry. Some captives were beheaded, but most were ransomed. The criminals had worked out a revenue scale: $5,000 (U.S. currency only) for a truck driver from Baghdad, $15,000 for a driver from Jordan, $50,000 for an employee of a major corporation. The Arab Americans on the division staff said they had not identified any "moderate" leaders who actually had followers inside the city. In Fallujah, if you were nice, you were seen as weak.

"The insurgents have lost up to a thousand killed in the past month," Mattis said. "How long to replace?"

"There are twenty thousand fresh recruits in there," LtCol Groen, the G-2, replied. "There are hundreds of former army officers to act as trainers. Give them a month, and they'll replace all their losses."

"That assumes a sanctuary," Mattis said.

"Sir, it is a sanctuary," Groen said.

"Not for long," Mattis said. "We'll execute our battle plan. We'll clean, hold, and bring in Iraqi security forces. We'll immediately start high-impact projects. Our Seabees are terrific at that. Hire men to truck out the garbage heaps, sweep away the rubble, clean up that shit hole. Offer thousands of jobs. Develop civic pride. Get enthusiasm going. Offer hope that the future's going to be better. Don't let them dwell on the past."

"Sounds good, sir, but the enemy's center of gravity is his intimidation of the people," Groen said. "That requires Iraqi leaders to break through. We can't do that. Once word goes out it's an American idea to clean up, they'll leave their city a shit hole."

"We have no idea how many are hard-core and how many are hangers-on who will shoot at us one day and pick up the garbage the next day," Dunford said. "We don't know where the tipping point is between intimidation and true allegiance. There's no historical precedent for how to defeat an insurgency that has no political cause or leadership hierarchy."

"We're not going to let Fallujah be a sanctuary," Mattis said. "Our guidance remains the Frag-O for offensive ops. When we're done, Governor Burgis owns Fallujah. We're conceding no special status to that city."

———

While Toolan and Mattis were holding their separate meetings, at the MEF Conway had received a phone call from Sanchez with a blunt message. The White House, Sanchez said, would never give the Marines the green light to take the city. The White House was under too much pressure from too many different directions. However, the Marines could remain in a cordon around the city. The White House still wanted the insurgents contained, but with the minimum casualties possible.

It was up to Conway to square that circle. Ambassador Richard Jones had left the MEF earlier that day believing the joint patrols were set for April 27. Since then Toolan had reported the patrols were unlikely. Due to the CIA channel, though, Conway had one ace in the hole.

Since the middle of April, he and his MEF staff had met several times with a team of Iraqis led by former Colonel Latif. A small man with a clipped white mustache, Latif, sixty-six, had been tending his banana trees in quiet retirement in Baghdad, when he had seen Rumsfeld on television discussing Fallujah. Latif contacted his old friend, former Major General Muhammad al Shawany, recently installed by the CIA as Iraq's intelligence chief. Through the CIA Shawany arranged for Latif to meet Conway.

Latif's pitch to Conway was simple: military-to-military relations based on shared professional ties, he stressed, could produce lasting stability. This was a matter for American and Iraqi military men, not politicians, to work out. Latif as a military man could reach out to the former military inside Fallujah.

Conway encouraged Latif, who seemed to have no hidden agenda, was anti-Saddam, and wanted the best for his country. In mid-April Latif met quietly with sheikhs from Fallujah, lauding the exploits of Marines in past battles, warning that Japanese on Iwo Jima and North Vietnamese in Hue City had learned the hard way not to tangle with Marines. This diplomatic touch, whether sincere or obsequious, flattered the listening Marines. How persuasive Latif would be with the insurgents was not clear, but he seemed to be a decent man. "He [Latif] is very well respected by the Iraqi general officers, you can just see the body language between them," Conway later said. "He demonstrates a level of leadership."

Latif brought in Major General Jasim Saleh and a few other former military officers living in Fallujah. When the joint patrols fizzled out, the MEF staff still had Latif's proposal to consider. Provided the Marines turned the city over to them, Saleh and Latif promised to turn insurgents into a Fallujah Brigade that would guarantee peace. As for the National Guard and the police, the Fallujah Brigade would not accept them into their ranks. The brigade would be comprised of former soldiers and insurgents defending their homes, not hacks like Suleiman's National Guard who pretended to fight in order to get a paycheck.

With former Baathists and generals in charge, the Sunnis would see they had a stake in the new Iraq. This would peel away support from the hard-core insurgents. Everything the Marines wanted they could have—provided they never entered the city.

Conway mulled the offer. He could not continue to tie down four battalions—half the division. He could not attack. Joint patrols had failed. Sanchez and Abizaid had offered no alternative. That left the vision proffered by Latif of using Iraqi generals, military men who seemed to share a sense of duty that transcended politics.

19

THE JOLAN GRAVEYARD

ON APRIL 25, THE CONCEPT OF joint patrols, announced by the president the day before, was rejected by the Iraqis who were being asked to risk the lives of their families. While the senior officers at division and MEF mulled what to do, the battalions kept watch on the lines around Fallujah.

Echo Company of Battalion 2/1 held a superb defensive position along the roofs of the city block on the northwestern edge of Jolan District. To their left was a city dump, acres of stinking garbage moldering in the dust. On the right the 3rd Platoon occupied a stout brick schoolhouse. A large cemetery lay to their eastern front, row upon row of headstones and crypts extending for hundreds of meters. For three weeks the Marines had exchanged fire across the cemetery with insurgents who sneaked into abandoned houses, shot for a few minutes, then scooted back a few blocks and mingled with civilians on the streets. Every few days a patrol from Echo poked through the houses on the far side of the cemetery to flush out any lurking snipers.

The next patrol, led by Capt Zembiec, was scheduled to leave the lines at 0400 on April 26. During the night Slayer—the AC-130—had cut down a few gangs, and the usual mortar shells and AK rounds had splattered randomly around the company perimeter. In the quiet before dawn Zembiec led thirty-nine Marines east across the cemetery. He had with him the 2nd Platoon, commanded by Lieutenant Dan Wagner, a Fire Support Team, and several Army special forces soldiers from Task Force 6-26. Zembiec had arranged to have two tanks standing by and had plotted locations for 81mm mortar strikes.

Once the patrol reached the far side of the cemetery, the usual confusion ensued as the point men scaled a six-foot courtyard wall and landed on the other side with thuds, clanks, and muffled curses. The fire team following behind paused, looked around, found an unlocked iron gate, and walked into the courtyard with no bruises. In the dark they set out trip flares and flash-bang grenades as warning devices, then entered two houses on a corner across the street from one another. The Marines searched from room to room, shining flashlights across empty walls, scaring each other as they burst through doorways. The commotion set the half-wild city dogs yapping and scampering down the empty street.

With the first smudges of light, the ululating, high-

pitched call for morning prayers echoed from a minaret two blocks to the north. Marine sentries at the
company position on the west side of the cemetery
warned that men with weapons were running out of
the mosque. Leaving a security detail behind in the
two houses, Zembiec led a patrol north three hundred
meters to the mosque.

After a long search turned up only a few AK rounds,
in the dawn light the Marines returned to the two
houses—neat, two-story tan-colored cement dwellings with flat, walled roofs and wide terraces off the
upstairs bedrooms. Set slightly back from the street
and shaded by a few palm trees, the houses would not
look out of place in southern Florida. About half
the Marines went with Zembiec into the house on the
southern corner of a paved street that ran east into the
city. Wagner took the others into the house directly
across the street on the northern side. The western
sides of both houses could be clearly seen from the
company defenses across the cemetery. On the east,
the houses were hugged by dozens of buildings, extending block after block, a maze of courtyards and
walls. After posting guards outside, the Marines inside
the houses rummaged through their daypacks for
oranges, crackers, and jalapeño cheese. For a day patrol they had come light on food and heavy on water
and ammunition, with three hundred rounds for each
M16 and fourteen hundred rounds for each SAW.

One moment they were sitting in the living rooms
and kitchens drinking water and munching on bread.
The next moment bullets were pelting the outside

walls like wind-driven rain. Salvos of dozens of RPG rockets were sailing by, hitting the telephone wires and palm trees, exploding with crumbling sounds in puffs of black smoke. The Marines were hit from the houses right next door, from adjoining courtyards and from farther down the street to the east. The insurgents hit both houses at once with a volume of fire that sounded like a radial saw, dozens of automatic weapons simultaneously tearing through magazines, the faces of the two houses peeling away in streams of gray dust, bullets pelting the cement surfaces and thwacking off at a thousand angles.

Out on the street the four Marines on guard flopped down and fired back. No one was firing at them, and they couldn't see any targets to shoot, so they threw rounds downrange at what they thought were likely firing positions. Lance Corporal Jeremiah Anderson lay prone outside Wagner's house and watched RPG rockets explode high in the trees. Seeing flashes from an alley to the east, he fired burst after burst in that direction.

In the first few moments it seemed to be raining rocket-propelled grenades, some streaking straight in like bullets, and others fired from adjoining streets, plunging down like mortar shells. In Zembiec's house on the south side, Private First Class Bernard Boykin counted six rocket hits against the outside wall next to the window he was guarding. In the north house, Lance Corporal John Sleight felt the floor shudder a bit as a rocket struck. While lacking the wallop to push through the cement walls, the RPGs burst loose thousands of cement chips that could lacerate and flay human flesh.

Lt Wagner quickly organized a two-tier defense. In the kitchen he stationed an SAW and an M203 gunner, while on the roof he sent in a machine-gun team and a sniper. The RPGs were now exploding on the outside walls as the insurgents aimed for the open windows. "Board 'em up!" Wagner yelled.

The Marines piled tables, couches, and drawers against the windows, leaving only small cracks to fire out. Sergeant John Neary peeked through a firing hole and saw a man in the open window next door, not fifteen feet away, loading an RPG. The man's face filled the red aim point in Neary's optical scope. When Neary squeezed the trigger, the man's face burst apart and the scope flared in a pink mist, causing Neary to flinch.

The Marines had a big problem. While they had been diverted at the mosque, hundreds of insurgents had sneaked through the back alleys and into the houses next door. Major Bellon, the intelligence officer for the regiment, had listened to radio intercepts suggesting the insurgents had organized a mobile reserve that moved in buses and trucks. Now, at nine in the morning the UAV hovering over the city was sending to regiment a live video feed of taxis and pickup trucks scurrying northwest into the Jolan District, where the battle was raging.

Wagner, a native of southern California, had loved visiting his relatives in central Pennsylvania, because the backyards were large enough for him to play baseball, his favorite sport. Now he was desperately wishing for a yard big enough to separate his Marines from the insurgents who had sneaked in next door, so close a man could leap from one roof to the next. The insurgents next door were leaning out the windows and over the low walls of the roof, firing wildly at point-blank range.

Corporal Richard Koci led his four-man machine-gun team up the outside stairs to the roof, with AK rounds bouncing off the cement of the steps. They dashed to the low wall next to the house occupied by the insurgents and hammered out a mousehole for the barrel of their machine gun. From nearby roofs, dozens of gunmen blazed away at them. Koci fired at the adjacent roof, hearing screams of pain and the screech of orders.

In city fights, protection means staying behind a cement wall. Shooters dart out, fire a burst from the hip, and duck back again, or they lie flat on a roof, stick the barrel over the low wall, and pull the trigger. So much hot metal flies downrange that sooner or later someone gets hit. The house next door to Wagner's group had a slightly higher roof, and the insurgents were lobbing down grenades. Eventually one found the range, wounding all four Marines around the gun. Lance Corporal Zackory Fincannon went down with severe wounds to his shoulder and arm. Koci grabbed Fincannon and the four staggered down the stairs and into the safety of the kitchen.

Not all Marines fought with equal skill or ferocity. One was reluctant to fire his rifle, and Wagner set him to collecting and redistributing ammunition. Most fought with a "battle buddy" in teams of two, encouraging and helping each other. And some were exceptional warriors. The bull in Wagner's platoon was Lance Corporal Carlos Gomez-Perez, a heavily muscled fireplug of a man who responded instantly in battle.

"What do you want me to do?" Gomez shouted at Wagner above the roar of the battle.

"Get up on the roof and throw grenades!" Wagner yelled back. "Don't let them get on top of us!"

Gomez's family had emigrated from Mexico in the early 1990s, and he had struggled to learn English. When he had returned from his first tour in Iraq, he plodded through the paperwork and qualified for citizenship. Governor Arnold Schwarzenegger swore him in at Camp Pendleton.

Gomez led a fire team up the outside stairs. They all knew the risk: on the roof bullets were cracking by. The Marines could hear them, snapping and hissing, some high, some low. They crouched, sprinted to the wall, and put out a fire caused by a Molotov cocktail, kicking clear of the flames a belt of 40mm grenade rounds. They threw down the stairs the damaged 240 Golf machine gun, a Mark 40 sniper rifle, and a PRC-119 radio. Then they crouched behind the low wall and hurled grenades up at the insurgents hiding on the adjacent roof.

On the street below, insurgents were arcing RPG rockets and dropping mortar rounds, trying to hit the four SAW gunners lying flat and covering the corner approaches to the two houses. A blast from an RPG rocked Lance Corporal John Paul Flores, and as he shook off the concussion, he felt wet, as though he had been in a shower. He stumbled into the north house and limped up the stairs to the kitchen.

"Sir," he said to Wagner, "I'm shot, I'm shot."

Flores was bleeding from his right arm and leg. Corpsman Benjamin Liotta hurried over but after one glance concluded he couldn't extract a piece of metal protruding from Flores's leg.

"It's a scratch," Liotta said. "It'll heal itself."

"I'm bleeding out," Flores said. "At least stop the bleeding."

"Flores, you're nuts," Wagner said, desperate not to lose the firepower of the SAW. "Get back out there and kill someone."

Flores limped down the stairs, passing his friend Lance Corporal Juan Sanchez.

"Dog," Sanchez said, "you're not going home. So conserve ammo. Long day coming."

"Fuck," Flores said, hobbling back outside.

A machine gun was hammering away from the east, RPG rockets were streaking by, grenades were exploding, and AK rounds cracked and snapped through the air. The SAW gunners were lying prone against the corners of the courtyard wall, and the bullets were snapping well above their heads. The insurgents seemed as intent at chipping away at the cement walls as at finding individual targets. Flores ripped through a two-hundred-round drum, momentarily reducing the amount of incoming fire. As he switched out the overheated barrel on the SAW, Capt Zembiec sprinted across the street and into the house.

"Can you hold?" Zembiec asked Wagner. "I'm calling for tanks and eighty-ones."

"We're good as long as I have the roof covered," Wagner said. "Fincannon's arm is really messed up. We need to evac him now."

"How many wounded you got?"

"Six, eight, I don't know. Liotta keeps patching them up and sending them outside. Fincannon's really hurting, though."

"I'll get on it," Zembiec said. "TAC one's clobbered. The whole goddamn world wants to talk to me. I'll go over the company net to get a medevac down here."

Zembiec opened the front door, waited while Flores laid down a long burst of suppressive fire, then dashed back across the street to the south house. Flores came into the north house for more ammo, and immediately the volume of enemy fire increased.

"We need to suppress! Somebody get outside!" Wagner yelled. "Don't sit on your asses!"

Lance Corporal Thomas Adametz rushed out with his SAW, momentarily grasping the barrel in his left hand and burning it badly. "Fuuuck!" he screamed, standing erect, wildly spraying bullets down the street, screaming at the top of his lungs, his welder-type shooter goggles completing the image of a man completely berserk. The Marines inside the house cheered and hollered. Flores said he looked like the wild machine-gunner in the movie **Full Metal Jacket.** When his drum was empty, Adametz ran inside, and

Lance Corporal Craig Bell took his turn in the tag game, shambling out with an I-don't-give-a-damn attitude, popping off a half-dozen 40mm rounds from his 203, then ambling back inside with a strut.

The small-arms fire was not abating. From the center of the Jolan District to the east, taxis were dropping off gunmen as though they were commuting to work. Zembiec received a radio report that a UAV was tracking two buses headed his way. The Jolan was the heart of the Fallujah defenses and the lair of the archterrorist Zarqawi. The "cease-fire" had provided the insurgents with weeks to organize their interior lines, and they were responding with reinforcements. From their perspective, this could be the beginning of the final attack that LtGen Conway had promised a few days earlier.

Lance Corporal Joshua Hill, lying behind his SAW across the street from Flores, watched as a truck with wooden slats slowed down as it crossed an intersection three hundred meters to the east. Hill saw at least twenty men standing up in the truck bed, hanging on to the slats. He sighted in and held down the trigger, sending dozens of rounds smashing into the wood and flesh, firing until the truck crawled out of view. Hill knew he should fire two hundred rounds, then change out a barrel and let it cool for fifteen minutes. He had burned through twelve hundred rounds, and still the insurgents were returning more fire than the Marines were putting out. Hill laid the red-hot barrel on his bipod and attached his third and last barrel. Smelling acrid smoke, he saw that the sizzling barrel had welded to the plastic on the bipod. He searched around for a substitute brace.

The insurgents in the adjoining house, no longer under fire from the roof, pressed forward. A small silver-colored grenade bounced off the outdoor steps to the roof and dribbled into the kitchen.

"Grenade!"

Eight Marines went flat, and the exploding shrapnel missed all except Lance Corporal Rafael Valencia, who felt his right leg go numb.

"I'm hit," he said as he collapsed in slow motion to the floor.

Liotta rolled him onto his stomach, slit open his trouser leg, and saw an ugly gash in the calf, with what could have been a chunk of metal. It was hard to tell with the blood gushing out, and Liotta didn't want to poke around with a forceps and pull out a tendon instead.

"Valencia, stop acting," Liotta said in his best bedside manner.

"At least stop the bleeding," Valencia said. "Then I'm out of here." Valencia thought, **Time to go back outside.**

Liotta wrapped a pressure bandage around the wound, and before Wagner could say a word, Valencia limped down the stairs and back into the fight.

The insurgents next door were peppering the north side of the house with rounds. LCpl Sleight was ducking instinctively and watched in amazement as Sgt Neary poked his rifle out the window at an angle and shot a man in the neck. Sleight saw another man with an AK leap up and run away. As the pressure against the north side of the house eased, Liotta radioed to the south house for help. He had eight wounded, two in tight tourniquets and three with metal sticking out of them. He needed an experienced medic to guide him.

Across the street in the south house, Zembiec was on the roof with a team of snipers, including Larry, from special Task Force 6-26. Delta Force soldiers like Larry were spread out in all the rifle companies, lending an unofficial hand. Larry had taken some shrapnel in the face and, like the five other Marines and Delta soldiers on the roof, had laid aside his sniper rifle to pitch grenades. Zembiec thought their position was secure. It was the casualties, not the fighting, that concerned him. No helicopter could evacuate the wounded from this beehive, and he didn't have an armored ambulance to call forward.

The forward air controller, Capt Michael Martino—call sign Oprah—was waiting for two Cobras to arrive. Battalion had refused the request for mortar support, lacking precise targets in a district teeming with civilians. Zembiec had yelled and yelled over the company radio net to bring forward the two tanks. In the din of the battle, he couldn't hear the response and kept shouting his coordinates.

"Red Three and Four, this is War Hammer. I am at eight four nine nine two six. When at my pos? Over."

The battalion and company frequencies on the PRC-148 had been cluttered with too many people asking him too many dumb questions, so he had put it aside and talked with Wagner over their handheld radio. When he picked up the 148 to again call the tanks, the company first sergeant came on the net.

"War Hammer six," 1/Sgt Skiles said, "I'm Oscar Mike in a Hummer. ETA three mikes. Out." Skiles would arrive in three minutes—in an unarmored Humvee.

Through a mouse hole in the terrace wall, Zembiec studied the street. A well-known wrestler at the Naval Academy, Zembiec was accustomed to concentrating on an opponent. He had never felt this alive and focused. His brain was whirling, anticipating the next move. The machine gun to the east and the AKs were still firing. Zembiec had counted more than sixty RPG rockets in the initial attack and another fifty since then. Now there was a lull in the rocket fire. **They're out of rockets,** he thought. **Poor fire discipline.** He beckoned to Dan, the Delta medic.

"Ready to run for it?"

Dan nodded. At twenty-eight, Dan was the youngest of the Delta soldiers with Echo Company. He was also calm, steady, and superbly trained in shock trauma medicine, treated as the leader by the younger navy corpsmen. The two men sprinted across the fire-swept street and up the stairs to Wagner's redoubt in the kitchen.

"Let's get the most seriously wounded downstairs," Zembiec said.

As the wounded were carried down, a Humvee skidded to a stop outside the house, rounds hitting the wall behind them. To Skiles, it sounded like a hundred angry bees were buzzing around him, and he wondered how they were going to make it back out. An empty AK magazine struck Skiles on his shoulder, and he pointed his 9mm pistol at the nearest roof but saw no one.

The Cobra helicopters had just arrived and were skimming back and forth, trying to frighten the shooters off the rooftops while aiming their guns farther to the east, the empty brass tinkling on the street. The SAW gunners were ripping both sides of the street, screaming at them to get the wounded the fuck out of there before they all were killed. As the corpsmen rushed the wounded out, a grenade bounced off the hood of the Humvee and sputtered out harmlessly.

Valencia helped to carry out four wounded, anxious for the Humvee to escape before an RPG rocket found it. He then lay down and fired up the street, yelling for 1/Sgt Skiles to get the hell out of there. When a Marine who had driven in with Skiles handed Valencia a fresh M16 magazine, Valencia thought, **What's he doing? Why's he not shooting?** Valencia grabbed the magazine, slapped it home, and resumed firing.

Wagner was crouched next to the Humvee when he heard through his handheld radio that he had another serious casualty on the roof. As Doc Liotta and Dan ran back up the stairs, Wagner shook his head.

"Too much fire, First Sergeant!" he yelled. "This Hummer is going to be chewed to pieces. Take off now."

With four wounded, the makeshift ambulance turned around and drove out of the maelstrom.

Wagner went back into the house just as Doc Liotta and Dan carried another Marine down from the roof. Behind them on the outside steps, Gomez was tearing through M16 magazines to suppress the enemy fire.

"Roof's clear," Gomez told Wagner. "No one can survive up there."

Gomez slumped in a corner while Liotta and Dan went to work on Lance Corporal Aaron Cole Austin, who had been shot in the shoulder, the bullet exiting his chest above his heart, a grievous wound.

"Tell my fiancée I love her," Austin mumbled.

"Tell her yourself, man," Lance Corporal Jose Cruz said. "You're getting out of here."

Gomez had a cut on his face and sat on the cement stairs leading to the roof, dripping blood and muttering that he should have done more. Walking past him, Liotta slipped in a puddle of blood. He looked more closely at Gomez and saw that the top of his right shoulder had been ripped away, leaving a hole the size of a Pepsi can. A round from a heavy machine gun had gouged out enough muscle to rip the arm off a normal-size man. Wagner looked at him in alarm.

"Sorry, sir," Gomez said, embarrassed to be out of the fight.

"You're a beast, Gomez," Wagner said.

Liotta bandaged the wound and turned to Austin, who had struggled to his feet and fumbled for his rifle.

"Gotta get back," Austin mumbled.

Wagner helped Liotta restrain the severely injured

Marine. In shock and a morphine haze, Austin weakly hit Wagner in the face.

"It's okay, Austin," Wagner said, laying him back down. "It's okay. You've done your job."

———

In the house across the street Zembiec was crouched on the roof, trying to figure out how to get out the other wounded. He glanced down at some movement in the side alley and saw a man pointing an AK right at him. He leaped back as bullets chipped the cement between his legs. He felt like he had been kicked in the balls and stumbled back, looking down at the tear where a spent bullet had ricocheted off the ceramic groin protector attached to his armored vest. It looked like a drooping diaper—Zembiec had felt a bit foolish wearing it that morning. His future progeny safe for the moment, he flipped a grenade down into the alley and turned his attention back to directing in the over-due tanks. Zembiec had more wounded to get out.

Downstairs Sergeant Joshua Magana had been out-side guarding the rear courtyard when he was shot, then was dragged inside by Sergeant Nunez and Staff Sergeant Willie Gresham. Corpsman Everett Watt pulled down Magana's pants and saw that the bullet had hit him in the buttock and exited through his pelvis.

"It hurts, man," Magana said as Watt rolled him on his side. "I can't feel my arm."

"That's 'cause you're lying on it," Watt said.

Watt didn't like the situation one bit, though. A yellowish tube protruded from the stomach wound, and Watt gently packed the entrails in battle dressings and applied an Ace bandage while Magana clutched a crucifix and a picture of his wife and daughter. After a while, he stopped staring at the picture and lay still, a blank expression on his face. In the south house, Gresham saw the unexpected Humvee and grasped Magana under the armpits, dragging him toward the back door just as mortar shells exploded in the courtyard.

"Where are we going, Staff Sergeant?" Magana said. "I want to go home."

"Not this way, we're not," Gresham said. "We're staying inside. You'll catch the next ride."

He lowered Magana to the floor in the kitchen.

"Take this letter." Magana held out a letter from his wife.

"Bring it home yourself."

Up on the roof Zembiec heard the sharp **bang** of a tank main gun, sounding like a giant sledgehammer hitting a manhole cover, and looked up to see the minaret at the mosque buckle and pitch forward. **It's about time,** he thought. The tankers assured him they were two minutes out, approaching from the schoolhouse to the west. They had been driven back once by a torrent of RPG fire, concerned about being struck in the rear. Now they were advancing with a platoon of riflemen covering them from the school.

Zembiec contacted Wagner over the handhelds. "We're getting the wounded back, Ben," he said.

"When the tanks get here, we're hoofing it. I'm coming across."

Again Zembiec darted across the fire-swept street and into the north house. In the main room on the second floor, Sanchez was applying CPR to Austin; Dan and Liotta had performed a tracheotomy to ease his breathing.

Zembiec ripped down a door. "Carry him on that," he said.

The walking wounded went out first, followed by Wagner and three others carrying Austin on the door, his shirt off, breathing hoarsely. Going downstairs, they slipped in the blood and Liotta caught Austin, hugging him to his chest and stumbling backward across the street. Liotta's foot tripped a wire, and he fell. There was a brilliant flash of light, and he rolled on top of Austin to absorb the blast. Nothing happened.

Thank God, he thought, **it's only a trip flare.**

Then hands were pulling them both up and propelling them into the south house. Lance Corporal Chris Hankins crossed last as the rear guard. He had gone out that morning with twenty-three magazines; he was down to two. They could hear the tank treads around the corner, and Zembiec ran back to the roof and grabbed his PRC-148.

"Red Four, pull into the street in front of us and fire to the east. We're getting the wounded back to the schoolhouse."

On the roof next to Zembiec, Lance Corporal Lucas Seielstad felt a hammer hit him in the right arm.

Dazed, he stumbled down the stairs and into the main room, where PFC Boykin was firing out a window.

"Oh shit," Seielstad said.

"Oh shit what?" Boykin said.

Seielstad gestured with his jaw at a bullet sticking out of his right bicep. "Looks cool," he said.

In shock and with a fractured right leg, he sat down and tugged off his glove, blood and chunks of flesh dropping onto the floor.

"What's that?" Seielstad said.

"Man, you're all messed up," Boykin said.

Zembiec looked around. Staff Sergeant Gresham was organizing the thirty-five Marines for the three-hundred-meter dash west to the schoolhouse, where 3rd Platoon was providing covering fire. Zembiec hesitated, then sprinted back to the north house, running alone up the stairs to the empty kitchen.

"Is anyone here? Marines? Any Marines here?"

He knew his questions sounded ridiculous, but he had to make sure. It was spooky, standing in a puddle of blood, yelling in an empty house, the sounds of the AKs, M16s, and .50 calibers on the tanks hammering away outside.

Careful not to slip in the blood, he scampered back down the stairs and ran across the street to the south house. Gresham was shepherding everyone out the back door and forming them up into teams in the walled courtyard. Zembiec went up to the roof for a final look around. Two Delta operators, Don and Larry, were glassing the rooftops, looking for targets. Below them a tank main gun fired, followed a few seconds later by the other.

"Fire's died down," Don said. "We can stay."

Don, Zembiec knew, was a master sergeant. His flat statement was almost a challenge. Larry, who was bleeding at the neck, nodded in agreement. They wanted to continue the battle.

"I have two urgent wounded," Zembiec said. "We've been killing these fuckers for a month. They'll be here tomorrow. Come on, let's go."

"Let me shoot my thermo," Don said.

To the envy of the Marines, Delta had brought some neat grenades and disposable one-shot rockets called thermobarics—new explosives that drove up the overpressure in confined spaces, creating tremendous destruction.

"All right, then we're out of here."

With Zembiec and Larry providing suppressive fire, Don knelt, aimed at the window on a troublesome house a block away, and fired the rocket. There was a muffled **whump!** as a corner of the building crumbled. Satisfied, the three ran downstairs. In the courtyard, Gresham lined everyone up two by two. No one was to make the run alone; every Marine had a battle buddy. Those with severe wounds were carried out first, followed by the walking wounded. Magana lay on a metal door, a Marine carrying each corner.

"Hey, you need to cover that approach," he said in a morphine-induced slur, gesturing vaguely around.

"Got you covered, bro."

The 3rd Platoon wanted to move forward to help. Zembiec told them to hold their position, fearing a loss of control and friendly fire if some Marines rushed forward while others pushed back. It was only three hundred meters, and they could see the schoolhouse. No way they could get lost or separated.

While the two tanks sat in the intersection and pounded both sides of the street, the wounded were carried out the back of the courtyard. The insurgents on the roofs saw what was happening and began yelling. Out of sight of the tanks, some ran down back alleys, firing from the hip whenever they glimpsed the withdrawing Marines. Behind the wounded, the rear guard of able-bodied Marines departed the courtyard in pairs. When it was LCpl Sleight's turn to go, he took off at full speed, head down, trying to make himself a small target. After running half a block, he glanced around for his battle buddy. No one was there. He looked back—and stared into the gun barrel of an Abrams tank. The tank commander was standing upright in the turret, waving both arms frantically, gesturing to Sleight to come back. He had been running full tilt the wrong way, heading for the center of the city. Sleight quickly scurried back.

For the first two hundred meters, Wagner carried Austin. Once he had to cross a ditch by embracing Austin in his arms. Both were covered with blood and sweat, and Austin kept slipping and fighting against Wagner's embrace. Wagner took that as a good sign that Austin would make it. When Wagner ran out of steam,

Sergeant Jason Rettenberger carried the wounded Marine. But LCpl Austin eventually succumbed to his wounds.

Corporal Joshua Carpenter had taken shrapnel wounds to his eyes fighting next to Zembiec on the roof. Corpsman Watt had placed a bandage over his eyes, shouldered both their packs, and was running with Carpenter by the hand, the rounds cracking around them and brass from the hovering gunship hitting them on the helmets. It was noon, and they had been fighting for their lives for three hours. Watt couldn't believe how exhausted he was. Getting to the schoolhouse with the two packs seemed like the longest run of his life. Toward the end he was wheezing and his stride faltered. He slowed to a walk.

Having none of that, Carpenter kept tugging at him. "Doc, why are we slowing down? Speed it up, man. I can hear those bullets."

Boykin and Liotta were supporting Seielstad, who hobbled along, blood dripping out of the right side of his mouth, his right arm dangling, his right leg bloody, fractured, and wobbling. Rounds were zinging by, and they were almost home.

"Motherfucker, you're going to get me shot. Hurry up," Boykin said to encourage Seielstad, who cursed back at his friend.

Zembiec, Don, and Larry brought up the rear. Don, the Delta command sergeant major, was the last to leave the field of battle.

The Jolan battle subsided shortly after noon on

April 26. Seventeen of the thirty-nine Marines had been wounded. The company loved the story that trickled back about LCpl Fincannon. Badly wounded in his left arm, LCpl Fincannon was being carried to a plane in Germany when the secretary of defense walked by.

"Don!" Fincannon had yelled. "Any word on Echo Company?"

———

Though shaken by how the insurgents had sneaked up on them, the Marines had taken care of one another, later laughing at their fears. The man who stood out in their eyes was LCpl Gomez. He was every man's image of a Marine—tough, stoic, determined, and caring. In the school courtyard Echo Company held a farewell ceremony and painted a sign for Cpl Austin, with a colored flag of his home state and the words "Texas stands proud."

For the next few days, Zembiec ran the battle over and over in his mind, looking for a way to get Austin out. "I pray," Zembiec said. "I mean, for my men, not for something selfish like myself or winning the lottery."

At an afternoon mass on the third floor of the apartment building housing the company, Father Devine, the division chaplain, gave a simple sermon.

"I was out with recon on a river patrol the other day," he said. "We searched a small boat. Instead of being angry at us, the two fishermen offered us the one fish they had caught. They didn't do it because they were afraid. They were good, simple men. Not all Iraqis hate us."

Before the mass ended, from the roof came the heavy **crack!** of the .50 caliber sniper rifle.

———

For Echo Company, April 26 was another day during a one-sided cease-fire that had extended for seventeen days. It made no difference if the insurgents lost a hundred men each time they fought. They had overwhelming manpower to send into the meat grinder. A war of attrition against Marines pinned to fixed lines created the ideal battlefield for them. The Jolan battle was the sort of encounter that could happen any day along the lines.

"The only thing the insurgents understand is violence," Zembiec said. "I think we need to go on the offensive."

20

A DEAL WITH THE DEVIL

LTGEN CONWAY HAD MONITORED ZEM-BIEC'S fight on April 26. One more Marine killed and seventeen wounded. That afternoon he decided to take Latif up on his offer. The Marines would pull out, and Latif and four or five hundred armed Iraqis—some former soldiers, some insurgents, some both—would take over the city.

"I didn't want my Marines sitting in a cordon," Conway said. "I called General Abizaid first to get some support, because I anticipated Sanchez might balk at the idea. But that didn't happen. Instead of an argument, I got an okay from both of them to try the alternative."

Conway told Latif and his deputy, MajGen Saleh, that the Marines would stay out of Fallujah and support the Fallujah Brigade with money and arms. In return, the brigade would ensure a real cease-fire. "In a very few days our first convoy will move through Fallujah. General Saleh will be expected to provide security," LtGen Conway said. "He'll do it, or we'll find someone who can."

The division, from Mattis through the battalion commanders, was quietly informed that Iraqis under Iraqi generals would replace the Marines on the lines. The MEF intended to gain "a strategic victory from a tactical defeat" by reenergizing the Sunni community, empowering former Baathists, and providing the basis for an Iraqi army.

The responses from the division were negative. Those opposed argued that "we are turning security over to the same guys we are fighting." The agreement was called "a deal with the devil." Because Sheikh Janabi, among others, had endorsed it, that meant the fix was in for the insurgents. With the Marines agreeing to stay out of the city indefinitely, the insurgents would take charge.

Asked for his judgment, Maj Bellon, Toolan's intelligence officer, said, "We're letting the muj off the canvas. They'll use Fallujah as a base to hit us."

Marines, however, adhere to iron discipline. The MEF was informing, not consulting the division. The decision stood as a done deal, and that was that. No leak sprang from the Marine ranks. Latif agreed to a series of meetings to work out the details before a public announcement was made.

In the meantime the fighting continued. On the night of April 27 the insurgents attacked Zembiec's lines, and the Marines responded with the AC-130 gunship, tanks, and machine guns. An Australian camera crew on a rooftop captured an hour of spectacular red explosions and streams of orange tracers, fed live to Baghdad. A Sunni cleric featured on Al Jazeera screamed, "They are killing children! They are trying to destroy everything!" Not to be outdone, the president of the Iraqi Governing Council repeated the charge that the Americans had changed from "an army of liberation" to "an army of occupation."

The next day the JTF spokesman, BrigGen Kimmitt, cited eleven violations of the cease-fire in the past twenty-four hours, charging that the civic leaders "had not delivered" on their promises. Outside Fallujah, Toolan had driven to the western side of Queens, where LtCol Kyser was pushing up with Battalion 2/2 against steady mortar and machine-gun fire. To straighten out the defensive lines, MajGen Mattis had authorized Kyser to move north and tie in with 1/5 on the right flank. Battalion 2/2 had taken seven wounded the day before, as small gangs in taxis and rumpled old cars drove down from the city, got out, and ran into abandoned houses, fired from several hundred meters away, and darted off. The streets were strewn with rubble, and each time the Marines moved forward, they found sandbags, binoculars, bipods, empty shells, and bloody bandages. Bullets snapped overhead.

"They're in that house six hundred meters to our front," Kyser said.

"If you have positive ID, take it out," Toolan said.

"Each time?" Kyser asked, not sure what a cease-fire meant.

"If you're under fire, you're in a fight," Toolan said. "Take it out."

Toolan and Kyser stood on the rooftop while the air officer, Captain Neil Sanders, picked up the handset of his radio.

"Ninety-nine Aircraft, this is Swami. Marines in southwest Fallujah in contact. Any aircraft audible?"

An air force AWACS command and control aircraft answered, giving Swami the frequency to reach Bud 2-1, two F-16s in a holding pattern south of the city.

"Bud two-one, this is Swami. Target is a house at eight six one two eight nine zero four. Forward friendly troops at eight six zero three eight eight four three. I'll talk you on."

Both Swami and Bud 2-1 were looking at the same 1:8,000 scale photomap with five-meter imagery that showed every one of the more than 24,000 houses in the city.

"Bud two-one, from the mosque at Donna and Henry, go three blocks south. There's an open field, right? Okay, go west one block. See the end house facing south? How many windows on the top floor?"

"Swami, there are two, with arches."

Swami turned to Kyser and Toolan. "I'll bring them in on a twenty mike-mike run east to west, then GBU it."

Kyser nodded. A few minutes later a burst of 20mm explosive rounds raised dust along the south wall of the house.

"Bud two-one, that was dead-on."

The Marines stayed under cover while a five-hundred-pound GBU, or guided bomb unit, blew through the roof of the targeted house and collapsed the walls. Toolan drove back to his headquarters, and Battalion 2/2 moved steadily forward.

In the forty-eight hours since Conway had approved the Fallujah Brigade, air force, navy, and Marine warplanes had dropped three dozen laser-guided bombs in Fallujah, destroying ten houses holding snipers or machine guns in 2/2's area. No civilians were seen in the area. Kyser appeared to be pressing up against the main line of resistance.

———

By April 29 Iraqi circles in Baghdad were buzzing with rumors about Baathists or former generals returning to power. Tony Perry, embedded with Battalion 2/1, decided to stake out the Fallujah Liaison Center and see who was meeting with whom. LtCol Suleiman drove up, accompanied by LtCol Jabar. That was normal and Perry was thinking he had wasted the day when MajGen Saleh strode into the narrow courtyard in his green uniform from Saddam's era, with the red beret and epaulets showing his rank. Latif, in an old blue suit and tie, walked behind Saleh, benevolently beaming at Suleiman's excited National Guard troops, who were leaping to their feet, saluting, smiling, and murmuring about "the generals."

Saleh swept by Suleiman without acknowledging him and disappeared into the conference room. Lieutenant General Conway and MajGen Mattis arrived a few minutes later and went into the conference room. Suleiman, red with anger, began spouting in English about "insult, insult." Toolan hurried over to take Suleiman and Jabar into a side office.

Perry stood against the wall, scribbling into his notebook. "The exotic life of the foreign correspondent," he said as Toolan walked by, shaking his head.

Behind the closed door Toolan, with SSgt Qawasimi translating, tried to calm Suleiman down. You have disgraced Jabar and me, Suleiman said. My goals in the city are like yours. First you put Hatim over me and now this. You don't know Hatim. I don't know him. I know Saleh. He is your enemy.

"Your men ran away," Toolan said.

"That is no reason to go over to the enemy," Suleiman replied. "Tell this new brigade to stay outside the city with you, like soldiers. Let me and the police go into the city. If they go into the city, you are finished."

"I will continue to support you," Toolan promised.

"You are in trouble," Suleiman said as he left, with Jabar trailing behind.

Toolan knew the score. A month ago the Marine plan had been to regain control block by block alongside the National Guard. That plan had walked out the door with Suleiman's tattered pride. The die was cast. The MEF had thrown in with a new team led by Latif, Hatim, and Saleh.

A few hours later the main meeting broke up. Perry pounced on Saleh as he walked out. "Are you a general?" Perry asked. "How do you spell your name?"

"Yes, I am in charge of the city," Saleh proudly answered.

Conway and Mattis ruefully said a few words, and Perry rushed off to file the story that the Marines had turned the city over to the Fallujah Brigade. That evening in Baghdad, Bremer read the story online, together with a scathing memo from the CPA diplomats in Anbar Province. The memo confirmed Perry's account that the Fallujah Brigade would replace the Marines immediately. The memo described the arrangement as a "stunning victory for the ACF [anti-Coalition forces] . . . the 'Brigade' will not fight the ACF." The memo ended by urging Bremer and the JTF to overturn the MEF's decision, adding that many Marines opposed it as well.

Bremer, who had not been consulted or notified about the brigade, was furious. A year earlier the president had relieved Central Command of authority over the creation of the new Iraq and had given that responsibility to Bremer, who promptly abolished the Iraqi Army. Now CentCom had turned around and appointed Iraqi generals to create a Sunni brigade to take control of a Sunni city-state. Many Shiites would see this as a double-cross. The American military would appear to be rewarding Sunni insurgents with paying jobs inside a sanctuary while gunning down Shiite youths who supported Sadr. Following less than a week after Bremer's edict authorizing the rehiring of Baathists, it would appear that Bremer had set the Shiites up, heightening political paranoia among

Shiites already suspicious that the Americans were working behind the scenes against the emergence of a Shiite democratic majority.

"This is an absolute disaster," Bremer said.

Ambassadors in Baghdad called CPA officials in the province. What are the Marines doing? they asked. Are they retreating? The officials said they didn't know; they hadn't been consulted. The last they had heard, the Marines wanted to finish the fight.

The CPA memo of dissent to CentCom's decision was read over the phone to Secretary of State Colin Powell, who was traveling in Germany. Powell demurred becoming involved in a tangle between the generals and the president's envoy to Iraq. Abizaid had already called a deeply skeptical Secretary of Defense Rumsfeld, advancing the argument that the Sunnis had to be given the chance of showing they could govern themselves responsibly. Rumsfeld agreed to back the decision made in the field, but his senior staff were not happy to be handed a fait accompli without having had a chance to discuss it.

The Iraqi national security adviser, Mowaffak Rubaie, and the interim defense minister, Ali Alawi, protested strongly to Bremer, calling the agreement "appeasement" and warning that the deal would backfire. The CIA station chief told Bremer that his agency had not been involved, saying he did not know by what channel Gen Shawany, the Iraqi intelligence chief, had communicated with LtGen Conway. Conway had said both Latif and Saleh had been vetted through the proper channels, but Shiite officials immediately accused Saleh of past repression and ongoing insurgent activities.

In ordinary times a major policy decision like the Fallujah Brigade would have been thoroughly vetted and debated by various staffs and been the subject of several sivits meetings among the principals. Instead Rumsfeld, Abizaid, and Sanchez said little about the Fallujah Brigade; all three knew they faced a much more politically charged crisis. For weeks their staffs had been investigating allegations of Iraqi prisoner abuse. The issue had not yet gone public.

At the same time that an angry Ambassador Bremer was reading cables from CPA diplomats in Fallujah recommending an overturn of the Fallujah Brigade concept, digital pictures of abused Iraqi prisoners at Abu Ghraib prison, ten miles east of Fallujah, suddenly ignited a worldwide firestorm of press and political attention. On April 29, CBS showed graphic pictures taken by American guards that depicted American soldiers forcing Iraqi men to lie naked in piles and stand blindfolded on stools with wires attached to their fingers, believing they would be electrocuted if they moved. As U.S. senators profusely apologized to the world, the press was bombarding defense officials for explanations about their roles in the scandal.

The entire American military effort in Iraq stood on trial for the injustices and criminal acts of a few. The president said the matter deserved the most immediate and thorough attention of the Pentagon. Congress demanded an examination of the policy directives by

Secretary of Defense Rumsfeld. Gen Abizaid received queries about the orders he gave to his subordinates, while LtGen Sanchez became the object of several high-level investigations. The political hurricane swept through Washington and Baghdad on April 29, blowing away any senior review of the precipitate decision to turn Fallujah over to the former Iraqi generals.

With the senior ranks of government preoccupied with a public scandal of the greatest proportions, Bremer could generate no consensus to overturn the Fallujah Brigade. Having urged the cease-fire and emphasized the dire consequences of an attack, he wasn't in a strong position to insist on an immediate reversal. The senior officials with the authority to do so were fully engaged in defending their own careers. The Marines had heeded Bremer's warning that to resume the attack jeopardized returning sovereignty to the Iraqis, which would be a severe embarrassment to the president. In any case, all parties—Abizaid, Sanchez, and Bremer—had agreed to the unusual step of assigning the chief negotiating role to the military field commander.

Conway had properly requested permission of Sanchez and Abizaid to negotiate the agreement. Neither one of them had chosen to inform or consult with Bremer on this highly sensitive political matter. American diplomats in Baghdad, knowing nothing about the agreement between Conway and Latif, expressed open distrust of the military, a feeling that was reciprocated. The civil-military relations in Iraq were described as "poisonous."

In the Pentagon a senior official called the situation "confusing . . . There's a disconnect here, and we can't figure it out." The chain of command for major decisions was clear. Secretary Rumsfeld issued a directive, and the chairman of the Joint Chiefs wrote a formal tasking. The order went to the theater commander as a directive from the secretary of defense. The theater commander then issued a directive to the JTF commander, who sent a directive to the MEF commander, who sent one to the division commander. This formal system ensured a written chain of custody so there would be no verbal misinterpretations. It also enabled each level of command to include amplifying instructions. But when Sanchez and Abizaid had approved the Fallujah Brigade in lieu of an attack on the city, CentCom had not sent a written order down the chain, with a copy up the chain.

A senior Marine described the situation to a **Washington Post** reporter: "We had all these different tracks going on. Ad hoc would be a kind [description]."

Deputy Secretary of Defense Wolfowitz asked his staff, "Have we turned Fallujah over to the old regime?" The staff, unable to find any memo or written agreement, replied that was not the case. In responding to a congressional question, Wolfowitz admitted the situation was confusing but insisted that a deal had not been struck. He characterized Conway's agreement with Latif as "conversations going on," not a coordinated plan.

General Conway had a very different perspective.

"The plan to employ an Iraqi battalion in Fallujah was closely guarded," he said. "However, the plan was not conceived in a vacuum. Every step was coordinated with the right individuals from Baghdad to the Beltway."

Conway's two seniors in the military chain of command were Sanchez and Abizaid. He had informed them of his decision to organize the Fallujah Brigade. Within the MEF's chain of command, Abizaid had provided the key endorsement verbally. That was all the MEF needed. It was Abizaid's responsibility to consult with the Pentagon, or to inform Rumsfeld after the fact. It was Sanchez's responsibility to inform the CPA, although Conway had not informed the CPA at the Anbar Province level.

General Myers, the Chairman of the Joint Chiefs of Staff, was publicly enthusiastic about the deal. "This is a microcosm of what we want to happen all over Iraq," he told Fox News.

Abizaid cautioned Conway that Fallujah must not become a "city-state." In his judgment, there was a high likelihood the Marines would have to go back in: "It may be necessary to have a strong fight in there."

Abizaid, though, had endorsed the extended "cease-fire" when the Marines had wanted to attack. The Marines were no longer preparing for "a strong fight." Three of the four battalions were decamping from Fallujah. The Marines weren't a debating society. Once the decision was made, the word went down the ranks: the Iraqis want to take care of the insurgents, and we as Marines are going to make it work. MajGen Mattis told the Marines they had done their job, and now it was time for the Iraqis to take over.

"We did not come here to fight these people," Mattis told the troops, "we came here to free them. We have to give them a stake in their own future."

The battalion commanders congratulated their men on how hard they had fought and praised the decision to give the Iraqis a chance to show what they could do. "This is an Iraqi solution to an Iraqi problem," LtCol Byrne said. "They know the populace."

Captain Johnson of India 3/4 said it was "tough justifying a political cease-fire to 168 pumped-up Marines who kept saying we should push west." That sentiment was prevalent at the fighting level. They had lost comrades and night after night had heard the imams' call to arms. In the midst of the battle so personal, they didn't want to be pulled off. Newspapers reported that the turnover "grated on many of the Marines" at the battalion level.

"Now it's going to get worse," Lance Corporal Julius Wright said. "We pulled out when we should have went in." Pulling out without defeating the insurgents "was a waste of time, of resources, and of lives," in the view of Lance Corporal Eduardo Chavez. "Everyone feels the same way, especially those who know someone who was killed."

While skeptical that the Iraqis would live up to the agreement, overall the squads took the news with good grace and biting humor. In Battalion 3/4 a corporal answered the phone by saying: "Peace Busters: you negotiate, we instigate."

Initially proving the skeptics wrong, Latif and Saleh moved with remarkable speed to implement the agreement. True to their word, on the afternoon of April 30 they assembled more than two hundred men, drawn up in formation, at the cloverleaf east of the city. The Marines were warned to stay three hundred meters away. Conway and Toolan met briefly with Gen Saleh, who proudly wore his green uniform and red beret. Handing over responsibility for the city was done with stiff handshakes, few words, and no smiles.

The **New York Times** ran a front-page, irony-tinged picture of a visibly pained Col Toolan shaking hands with the redoubtable Gen Saleh. The accompanying story, by John Kifner, reflected the caution if not outright skepticism of the embedded reporters about the sudden reversal of fortunes in Fallujah.

On May 1, when Conway met with the press to explain the Fallujah Brigade, he answered their questions directly. Tony Perry from the **Los Angeles Times,** noting that the deal was not in writing, asked whether the Iraqi generals were trustworthy. "I have enjoyed working with these people to date," Conway said. "I find that words like 'honor' and 'pride' and 'trust' are vital parts of the conversation."

John Kifner asked why the battle plan for seizing the city had not been carried out.

"Our orders changed," Conway said.

"Orders from higher, like Washington?" Kifner asked.

"I don't ask those questions," Conway said. "We were probably going to mount up and those [orders] simply changed and that's not uncommon."

"But the orders that you received changed?"

"Well, there were never orders, just verbal orders."

———

On May 2, Gen Myers went on the Sunday talk shows to explain that the deal had been made "from the bottom up," resulting in "a policy to catch up with what is happening on the ground." The mission of the Fallujah Brigade, he said, was to "deal with the extremists, the foreign fighters, get rid of the heavy weapons and find the folks who perpetrated the Blackwater atrocities." Myers then publicly fired Gen Saleh, saying his involvement had been a mistake.

At the same time Myers was speaking, armed men inside Fallujah jubilantly took to the streets. "We won," a militiaman told Rajiv Chandrasekaran of the **Washington Post**. "We didn't want the Americans to enter the city and we succeeded."

LtGen Conway had a different view. "They [the Fallujah Brigade leaders] understand our view that these people [the hard-core and the foreign fighters] must be killed or captured," he said. "They have not flinched."

In the view of the MEF commander, the agreement was based on trust among military men. The day of reckoning for the hard-core insurgents was soon to come.

Saleh's firing by the Chairman of the Joint Chiefs of Staff left Latif, who had been growing bananas in retirement, at the core of the brigade. Referring to the officers in his brigade, Latif, who drove back to Baghdad each night, told a reporter, "I don't know many of these men."

The concept was a political hope in an alternative future. Politics had prevented LtGen Conway from seizing Fallujah, so Conway had taken a political gamble to get out of the box and relieve the Marine battalions of their siege position. The hope was that Sunni Baathists and army officers would quell the rebellion by showing the Sunnis that they were included in the future of the new Iraq.

"The word 'brigade' is a misnomer. It was not a military organization by our standards," Conway said. "It was an effort to split the hard-core ACF [anti-Coalition forces] and the terrorists from all those others who were fighting for their city."

———

By the beginning of May, the spotlight of national publicity had swung completely away from Fallujah and onto the Abu Ghraib scandal. The prison abuse story also pushed Sadr's rebellion to the back pages. MajGen Dempsey had backed Sadr and his bruised militia into a corner in Najaf. Instead of arresting him, the Iraqi politicians agreed to let him go free.

The reason they gave was that the Coalition could ill afford to make him a martyr at a time when the Arab press was showing the Abu Ghraib pictures as proof that Americans were the oppressors in Iraq. Sadr was allowed to leave Najaf and resume his plotting, with the warrant for his arrest abated.

On May 8, Bremer and Blackwill met with Sanchez and Conway in Baghdad. Bremer's staff expected fireworks, but instead the meeting was civil. Conway had shown verve, and no one had had a better idea. Blackwill followed up with a visit to Mattis. Again, the meeting was collegial. Conway and Mattis stoutly defended the Fallujah Brigade concept. During the siege the Iraqi officials had lectured about how Americans misunderstood the resistance and how Fallujans wanted to control their own lives and live peacefully. Now they were being given the chance to do so.

To demonstrate that he had control, Latif urged Mattis to visit the Government Center with only a few Marines; too many Americans would be threatening. When Mattis eagerly accepted the offer, everyone in the division knew what was up. Insurgent stupidity would be their last chance of taking the city. The insurgents had attacked Abizaid; maybe they'd be dumb enough to shoot at the next visiting general.

On May 9, Mattis and Toolan drove to the outskirts of Camp Fallujah to meet with Battalion 3/4. McCoy proudly showed off a sand table his staff had built as a replica of the city. Laid out with string and cardboard signs were the major streets, checkpoints, and phase lines. McCoy stepped over one line of twine after the

other, pointing out the firing lanes and geometries of
fire for his vehicles. Only seven Humvees and LAVs
would go in with Mattis. Toolan would be airborne in
a command helicopter, while most of 3/4's vehicles
and tanks hid behind a berm outside town. When the
firing starts, McCoy explained, each of his companies
knew which streets to race down.

"Bryan, I expect they're going to shoot," Mattis said,
"but those bastards might be smart enough not to.
You're not to start World War III by yourself. If they hit
me, get us out. You are not to take the Jolan by yourself.
We'll come back and finish the job. There's nothing I'd
rather do than stand on the Euphrates smoking a cigar
with my new best friends, those bastards."

———

On the morning of May 10, Mattis drove at high
speed down the highway from Ramadi to the assembly
point east of the cloverleaf. As his LAV swung onto the
side road in a swirl of dust, a four-door white Toyota
approached from Fallujah and cut in front. Fearing a
suicide bomber, the sentries opened fire—three short
bursts from an M60 machine gun—and the Toyota
bucked to a halt, steam rising from a perforated radiator and air hissing out of the front tires. Three stocky,
bearded men hastily flung open the car doors and dove
to the ground, arms high in the air, one of them shouting "American! Don't shoot! American!"

Mattis climbed down as the men stood up and
wiped off the dirt. Their leader was a CIA agent who
earlier that morning had watched video from a UAV

that showed that the insurgents were permitting cars to proceed without stopping them. So he had driven the route Mattis would soon take. He told Mattis one idiot had blown himself up trying to plant an explosive device outside the Government Center and that he had seen two trucks with mortar tubes. But he hadn't seen a prepared ambush.

McCoy, who had walked over to listen, looked disappointed. Mattis ambled over to the Marines in their battle gear, inviting the Iraqi police, who had driven up in orange and white Toyota pickups, to join him. LtCol Hatim, in pressed chinos and a clean white shirt, was in charge. LtCols Suleiman and Jabar were nowhere to be seen. The police were startled by the friendly atmosphere. The Marines, expecting a fight within the hour, saw the police as bystanders caught in the middle, neither allies nor enemy. Mattis told a police captain he would like to visit his precinct. No, the captain said, Americans were not permitted into the city after today. Mattis shrugged and climbed into his LAV.

Primed for combat, the Marines said they didn't have room for reporters. Shooters filled every spot in the few vehicles. Perry and Kifner, though, were plucked out of the crowd and shoved inside an amtrac. They had been with the battalions for a month and had earned admittance.

"I don't advise this," Mattis said, smiling at them. "You may not get a chance to file."

At the front of the column Hatim sat in a pickup

packed with policemen in blue shirts clutching AKs. An Iraqi flag on the cab roof flapped in the breeze. With four pickups in front of the half-dozen Marine vehicles, the strange parade drove into Fallujah, following the same route taken six weeks earlier by the four Blackwater contractors. On their left they passed the grungy industrial sector seized by Battalion 1/5—squat rows of repair shops, twisted piping, rusted hulks of cars, and puddles of mud and oil. On the right was East Manhattan, the middle-class residential area controlled by Battalion 3/4. At every intersection stood a blue-shirted Iraqi policeman, most looking up the empty cross streets and ignoring the armed convoy as it passed.

At the Government Center, Latif and the mayor welcomed Mattis, who sipped tea with them in the long council room. Two dozen local dignitaries in flowing robes and headdresses sat in overstuffed chairs along walls unadorned by a single picture or map. Arab and Japanese TV crews bustled to capture the scene. Mattis stayed the agreed-upon fifteen minutes, then walked back to his LAV.

Outside the courtyard Gen Saleh, with no rank showing on his green uniform, was giving orders over a handheld radio. Dozens of men, with police and National Guard soldiers among them, lined the sidewalks, arms folded, glaring at the Marines. No words were spoken. Many were holding up their two forefingers in the V for victory sign. Others turned their backs and gestured as though defecating.

In the amtrac holding the reporters, Sergeant Victor Gutierrez, a huge man who wrote for the division newspaper, sat in a corner.

"No, no," Perry said, "you stand up here. You get your pictures, too."

"And bring your M16," Kifner added.

As the Marines drove out of the city, not a shot was fired. The Iraqi men stood on the sidewalks and jeered or glared. Perry bet one hundred dollars no one could get a wave from the crowd.

"That drive was a goodwill gesture that proved nothing," BrigGen Kelly, the assistant division commander, said later. "We don't want to call on Killer McCoy every time a convoy drives though town."

The next day Toolan sent Battalion 3/4 back north to rejoin Col Tucker. Battalions 1/5 and 2/2 had earlier departed Fallujah. Battalion 2/1 also pulled back.

The city belonged to the Fallujah Brigade.

PART III

REVERSAL

May to October 2004

21

THE BOMB FACTORY

ONCE MAJGEN MATTIS DROVE AWAY FROM the Government Center on May 10, the insurgents proclaimed victory and began to celebrate. Pickup trucks with horns honking and men waving AKs, some with colorful bandannas wrapped around their faces, others bare-headed and grinning, drove up and down Highway 10, shouting **Abu akbar!** Men with RPGs stood on the rooftops, waving. Banners praising the heroic martyrs of Islam were strung across forlorn storefronts: **We have defeated the devil Marines! Jihad has triumphed!** Shop owners threw handfuls of candy at passersby as music blared from the minarets. The initial burst of exuberance was widespread. Police, National Guard soldiers, the Fallujah Brigade, jihadists, merchants, local gangs, foreign fighters, and young boys delighted that the city was theirs.

American reporters venturing into town over the next several days described checkpoints manned by insurgents, while the soldiers of the Fallujah Brigade stood by. Asked about this, residents replied that everyone was a mujahedeen. Such boasting provoked questions about the wisdom of canceling the attack and creating the Fallujah Brigade.

Before he left to take a command in Germany, LtGen Sanchez said those decisions were a matter of civilian politics. "We are a civilian-controlled military," he said, "and it is our business to stay out of politics."

The White House, though, placed responsibility for the Fallujah decisions on the military. "Our commanders," Mr. Bush said in a speech at the Army War College, "consulted with Iraq's Governing Council and local officials, and determined that massive strikes against the enemy would alienate the local population, and increase support for the insurgents. So we have pursued a different approach. We're making security a shared responsibility in Fallujah . . . our Marines will continue to conduct joint patrols with Iraqis."

The Marines, though, had pursued a different approach because they had been told that the president wanted an alternative to attacking Fallujah. Disaster being an orphan, no one was rushing forward to claim credit for reining in LtGen Conway who, fed up with the empty promises of the Iraqi negotiators, had said on April 21 that he was going to attack within a few days.

The political fortunes of the president were ebbing. By mid-May only 40 percent of the electorate approved of his handling of Iraq, while 55 percent disapproved, the lowest approval rating since the war had begun. One hundred and thirty Americans had died in Iraq in April, the highest monthly total in the war. Sadr, having lost in his rebellion, had negotiated his freedom and remained at large. The press focused on the administration's reaction to the garish pictures from Abu Ghraib, which a former secretary of defense described as the "Animal House" criminal behavior of an unsupervised squad on night duty.

The press and Congress, however, were looking to affix senior responsibility, stirring up speculation that the president might fire Rumsfeld or LtGen Sanchez. Given these negative developments, it did the White House no good to have a postmortem discussion of why the Marines had been ordered to seize Fallujah and now were handing it over to the politically androgynous Fallujah Brigade.

The JTF commander replacing Sanchez, Lieutenant General Thomas Metz, framed the Marines' withdrawal in terms of its strategic benefits, rather than whether the military or the civilians had forced the decisions. "We had the combat power necessary to finish that job in a couple of days," he said. "But having done that, there were many who thought the strategic value of that was not only zero, it could have been negative. The route we chose to go clearly saved a lot of lives."

Marine spokesmen, in support of the rationale of saving civilian lives, had adopted what **Los Angeles Times** reporter Perry called a "mantra," repeating over and over again that the MEF didn't want to turn Fallujah into a Dresden. In Fallujah in the month of fighting there had been approximately 150 air strikes, and 75 buildings and two mosques were destroyed by approximately a hundred tons of explosives. In Dresden 1,100 allied bombers in a single night dropped 6,600 tons of explosives, destroying tens of thousands of buildings and killing between 35,000 and 45,000 civilians. In Fallujah civilian deaths ranged from 600—according to Al Jazeera—to 270, according to the Iraqi Ministry of Health. Dresden was a tragedy one hundred times the size of Fallujah.

Other spokesmen trotted out the cliché of "not destroying the city to save it." Both infelicitous examples referred to the application of massive firepower without regard for civilian casualties—scarcely what the Marines had intended to convey about their planned attack in Fallujah.

The prevention of destruction rapidly became the public rationale for stopping the attack. Although not intended as legerdemain, the rationale confused costs with goals and raised the question why Fallujah had been attacked in the first place. If avoiding casualties was the strategic objective, it was illogical to go to war.

————

The Marines would not be judged, however, by historical analogies or by political rationales. What mattered was what happened on the ground.

The first returns were inauspicious. Twenty-three-year-old Nicholas Berg, a friendly Californian—part entrepreneur, part youthful wanderer—was traveling by himself in Baghdad when he disappeared in mid-April. In mid-May the terrorist Zarqawi posted a video on his website, Al Ansar. The grainy pictures showed a bearded and gaunt Berg, clad in an orange prisoner jumpsuit, sitting in a white plastic chair in front of a beige wall. Five men clad in black, with facemasks and green chest vests holding AK clips, stood behind Berg as Zarqawi proclaimed retaliation for the abuses at Abu Ghraib. Then shouting "God is great!" Zarqawi drew a long knife and leaped upon Berg. There was a scream, and a few seconds later Berg's severed head was placed on his bloody torso. The gory videotape made the prime-time news on Al Jazeera.

The timing of the video's release, a few days after the Marines turned over control of the city, seemed either a mockery of the Americans or a celebration, or both. The CIA believed Zarqawi's torture studio was located in the Jolan District, but no one knew where to look within that devil's den of twisting alleyways and backstreets. So a raid was not possible.

Instead, Mattis proposed immediate joint patrols through the Jolan to shake down the district from top to bottom. Latif demurred, insisting that the timing was not right. Trust had to be established first. All right, Conway and Mattis countered, let's build trust and then get Zarqawi.

The Marines offered $40 million for reconstruction, plus U.S. Navy Seabee engineer teams. The owners of every building hit by air strikes would be compensated; the contaminated water supply would be purified; electric power restored; garbage dumps plowed under; thousands of men employed and paid immediately. For a few days a dozen city engineers flocked to the Fallujah Liaison Center, excitedly exchanging blueprints with the Seabees. Then they didn't come back.

Latif and the city elders met with Mattis, explaining that the people of Fallujah wanted no help from outsiders. No American soldier could enter the city. It made no difference if he was coming with a tank or an electric generator. Latif denied there were any foreign fighters in the city. Mattis shot back that he was willing to give Latif a little time to get the Fallujah Brigade organized to attack "those murderous bastards."

In late May the rate of attacks along the nearby highways dropped, provoking a burst of optimism among senior officials. General Myers argued that "this is the right way to do it . . . We need to know when to back off." In testimony before Congress, the Commandant of the Marine Corps, Gen Michael Hagee, said that the critics of the Fallujah Brigade did not know what they were talking about. "If that's a defeat," he said, "we need more defeats like that."

Efforts to be upbeat contrasted with the stories reporters gathered at high personal risk. Iraqi police gave false directions in the hope of capturing American reporters. A news crew was kidnapped and released only after tense negotiations. A **Washington Post** reporter escaped as his armored SUV withstood repeated bursts from AK-47s while careening down the highway to Baghdad at ninety miles an hour.

Correspondents from Reuters, the **New York Times,** NBC News, the **Washington Post, Harper's** magazine, and the **Los Angeles Times** sneaked into the city. They described gangs of insurgents searching cars, manning checkpoints, and conducting patrols while the Fallujah Brigade soldiers stood idly by or joined them. They reported residents basking in the apparent insurgent victory and making boastful proclamations. "I believe the U.S. forces went through one of their toughest times here, meeting the resistance they did," said a government worker in the city. "We believe God saved our city. And we believe they learned a lesson: not to mess with Fallujah."

The imams declared the city would be governed in accord with the strictest interpretation of the sharia. Those selling alcohol were stripped, flogged, and driven through town, bare backs bleeding, to be ridiculed and spat upon. Barbers were beaten if they offered "Western-style" haircuts. Students with long hair were rounded up, mocked, and shorn. Anyone caught drinking beer was beaten and paraded through the streets. Residents were whipped for petty transgressions such as talking back to a mujahedeen fighter. Shop owners selling lipstick, American-style magazines, or pop music CDs were beaten and their meager goods smashed or stolen.

The regiment's intelligence officer, Maj Bellon, had contempt for the imams advocating Islamic fundamentalism. "Wahhabism itself isn't the motivating force in Fallujah. The imams use the mosques to gain control over ignorant people. They preach hate, and that's not a religion," he said. "I keep the book on these guys. Most of them are criminals. They own the real estate, they send out thugs to shake down the truck drivers doing the run to Jordan, they fence the stolen cars and organize the kidnappings. They get a cut of every hijacked truck. They could teach Al Capone how to extort a city. They use young, gullible jihadists as their pawns. Don't think of them as clerics. Think in terms of a Mafia don. They stand there in a religious costume, because that is exactly what it is, and inspect the latest haul before saying afternoon prayers."

Foreign fighters from Syria and Saudi Arabia trickled into the city. The insurgents organized a ruling council, called the Mujahedeen Shura, which moved into a mosque in the center of the city and issued written passes for Arab journalists to visit the "liberated" city. Truck drivers passing by on the main highway to Jordan were forced into the city and executed or held for ransom. Neighborhood militias sprang up, manned by teenagers who perhaps joined out of intimidation but soon cheered as hapless Iraqis were disemboweled at the whim of the mobs. The reign of the Taliban had descended on Fallujah.

The loose gangs of jihadists resembled the Jacobin communards of Paris in 1793—gang rule by a bloody hand with no political ideology or organization. Though Secretary Rumsfeld had labeled the insurgents as "dead-enders," the rule of the Terror in France suggested that tenacity fed by blood could persist for years. Between 1793 and 1795 more than a hundred thousand French citizens were murdered by their neighbors as society was trapped in a paroxysm of psychotic betrayals. Finally, Robespierre himself was led to the guillotine.

Like Robespierre, Zarqawi's weapon was terror wrapped in fuzzy ideology. His campaign of blowing Shiites to bits was intended to provoke retaliation against the Sunnis and lead to large-scale civil war. He would improvise where he would go from there. Neither the American nor the Arab press called particular attention to the proliferation of terrorist safe houses in Fallujah, while the city elders vehemently denied Zarqawi existed.

At the end of May Zarqawi kidnapped in Fallujah thirty-four-year-old Kim Sun-il, a missionary fluent in Arabic who worked as a translator for a South Korean company. A videotape delivered to Al Jazeera showed Sun-il denouncing the Coalition and pleading with the South Korean government to withdraw its 3,500-man construction battalion in exchange for his release. Weeks of debate in South Korea, featuring the tearful anguish of Sun-il's family, followed. When the South Korean government held firm, Zarqawi beheaded Sun-il and distributed the video to the Arab television networks.

A **Washington Post** reporter observed that, although President Bush had declared "security a shared responsibility" inside Fallujah, the insurgents controlled the streets, sharing power with nobody. Publicly, the MEF was reluctant to agree: "It is only a supposition that Fallujah is a sanctuary for insurgents," said the operations officer for the MEF.

Trends, though, were emerging that supported the supposition. When Fallujah was under siege in April, there were five bombings of civilians across Iraq; in the six weeks after the siege was lifted, there were thirty bombings. The Marines retaliated with air strikes against safe houses inside Fallujah, using unmanned aerial vehicles with video cameras to follow the terrorists to their lairs. The insurgents reacted by dispensing roving gangs to accost strangers, executing fourteen Iraqis as spies.

As the jihadists were consolidating their power, the Fallujah Brigade was doing nothing. Latif's compound on the outskirts of the city was mortared, killing and wounding a dozen Iraqis. When he was unable to gather a force to retaliate, his effectiveness ended. After that the brigade officers treated him as a figurehead useful for delivering cash from the Americans. Sometimes the officers didn't even stand when he entered the room. One month after the brigade had replaced the Marines, none of the agreed-upon conditions had been met. No heavy weapons had been turned in; the foreign fighters and perpetrators of the mutilations remained at large; the insurgents were controlling the city; no military convoy dared to drive through the city; kidnappings were a daily occurrence; and terror bombings had increased.

———

Mid-June marked the end of the third month of daily dealings between the Iraqis and the Fallujah Liaison Team, comprised of civil affairs officers, intelligence operatives, and Arabic speakers from the division. They reported directly to Toolan, who also met daily with Iraqi delegations. After hundreds of meetings, supplemented by intelligence profiles, the regiment had a good mosaic of the city's political structure and leaders. The CIA had several excellent informants, and SSgt Qawasimi had recruited four others. About once a week Qawasimi went a few days without a shower, put on a dishdasha and kaffiyeh headdress, stripped off all American-type items, picked up a worn AK, and slipped out after dark to meet with informants. In exchange for used cars and cash payments of $200 he bought information on Zarqawi's cells, the Syrian gangs, the Wahhabi clerics, and the rich, shadowy Baathists.

When Qawasimi had the names, descriptions, and addresses of the safe houses, he turned over the folders to Bellon. What drove Bellon to distraction was the casual Iraqi approach to identifying the precise house. Agents were given GPS sets with accuracy within fifteen feet, as well as other devices. After an agent was caught with GPS and beheaded, the other agents were reluctant to carry such equipment. Bellon's best homing source were the crews of the unmanned aerial vehicles. The video feeds included a continuous GPS update, while the crews became expert at tracking individual cars and men down any street or alley.

Putting together the pieces, Bellon told Toolan he estimated there were seventeen separate insurgent gangs in the city and about a dozen key leaders. Aside from the Syrians and Zarqawi, they were home-grown and not into exporting suicide attacks. They were primed to fight, though, still on an emotional high, thinking they had defeated the division in April.

Yet those street gangs couldn't go anywhere; the regiment held the highways. The Fallujah Brigade was being paid, and their officers were holding back 10 percent to share with all the insurgents who hadn't climbed on the gravy train. Mattis wanted to meet face-to-face with the enemy and explain how stupid the fighting was. They were living in their own city; no one was bothering them. It was time to get on with their lives, not drive around in stolen police vehicles looking tough, without enough money in their pockets to consider marriage or a future.

Toolan and Mattis wanted to talk directly to leaders with influence. All strands of intrigue led back to Sheikh Janabi. He preached a radical brand of Wahhabism in his large mosque in the center of the city, but he had been a businessman and smuggler for decades before embracing religion. His family had exercised power in city circles for three generations. While not as rich as Sheikh Ghazi, Janabi, according to Bellon's reports, was raking off 10 to 20 percent from every hijacking. He was the go-to man who could return a kidnap victim before Zarqawi got hold of him. He was hauling in serious money, between $20,000 and $40,000 a month. Most of the gangs asked favors of him, or at least dropped by his mosque grounds once a week.

Toolan talked to Suleiman about approaching Janabi. Toolan had intervened when Hatim, correctly claiming the city council had chosen him, tried to take over command of the National Guard battalion. Toolan said Suleiman would stay in charge if the soldiers wanted to keep being paid by the Marines. Suleiman, who was straightforward, kept his distance from the Marines and didn't curry favor. He refused to play the middleman and act as a bridge to Janabi.

Hatim volunteered to be the intermediary, endorsed and assisted by Jamal, the mufti released from prison by Bremer. Although Jamal seemed sincere about toning down the sermons of other imams, rumors persisted that he was supporting the insurgents. All the elders who lived in the city seemed to have two faces, saying one thing to the Marines and another to the insurgents. Toolan sent half a dozen messages to Janabi, who demanded a letter signed by Ambassador Bremer guaranteeing he would not be arrested. Eventually, he offered to meet if MajGen Mattis signed the letter and came personally to the Government Center. Mattis agreed.

In mid-June Mattis met Hatim at the cloverleaf east of the city. Hatim vehemently insisted that only nine vehicles could enter the city, not a good sign. With Toolan up in a command helicopter and a Quick Reaction Force standing by, Mattis agreed to nine and made his second trip into Fallujah. In mid-May Latif had been the guest of honor at city hall among a crowd of Arab dignitaries and Arab TV crews. This time Latif wasn't even invited. Instead, Janabi was the central figure, a short, trim man in his early sixties with a long beard and sharp features, wearing a white dishdasha and a full Arab headdress.

While the perfunctory introductions were being made, Sheikh Ghazi exchanged a few words with Qawasimi.

"Marines are no good," Ghazi said, visibly angry.

His smuggling had dried up during the siege, his hand-picked mayor (Ra'ad) was in prison, and no contract money from the Americans was coming his way. Qawasimi shrugged and walked away.

As in May, dozens of sheikhs sat along the walls, craning their heads to hear. None spoke. This was a meeting between the Marine combat leader and the guerrilla leader. Putting aside small talk, Mattis and Janabi politely exchanged terse verbal blows.

"For the sake of your city," Mattis said, "you must tell Zarqawi and the Syrians to leave. They are killing your innocent fellow countrymen. We intend to kill all terrorists. That means more bombing and fear in the city. This is unnecessary. I am sure a man of your power can put a stop to it. Get them out."

Qawasimi was translating, sitting behind Mattis.

"Someone gives you bad information," Janabi said with a glare at Qawasimi. "There are no foreigners here. You bomb innocent people. We only protect our homes when you come to destroy."

"We are here to help—to make the water safe for your children, to bring electric power into the schools, to clean out the garbage that spreads disease," Mattis said. "We have the money. We can pay your contractors right now, beginning today."

"The people do not trust you after all this war," Janabi said. "Give us your money and let us take care of ourselves. That is the best way."

The two men continued to spar verbally, neither giving an inch. Mattis's message: **Terrorists hiding in Fallujah are killing innocent Iraqis. You can stop that. Together we can build a safe, healthy city.** Janabi's message: **The killing is all your fault and everyone here wants peace. Leave Iraq. You are not welcome.**

Hatim waved his arms at Qawasimi to end the talk. They had agreed to stay only fifteen minutes. Hatim was agitated, certain that mortars and machine guns would open up at any moment, as they had when the Marines and soldiers from the 82nd had come in March.

"We may be in for it," Qawasimi murmured to Mattis as they got up to leave.

"I hope so," Mattis said.

He grimly shook hands with Janabi and walked out. He had been warned that Janabi had previously plotted to assassinate him. In his role as commander, he had brushed off the warning. Privately, he had an emergency plan. If they were hit inside the Government Center, as had happened in March, he was arresting Janabi. If that provoked a firefight inside the room, he was going to put two rounds in Janabi's head. As Qawasimi, a few steps behind Mattis, walked by Janabi, the sheikh uttered a quick, low curse: "Traitor."

A relieved Hatim watched as the Marines drove out of town. As in May, men stood on the street corners. This time they were more aggressive in their ridicule, some shoving their hands up rudely in the air, others gesturing at their groins as if masturbating. The Marines sighted in on the rooftops, waiting for the first RPG gunner to show himself. Toolan's Huey circled overhead, while outside town the tank crews sat in their hatches and hoped for battle. But the tiny convoy exited without a shot being fired.

Once back at Camp Fallujah, Mattis and Toolan asked Qawasimi for his take on the meeting.

"Janabi's the boss man, sir," Qawasimi said. "That's his city now. I recommend we invite him to a big meeting outside town, then arrest him."

Bellon objected, arguing that would set a terrible diplomatic precedent and be a public relations disaster. To Qawasimi's distress, his idea was vetoed.

"Anything else?" Mattis asked.

"It was obvious you don't like him, sir. I think he sensed you want to fight him."

"He's got that right."

The meeting with Janabi put an end to Qawasimi's night forays to meet with his agents. Toolan ordered him to stay put.

"They'll set you up and kill you," Toolan said, "just like you want to set up Janabi."

"KEEP THE NOISE DOWN."

THERE WAS A BRIEF FLURRY OF conjecture
that the Fallujah Brigade constituted the model for
quelling the Sunni insurgency. Deputy Secretary of
Defense Wolfowitz, who had visited Iraq in late June,
had heard contradictory assessments. One senior
Iraqi official had whispered that the solution was
"Gaza," meaning that the Americans should withdraw completely from the area, as the Israelis had
promised to do in Gaza. Some Iraqi officials had
looked Wolfowitz in the eye and claimed there were
no terrorists or foreign fighters in Fallujah. Some
American officers had claimed the brigade still had "a
faint heartbeat."

Yet the Marines had launched two air strikes and
fought an all-day battle in Fallujah at the time of Wolfowitz's visit and had followed up by dropping four
five-hundred-pound bombs and two thousand-pound

bombs on a terrorist safe house. A few days later the chief of staff of the MEF, Col J. C. Coleman, publicly presented an optimistic view about the trends in the city. "Fallujah," Coleman told the **New York Times,** "is moving ever so slowly in the right direction."

Wolfowitz was taken aback. While intelligence reports pointed to an accretion of insurgent rule in Fallujah, some Iraqi and American officials were refusing to admit the fact. Trained for battle yet fiercely loyal to orders, the Marines were struggling with contradictory impulses. They wanted to be optimistic about the Fallujah Brigade while not appearing naïve about the enemy. They rejected suggestions that suicide car bombings in other cities were linked to Fallujah "because you build truck bombs near where you detonate them." CPA officials who had been excluded from the decision to create the Fallujah Brigade wondered whether some Marines had been affected by Stockholm syndrome and were "trying to put lipstick on a pig."

The deputy secretary of defense came away from his trip to Iraq convinced that turning Fallujah over to former Baathists and Iraqi generals was a serious mistake. "Fallujah is not a model," Wolfowitz told CNN. "I mean, Fallujah was probably the worst place in the country."

By the end of June, the press was describing Fallujah as "a nest of vipers" controlled by "mujahedeen-run fiefdoms" and a training ground for "the new jihadists." The **Washington Post** ran a front-page story saying that Iraqi and American officials believed the decision to pull back the Marines had created "an incubator for insurgency recruits."

Speaking with reporters as he turned over command of the JTF at the beginning of July, LtGen Sanchez criticized the decision to cancel the Marine assault. "The lesson [from Fallujah] is to use massive force," he said, "not precision strikes." In April Sanchez had warned Conway that White House support for attacking Fallujah had been undercut by the objections of the British, but Sanchez had remained firm in his belief that a full-scale attack was the only sensible military option.

After Sanchez left, Fallujah continued to deteriorate. As the residents of the city sweltered in the July heat, Janabi found his leadership position challenged by an upstart, Omar Hadid, a former electrician who lived with his mother in a lower-class section south of the Government Center. Janabi enjoyed the perquisites and prestige of representing the Mujahedeen Shura Council that met in a spacious mosque a few blocks from his upscale compound. Equality among men was a principle tenet of the Islamic religion, and among the insurgents, unlike the case in the Iraqi Army, leaders were encouraged to rise from the ranks. Like Al Pacino's character in the movie **Scarface**, Hadid, a thick-set man in his forties with a bushy beard and a tangle of long black hair, combined natural leadership with a flair for offhand, blood-chilling savagery. Zarqawi took him under his wing in April, and by July Hadid was a local legend, the survivor of numerous brushes with the Marines and the killer of

traitors. Local youths looked up to him, and he reciprocated by making the rounds at night, stopping by
gang houses to chat and leave fresh bread.

His leadership threatened, Janabi responded by
embracing more tightly the extreme jihad precepts of
Wahhabism. He became less the cunning businessman seeking a profit and more an advocate of anti-
Western violence for its own sake. The **Asia Times**
referred to Fallujah as "the Islamic Emirate," where
the mujahedeen believed, that having pushed out the
Marines, they could win the rest of Iraq, just as the
Taliban had recently ruled Afghanistan.

On the Marine side, Toolan had emerged as the primary point of contact for negotiating with Iraqis of all
stripes in Fallujah. LtGen Conway was busy coordinating with the new U.S. military and Iraqi teams in
Baghdad, and MajGen Mattis operated from Ramadi.
By July some said that sitting near Mattis in negotiations was like watching a wolverine circling a baited
trap. As Toolan took the reins in the daily sessions, he
conveyed in measured tones a firm message: Iraqis
had to stand up for their country. At the end of one
session replete with doggerel, he acknowledged to a
reporter that he was frustrated in his search for real
Iraqi leaders.

Latif never established leadership over the Fallujah
Brigade. The second-in-command, Major General
Abdullah Muhamdi, exerted more influence over the
soldiers but was distrusted. He once claimed Marines
were harassing a family near the railroad station. A
skeptical LtCol Olson insisted that Abdullah and

Latif immediately accompany him to investigate. When they arrived at the house in question, the bewildered family said they had had no dealings with Marines. Latif turned on Abdullah, calling him a liar and a disgrace. Leaving behind a glowering Abdullah, Latif then drove back to Baghdad. That was his last hurrah. By late July Latif, knowing he had no influence, no longer visited Fallujah.

By August, Abdullah avoided the Marines entirely, except to pick up pay. Suleiman emerged as the reliable military leader, just as he had in February. Not strong enough to stand up to the insurgents inside the city, he kept his battalion together on the peninsula west of the trestle bridge where the American contractors had been mutilated. Toolan drove over weekly to chat with him. Once while they were talking outside, they came under fire and Suleiman stepped in front of Toolan, shouting at the shooters to stop. Another time an IED exploded near Toolan's Humvee. Toolan stopped and called Suleiman on his cell phone, testily suggesting perhaps he had been set up. Fifteen minutes later Suleiman drove up and escorted Toolan to his compound. From then on Toolan was provided an escort on every visit.

Based on more than a dozen meetings, Toolan had concluded that Suleiman was a straight shooter. He was a small warlord on a small peninsula. His family was highly regarded in the Abu Mahdi tribe, supposedly staunch fighters, and each night he drove fifteen kilometers to his guarded house in Habineah. He avoided trips into Fallujah, where Jabar, the other

National Guard commander, stayed holed up at the Government Center. Suleiman warned Toolan that inside the city the Fallujah Brigade answered to Janabi, who was becoming "more bad." As long as he minded his own business and retained the loyalty of armed followers, he was left alone. Suleiman, who knew all the sheikhs and insurgent leaders, betrayed no trusts and received no support from any officials of the Iraqi government. The writ of Baghdad did not extend to Fallujah.

————

If Fallujah was the worst place in Iraq, it seemed in July to also be a backwater. While it was lurching out of control, it was isolated. That still left the question of how to proceed against the Sunni insurgency as a whole.

The end of June had marked the return of Iraqi sovereignty. Ambassador Bremer dissolved the CPA, turned the country over to an appointed interim government, and flew home. The new Iraqi government faced the tasks of quelling the Sunni insurgency, reassuring the skeptical Shiites about elections in January, marginalizing Sadr, and rebuilding the country. Of 2,300 construction projects promised by the CPA, only 140 were under way. The return of sovereignty had no noticeable effect on security in the country. The CPA plan had envisioned twelve thousand trained soldiers in the field by June; instead, there were about four thousand. Over the previous year the

Iraqi security forces had not emerged as a significant force.

The new American ambassador was John Negroponte, a seasoned diplomat. In July Negroponte doubled the size of the Iraqi security budget that had been advocated by Ambassador Bremer and increased the police force by 40 percent. It would be a year, though, before the funding increase resulted in trained Iraqis on the streets.

The central government was too weak either to provide security or to enforce allegiance to the commonweal. Having dominated the Shiites and Kurds for centuries, the Sunni-based insurgents had the self-confidence to reassert control the moment the Coalition army left. Yet the Coalition army no longer decided how and when to combat the insurgents. Decisions about Fallujah and all other locales rested with the interim Iraqi government in Baghdad. The newly appointed president, Sheikh Ghazi Yawar, and the prime minister, Ayad Allawi, had both ardently argued against the Marine offensive in April. They were enthusiastic boosters of selectively reempowering Sunni Baathists. They would decide what to do about the Fallujah Brigade.

On the American side, there was a new commander as well. Four-star Army General George Casey had been appointed to the new post of Commander of the Multinational Force. Casey, who came from a distinguished military family, was comfortable in command, with the knack of treating everyone as an equal.

_____

At the end of July Gen Casey met with Mattis in Ramadi. Casey began his visit by listening to the troops who did the fighting, and Battalion 2/4 was the most combat-seasoned unit in Iraq. The battalion averaged three attacks a day from small arms, indirect fire, or IEDs, and it had taken 31 killed and 284 wounded.

Casey wanted to know if Iraqi security forces could take over local control by December. No, the Marines said. The insurgents had changed tactics since they tried and failed to stand toe to toe with the Marines in April. The insurgents had reverted to IEDs and shoot and scoot attacks against the Americans while assassinating any Iraqi police or National Guard who dared to challenge them. The result was a city where the Americans held the main avenue, while the insurgents controlled the marketplace by both intimidating the people and gaining their sympathy.

"Every neighborhood knows Joe Muj, yet the Iraqi police say they can't go where the people don't want them," Capt Bronzi said. "And they won't patrol with us because the enemy threatens them and their families."

Prior to the battalion's arrival in March, the civilians like Keith Mines and the officers in the previous battalion had immersed themselves in the byzantine politics of Sunni Islamists, tribal sheikhs, former Baathists, and opportunists of every persuasion. There were endless meetings with sheikhs, imams, and local officials.

There were lists of the likes and dislikes of every subtribe. All sheikhs claimed to have influence and therefore to deserve payment. General Abizaid had personally met with the sheikhs.

LtCol Kennedy told Casey the insurgency had matured, weakening the influence of tribal sheikhs. The police and National Guard remained hunkered down in their compounds, permitting the insurgents to move freely wherever the Marines were not present. Contractors trying to improve even the basics like the water plant were scared away.

Kennedy placed more stock in Governor Burgis, a former police chief who was struggling to bring municipal services and hope in the future. Kennedy agreed with the assessment of the diplomat Keith Mines that Burgis was first rate. He was honest, hardworking, and respected by the sheikhs. Burgis, though, was convinced his office was penetrated by spies. Kennedy kept a platoon on duty twenty-four hours a day at the government center to protect Burgis, while the police guarded his home.

General Casey said the Iraqi forces had to face up to the basic challenge: It's your country—now fight for it. "That's what they should do," Kennedy agreed. But the Iraqis were scared, intimidated.

A few days after Casey's visit, the insurgents attacked the governor's house while he was away. His two sons were kidnapped and the house burned. The policemen on duty dropped their weapons and fled without raising any alarm. Burgis asked Kennedy to please not help him; any American interference would doom his sons. A week later a video on Al Jazeera showed Governor Burgis, with tears running down his face, apologizing for betraying Islam by working for the infidels. After Burgis had been humiliated before millions, his sons were released and he fled to Jordan with his family. The next day Prime Minister Allawi shut down Al Jazeera's office in Baghdad.

Casey and the new Iraqi government were facing a crisis of much larger proportions than the setbacks in Fallujah and Ramadi. Sadr was again leading a revolt that threatened to convulse the Shiite south and doom the government. On August 5, after attacking the main police station in Najaf, Sadr took up lodging inside a fortified compound on the outskirts of Mosque of Ali, a sacred site that attracted Shiite pilgrims from around the world. Grand Ayatollah Ali Husaini al Sistani and the elder clerics of the Iraqi Shiites also resided in Najaf. Sadr represented a mortal and immediate threat. If he emerged as the leader among the Shiites, Iraq would be thrown into chaos.

Casey moved swiftly, sending the 11th Marine Expeditionary Unit to cordon off Sadr's militia inside Najaf. The tactical challenge was to apply force while not damaging the holy sites that Sadr's men were using as hideouts. Day by day in temperatures of 120 degrees, Battalion 1/4 inched forward. They fought from tombstone to crypt across the gigantic cemetery outside the Ali mosque where Sadr's 120mm mortars fired with impunity from the courtyard. The tankers fought with IV needles inserted in their arms. Every three hours they got out of their tanks and lay on stretchers while pints of liquid flowed back into their veins. Once rehydrated, they went back into the fight.

In the second week in August, the 2nd Battalion of the 7th Cavalry Regiment joined the fight, bringing in armor to squeeze the militia from the east. Daily, the two battalion commanders—LtCol John Mayer (1/4) and Lieutenant Colonel Jim Rainey (2-7)—had to explain to their troops why they could not fire back at certain sites. The tactical end was in sight, but the soldiers and Marines weren't permitted to capture Sadr or to finish off his militia due to concern about the political consequences. Instead, Prime Minister Allawi engaged in a tortuous minuet, attempting to negotiate through a maze of intermediaries with the crafty Sadr.

The relationship between American military force and Iraqi diplomacy was ambiguous. Allawi set the parameters, and Casey executed. The Americans did the fighting but could not finish the fight—that was Allawi's call. Allawi proved as changeable as Sadr, issuing ultimatums, then backing down, then allowing the U.S. forces to press forward, then calling a halt and urging Sadr to negotiate. American forces pummeled Sadr's militia for two weeks, drawing the noose around them tighter and tighter. On August 20 the militia was down to its last stand. Under pressure from Sistani, at the last minute Allawi allowed Sadr and his henchmen to go free. As in April, Sadr had provoked a rebellion, lost a battle, and remained at large.

The American military role in local governance had diminished since Casey had directed that local security be taken over by the Iraqis. It was no longer the responsibility of tactical leaders—battalion and company commanders—to meet daily with Iraqi politicians, sheikhs, and officials to work out the everyday problems of municipal governance. Much of the training and equipping of the Iraqi security forces would now be done by a training unit separate from the U.S. divisions, commanded by Army LtGen David Petraeus. The details and machinations characteristic of a colonial administration, such as trying to play one sheikh off against another, became less relevant once Iraq was again a sovereign nation.

The insurgency was a confederation of Baathists seeking a return to power, Islamic extremists, criminals, former military and intelligence officers, radical Sunni imams, and young men motivated by revenge or a desire to fight against the infidel occupiers. Americans could not drive ideological wedges among the various insurgent groups, but Allawi believed he could.

Allawi was playing a complicated game, reaching out with blandishments to the Sunni and Shiite rebels while employing the American forces as his hammer. He used the channels he had set up in April to continue to meet with Jamal and Janabi, who were sending insurgents in stolen police cars from Fallujah to join Sadr's rebels. That military contribution was trivial; the morale implications were more troublesome. In Mattis's view, the clandestine negotiations by the Iraqi government encouraged the insurgents and delayed the inevitable day of reckoning.

While the major fight in Najaf was playing out, Col Toolan was working patiently to encourage the National Guard under LtCol Suleiman. A black belt in karate with a good sense of humor, Suleiman had become the regiment's favorite Iraqi officer. He kept his word and never curried favor. He was trying to walk a fine line, staying independent of the Americans while avoiding a blood feud with the hard men in town.

In mid-July the house of Suleiman's bodyguard had been blown up, and then the unfortunate man had been kidnapped and presumed killed. Flyers had been distributed in Fallujah urging the death of "Suleiman the traitor." Although Toolan wanted his Marines to patrol with the Iraqi soldiers, he accepted in good faith Suleiman's refusals.

"Colonel Suleiman is my friend. I've worked with him for five months," he said in late July. "When he tells me 'this I cannot do and keep my family alive,' I believe him."

On August 9 one of Suleiman's officers, a captain, was kidnapped and taken to the Maqady Mosque in midtown Fallujah. An angry Suleiman called Toolan and said he was going to get the captain—a member of his tribe—back. Toolan asked him to wait for a backup force of Marines. No, Suleiman said, I have to take care of this myself.

Dressed in workout clothes, Suleiman raced over to

the mosque with a dozen soldiers, where an imam accused him and the kidnapped officer of conniving with the Americans. Suleiman slapped him across the face and drove off, shouting that he expected the officer to be released or he was returning with his whole battalion. There were reports of an ambush and a brief firefight as Suleiman drove back to his compound on the peninsula. Over the next hour insurgents gathered outside the gates, brandishing RPGs.

Before shooting broke out, several imams arrived, assuring Suleiman that it had all been a mistake and that the officer was waiting for Suleiman to pick him up. When Suleiman drove back to the mosque, Janabi was waiting.

A few hours later Hadid called Toolan's headquarters on Suleiman's cell phone. The message was garbled, but the phone number was clear. Minutes later Hadid mockingly called Suleiman's wife, who became hysterical, convinced that her two daughters would never again see their father.

Later that day LtCol Jabar, who commanded the other National Guard battalion, was also kidnapped. Toolan wanted to organize a raid but didn't know where to look in the city. He called in the city elders and officers in the police and the Fallujah Brigade, warning them to secure Suleiman's release. They professed knowing nothing. A day later they said it was all a mistake that was being taken care of. A day after that they reported more ominous garbage about

Suleiman entering a mosque in a tracksuit instead of in uniform, so he did not merit the protection of the **shura**. Suleiman's tribe was trying to buy him back. It sounded like he would be beaten, then released. That had been the punishment meted out to the son of a less powerful sheikh a week earlier. The soles of the man's feet had been beaten to bloody pulps and he would walk with canes for the rest of his life, but he was alive.

Toolan hoped that Suleiman's tribe—the Abu Mahdi—would react, but the tribe was cowed by the ruthlessness of Janabi and Hadid. Several days later Suleiman's pulverized corpse was dumped on a road south of the mosque. The torso was burned pink, and the feet and legs were swollen and black. Toolan heard that Janabi and Hadid hadn't set out to kill him. The usual beating had begun—bamboo canes lashing the soles of his feet, then proceeding up his legs. Instead of whimpering and agreeing to a confession, Suleiman had cursed his torturers, who responded by pouring boiling water on his chest. They then propped him up and videotaped his halting monologue that he was an American spy, working for Toolan. Hadid then sawed off his head.

The next day the videotapes circulated in town, showing a weeping Suleiman, moments before his death, begging forgiveness for betraying the Iraqi people and an abject, sobbing Jabar pleading for his life, claiming that Suleiman had been an American agent. Janabi sent his minions to the compounds of the two National Guard battalions, where the soldiers promptly deserted, leaving behind their trucks and weapons. Jabar was never seen again. Terror had spawned its own biogenesis, the malevolence passing from Zarqawi to Hadid to Janabi, who had mutated from business opportunist to gangster to zealot torturer.

When the CIA quickly turned up evidence that members of the police and the Fallujah Brigade had helped to engineer the kidnappings, Toolan exploded. In white-hot fury he summoned the leaders of the brigade, the police, and the National Guard to the Fallujah Liaison Center. There he accused them of betrayal and murder. The brigade and the police are finished, Toolan told them. "Insurgents have taken control of the town. I am not going to negotiate with them," he said. "We fight right now to prevent losing Iraq, or else we'll be paying the price for years to come."

He said anyone loyal to the Iraqi government had one week to get his family out of town. After that the Marines were treating everyone in that city with a weapon as an enemy, to be dealt with accordingly. "Everyone who wants to fight for the new Iraq," Toolan said, "join us. If not, we'll see you inside the city."

Staff officers in the MEF next door were furious that Toolan had taken matters into his own hands and had reacted without checking up the chain of command. But no senior Marine officer disagreed with

Toolan's command decision. At best the Fallujah Brigade had capitulated to the enemy; at worst it had been the enemy from the beginning.

LtGen Conway and MajGen Mattis had returned to Iraq in March intending to work alongside the Iraqi forces while respecting the Sunni population. The decision to seize Fallujah and then not to seize it had knocked that strategy off course. Well-intentioned compromise had emboldened the insurgents. Now the theory that secular Baathists and senior Iraqi officers aligned with Baghdad could reclaim status and power in Fallujah lay in ruins.

Mattis had made no secret of his judgment. "There's only one way to disarm the Fallujah Brigade," he said. "Kill it."

Toolan rolled tanks south outside Queens. As he expected, the insurgents rushed to man the earthen berm they had thrown up around the outskirts of the city, firing barrages of RPGs. The Abrams tanks maneuvered forward and eagerly returned the fire. The battle raged for several hours; the sounds were clearly heard back at the regimental headquarters. The staff called the episode "Toolan Tunes." The regiment was straining at the leash.

According to the **New York Times**, Allawi, despite Suleiman's murder and UAV videos of terrorist safe houses, had promised not to permit large-scale American attacks while Janabi was considering halting insurgent attacks. "Keep the noise down," higher headquarters in Baghdad told the MEF, not wanting a full-scale battle in Fallujah to upset Iraqi political maneuverings. The MEF was sympathetic with Toolan's instinct but had to call him off. The tanks pulled back after a battle of several hours.

"Keep the noise down," the MEF told a simmering division.

23

ALL OF THIS FOR NOTHING?

WITH THE IRAQIS, IT WAS DIFFICULT sorting out friend from foe and what motivated resistance. Stability in the Sunni areas required an amalgam of political compromise, economic blandishment, and superior firepower. It was a Mafioso game that only Iraqis could master, and in late summer the new Iraqi government was off to a slow start.

Spontaneous professions of gratitude for the sacrifices Americans had made to liberate Iraq were few. When President Bush congratulated Iraq's soccer team for its excellent play during the August Olympics in Athens, the team reacted with outrage. The coach exclaimed, "Bush helps destroy our country." Ahmed Manajid, a midfielder and a resident of Fallujah, said his cousin had been killed fighting as an insurgent, and if he weren't playing soccer, he too would be an insurgent. "I want to defend my home. If a stranger invades America and the people resist, does that mean they are terrorists?" Manajid said. "Everyone [in Fallujah] has been labeled a terrorist. These are all lies. Fallujah people are some of the best people in Iraq."

The best people, however, weren't opposing the insurgents who had taken over their city. Finding volunteers for the National Guard in Fallujah while its athletes went to Athens was proving next to impossible. Under Ambassador Bremer's plan of a year before, the U.S. Congress had authorized $18 billion in aid for Iraq over a two-year period; less than 20 percent of the funding was to go to Iraqi security forces. The CPA view was that the rebuilding of the infrastructures of electricity, oil, water, and sewage would provide the underpinnings for a burgeoning economy offering jobs and undercutting the insurgency. A year later most monies had not been spent due to the skyrocketing costs of protecting the workers, congressional "Buy America" restrictions, and the challenge of administering contracts during a war.

While the CPA had planned on deploying at least twelve thousand trained Iraqi soldiers by September, the actual number deployed was half that. The new U.S. ambassador, John Negroponte, had requested that the security budget proposed by Bremer be doubled to $6.6 billion. Money, though, wouldn't put effective Iraqi soldiers on the streets in Ramadi or Fallujah as long as the insurgents were the intimidators fighting with the blessing of the Sunni imams.

Allawi's strategic alternative was to reduce the number of insurgents by persuasion instead of by battle. Moderate Sunni Baathist insurgents appeared to be an oxymoron, but wooing them was the course Allawi doggedly was pursuing as the summer ended.

While in exile in London a decade earlier, Dr. Allawi and his wife had been severely wounded by Saddam's ax-wielding assassins. Despite those terrible wounds Allawi tried to work with secular Baathists, believing that goodwill and dialogue could substitute for raw force and violence. At the least negotiations would indicate he had tried to be reasonable. Allawi was convinced that rational dialogue would yield beneficial results. "I said to them, and to [delegations from] Ramadi and Fallujah, 'Okay, for the sake of argument, let me assume the multinational forces will leave. What do you think will happen?" Allawi said. "You know what they answered? I swear to God, they said: 'Catastrophe. Iraq will be dismembered.' "

Allawi met in Baghdad with the leaders from Ramadi, pitching that Ramadi should not embrace impoverishment for the cause of radical Islam. Not one post in the Iraqi government was held by a representative from Anbar Province. Baghdad could treat Ramadi as hostile, controlled by military force and neglected economically, a mirror image of how the Sunnis had treated the Shiites and a sure guarantee of a never-ending insurgency. Allawi indicated that that path was self-defeating for all parties. Instead, the city elders had to marginalize the insurgents and turn them away. If they did not, Ramadi faced a bleak future.

Ramadi was not improving. Having lost in open battle in April, the insurgents had reverted to their tried-and-true intimidation tactics. The humiliation and exile of Governor Burgis had gravely weakened the city's political structure. The security was similarly damaged by the downfall of the top cop. The provincial police chief, Jaddan, had been the friendly rascal in Ramadi who had befriended LtCol Mirable a year ago and had warned Kennedy about the attack last April. The 82nd staff knew he was padding his payroll, but he turned in IEDs and wanted to get along. He wasn't mean or thuggish; his police didn't beat up people. He was taking a cut when he could, trying to navigate a nice, reasonable life through swift currents.

The insurgents tried to kill Jaddan three times during the summer. On the last attempt, in July, his eighteen-year-old son lost his leg. LtCol Kennedy wasn't sure whether the assailants were insurgents or criminals disgruntled about a botched payoff. Whatever the reasons, Jaddan began to cooperate with the insurgents. After Governor Burgis fled to Jordan as a broken man, ODA had dug into the actions of the police who had abandoned their posts. In late August Kennedy arrested Jaddan for complicity in the kidnapping of the governor's sons.

In early September Battalion 2/4 and LtCol Kennedy returned to the States, understanding of but not sympathetic to Ramadi's basic contradiction: the residents feared turning into another Fallujah, under the whips of the jihadists; yet they were fence-sitters who, as had happened in Fallujah, in a frenzy would drag an American body through the streets. Americans could keep a lid on the military growth of the insurgents, but only Iraqi leaders could bring the city over to the government's side. And in Ramadi, where the governor had fled and the police chief had been arrested, that wasn't happening. Ramadi had settled into a routine of short, desultory skirmishes punctuated by IEDs and suicide bombers. The insurgents controlled the population, while the Americans controlled the main streets and highways. The Iraqi government had yet to make an impact.

———

In late August MajGen Mattis was nominated for three-stars and left to take command of the Marine Corps Combat Development Command in Quantico, Virginia. LtGen Conway would also be leaving. All the battalions in the division would follow in the next several weeks as their seven-month rotations ended.

Mattis understood the nature of the combat. His small "jump" command element convoy had been hit by IEDs on three occasions and engaged in three extended firefights. In April his aide, Lieutenant Steven Thompson, was severely injured. In May Staff Sergeant Jorge Molinabautista was killed outside Fallujah, and in June Lance Corporal Jeremy L. Bohlman was killed in Ramadi.

"Staff Sergeant Molinabautista was devoted to his family and kind towards the young men in the

Jump—I trusted him totally," Mattis said. "Bohlman was keenly attentive on patrol and high-spirited off duty. He was a lot of fun for the rest of the team to have around."

On the eve of the campaign to overthrow the Saddam regime in March of 2003, Mattis had told his Marines that "on your young shoulders rest the hopes of mankind." When he left Anbar Province in August of 2004, he did not talk about the liberation of Iraqis. At the end of their tours, MajGen Swannack and LtGen Sanchez had spoken in optimistic tones about progress in Anbar. When Mattis left, he exuded no such confident optimism. There was no soaring rhetoric. Instead, he focused on soldierly virtues. He read to his Marines a poem by Lieutenant Andre Zirnheld that stressed ascetism and belief in each other.

" 'Give me, God, what no one else asks for;
I ask not for wealth, or for success or health;
People ask you so often for all that,
That you cannot have any left.
Give me what people refuse to accept from you.

" 'I want insecurity and disquietude,
I want turmoil and the brawl.
If you should give them to me,
Let me be sure to have them always,
For I will not always have the courage to ask for them.'

"May God be with you, my fine young Marines,
As you head out once again

Into the heat of the Iraqi sun,
Into the still of the dark night,
To close with the enemy.

"Beside you, I'd do it all again. Semper Fidelis."
s/ Mattis

September marked a turnover month. Olson's battalion (2/1), responsible for patrolling outside Fallujah, had few Iraqi security forces to turn over to the next battalion. After Suleiman was murdered, it was a week before some Iraqi soldiers straggled back to their looted posts. Since then they had been provided new officers, but the officers showed up for duty only haphazardly and avoided any encounters with the insurgents.

"We have to start from scratch," Olson said.

On September 7, as Battalion 2/1 was preparing to turn over its area, a suicide bomber drove a car into a convoy from Fox Company, killing seven Marines. Toolan struck back the next day, sending a tank company down the highway south of the cloverleaf and parallel to the filthy industrial zone where Byrne's 1/5 had fought in April. Sure enough, the insurgents rushed out to the berm and began firing RPGs and mortars. The fight raged all day, with the Marines surging forward three blocks deep. But lacking any authority to prosecute an offensive operation, at the end of the day the regiment withdrew its forces from the city.

The tragedy of the suicide bombing was a bitter send-off to a stalwart unit, deepening the resentment toward the sanctuary of Fallujah, which the Marines called "the bomb factory." Lingering among the Marines was the basic question: what are we going to do about Fallujah?

In early September the mother of Corporal Nathan R. Bush spoke for many Marines in an interview. "It appears to me that not a lot has changed," she said. "They went in there to bring Fallujah back to the norm and get rid of the insurgents and that didn't happen. I don't like to think my son went through all of this for nothing."

———

By early September, from Toolan's regiment to the White House, there was a solid consensus that the status quo in Fallujah was intolerable. "The whole Fallujah Brigade thing was a fiasco," said Colonel Jerry L. Durrant, who oversaw the MEF's training of Iraqi forces. In Washington the secretary of defense was similarly blunt. "The Fallujah Brigade didn't work," Rumsfeld told reporters. The Chairman of the Joint Chiefs of Staff agreed with the secretary. "The situation in Fallujah is unacceptable," Gen Myers said.

In Baghdad, Prime Minister Allawi's negotiations with Janabi had gone nowhere. As for the performance of the Iraqi security forces, he accused the CPA and Ambassador Bremer of leaving him with "confusion and the problems of the military and police." The fifty-nine-year-old formerly exiled leader was equally critical of the Fallujah Brigade. "We did not want this brigade to persist. It was a wrong concept," he said. "We don't want militias to be formed in provinces. We don't agree with what the CPA did."

Making no mention of his own wooing of former Baathists or his opposition to the Marine attack in April, Allawi disbanded the Fallujah Brigade, formally finishing what Toolan had done weeks earlier.

It was a maestro bureaucratic performance all around. Senior American and Iraqi officials proved equally nimble in lauding the Fallujah Brigade in May and damning it in September, without explaining how the Coalition's boldest political-military gamble since the fall of Baghdad had ended so disastrously. After Toolan demanded they choose sides, only four of the six hundred members of the Fallujah Brigade crossed over to the Marine side. Every institution involved in establishing the Fallujah Brigade castigated it later and acted as if it had nothing to do with its creation.

In the States, Senator John Kerry, the Democratic nominee for the presidency, was criticizing President Bush for vacillating about Fallujah. He was tilting at a windmill, however, as the newspapers were full of stories about the Marines preparing to reattack.

"From the regimental perspective, in mid-September it looked like someone high up threw a switch," Major David Bellon said. "No more keeping the noise down. Instead, suddenly we're told: Get ready to go in. It was great, great news."

To prevent any backsliding, the Marines kept the pressure on by using the press to convey what they believed had to be done. "We need to make a decision on when the cancer of Fallujah is going to be cut out," a senior Marine commander said in mid-September, repeating what LtCol Drinkwine had recommended eight months earlier.

The continuous string of kidnappings, beheadings, and car bombings had shaken the city's staunchest supporters among Baghdad's political elite. Sunni politicians like Hachim Hassani were quiet. Allawi began a two-pronged campaign, privately agreeing with Gen Casey that planning for an offensive to seize Fallujah should proceed, while publicly urging Fallujah's city elders to negotiate.

"We waited so long," Dunford said, "because Baghdad looked on Fallujah as a sideshow. The division wanted to seize Fallujah quickly in August, even though the fight at Najaf was ongoing. But the links among suicide bombings across Iraq, foreign fighters, IEDs, kidnappings, and the Fallujah sanctuary weren't as clear to others. It took higher headquarters longer to see the consequences of allowing the sanctuary to grow."

By mid-June the division had been convinced of the perfidy of the Fallujah Brigade. But with the return of sovereignty only two weeks away, the timing was wrong to push for an attack. During July, Prime Minister Allawi and Gen Casey were adjusting to their roles and working out a satisfactory path to their opaque command relationship; Casey could not undertake major operations without Allawi's approval and Allawi could not conduct operations without the American forces commanded by Casey. In August, Sadr's revolt demanded the attention of both men. By September, Allawi's standing was high in Iraqi polls; his first confrontation had been against a fellow Shiite, giving him the political room to maneuver against the rebellious Sunni city.

———

The stage was set to clean out Fallujah. As his first step, Allawi had closed Al Jazeera's bureau in Iraq, depriving the insurgents of the strategic weapon that had saved them in April. With the intent of emptying the city, he then issued repeated warnings in September that time was running out. As he made it more and more clear that he intended to attack Fallujah, the insurgents repeated the diplomatic tactics that had succeeded for them in April. First they sent a delegation of city elders to meet with the interim government. President Ghazi Yawar, who had negotiated to stop the attack in April, agreed publicly with the delegation that any attack would be an unjust punishment of an innocent population. This time around, though, no major Iraqi official, including Yawar, threatened to resign. There were scores of Iraqis eager to replace any minister who chose to step down. Yawar was playing a politician's standard gambit, publicly appearing sympathetic to his fellow Sunnis by decrying the impending attack, while behind the scenes doing nothing to prevent it.

Highly publicized negotiations between Baghdad and representatives of the insurgents continued throughout October. At one point the Marines waited until the chief negotiator, Abdullah Jumali, and the police chief, Sabar, felt safe enough to visit outside Fallujah, then arrested them for complicity in multiple murders, including that of LtCol Suleiman. Allawi, however, ordered them released because he had promised safe passage. The Marines hoped to meet them soon on the battlefield.

When the insurgents failed to gain support from the interim Iraqi government and when the UN and the Arab world remained muted, the insurgents tried their final gambit. They claimed that their council, the shura, had voted by ten to two to throw out the foreign fighters (whose existence they had denied for months) and to allow the Iraqi National Guard to enter the city—provided of course that the U.S. Marines stayed out.

This time, however, Defense Secretary Rumsfeld did not leave negotiations to the regular military and diplomatic chains of command. In April he had been informed after decisions had been made in Iraq. In mid-October he flew to Baghdad for discussions with Prime Minister Allawi and General Casey. Allawi then told the shura to hand over Zarqawi. That, he said, would prove they were serious about ridding the city of foreign fighters. The shura, of course, refused. Rumsfeld and Allawi had called their bluff.

At the same time the press was describing how the Marines were edging up to the line of departure. Nothing in their training or their nature comported with staying on the defense outside an enemy sanctuary, steadily losing men. In early September one suicide bomber had killed seven Marines from Battalion 2/1. Then in mid-September it was Toolan's turn, as Mattis and Conway had done, to return to the States. A few hours after his change of command, a rocket slammed into the regimental headquarters, killing the regiment's popular and outgoing communications officer, Major Kevin Shea. In late October another suicide bomber killed nine Marines from Battalion 1/3 that had just arrived at Fallujah.

Enough was enough.

PART IV

ATTACK

November to December 2004

24

THE WATCHDOGS

FOUR DAYS AFTER GEORGE W. BUSH was reelected, Prime Minister Allawi, who had pledged not to allow Fallujah to keep drifting, ordered the attack against the city. This time around senior American and Iraqi leaders had taken the time and care to shape the strategic setting before commencing the operation. Since April the Sunni insurgency and the terrorist bombings across Iraq had grown in intensity, while the reelection of President Bush had reassured the Iraqi government. The intransigence of the insurgents and the duplicity of Fallujah's city elders had exhausted the sympathy of most Shiites, who knew the terrorist bombings were intended to prevent them from gaining political power. The Sunni hierarchy—a few small parties and a large group of clerics—complained that the forthcoming election lacked security and therefore shouldn't be held. They then declared a boycott of the election scheduled for January and became a marginal factor. Sunni imams in a dozen cities railed and postured, threatening a popular uprising if Fallujah were attacked. Allawi ignored them. As prime minister of a sovereign nation, he was better able than American diplomats to gauge popular support and to sense when his fellow Arab leaders were bluffing.

Sadr mouthed support for "the holy warriors of Fallujah" but, true to his nature, did nothing to help them. The pro-Sunni voices of UN representative Brahimi, King Abdullah of Jordan, Mubarak of Egypt, and Iraqi notables like Hassani ensconced in Baghdad—all shrill in April—were silent in November. Prime Minister Allawi had shut down Al Jazeera in August, which resulted in restraint on Al Arabiya's reporting as well.

Gen Casey asked for a British battalion from Basra to guard a highway outside Fallujah, freeing up a Marine battalion for the assault. As part of the attack, the British didn't have the luxury of criticizing American tactics from the outside.

Day after day senior Iraqi and American officials signaled the proximity of the attack, urging the civilians to leave. Rumsfeld added to the public pressure by telling the press that this time around there would be no cease-fire. Military planners estimated that the population of Fallujah, knowing the assault was coming and terrified by the daily bombings against terrorist houses, had plummeted from 280,000 to less than 30,000. In June the insurgents had zipped jauntily through town in white-and-red-striped Nissan pickups seized from the police and National Guard.

Throughout the summer the Marines had confiscated all police vehicles leaving the city, and each night the AC-130s had destroyed any truck seen with a weapon.

By October video from the UAVs showed that the clotheslines throughout Queens were empty, indicating the families had fled. Agents reported that Janabi was directing a steady flow of foreign fighters to take up residence in Queens, choosing whatever house they liked. In the middle-class districts north of Highway 10, each day fewer residents were seen. By November, Fallujah looked like a scene from the film **Blade Runner**—block after block of squat, unpainted cement houses and grubby streets littered with trash and dirt, bereft of vehicles and people.

———

In April, Fallujah was defended by about five hundred hard core and a thousand part-timers. Seven months later the estimate had doubled to a thousand hard core and two thousand part-timers, although how many had fled in late October was unknown. Eager to show they were ready to repel the Marines, the insurgents welcomed Arab reporters. From press stories and numerous agent reports, a composite picture of the insurgents emerged. They were clustered in groups of four to twenty, each with a leader and a spiritual commissar. Their daily training consisted of weapons handling, studying the Koran, and watching videos of suicide bombers and attacks on Coalition forces.

With months to prepare, they had dug trench lines, rigged daisy chains of explosives along alleyways, hauled buses and trucks as barriers across the main streets, and planned fallback positions. To the south, they had bulldozed earthen berms on the outskirts of the industrial sector and Queens, inserting land mines and RPG revetments. In the northwest, where Zembiec had fought, they dug trench lines and threw up a huge berm. Where McCoy and 3/4 had assaulted from the northeast, they placed Hetsco barriers—massive sandbags filled with dirt and wired together to yield solid protection. At whatever point the Marines had previously entered the city, the insurgents prepared to repulse a return visit.

As in Ramadi, the gangs relied on dispersion and cover inside cement houses and mosques to withstand the firepower of the Marines. As in the April battle, the Jolan loomed as the redoubt of the key leaders and the area south of Highway 10 west of the Government Center seemed the likely rallying spot for the defenders. The insurgents had limited running room in a city measuring roughly five by five kilometers. Offsetting that, though, the city contained 39,000 buildings and almost 400,000 rooms, most offering solid protection against small-arms fire. The insurgents knew every alleyway and back door. They could slither around, allow the Marines to surge past them, then fire from the rear.

Some planned to die as martyrs, lurking inside a house to shoot an American before being killed. Most planned to hit and run, joining with other groups to rush forward and, when the pressure became too great, to sprint away down the alleys. The Americans would roar through in their armored vehicles and declare the city taken; then the holy warriors would slip out night after night, destroying the Americans piecemeal, as their fellow Muslims had done to the Russians in Chechnya.

———

The MEF planners believed the most deadly weapon would be the IED in all its variations: buried under streets, rigged inside houses, taped to the sides of telephone poles, stuffed into manholes, hidden under loose lumber, or wired inside abandoned cars. The greatest danger was a thousand pounds of explosives detonated inside a house after a squad of Marines had entered.

The new MEF commander, Lieutenant General John F. Sattler, had taken over from LtGen Conway in September. An experienced infantryman, Sattler was determined to conclude the fight by overwhelming force. The main job of the MEF was to arrange the pieces on the military chessboard and work out the overall game plan with the division. All prudent battle plans begin with the marshaling of supplies. For several years both the army and the Marines had been moving toward the "pull" model of logistics championed by Wal-Mart, the world's largest merchandiser. The infantry battalions, as the end users, determined their rates of consumption and informed the logisticians, thus "pulling" the items they needed rather than having items "pushed" to them based on determinations made in the rear. To avoid overstocking and unnecessary transportation, the logisticians tried to fill the requests on a "just-in-time" basis.

In April, though, as the spontaneous Sunni uprising swept through the villages, convoys headed for Baghdad came under repeated attacks, at one point reducing fuel on hand to two days' supply. To avoid supply problems during the Fallujah attack, Sattler and Brigadier General Richard S. Kramlich, in charge of Marine logistics in Iraq, reverted to the old method of building several "iron mountains" of supplies, munitions, and fuel around Fallujah, ensuring the attack would not slow regardless of attacks on the highways.

Sattler then turned his attention to the air component. Major General James F. Amos, commanding the air wing, had a plan for twenty-four-hour army and Marine helicopter evacuation of the serious casualties. No heliborne raids were needed inside the city, and the Cobra gunships would work the flanks of the city but would not fly downtown. There was more than adequate fixed-wing air to strike the hard points without losing a rotary-wing gunship to the air defenses inside the city. The heart of the air effort would be precision bombing against targets identified by the forward air controllers assigned to the twelve rifle companies.

With the logistics and air set, Sattler next aligned the ground forces. In April, Mattis had been poised to attack with four battalions, with another three providing an outer ring. The new division commander, Major

General Richard F. Natonski, retained that basic concept, adding several new aspects. Colonel Joseph Letoile, the experienced operations officer who had been with the division in its march to Baghdad, and Dunford (recently promoted to brigadier general) proposed to Natonski that this time the main effort by Regimental Combat Team 1 should come from the north, because the insurgents were expecting the attack to come again from the south and east, as in April. The Jolan and the Maqady Mosque south of the railroad station in town comprised the command center and the hub of the defense, Dunford said, so let's seize the Jolan and that mosque right away and drive a stake into the heart of the enemy.

Natonski approved the concept, directing RCT 1 to run a series of feints from the south to misdirect the insurgents. As in April, the division brought Regimental Combat Team 7 down from the north to provide the supporting effort. This time, though, RCT 7, still commanded by Col Tucker, would attack from the northeast alongside RCT 1. Natonski wanted two armored battalions to charge south to control the city's main arteries, followed by the four infantry battalions that would clear the buildings. The first priority was seizing the Jolan, the main mosques supporting the insurgents, and the Government Center, all on the north side of Highway 10. After that the attack would continue south into the industrial district and Queens.

He brought the plan to Sattler, asking for armor. Sattler called LtGen Metz, who in July had replaced Sanchez as JTF commander. "Tom, I need two-seven again," Sattler said, referring to the army mechanized battalion that had fought aggressively alongside the Marines in Najaf in August. "Oh, and two-two as well."

"John, you know you're to ask for capabilities, not specific units," Metz said.

"Let me amend my request," Sattler said. "I need two hard-charging mounted battalions with the capabilities of two-two and two-seven. Oh, by the way, Rich [Natonski] needs something like the Blackjack Brigade to surround the city."

Metz laughed. "All right, you get all three. But that's it for this way of doing business. We don't want to be accused of playing favorites."

Sattler still needed a dependable outfit to patrol the main highways to the east. In April the insurgents had almost cut off Baghdad. This time Metz called on the British as the force with the right skills. Turning aside protests in Parliament, Prime Minister Blair approved the temporary shift of the Black Watch Battalion to the Fallujah region—a move that was criticized in the United Kingdom as "politicized."

Western troops could crush the insurgents, but they couldn't control the city. That would require reliable Iraqi units, an ingredient MajGen Mattis had been unable to find last April. In November, however, Lieutenant General Dave Petraeus, in charge of training the Iraqi forces, assured Sattler that three Iraqi battalions would be ready for D-Day.

As the MEF commander, Sattler had assembled one British, three Iraqi, six Marine, and three army battalions. Natonski would fight twelve thousand troops as a composite division. A major task would be coordinating the movement of the battalions across a six-kilometer front, maintaining momentum while avoiding friendly fire.

———

The attack began at dusk on November 7 with the seizure of the hospital on the peninsula west of the city. The insurgents regularly met there, and during the siege in April, the hospital staff had daily bombarded the press with wild charges of horrific civilian casualties. That wouldn't be repeated. Electric power had been cut off days earlier to induce the few remaining civilians to leave, and Allawi had warned all Arab reporters to join the press pool set up by the MEF and not to enter the city unescorted.

Supported by the 3rd LAR Battalion, the 36th Iraqi Battalion and its U.S. Army Special Forces advisers surrounded the hospital as dark fell. The moon was down and the Iraqi night was black as pitch. Yet from several thousand feet above the hospital, the scene looked as bright as day to the forward-looking infrared radar (FLIR) camera mounted on a Pioneer unmanned aerial vehicle. A line-of-sight video link projected the images onto a pair of flat twenty-six-inch screens inside a tent ten miles southwest of the city. A dozen Marines from VMU-l—"The Watchdogs" that flew the Pioneer—peered intently at the video screens.

The black edges of the hospital roof stood out in sharp contrast to the white thistle clumps of palm trees in the courtyard below. A line of white ghosts snaked around the trees and flowed onto the roof. "Those guys are wearing packs," Lieutenant Colonel John Neumann, the mission commander, said, watching figures climbing onto the roofs. "They're friendlies."

"LAR wants us to scan across the river," Corporal Robert Daniels said, reading a chat-room message that had popped up on his computer monitor. "Someone's firing at them."

"Take us east across the river," Neumann said over his shoulder. "Shift from white-hot to black-hot."

Behind him the Marine at the remote controls of the UAV adjusted the flight path as his partner tightened the focus on the infrared camera. The images on the screen jumped slightly and zoomed in on two black shadows hopping from spot to spot behind an earthen berm along the bank of the Euphrates.

"Watch their right arms when they run. I confirm weapons," said Sergeant Jenifer Forman, an imagery analyst. "They're shooting across the river."

The two black spots darted back and forth, firing in the direction of the hospital. As the camera tracked them, the two figures bobbed together to discuss something. The screen suddenly bloomed white, then settled back into focus, showing a thick gray cloud and a scattering of small spots, like someone in the cloud had thrown out a handful of black rocks.

"Direct hit," Neumann said. "Tankers picked them up on their thermals. They're scratched."

The dead insurgents were proof that human beings embrace contradictory thoughts without reconciling them. For months the Marines had hit them night after night on streets empty of civilians. Yet still they ventured out after dark, albeit in dwindling numbers. During World War II, May was the month of the Germans' heaviest casualties to artillery, because the soldiers were loath to dive into the sopping mud when they heard shellfire. Similarly, the insurgents knew they were being watched, yet clung to the hope that what the Marines called "the finger of God" would point to someone else.

"Scan up Fran," Neumann said, referring to Highway 10.

The Watchdogs flew the Pioneer east, its camera tracking up a wide, empty boulevard bordered by ramshackle warehouses, tin-roof repair shops, and dingy apartment buildings. Two other UAVs—part of the Marine fleet of one hundred UAVs in Iraq—were flying over the city farther to the south. A few hundred meters east of the trestle bridge where the bodies of the American contractors had hung in April, four dark spots huddled against a corner of a large concrete warehouse, with three other spots around the corner.

"One's lying down," Neumann said, "manning a crew-served weapon pointed at the bridge. Tell Regiment we have targets for Basher."

Daniels glanced at the numbers on the video, typed in a grid location accurate within a few meters, and sent the data to Regiment. Seconds later Regiment sent a one-line response: **Basher on the way.** In April, when McCoy had called for the air force AC-130, its radio call sign had been Slayer, which some considered too bellicose. So now the AC-130 was Basher, a still-apt name for the single most fearsome weapon on the battlefield.

Inside the ops center Marines stopped what they were doing and clustered behind the screens. A minute went by. On the screen the four dark spots bobbed back and forth in the shadow of the warehouse. A ball of black abruptly plumed outward from the edge of the building, sending huge black chunks of concrete flying. Another black ball, then another and another enveloped the dark spots crouched along the side of the building.

Basher, an air force AC-130 four-engine aircraft, had illuminated the ambushers with its huge infrared spotlight and was pounding them with 105mm artillery shells, each round packing fifty pounds of high explosives. Gray smoke rose from the scene.

"Watch for leakers," Neumann said. "There's one now, heading north. Stay with him."

A black spot had broken out of the smoke. Against the background of the macadam on the street, the man's silhouette stood out plainly. He was running with the speed of a sprinter.

"Ten to one he's headed for the nearest mosque," Neumann said.

"Same as always," Lieutenant Jerry Parchman said as he watched the runner climb over a wall. "He's made it."

The insurgents knew the rule: once they reached a mosque, they were safe. While Basher moved on to another target, the Pioneer UAV circled the building to assess the battle damage. A large door in the back slid open, and two men ran around the side and quickly returned, dragging a body. The Marines watched as this was repeated a few times.

"Are they carrying a heavy weapon or a guy's leg?" a Marine asked.

"Don't know. I confirm four down," Lt Parchman said. "Mark this as a safe house. We'll come back later to reassess."

The Pioneer flew on for a look along the river's edge. It looked like a boxy model aircraft you could buy from a local hobby shop, assemble in the garage, strap to the roof of the SUV, and haul to the nearest park for a day of fun with the kids. With radio-controlled landings and takeoffs, the Pioneer provided a stable platform for its optical day and FLIR cameras. In four months at Fallujah, VMU-1 had flown more than four hundred sorties with only two malfunctions (and several UAVs returning with bullet holes). Flying at under a hundred miles an hour, the Pioneer could loiter over Fallujah for a few hours at a time; its annoying noise announced its presence, but it was usually not detectable visually at several thousand feet.

Surveillance by UAVs has been going on for decades, and both the Israelis and Americans had employed UAVs occasionally for real-time target acquisition. What made VMU-1 and similar units in Iraq different in 2004 was that acquisition became routine at the lowest tactical level. The insurgents had no place to hide. When they came out of doors, they were seen, tracked, and attacked—day after day since May, when the Fallujah Brigade had taken over.

Several times the Watchdogs had seen a pickup suddenly swerve into an empty lot; the occupants would jump out, set up a long tube, fire a few rockets, and scurry off before a response attack could be launched. "We followed one pickup after it fired some rockets," Staff Sergeant Francisco Tataje, the intelligence chief, said. "It swung up onto the main highway, and we had it intercepted. The driver had perfect ID. No incriminating stuff. So we gave the interrogation team a copy of our video. The team called back to say the guy confessed after they told him the route he had taken."

The Watchdogs had followed one pickup from a mosque to a highway outside town, where three men with their arms bound were pushed into a ditch and shot. The pickup then drove back to a house, and the Watchdogs added it to their list of "safe houses," tagged for later bombing. After each safe house was struck, they would watch dozens of men converge on the ruins, take bodies to the hospital to the west across the river, and from there drive to the Cemetery of Martyrs, where long trenches awaited the dead.

———

With the western peninsula and the hospital secure, on November 8 the battalions moved into their attack positions a few kilometers north of the railroad tracks.

Preparatory fires during the day were lit. The division had more than two hundred targets confirmed by reliable sources such as the Watchdogs. But the military coalition at the Baghdad level, fearing adverse press coverage and collateral damage, approved strikes on fewer than twenty targets. Concerned about their own casualties, more than a few Marines were angered by the approval process.

Additional strikes were permitted upon positive sightings of the enemy. The Watchdogs were assigned to Queens, the four-kilometer-square district to the south of Highway 10. Long the lair of criminal gangs, terrorists, and foreign jihadists, Queens was a jumble of four thousand drab cement two-story houses, many half-finished, and dirt roads, with scant vegetation. For most of the day the UAV team had watched groups of three to five men run from one house to another, offering no chance for a fire mission. In mid-afternoon, though, the daytime optical camera on the Pioneer picked up a series of quick red flashes from a mosque courtyard.

The half-completed mosque looked like a small soccer stadium, surrounded by an oval-shaped courtyard wall several stories high and an empty interior court. In the center of the court a single mortar tube pointed north toward Camp Fallujah, which included the command centers of the MEF and RCT 1. Every ten minutes or so the Watchdogs watched three insurgents sprint from a large house a few hundred meters north of the mosque and disappear under the eaves of the wall. Seconds later, one by one, they dashed out, dropped a shell down the tube, and madly sprinted back to the house.

After six mortar rounds had exploded inside the huge Camp Fallujah, Major Kelly Ramshur, the Watchdogs' mission commander, took a phone call from the regimental fires section, which was assigning targets to firing units. "Air's not available," Ramshur said to his ten-man crew clustered around the two video displays and four computer monitors. "Arty has the target."

This brought a murmur of disapproval from the crew. Artillery was an area-fire weapon, most useful against troops in the open and not intended for point targets.

The crosshairs on the Pioneer's optical camera centered on the mortar tube and a ten-digit grid that appeared on the screen. The coordinates were typed and sent to the firing battery. The crew waited for several minutes, saying little, as the Pioneer circled several thousand feet above, camera locked on the black mortar tube.

When Kelly said, "Shot out," they craned forward to watch as a large gray puff popped up a football field outside the mosque. The crew measured the miss distance and typed in, **Add one hundred, right fifty.** Three minutes later a large cloud of dirt erupted inside the courtyard. Among several cries of **All right!** the next command typed in was **Fire for effect.** A few minutes later two bright orange flashes lit up the courtyard, with a third about a hundred meters to the south. When the smoke cleared, the tube was still standing. The crew called for another volley. Same result—close but not effective. No secondary explosions. No visible damage to the tube.

During the ensuing lull the three insurgents again ran from the house to the mosque wall, picked up shells, dropped them down the tube, and ran back to the house.

The Watchdogs exchanged admiring exclamations. "They're hanging in there."

"You wouldn't catch me playing dodge with 155s."

"Suckers are dead meat if they guess wrong when the next volley is."

"We're getting a Predator," Neumann said.

The Predator UAV, which carried a Hellfire missile, was controlled by air force pilots following its video feeds back in Nevada. A few weeks earlier the Watchdogs had directed a Predator onto a pickup with a machine gun. The Predator and Pioneer crews used e-mail chat over nine thousand miles to align their UAVs.

Televised football games are controlled by a producer who cuts the video feeds so that the audience can see the play from different angles. That sort of instant replay wasn't yet available on the battlefield. The bandwidth required to exchange battlefield imagery was enormous; it would be a few more years before the Watchdogs in Fallujah and the Predator crew in Nevada could see each other's video. In the interim the crews updated each other by e-mail.

As Neumann sent updated coordinates to direct the

Predator, the regiment became impatient. More mortar shells were exploding inside the camp.

"Break, break," Neumann said. "Regiment has shifted the mission from Predator to Profane. Stand by for a talk on."

Profane was the call sign for two Marine AV-8B jets hovering at nineteen thousand feet above the city. The Watchdogs would use voice and data to talk to the forward air controller airborne (FACA), who would line up the jets for the attack. In the meantime the insurgents had made another round-trip sprint. At least twelve rounds had struck Camp Fallujah.

"What do you think, guys?" asked Neumann. "Hit the tube or the house?"

"House!" came back the chorus.

The two-story cement house where the insurgents were hiding between rounds had a dome roof, a large courtyard with an outside wall, and an overhang at the front door, where a sentry was posted. The Watchdogs had counted more than twelve men entering or leaving the house.

Once Profane had locked on the mosque, Neumann talked the FACA on. "Do you see the mosque? Okay, the target is the first house north of the vacant lot on the northeast corner. Wait—it's where that truck is. Got it?"

A truck had pulled up and five men had walked inside, carrying something in their arms. Three dogs had trotted up.

"Suppertime," Sergeant Roneil Sampson, an imagery analyst, said. "Domino's delivery."

"Cleared hot," Neumann said.

Word had spread about the insurgent mortar crew that wouldn't quit, and over two dozen Marines were squeezed into the small ops center, murmuring back and forth. The GBU, a guided bomb unit, was less than a minute from impact.

"I like dogs. Get out of there, dogs."

"Stay in there, muj. You're almost in paradise. Don't leave now. Don't leave."

The courtyard door opened, and a man walked to the truck and slowly drove away.

"Boot muj sent out to get the Coke. Luckiest bastard on the planet."

Both video screens suddenly flashed a bright white, as if a fuse had blown. There was a collective **Damn!** from the watching Marines. The center of the roof was now a huge black hole.

"That's a shack," Neumann said. "That's what I call a shack! Scratch a dozen muj."

"I feel sorry for the dogs," someone said.

———

Several mortars and rocket positions inside the city were firing at the American units massed to the north. As the Watchdogs were destroying the mortar crew, two CH-46 helicopters were transporting the first casualties from the insurgent fires to the Shock-Trauma Platoon at the Taqaddum base outside Fallujah. STP provided immediate stabilization for the wounded and decided who should be sent to what hospitals. When the casualties were carried off in the birds, Colonel John Dietrich, who supervised the helicopters, drove over from the flight line to see if additional help was needed. Inside a large tent three men and four women in brown T-shirts, short white hospital gowns, and green disposable surgical gloves were tending to three soldiers lying on stretchers. One medic was collecting a heap of ripped or cut cammies lying on the floor, while another mopped away the blood. With IV tubes protruding from the blankets, the soldiers lay quietly, two with their eyes closed, the third looking at the tent ceiling.

A nurse took Dietrich aside. "Any fatalities?" Dietrich asked.

"No, sir," she said. "We had one amputee above the knee. We just moved him out."

Due to the armored vests and immediate medical care, in Iraq there were eleven wounded for each death, almost twice the survival rate of past wars. Once at the STP, the chances that the doctors, nurses, and corpsmen would keep a soldier alive were 95 percent. At Taqaddum, one surgical team worked for thirteen hours to save the life of one Marine.

"And we took a pound of shrapnel out of the soldier behind you. Colonel," the nurse said. "He's going out next. He should be fine. We're giving this to him as a souvenir." She held up a twisted black piece of metal the size of a man's fist.

"How was the movement in? Comm working?" Dietrich said. "Dust under control? Anything I can do from my end?"

A reservist who in civilian life was a FedEx pilot,

Dietrich wanted to ensure that his CH-46 heli-copters, which entered Marine service in 1966, were performing well.

"They're fine. We—"

Bam, bam, bam. The tent shook as three rockets slammed in. In one quick motion the nurses grabbed the ends of each stretcher and placed the wounded on the floor, bending over to shelter them. Dietrich ran out to check on the helicopters. He returned a few minutes later.

"Flight line's okay," he said. "Chapel may have taken a hit, though. Good job with the wounded. It's going to be a busy week."

25

MERRY-GO-ROUND AT THE JOLAN

THE MAJOR GROUND ASSAULT BEGAN AFTER dark on November 8 with the blinding flashes and monstrous claps of tank rounds, artillery shells, and mortar rounds, all bursting in blooms of lava red, while Basher hovered above the apex of the shells and pounded away. The insurgents responded with an unaimed barrage of rockets and mortars that traced arcs of red sparks across the night sky. It was raining intermittently, with a cold wind gusting from the east. Through-out the city the few residents re-maining huddled behind thick cement walls.

The composite army-Marine-Iraqi division surged forward and swept south. The intent was to over-whelm the enemy. Six battalions attacking at night through three cuts in the berms on a three-mile front required meticulous coordination. General Natonski by nature was an upbeat, can-do leader, and this assault required all his confidence in the dozens of lieutenants and staff sergeants leading the platoons and running the company Fire Support Teams. Vectored at a wrong angle, any one of more than five hundred heavy weapons would inflict substantial casualties on a friendly unit. Natonski ran the risks of a night attack because the critical point of vulnerability occurred when the battalions were tightly packed along the line of departure. In the dark the insurgents could not concentrate aimed fires.

———

As the sun came up on November 9, the fighting began with a rhythm that became common to all the battalions. There were two types of enemy, the jihadist isolationists and the Main Guard. The jihadists hid in back rooms, prepared to fight to the death. In contrast, the Main Guard possessed more military training and employed a mobile defense. Once there was enough morning light to see, the Main Guard insurgents dashed forward up the alleys in small groups, darting out into the streets to launch RPG rounds while others used the cement buildings as pillboxes.

The initial mortar barrages by the insurgents on November 9 were disconcertingly accurate. As the shells walked systematically down the streets, the Marines hastily shot the locks off courtyard doors and broke into houses to find shelter. To drive the mortar crews away from their tubes, the Marines called in their own artillery and mortar fires two hundred to four hundred meters to the front.

As Battalion 1/8 advanced, mortar rounds walked up the street to greet them. The Charlie Company commander, Captain Bo Bethay, radioed to the fire support center.

"Turn it off!" he shouted angrily. "That's too damn close!"

"We're not firing!" Captain Steve Kahn yelled back. "We're not that inaccurate!"

Under cover of the mortar barrage, a group of insurgents rushed toward a tank, only to be driven back by a hail of bullets from the Marine riflemen. One insurgent didn't seek cover. He stood in the street, a bulky vest over his blue work shirt, looking around as though confused. Then he blew himself up, disappearing in a huge black cloud. The Marines ducked as the shock wave hit them. They were lying prone when the red wet mist floated down and gobs of flesh fell on them like large rain drops.

The first day, with set geographical objectives to reach, most battalions weren't systematically searching each house, and every company encountered the challenge of the random, close-quarters firefight.

There were no telltale signs signaling which house held jihadist isolationists. The first platoon of Lima Company, 3/1, had searched two dozen houses and found no one. At nine in the morning, entering a house through a hole blown in the south side of the wall, suddenly there were grenades rolling across the floor and AK fire from all sides. The explosions kicked up clouds of dust, making it impossible to see the locations of the hidden insurgents. Two Marines fell, mortally wounded. Dragging their comrades outside, the squad backed off while Lance Corporal Evin Marla, who looked barely heavier than the SMAW rocket he was carrying, fired a thermobaric round through a window at a range of fifteen feet. When the insurgents continued to fire, the squad sneaked up to three windows, pitched in grenades, sprayed the inside with hundreds of rounds, then burst through the door and killed the last remaining defender. The platoon dragged five bodies out of the wreckage, smashed their weapons and proceeded down the street.

During the next six hours, the platoon searched fifty-four houses without a fight. They found a handful of civilians in six houses and all waved white flags when they heard the platoon approaching. With scant civilians in the city, the usual tactic was to throw grenades over the courtyard wall, blow the lock on the metal gate, rush a four-man fire team into the courtyard, and shout and bang on the windows and door to the house to draw fire. There weren't enough explosives to blast an entrance in the side of thousands of buildings. If nothing happened, then the most risky step followed: smashing through the doors and searching room by room down narrow, gloomy corridors.

Most of the insurgents, though, preferred to fight in groups, firing from inside and around buildings then falling back. Time and again an insurgent running across a street would be hit and fall. Almost invariably his comrades would dash out to drag away his body, a feat that impressed the Marines.

———

Natonski had assigned an Iraqi battalion of about four hundred soldiers to each regiment. Not trained for urban combat, they moved behind the lead American units. During the night of November 8, the 2nd Battalion of the Iraqi Intervention Force, which had mutinied on the way to Fallujah in April, trailed behind 2-2 and moved into a schoolhouse in the northeastern section of the city. The 2nd Battalion was assisted by a team of six American advisers.

As the sun came up, the schoolhouse came under fire from all directions from several groups of insurgents, some only a few doors away. Crouching in the street, Army Staff Sergeant Trevor Candellin peered through the twenty-four-power sniper scope he had personally bought and mounted on his M4 carbine. Three hundred meters down the street he saw a man in a black tracksuit with a red bandanna around his neck shooting RPGs up at an angle, so that they would arc down like mortar shells. Resting his M4 on the hood of a Humvee, Candellin aimed in and shot his first insurgent.

Excited, he turned to Army Staff Sergeant Todd Cornell, hoping to be congratulated. Instead, Cornell was peering through the window of the house next to them, pointing to a stack of Iraqi uniforms and boots. They had stumbled onto a safe house where the insurgents intended to change into the uniforms of National Guard soldiers and infiltrate the American lines. While Candellin ran across the street to inform the senior adviser, Army Major Fred Miller, Cornell moved up the block with Iraqi Lieutenant Hida and five **jundis,** the advisers' term for the Iraqi soldiers. Coming under fire from a yellow house in the middle of the block, the platoon climbed to the roof of the house next door and jumped over a small wall onto the yellow house. Below them three insurgents with rifles ran out the front door and were shot down.

In the center of the gravel roof there was a small covered entrance to a stairwell. A dozen cement steps led down to a landing. From there another half-dozen steps set at a right angle led down to the dark, unfinished ground floor. Hearing men yelling in Arabic, Cornell rolled a grenade down the steps.

A few seconds after the grenade went off, firing erupted from downstairs and from adjoining roofs. As he scrambled for cover, Cornell tripped and fell backward, his 9mm pistol flying from his hand. The Iraqi soldiers had ducked behind a small wall, and Cornell lay on his side near the entrance to the stairwell, trying to catch his breath and figure out his next move. Suddenly an Iraqi man appeared in the doorway three feet away, clutching an AK. Seeing Cornell's pistol in front of him, he snatched it up as Cornell lurched forward. Before the Iraqi soldiers could do anything, the man shot Cornell in the face, killing him instantly. Lieutenant Hida fired back with his AK, and the man toppled down the stairs.

Not knowing what to do next, the six Iraqi soldiers hopped over to the next roof, ran down the outside stairs, and retreated to the schoolhouse half a block away. The fight around the schoolhouse was still going on, and Candellin was ducking from one spot to another, aiming in, shooting, and moving. The Iraqi soldiers and their lieutenant kept trying to get his attention, and he kept gesturing at them to take up firing positions. Finally Lt Hida sliced a finger across his neck, saying, "Army, army," and shaking his head. Candellin frantically looked around the schoolyard for Cornell. Not seeing him, he turned back to Hida, who pointed down the block at the yellow house.

Candellin grabbed Miller and they ran up the street, gesturing at the Iraqi soldiers to follow. When none did, they posted up on both sides of the front door of the yellow house and burst in firing. Hearing them approach, the insurgents had run up the stairs leading to the roof. They were now firing down the stairwell.

Standing directly beneath the stairs and looking at the body of an insurgent crumbled on the landing, with bullets zinging around, Miller turned to Candellin. "I'll suppress," he said. "You throw your grenade up there."

"I'm not stepping out and getting shot. Besides, it'll bounce back down. Here," Candellin said, handing the grenade to his boss, "you throw it."

Conceding the point, Miller agreed that throwing the grenade was a dumb idea. Instead, he radioed for help. Led by Lt Hida, eight Iraqi soldiers ran from the schoolhouse, climbed to the top of a nearby house, and began firing at the insurgents on the roof above the two advisers. Battalion 2/2 sent a tank to help them. As it rumbled up the street, three insurgents burst out of the shrubbery and were cut down. Taking fire from all directions, the insurgents pulled back. Together, the advisers and the Iraqi soldiers carried SSgt Cornell's body back to the schoolhouse.

————

All day the infantry had dog-trotted across the wide streets and poked down the side alleys, weighted down by seventy pounds of armor and ammo. The night brought little rest for the keyed-up grunts. Most hadn't slept for forty hours, and once they were set in platoon defenses inside large houses, the night chill crept into their sweat-soaked cammies. The seven-tons and am-tracs pulled up, dropping off food and ammo. Some grabbed the right packs and unrolled their sleeping bags; others scrounged around the houses for blankets and cushions. Most sat shivering in the cold as the insurgents continued to lob mortars and RPGs in unpredictable directions. From the mosques came the usual incessant chants and exhortations for glorious death. The washing-machine racket of Basher echoed up and down the streets, punctuated by successive blasts.

Inspired by the musical shenanigans of Byrne and McCoy last April (the Lalafallujah), the army psyops crews roamed around in their Humvees, filling the streets with the sounds of men and women screaming, or cats fighting, or Guns 'n' Roses. The top chiller was the deep, sinister laugh of the monster in the movie **Predator,** played in low bass at one hundred decibels, echoing off the pavement. After one round of demonic laughter, the fire team on outpost half a block to the front of Lima Company, 3/1, called the company commander, Captain Brian Heatherman. "Sharkman six, that's not funny anymore. You keep that shit up, and we're coming back in." Heatherman sent his executive officer out to reassure them.

After midnight the battlefield quieted. The insurgents, out of adrenaline, dispersed to their safe houses to sleep. Both sides were exhausted. Even with their night-vision goggles, the Marines were loath to search room by room in the dark, because NVGs deprived them of depth perception, resulting in tripping over stairs and shooting at the wrong angle into rooms.

Urban fighting tended to be a daylight affair.

———

On the morning of November 10, the 229th birthday of the U.S. Marine Corps, Natonski knew he had the insurgents reeling. All battalions continued to attack south.

Of the ten battalions in the fight, 3/5 was the only one with the mission of clearing building by building from the first day. Lieutenant Colonel Pat Malay, commanding 3/5, called his battalion's tactic the "squeegee" effect. The other battalions had pushed quickly through, in effect rubbing the dirtiest spots off the window. It was up to 3/5 to apply a thorough wiping.

Malay set the rhythm his battalion would follow for the next ten days. He placed three companies abreast with two tanks per company on the main streets, slightly in advance. Humvees and amtracs used the narrower side streets, moving behind. As light came up, the insurgents stirred and bullets snapped over the roof where Malay and his small staff crouched, watching the companies deploy. Volleys of artillery shells and mortar rounds were called against distant intersections and buildings to drive the insurgents off the streets and roofs.

Each platoon was assigned two blocks, a squad working each side of the first block, while the third squad took half of the second. Each set of houses inside a courtyard wall took about twenty minutes to clear, with one fire team staying outside to provide cover while two others entered and searched. Upon receiving fire from a house, the line held up while tanks moved forward, sending shell after shell into the house. When the AK fire stopped after ten or twenty shells had pierced the building, the Marines advanced, pulled out the crushed bodies, and walked on.

By noon, after the battalion had found seven large caches of munitions, Kilo Company came under sustained fire from an apartment, with muzzle flashes winking in a dozen windows. The company responded with a mortar barrage to clear the roofs, joined by direct tank fire against the windows. The insurgents fell back to a two-story house, where they called out, "Mister, mister, help us! Family! Family!" The Marines rolled up the tanks and flattened the building.

By one in the afternoon 3/5 was pushing through an area along the river called the Palm Grove. Major Bellon had provided RCT 1 with a photomap of Fallujah showing 108 target houses. The Palm Grove was among his top ten. One of the ringleaders in the mutilations of the four American contractors owned a large house in the Grove, as did two brothers known as insurgent leaders.

Corporal Michael Hibbert was leading his squad toward an opening in the wall of what appeared to be a warehouse. Sniper fire had stopped ten minutes earlier, and Hibbert suspected the insurgents had fled into the bulrushes along the riverbank. In the drainage ditch surrounding the wall, Hibbert saw three artillery shells lying on their sides, rigged to wires. After engineers cut the wires, Hibbert blew a hole in the side of the building and his squad swarmed into a large bay, loaded with RPGs and 122mm rockets.

In a smaller side room with a safe against the wall, Hibbert heard a noise. The Marines dragged the safe aside and followed a hidden passageway into a fetid crawl space, where an Iraqi was chained hand and foot. He was the taxi driver for two French journalists captured in August. The journalists had protested that they and their government opposed the war. After negotiating with the French government, the terrorists had taken the journalists out of Fallujah to be eventually released. They had chained the taxi driver and left him to starve to death.

Hibbert continued his search. The third door he

kicked in led to a film studio with the green and black flag of Zarqawi's terrorist gang, Al Ansar, on the wall and black blood on the floor where Nicholas Berg had been decapitated in May. On a table was a glass of water with ice in it. In the next room were two computers, klieg lights, a CD burner, two video cameras, VHS tapes, a television, a VCR, and a recording schedule typed in English. The schedule included what time a prisoner was to be brought out and washed up, when his confession had to be taped, when the execution should be done, how long it would take to digitize the video and make copies, and when to leave Fallujah in order to deliver the tape to the Al Jazeera studio in Baghdad to be shown on prime time.

Late in the day Battalion 3/5 made another discovery at Jolan Park, a kilometer east of where Berg had been beheaded. The park was a large rectangle of grass flanked by a mosque and a row of middle-class houses. In the center of the park, untouched by any shells or explosions, were a Ferris wheel and a merry-go-round with "United States" painted on the center pole in large English letters, embossed with blue and red stars. The corner house on the street next to the mosque looked like an average, modest two-floor dwelling. But when his troops called LtCol Malay over to look inside, the first thing that struck him was the stench of death. Inside the foyer the floor was hardened mud, with a narrow, dark corridor leading back to a rusty cell door. Inside a man in a tan, tattered dishdasha lay with his shriveled head thrust back in a paroxym of agony. Both his legs had been chopped off above the knees. Behind him a second cell door led to a room with another legless corpse twisted in agony, clearly visible in the light flooding through the cell window. The window faced the city street, and through the flimsy glass the screams had echoed through the park.

———

At the eastern end of the city, Battalion 1/3 was pushing through the section where Battalion 3/4 and Killer McCoy had fought in April. The Marines came under heavy fire from the same house where Cpl Amaya had been killed. Corporal Peter Mason was hit by twelve bullets and knocked off his feet. But his armored vest saved him and he scrambled outside the courtyard. The Marines then backed off and pulverized the house. Insurgents streamed out the rear, where the 25mm fire from an LAV trapped them against a wall. Many were high on drugs. One man hobbled down the street on one leg, the other having been blown off. He made it half a block before collapsing. Over twenty-five bodies were found in the ruins, the largest number killed in a single house in the Fallujah battle.

By dusk on November 10, Battalion 1/3 had seized the Mujahereen Mosque north of Fran and halted to observe the Marine Corps birthday, an annual ritual observed at thousands of balls around the world. In a formal service steeped in tradition, Sergeant Major Michael Berg had the army psyops Humvees play the

Marine Corps hymn over their loudspeakers while he cut a slice of pound cake from an MRE and presented it to the youngest Marine. As he did so, the insurgents fired a brace of RPGs.

"Shut those bastards up!" Berg yelled.

Over two hundred rifles and machine guns blazed away for several seconds.

"Cease fire!" Berg yelled.

The battlefield was silent.

"That's more like it," Berg said. "Continue with the ceremony."

———

Lieutenant Colonel Michael Ramos, 1/3's battalion commander, had assigned a company from the 5th Iraqi Battalion to fight alongside each of 1/3's rifle companies. Led by their American advisers and company-grade officers, the Iraqi soldiers took the lead in searching the mosques, where leaflets showed a Marine and a tank engulfed in flames, with the Arabic words "Fallujah—April turning point victory over the Americans."

After dark on the tenth, the insurgents were lobbing RPG rounds and probing for weak spots in the Iraqi battalion's defenses. The 2nd Company was holding a three-story building, but the soldiers were eating instead of standing guard. The frustrated company adviser, Master Sergeant Andreas Elesky, found himself alone on the roof, dropping grenades onto small groups of insurgents who were darting down a cramped alleyway, shooting at the roof and windows. Having gone sixty hours without sleep, Elesky found himself thinking, **What if I doze off?**

An army Bradley roared by on the main road, gun chattering. A moment later a Humvee pulled up, and seconds later Major Andrew Milburn, sent from Quantico, Virginia, to analyze "lessons learned," was kneeling next to Elesky. "Want an assistant?" Milburn said.

"Bring your own grenades?" Elesky asked.

"Six, plus fresh batteries and strobes to fix our pos," Milburn said. "In case we want to call in something a bit heavier."

Back at MEF headquarters, the word had gotten out that the advisers were understaffed. To lend a hand, staff officers from the MEF had slipped forward. Out on the lines, no one questioned majors who simply appeared and quietly obeyed the directions of sergeants.

PHASE LINE HENRY

BY NOVEMBER 11 THE NORTHERN HALF of Fallujah had fallen days ahead of schedule, and Col Tucker, commanding RCT 7, had sent Lieutenant Colonel Peter Newell's armored battalion, 2-2, south into the industrial sector and Queens. Hundreds of insurgents were hiding from the armor amid the thousands of houses. So Tucker ordered Battalion 1/8, holding the Government Center, to root them out. Lieutenant Colonel Gary Brandl, commanding the battalion, designated Alpha Company to lead off. All day on the tenth the company had exchanged fire with snipers and bands of gunmen hidden in two large apartment buildings one hundred meters away on the south side of Highway 10.

For four hours Corporal Timothy Connors and his squad from 2nd Platoon had been firing from prone positions along the lip of the roof on the mayor's office. There was a low retaining wall in front of them, and they wiggled from spot to spot, popping up, aiming in with their ACOGs, snapping off a burst at a window in an apartment building, and crawling away as a return hail of bullets peppered the wall. Occasionally they yelled to one another "RPG!" and sneaked a look at the red, spiraling glow spinning toward them. Not one Marine had been hit, and they were giggling and laughing at the insanity of knowing death was zipping and cracking by or exploding against the concrete to their front. Once Connors stole a glance and was sprayed by chips of cement as bullets hit the wall under his chin.

The platoon commander, Lieutenant Ryan Hunt, called for air to strike the apartment across the street. The sixty-pound hatch on an amtrac had slammed down earlier that day on Hunt's fingers, almost severing them. But he refused to leave the battle. After the forward air controller called in the target, the Marines huddled along the wall to watch. They saw the plane pass overhead and the bomb release. Cool. Then the bomb plunged toward them. Connors heard Hunt screaming "Abort! Abort!" and turned his head to see the lieutenant gripping the handset, blood spurting from white bone, all flesh torn away. Hunt seemed oblivious to the pain.

The five-hundred-pound bomb smacked into the courtyard next to the building and rammed through the macadam with a heavy thud. Connors held his breath, tucked into the fetal position. Nothing happened. Thank God, a dud.

Booom! The shock wave was so powerful, the Marines never heard the explosion. Connors looked up to see a vertical geyser of dirt and chunks of cement rocketing straight into the air, hanging, defying gravity, then pausing and falling back down. He could plainly see parts of the street plunging toward his head. He tucked his rifle under him and squatted down, trying to draw his legs under his armored vest and thrusting his helmet forward so that it banged against the helmet of the Marine next to him. They pushed their bodies toward each other, hoping the Kevlar and the heavy plates on the backs of their armored vests would absorb the blows. They were buffeted and thrown off balance by the rain of rocks and stones, but they considered themselves lucky when it ended and they saw a slab of concrete as long as a man lying next to them.

"Brown's arm is a mess!" a corpsman yelled. "Desiato's down. Medevac!"

Lance Corporal Travis R. Desiato was lying on his back inside a window, knocked out by the blast. After a few minutes he groggily stumbled to his feet, refusing to be evacuated. Staff Sergeant Richard Pillsbury, the platoon sergeant, rushed over to Hunt.

"Hummer's out back for Brown, sir," he said. "Time for you to go."

Hunt shook his head.

"I'm not arguing with you, sir," Pillsbury said. "Colonel Brandl's here. I'll get him if I have to. Doc says you'll lose your fingers if you stay."

The firing on the roof above them had increased.

Connors was lying on the lip next to a Force Recon sniper team. Through a mousehole he saw a flash from a window and poked the spotter next to him.

"See that?"

The spotter squinted at the target, rolled onto his back, and checked his grenade launcher. Then he nodded at Connors, rolled over, knelt up, fired at an angle, and ducked back down. A half-dozen Marines edged up the wall and watched the black dot arc out and down, exploding inside the target window. The Marines cheered and laughed. It was like watching a hole-in-one shot at the golf course.

Two floors down, LtCol Brandl sized up the firefight. He had brought the battalion surgeon forward to the Government Center, determined to have medical aid as close to the frontlines as possible. In the past two days, he had lost ten killed and over seventy wounded and was struggling to wall off his emotions. He told himself, **I'm the leader and this is the battle. Get it done. Focus on the mission.**

Getting it done meant crossing the main highway and keeping the pressure on. **I wish I had flame,** Brandl thought. Instead, he had Basher lurking overhead and the Marines owned the night. That was the time to move.

"This is where they're making their stand," he said to Captain Aaron Cunningham, the Alpha Company commander. "Get a foothold behind those apartments after it's dark, then proceed down Henry and roll them up."

Just west of the Government Center the highway

split into a Y, with each broad avenue leading to a
bridge across the Euphrates. A cluster of restaurants
and shops called the "pizza slice" occupied the center
strip at the fork in the Y. Captain Cunningham told
Lieutenant Elliot Ackerman to gain a foothold in the
pizza slice for the company.

As a young boy, Ackerman had decided he wanted
to be a Marine, although there was no Marine heritage in his family. At Tufts College he had joined
Marine Corps ROTC and volunteered for extra training courses every summer to bolster his chances of
being selected by the infantry branch. Before leading
his platoon across Highway 10, Ackerman asked
Basher to work over the building he had marked as his
objective. Basher obliged with a barrage of 105mm
shells.

At three in the morning Ackerman trotted across
the highway with the forty-six men of 1st Platoon.
Not a shot was fired. The pizza slice was empty.
Basher had done such a thorough job that the building the platoon was to hold had collapsed. So Ackerman decided to push on south in the dark. The
platoon crossed the avenue called Fran, chose at random a four-story building, broke open the door, and
took up positions at the windows on each floor.

At first light the Marines saw that they had taken up
lodging behind enemy lines. On both sides of their
building, insurgents were slipping forward in bands
of four and six. Wearing civilian clothes, most had on
either black trousers or a black shirt, with a chest rig
for their AK magazines. They were unaware of the

Marines until the M16s opened up, hitting three or four before the others ducked into the surrounding buildings. With his ACOG three-power scope, Corporal Ramon Bajarano sighted in on a man standing in the middle of the street, not knowing which way to run. Using the window ledge as a rest for his M16, Bajarano shot the man in the chest, swung his rifle slightly to the right, and shot a second man smashing in the door to an apartment.

The insurgents scattered for cover, then converged on the platoon. Within minutes the fighting fell into a pattern. The platoon held a stout building with open ground on all sides, which made a frontal assault suicidal. Instead, enemy snipers, RPG teams, and machine-gunners were running from floor to floor and across the roofs of the adjoining buildings, looking for angles to shoot down. They stayed away from the front of the windows and bobbed up and down along the low rooftop walls, trying not to expose themselves for more than a few seconds.

The Marines tried to pick out a window or a corner of a building where an insurgent was hiding and smother it with fire. The shooters on both sides were like experienced boxers, jabbing and weaving, never leaving themselves open. The Marines punched mouseholes in the walls and threw up barricades in front of their machine guns, shifting from room to room every ten minutes.

One insurgent sniper had a fine field of view from a window that looked down on the platoon's building.

Every few minutes a well-aimed round drove a Marine back from his firing position.

"I can nail that bastard," Corporal Dylan Rokos said. Rokos was an assault squad leader, an expert in blowing breaches in walls and employing the SMAW. He ducked outside with his gunner and climbed onto the roof of the carport to sight in on the sniper's window. With bullets flicking by, the SMAW team set up. Rokos tapped the gunner to take the shot. Just as the rocket was fired, Rokos looked around, saw a Marine crouching in the backblast area, and dove backward, knocking the Marine clear. No one was seriously injured.

Ackerman had gone up on the roof to call in artillery. The air sounded full of invisible hornets and bees buzzing and snapping, the **cracks!** of the AKs sounding distant and remote, almost disconnected from the bullets whizzing by. The platoon commander was amazed to see SMAW team after SMAW team repeat what Rokos had done—breaking from cover, kneeling in the street, taking a shot, and then ducking back inside.

With his GPS, Ackerman had an exact fix on his position and called 81s and 155s on the buildings to the west. The red tracers from the platoon's machine guns marked targets for the main guns of two tanks. Sometimes air joined in, hitting buildings two hundred meters south. But tires were burning up and down the main streets, and a brisk westerly wind mixed the smoke and the dust of the battle, obscuring target observation.

Most of the firing was at suspected locations inside buildings. With rifles resting on chairs and window-sills, both sides could hit any target they could fix. Insurgents ventured outside only to sprint across openings. It was rare to see a man for more than two or three seconds.

The platoon had the upper hand, with ample supporting arms and clear fields of fire. No Marine had been killed. Capt Cunningham was satisfied to let Ackerman fight from his redoubt while the company attacked on an axis one hundred meters to the west. That would relieve the pressure and they could join up later.

At around noon Ackerman's platoon sergeant, Staff Sergeant Michael Cauthon, and Sergeant Corey Menard were crouching near a window behind a machine gun trying to get a fix on a persistent sniper when a bullet zinged off Menard's helmet. Cauthon pushed him out of the way and was struck in the helmet by the next bullet. Cauthon went down as though hit with a hammer, then crawled up on his knees and shook his head.

"I'm okay," he said. "Just a little woozy."

When he tried to stand, the room swirled about, and he had to sit down. The next bullet struck the machine-gunner, Lance Corporal Matthew Brown, in his right thigh, nicking the femoral artery and causing profuse bleeding. Cauthon provided covering fire while Brown was pulled back to cover. When he tried to stand, he had no feeling in his arms or legs.

"You're gonna have to help me to a firing pos, Lieutenant," he said.

"No way. You're getting out of here with Brown," Ackerman said.

The platoon commander called for a medevac and the company first sergeant came forward with an amtrac, supported by Humvees with Mark 19s. The insurgents concentrated their RPG fire on the amtrac, setting it on fire but not crippling it. Tanks swung up to protect the amtrac while Ackerman put his wounded in the Humvees. The first sergeant took out seven wounded.

After the casualties were evacuated, Cunningham crossed Highway 10 with the company and attacked south. A six-lane avenue with a grass median, called Phase Line Henry, ran north-south along Cunningham's west flank. He radioed Ackerman to move out and cover the east flank. Ackerman stuck his head out the front door and flinched. From the south an RPK machine gun was beating a tattoo on the outside of the building. Anyone venturing onto the street wouldn't last five seconds. Needing his flank protected, Cunningham was yelling over the radio at his platoon commander to get moving.

"I got you covered, Lieutenant. We'll go out the back," Corporal Luke Davy said.

Davy, the leader of the engineer team, packed a wad of C-4 against the back wall and blew a large hole through the cement.

"That should be big enough," he said, giving Ackerman his patented toothless grin. Davy had no front teeth, and months earlier his false teeth had been lost in a fire.

The Marines crawled out the hole, waited for two tanks to take the lead, and headed south. The insurgents were running down the side alleys, and when they ducked into a building, Ackerman would pick up the phone hooked to the back of the tank and request a shot. When a tank fired, Marines were supposed to stay over sixty meters to the rear, with fingers in both ears. On the narrow streets that wasn't possible. If the Marines knew the shot was coming, they'd bend away, crouch, cup their ears, and brace for the shock. When the 120mm gun went off, rocking all sixty tons of the tank and raising clouds of dust, the shock wave would batter the Marines. The water in their bodies vibrated, and the blood dropped from their heads to their toes, as if they were trapped in an elevator whose cables had snapped. Their lungs felt like they were being sucked from their chests, and their hearts seemed to expand. They stood wobbly-kneed in the dust, not able to hear a thing, not wanting to feel what it was like on the receiving end.

The insurgents bailed out of the buildings in front of the tanks and ran up the narrow alleys between the rows of buildings. Behind the tanks and the platoon came the Humvees hauling water and ammo. As they passed the alleyways, the gunners were opening up, frantically yelling "Stop! Stop! I got targets!" Walking and trotting northward up the alleys were RPG teams and men with AKs in their hands. Many had green ammo pouches slung across their chests. As the Mark 19s opened up, they hammered on gate locks and climbed over the walls to escape. The Humvees leapfrogged each other, each driver trying to claim an open space looking down an alley.

The infantry on the flanks and the insurgents were colliding in dozens of five-second encounters, throwing grenades, shooting at rooftops, and ducking around courtyard walls. RPG and SMAW rockets were whizzing back and forth, the explosions hurling small shards of cement at a hundred miles an hour.

After advancing two blocks, Ackerman had to send the second squad forward to take over for the first squad, which had seven injured. Reaching the next intersection, Ackerman heard a garbled radio transmission from Cunningham. "Go firm!" Cunningham shouted. "Get your people off the streets! Let them come to us!"

Ackerman screamed at his men. No response. So deafening was the roar of the M16s, AKs, machine guns, tanks, mortars, RPGs, and SMAWs that Ackerman couldn't hear his own shouts. He ran out into the street, waving his arms like a crazy man, then sprinted into a doorway, arms still above his head, hoping his platoon would follow to protect their suddenly crazed leader. They did. As one fire team after another piled into the building, Ackerman told them to stay inside.

A few minutes later Cunningham radioed again, telling them to pull back to a three-story house to give the tanks room to work. After two squads made it across, the insurgents concentrated all their fire on the intersection, pinning down the second squad. Lance Corporal William Long, who had fought in Fallujah in April with 3/4 and had volunteered to extend, had taken over after the squad leader had been wounded. Insurgents had hopped onto the roof of the building and were moving around on the second floor.

"We gotta get out of here," Long radioed to Acker-man.

Across the street, two Iraqi Army machine-gun teams that had been moving behind the Marines were hun-kered down in the three-story house. Sergeant Garret Barton, who was teaching himself to speak Arabic, led the Iraqis onto the roof. From there they placed beating fire on the insurgents circling Long's building.

Inside, Long posted himself at the foot of the stairs, firing up and driving the insurgents back. Then the Marines ducked out and ran across the street under the protective machine-gun fire.

Ackerman brought up a Marine machine-gun crew to reinforce Barton, and soon all three guns were ham-mering away. The insurgents responded by climbing to adjoining roofs and lobbing RPGs. Too exposed, Akerman ordered everyone off the roof while he stayed to call in fires.

An argument broke out. "It's my machine gun, sir," Cpl Bajarano said. "I can do more damage than you can. You go downstairs, and I'll stay here."

The Iraqis, who had accepted Barton as their leader, refused to obey Ackerman.

"Sir, you can't drag my gun crews out of here," Bar-ton said. "We got here first. Benjy goes, not us."

"I'm tired of this macho bullshit," Ackerman said. "We all get under cover—now."

They pulled off the roof and set up firing posts on

the floor below. For the next hour the three machine guns provided streams of red tracers to direct the fires of the tanks. As darkness fell and the firing dropped off, the 1st Platoon slumped over their weapons in exhaustion, too tired to trudge half a block to the seven-ton carrying their gear. During the twelve-hour battle the platoon corpsman, Hospitalman 3rd Class Jordan Holtschulte, had treated twenty-three Marines for wounds and heat exhaustion. While eight had to be evacuated to the States, none had died.

After talking with Capt Cunningham, LtCol Brandl changed the tactical pattern of his battalion. Instead of attacking in the morning, 1/8 would move forward at night when the insurgents were scattered in their safe houses. Brandl told Alpha Company to get some rest before resuming the attack at three the next morning.

On November 11 the 1st Platoon of Alpha Company 1/8 had begun the day with forty-six Marines and ended with twenty-one.

———

While Battalion 1/8 was taking a rest, to the north Battalion 3/5 had finished another day of squeegee tactics and formed into defensive lines. It was the best time of the day, when the squads unloaded their packs from the seven-tons, straightened out the night's guard duties, scrounged cushions to sleep on, boiled water for coffee, and ate MREs while swapping tales of the day about near misses, wild jihadists, and feral animals. Abandoned cats and dogs, starved for weeks, were eating the corpses, and everyone had a story of a kitten with a human eyeball in its mouth and or a cat gnawing on the cheek of a dead insurgent.

Around midnight, on the roof where Kilo Company had set up its command post, those not on watch were sacked out in their sleeping bags when a man ran out of the stairwell and bumped into a Marine, almost knocking him over.

"Dammit, watch where you're going!"

The man disappeared in the dark as the company's translator ran up the stairs shouting, "Irahabin! Ira-habin!" From the dark came a wild burst of firing. The startled Marines rolled out of their bags, clicked off their safeties, formed a skirmish line, and slowly walked across the roof, ready to fire. Nothing happened. They reached the edge of the building and peeked over. Again, nothing—no ladder, no rope, no secret exit. They searched for an hour, poking into the smallest crannies. There was no place he could be hiding. The man had disappeared.

No one wanted to go to sleep with a wild jihadist lurking in their midst. The only structures on the roof were a covered cistern and a square tank filled with heating oil. Standing next to the tank, a Marine heard a slight metallic tap. As he looked at the surface of the oil, a man's nostrils and closed eyes appeared. The man drew in a long breath and submerged. Two Marines aimed in, while the others drew back to be out of the line of fire. When the man bobbed back up, they shot him and returned to their sleeping bags.

On the morning of November 12, Col Michael Shupp, commanding RCT 1, sent Battalion 3/1 south across Highway 10 to the west of Battalion 1/8. The dividing line between the two battalions was the avenue called Phase Line Henry. Kilo Company, led by Captain Timothy Jent, took the lead heading down Henry. Jent's Marines were immediately swarmed by gangs of insurgents rushing out of side alleys and firing from the windows of dozens of buildings. Loath to direct the tank guns to the east where Battalion 1/8 was, Jent employed Mark 19s and machine guns, advancing at a steady pace with two platoons up and one back.

The 3rd Platoon was to guard the rear and blow the caches of IEDs, mortar shells, and small-arms ammunition found on every block. This was the second day Marines had attacked south down Phase Line Henry, and the insurgents were adapting. They tried to stay out of the line of fire of the lead platoons and run around the flanks to shoot from the rear.

Hearing the heavy fighting to their front, Lieutenant Jesse Grapes, the 3rd Platoon commander, gathered his squad leaders inside a blown-up retail store to discuss their attack. "There's no point getting jammed behind Second Platoon," Grapes said. "We don't want to be stuck on the road with no fields of fire or room to maneuver."

Corporal Robert Mitchell and Sergeant Christopher Pruitt, who had been with the platoon for two years, argued to place squads on both sides of the street to be able to shoot in all directions. At first, Grapes was not convinced. With sniper fire pinging against the storefront, they peeked around the corner and watched the other platoons fighting farther to the south on Henry.

"We had a hard time controlling two squads yesterday," Grapes said.

"We were bunched up then," Pruitt said. "Henry's large enough to work both sides."

"Okay, two squads up," Grapes said, "one back with our Humvees for rear security and medevac."

A bullet struck the doorway a few feet over Grapes's head, and he ducked back. A few seconds later a second round hit in the same place. Pruitt pointed to a second-story barred window in a sturdy, gray concrete home about a hundred meters away.

"Get a rocket in there!"

Sergeant Christopher Heflin and Private First Class Christopher Davis grabbed an AT-4 rocket and lay down behind some rubble. Grapes snapped off a string of red tracers to mark the target, and Davis put the rocket right through the window.

A Bradley fighting vehicle from Battalion 2-7 was passing by, saw the explosion, and pulled over. "Want it hosed?" the driver yelled to Heflin.

"We'd appreciate it," Heflin said.

The Bradley's 25mm chain gun proceeded to pour rounds through every window in the building.

"I think that does it," the driver said as he drove off.

Many of the houses enclosed the rooftop entry to the stairs in a cement box that made an excellent sniper post. Under fire from the cement shack on another house, Grapes called up the TOW and Javelin Humvees that were supporting his platoon. The TOW was a wire-guided sixty-pound warhead that could knock a huge hole in any building. But it required a direct shot and, with all the telephone wires dangling at wild angles, had to be employed with caution lest it explode or go off course.

"It's that house with the tall stack," Grapes said, pointing.

The gunner adjusted the thermal sight on the Javelin, snapped a picture of the target, and transferred it to the warhead. Seconds later he fired the Javelin. The missile shot straight up in the air, curled over, and plummeted straight down, obliterating the rooftop box.

Casualty reports were flooding Kilo Company's radio frequency. The 1st and 2nd Platoons had taken close to twenty casualties, including one KIA. From their position, 3rd Platoon watched the arcs and explosions of RPGs down the street. Small-arms fire was tearing the air in all directions.

"Third herd, close it up," Jent radioed to Grapes. "Cover my rear."

With six tanks in support, the path of Kilo Company was marked by tumbledown walls, splintered telephone poles, demolished cars, and sagging apartment buildings. Slugging its way down Henry in four hours, Kilo fired 160 TOW rockets and 180 main tank rounds into walls and through windows at the firing positions of the insurgents, following up with air strikes whenever resistance stiffened. Fixed-wing air circled in a cloverleaf formation called a keyhole, enabling four air strikes to be controlled simultaneously inside the city. Kilo's forward air controller was Captain David Smay, an F-18 pilot with the call sign Porkchop. The F-18 pilots waiting in the stack knew Porkchop personally and on his command had dropped two five-hundred-pound bombs two hundred meters in front of the lead platoon. Fires smoldered in the shattered buildings, the mounds of shattered concrete and cement preventing the flames from spreading. Columns of black smoke marked the progress of Kilo.

India Company was advancing on Kilo's left flank, a few blocks east of Henry. Like Kilo, India had tanks up forward with the lead platoons. As Master Gunnery Sergeant Ishmael Castillo maneuvered his tank, he could see Iraqis in civilian clothes darting from house to house on both sides of the dirt road. The pock-marked track was barely wide enough for his tank to squeeze by the courtyard walls. From his open commander's hatch eight feet above the ground, he could look over the walls and shout warnings to the Marines trotting behind his tank. Two insurgents lobbed grenades that bounced off the armored plates and exploded harmlessly. He thought of buttoning down the hatch but decided against it so he could continue to warn the grunts. Instead he swiveled—"pivot-steered"—the tank back and forth on its treads, smashing in first one wall, then another. An RPG shell skipped off the tank's front plates without detonating. Another struck the side of the tank and exploded without doing any damage.

With the grunts urging him on, Castillo rumbled down the dirt track, firing the 7.62 and .50 caliber machine guns into the doors and windows of every house. Using the infantry phone on an outside box in the back of the tank, the squad leaders directed the fire of the tank's main gun. One shell exploded against the side of a house and threw an insurgent into the courtyard, where he lay like a rag doll. Castillo watched as a huge D-9 bulldozer clanked across the courtyard to demolish the house, squashing the body.

The tanks advancing with India and Kilo Companies were smashing down dozens of walls, the shock causing hidden jihadists to fire blindly, giving away their hiding places. North of Highway 10 Kilo had encountered suicidal jihadists in about one in every fifty houses; advancing down Henry, it seemed one house in every twenty contained enemy fighters.

"Enter every room with a boom" was a standing order.

Jent slowed down Kilo's advance so that Grapes could catch up. On the rooftops the snipers were shooting at the insurgents flushed by the tanks while SMAW gunners systematically destroyed the houses designated by the squads. It was exhausting, dangerous work clearing

Henry, walking down narrow, dust-clogged alleys behind the growling tanks, barely able to hear the shouts of the fire team and squad leaders, hurling grenades in windows, slapping C-4 to door fronts, ducking from the blast, waiting for the dust to clear a bit, then bursting in, a stack of four or six Marines with rifles and pistols, firing and blasting from room to room.

Grapes pushed his platoon at a fast pace for about three hundred meters, then slowed his advance. "I think I'm close enough," he radioed to Jent.

The platoon had cleared a few more buildings when Mitchell called to Grapes. "Bradleys coming north," he said.

A column of Bradley fighting vehicles from 2-7 was heading to a resupply point, having finished their advance-guard "gun-run" for the company. When they were abreast of the platoon, one of the Bradleys slowed to a stop in a ball of smoke as an RPG hit its side. Three more RPGs exploded near the vehicle.

As the crew leaped out, Grapes saw Corporal Francis Wolf run toward a two-story concrete building.

"They're shooting those fucking RPGs from there!" Wolf yelled.

Before he had run a dozen steps, fire erupted from a half-dozen houses not fifty feet to his front. Wolf and the rest of the squad ducked behind courtyard walls and the scrap metal piles that littered the streets. Over the screaming orders of NCOs, Wolf kept pointing at the house in front of him, gesturing for others to move up. Grapes called back for the platoon's four Humvee gun trucks to come up, while Mitchell and Private First Class Alexander Nicoll linked up with Wolf. When the first Humvee rolled up, Grapes pointed at the house, and the Mark 19 gunner proceeded to hammer the building with hundreds of grenades.

"We could never use this much ammo in training!" Grapes said to Mitchell.

Once the Mark 19 ceased firing, Wolf and Nicoll kicked open the gate and threw a grenade inside the front door. The explosion ignited some propane tanks in the front rooms. With smoke pouring out the windows, Wolf yelled, "Go!" and he and Nicoll charged inside, putting rounds through every door they passed. The insurgents fled up the stairs to the second story. In the courtyard, Mitchell and Grapes were scanning the rooftops for the insurgents who had been throwing down grenades.

"First floor clear! We're going up top!" Wolf yelled at them.

Mitchell and Grapes laughed. Wolf was crazy.

On the western side, AK rounds were impacting all around Corporal Jose Sanchez and Private Rene Rodriguez. They dove behind a rusty engine block lying on the curbside. Peeking out, they saw six or eight insurgents firing from roofs on the eastern side, a few blocks in from Grapes. Sanchez wanted to warn Mitchell and Grapes, but he had no radio, and if he stood up to wave at them, he'd be hit.

"We need a fucking tank or something to go get those muj," he said to Rodriguez. "They're too far back for Mitchell to chase them."

Sanchez kept waving his arms, and finally Grapes got the message. He looked up just as one insurgent popped his head over the edge of a nearby roof. Fifty feet apart, the two men stared at each other. Grapes felt he was paralyzed by the man's gaze. They stared at each other for perhaps a second before the insurgent ducked back down.

"Wolf! Nicoll! They're on the roof with you!" Grapes hollered.

The two Marines already knew that. They had burst onto the roof as an insurgent was jumping over to the rooftop of the next house. They let loose a barrage of fire, and Nicoll threw a grenade, wounding the man. They were about to jump over the roof in pursuit when rounds snapped over their heads, too close to be random fire. They lay down and began to return fire, not seeing any clear targets.

Down in the courtyard, Lance Corporal James Crossan had run up to Grapes and Mitchell. Out of breath, he yelled. "Farmer's in a big fight up the street! He has a man down." Lance Corporal Tyler Farmer was prone to aggressive action.

"I'd better get up there," Grapes said to Mitchell. "You stay here to cover Wolf. I'll send someone to help out."

Grapes and Crossan ran out onto Phase Line Henry just as a Humvee firing its Mark 19 came down the street.

Grapes yelled at the driver, "I need someone to help out Corporal Mitchell."

The Weapons Company first sergeant, Bradley Kasal, was sitting in the backseat, supervising the TOW and Javelin crews.

"I'm in!" Kasal said, jumping out of the vehicle.

Kasal was a salty combat veteran and Kilo Company's former first sergeant. He knew every one of the Marines.

While Kasal went to help Mitchell, Grapes ran south a hundred meters, diving to the pavement as enemy machine-gun fire poured out of a connecting alley onto Phase Line Henry. Behind him Lance Corporal Clay Narey was being carried back to the medevac vehicles, blood pouring from his leg.

LCpl Farmer gestured to Grapes. "I'm on it, sir," he said. "I see the bastards."

Farmer grabbed a SAW gunner, Lance Corporal Dennis Stephens, and a rifleman, Lance Corporal Andrew Wright, and positioned them to shoot down the alley at a courtyard a block away.

"They're behind that wall," he said. "Keep them pinned. I'll get up on a roof."

Farmer and Lance Corporal David Stone climbed to the roof of a large two-story building and looked down to see three insurgents in the courtyard fifty meters away. Farmer nodded at Stone, and they opened fire. Stone, normally a quiet, even-tempered young man, ripped through a two-hundred-round drum in his SAW, screaming, "Yeah! Get some! Come on, motherfucker! Get some!" Farmer burst out laughing.

Grapes yelled up at him.

"We got targets, sir!" Farmer yelled.

Grapes grabbed a SMAW rocket team and headed to the roof. As bullets snapped overhead, Farmer pointed out a nearby roof to the rocket team leader, Corporal Jermaine Nelson. "Hit that window over there," Farmer said. "They're right behind it."

"Dog, there's no way I'm standing up to shoot this thing unless y'all give me some cover fire!" Nelson said.

Farmer looked at Grapes and Stone. "Okay," he said. "On three we all go. One, two, three."

They popped over the lip and fired wildly. Nelson and his gunner, Lance Corporal Scott Viera, lined up the shot and put a rocket right inside the second-story window.

"Perfect!" Nelson said.

Farmer grabbed Stone to assault the building and yelled to Nelson for support.

"Fuck you, dog, I'm outta here!" Nelson hollered back and ran down to the street.

Great, Farmer thought, **so it's just me, Stone, and the lieutenant. Well, let's get on with it.**

They rushed down to the street. As they moved up the alley, Lance Corporal John Winnick, a machine-gunner, ran toward Grapes with an RPG launcher and a bag full of rockets. "Sir, can I shoot these back at them?" Winnick yelled.

"Do you know how to use that thing?" Grapes asked.

Winnick had never held or fired an RPG. "Yes, sir! Fired one in a threat weapons course!" Winnick said.

"Then start firing!"

Farmer pointed to the gate to the building where the insurgents were holed up. Winnick loaded an RPG, sighted in, fired the rocket, and smacked the gate dead on, blowing it wide open. "Whoa!" the Marines cheered. Winnick grinned, reloaded, and put the second round through the doorway, hitting a fuel drum. In minutes the fire had spread through the first floor, and the insurgents had fled.

Jensen yelled, "Crossan's hit! We need a medevac!"

Grapes headed to the urban shack where Jensen was bandaging up Crossan.

"He took shrapnel right through his tricep," Jensen said. "That'll sting."

A Humvee swung up to provide the medevac. For the rest of the fight Grapes would be without the radio operator who had been his trusted companion for two years.

Further down Henry to the south, Mitchell, Wolf, Nicoll, and Kasal were still pressing the enemy when Mitchell was hit by an AK burst from a window. Wolf cut open Mitchell's camouflage blouse with his K-bar and applied a pressure bandage to Mitchell's arm.

"Stay here, man, I've got it," Wolf told Mitchell. "We'll clear this section and come back to pick you up."

Wolf hollered to Kasal and Nicoll to press forward. Lance Corporal Samuel Severtsgard joined them, and the four jumped over a dividing wall, landing in the next yard with a cluttered thud. AK-47 fire ripped the yard up around them.

"Back! Back!" Wolf yelled.

"Let's go around the other side," Kasal said. "Catch them in the rear."

Severtsgard led the charge, pulling the pin on a grenade as he ran around the corner and saw there was no entrance to the house from that side. Severtsgard, still holding the spoon down on the grenade, looked at Mitchell, not sure of what to do. Neither of them had any idea how long this firefight, now raging for almost two hours, was going to last or when they would get a resupply. Severtsgard didn't want to waste the grenade.

"Can you hold it?" Mitchell asked Severtsgard.

"I guess," Severtsgard replied.

Joined by Mitchell, the Marines tried to work their way up a back alley, only to be again driven back. As he turned around, Severtsgard tripped and fell, clutching the grenade tightly. He stumbled to his feet and ran after the others. When they stopped to catch their breath and figure out their next move, Severtsgard came to his senses and heaved the grenade into a courtyard.

Back on the street, Mitchell had had enough of the insurgents holed up in the house. "Sir, I want to take their position out with a TOW!" he radioed to Grapes.

"Do it!"

Mitchell marked the target and cleared the TOW

gunner hot. **Shwackk!** The missile blew in the side of the house and collapsed the roof onto the defenders.

After fighting their way nine hundred meters down Phase Line Henry, the 3rd Platoon joined up with the rest of Kilo Company and picked out a large house to serve as their base for an evening meal and a few hours' rest before moving forward again.

THE HOUSE FROM HELL

ON THE MORNING OF NOVEMBER 13 Kilo Company set out to clear the dense blocks of houses stretching from Phase Line Henry west to the Euphrates. Captain Jent told 1/Lt Grapes that his platoon would take the lead, and Grapes assigned a block to each squad. After the previous day's fight, the platoon was tired but excited, expecting immediate action, but the insurgents had retreated to the south and no contact was made in the first block.

The 3rd Squad began searching the second block by shooting and hammering at an unyielding lock on a courtyard gate. Admitting defeat, Corporal Ryan Weemer sat down to smoke a cigarette.

Screw this one, he thought. **Second Squad has some C-4. They can clear it later.**

Sergeant Pruitt, the platoon guide, ran across the street to pry open a side gate of the next house. Tough and muscular, Pruitt had a challenging nature and never relaxed. "Hey, this gate's open," he yelled. "Let's go!"

Weemer threw down his smoke and hustled over with Sergeant James Eldridge and Lance Corporals Cory Carlisle and James Prentice.

The five Marines slipped into the courtyard, and Pruitt looked inside the outhouse. Fresh shit.

"They're inside!" Pruitt whispered.

The house looked typical of Fallujah—two stories of thick cement squares. Usually on the first floor you entered a foyer with a large living room off to the right, a large common room straight ahead, a kitchen and bathroom with a one-hole toilet in the rear, and uneven cement steps leading to an upstairs corridor with doors opening onto three or four bedrooms. This house, though, had a raised cement dome with skylight windows in the center of the roof, an unusual addition.

The house looked too small to hold more than a few enemy. So rather than wait for a tank, the Marines decided to assault. Weemer, who had gone through the Close Quarters Battle (CQB) special training, posted Prentice as rear security and gestured to Carlisle and Pruitt to stack behind him. He slung his M16 and took out his pistol. Drawing a deep breath, he kicked down the door and charged across the room. He was "running the rabbit," a technique where the point man rushes across the room to distract the enemy while the second man in the stack does the shooting.

As Weemer sprinted across the entryway room, he glimpsed an insurgent with an AK hiding next to the door. As he ran by, Weemer fired three rounds into the man. Carlisle burst in after Weemer, almost bumped into the gunman, and jumped back, spilling into Pruitt.

"Go!" Pruitt yelled, shoving him back into the room.

Carlisle stepped forward and fired a long burst into the insurgent, who sagged to the floor. Carlisle then fired another burst into the dead man.

"Stop shooting and get over here!" Weemer yelled.

Carlisle ran across the room and flattened himself against the wall next to Weemer.

"Ready to clear?" Weemer said, gesturing at the open doorway to his left that led to the main room.

With Carlisle at his hip, Weemer charged in and was blinded by the pulsing white flashes of an AK muzzle exploding in his face. Weemer thrust out his right arm and fired eight bullets into the insurgent. The two were standing five feet apart, looking into each other's eyes, firing furiously. Weemer could feel bullets whizzing by his face. Chips of brick and concrete were pelting him on the cheeks, his ears ringing.

Weemer was a qualified expert shot with a pistol. There was no way he had missed with a dozen bullets. He was close enough to slap the man. The man would not go down.

Weemer was running out of bullets. He shuffled toward the door, still firing, and pushed Carlisle back into the first room.

The AK rounds that missed Weemer as he made entry had passed through the door and struck Pruitt and Eldridge. Bones were shattered in the wrist of

Pruitt's firing hand, and Eldridge was hit in the shoulder and chest. They staggered out of the house, and Pruitt tripped and fell near the front gate. As he struggled to get up, an insurgent on the roof opened fire, the bullets kicking dirt into his face. He dove around the wall and joined Eldridge on the street.

Inside the house Prentice, who had slid inside the doorway, saw a man wearing a green camouflage jacket and black pants rush out from a back room. Prentice fired a long burst from his SAW, hitting the man in the chest and head, killing him instantly.

Weemer turned back to Carlisle. "Reload, and we'll finish that other fucker."

Keeping his eyes on the doorway, Weemer patted his pistol leg-holster. **Where's my extra mag?** he thought. **Fuck.**

He dropped his pistol and unhooked the M16 from his back. He heard someone stumbling toward them and backed up as the insurgent hobbled out from the main room. Weemer shot him in the legs and, when he fell, shot him twice in the face. The man, wearing black body armor over a blue denim shirt, was light-skinned, with a red bandanna tied around his curly hair.

Hearing the firing and seeing the wounded, other Marines were rushing to the house. LCpl Severtsgard burst into the entry room. As he had done in yesterday's fight, Severtsgard was holding a grenade.

Weemer nodded at Severtsgard, who pitched the grenade into the main room. Immediately after the explosion, Weemer and Carlisle rushed in. The air was filled with black smoke and the acrid smell of gunpowder. Weemer broke right and waited a moment for the dust to settle. He saw a stairwell against the left wall and quickly raised his M16. Above him was a dome-shaped skylight and a circular catwalk with a solid three-foot-high cement guard railing. The stairs led to the catwalk.

As Weemer brought his rifle up, he saw an insurgent leaning over the cement railing, sighting in. The M16 and the AK began firing at the same time, the sound deafening. Weemer felt his leg buckle. A hard blow rocked back his face.

To his left, Carlisle was struck down in a fusillade of bullets, the shooters taking dead aim from the catwalk overhead. Deafened by the din, Weemer hobbled back to the entryway. In the dust-filled room he didn't see Carlisle lying with a shattered leg, and he couldn't hear his screams.

His face numb and dripping blood, Weemer limped out to the courtyard. He had flashbacks of a jihadist whom his team had shot in the face a few days ago. He saw Prentice squatting next to the doorway covering the roof. "What's wrong with my face? How bad is it?"

Prentice barely glanced at him. "You're cut above the eyebrow. It's nothing."

Weemer took off his Kevlar and found a spent bullet lodged in the webbing.

Carlisle was screaming in the main room, lying directly below the catwalk. The insurgents were using him as bait instead of killing him.

The platoon sergeant, Staff Sergeant Jon Chandler,

heard the screams and ran to the house, followed by Cpls Farmer and Sanchez. They huddled with Severtsgard.

"We're gonna flood the room, okay? It's the only way," Chandler said. "Everyone point their muzzles up high and blast away until we can pull Carlisle out. All right, let's go! Sanchez, you're number-one man, I'll follow."

Farmer thought it was a good plan. "Let's do it," he said.

Sanchez thought, **Oh shit, here we go**, and his mind went blank—just doing, not thinking.

Severtsgard thought, **Throw one grenade, then enter.** He pulled a grenade from his deuce gear and thumbed the clip.

Carlisle screamed again. **What am I thinking?** thought Severtsgard, as he pictured Carlisle lying in the middle of the room. **Hope nobody saw that.**

He slipped the grenade back into its pouch.

Chandler kneed Sanchez in the buttocks to signal "**Go!**" and they flooded the room. Sanchez ran straight across the room. Chandler and Severtsgard broke right, aiming up at the catwalk. Farmer was the last one to the door, where he froze for a moment, trying to convince himself it wasn't fear. A second later a grenade landed in the middle of the room and exploded right where he would have been standing.

Farmer was blown off his feet back into the foyer. Severtsgard and Chandler disappeared in a huge swirl of dust and debris, as the deafening roar of AKs filled the main room. Chandler fell instantly, three bullets in his leg and both his shoulder and leg shredded by the grenade shrapnel. Severtsgard was also torn up, with shrapnel in his leg and foot. With one hand he dragged Chandler from the kill zone into the kitchen.

Sanchez, who had raced across the main room, turned around and saw no one. **What the fuck? Where did they go?** he thought.

In front of him was the door to a small room. Sure he was going to be shot, he kicked open the door and stepped in alone. The bedroom was empty. He propped his rifle against the wall and ran back into the main room. He grabbed Carlisle under his shoulders and pulled him into the shelter of the small back room.

Bullets were ricocheting off the walls and skipping across the floor. From behind the cement guardrail on the circular catwalk, the insurgents were darting back and forth. Their fires covered all angles of the main room below them.

In the kitchen, Chandler was howling in pain. Severtsgard had his rifle trained on the door so no one could enter and finish them off. After a minute or so Chandler calmed down.

"Hey, man, the Corps will send us home now," Chandler said. "We're all messed up."

Severtsgard smiled and kept watch on the door.

Farmer was lying on his back in the foyer, his trigger finger and thumb badly shredded with shrapnel. He couldn't hold his rifle. He leaned against the wall and let loose a barrage of profanity. "Fuck! Those motherfuckers! I'll kill 'em. Those fucks!"

More Marines rushed to the house. Private Rene Rodriguez stood in the courtyard for a minute to sort things out. He had seen Sgt Pruitt stagger down the street with a shattered hand. He had seen Weemer limp out yelling for reinforcements. The platoon's corpsman, Doc Edora, was kneeling by the wall treating Eldridge for gunshot wounds in his chest. The word was the platoon sergeant and two or three more were down inside. And his fire team leader, Cpl Sanchez, was in there somewhere, unaccounted for.

Rodriguez grabbed Lance Corporal Michael Vanhove and ran inside.

"Corporal Sanchez! Sanchez?" Rodriguez yelled.

"I got Carlisle!" Sanchez yelled. "We're in the front room. Watch your ass. The center room's a kill zone!"

Rodriguez and Vanhove sprinted past Farmer, past the sprawled Iraqi bodies, past the weapons, shell casings, and blood. The insurgents above them opened up with a long burst of AK-47 fire. The rounds hit between the two Marines, forcing Vanhove to dive back into the foyer. Rodriguez plunged through the fire and into the bedroom with Sanchez and Carlisle.

"Take security on the door!" Sanchez said.

———

Sanchez had taken his pressure bandage from his shoulder pocket and was straightening Carlisle's leg, which had twisted backward from the force of the bullets. As Carlisle screamed, Rodriguez's stomach turned over. Sanchez spoke jokingly to Carlisle as he tried to staunch the flow of blood: "Clean the wound, direct pressure, bandage, more pressure . . . just like in Doc's classes."

There was no back door, only a small window covered with sturdy metal bars. The insurgents were steadily shooting at the doorway.

A block away Pruitt and Eldridge were wobbling up the street toward the medevac Humvees. First Sgt Kasal from Weapons Company was walking forward next to a Humvee. Kasal ran to Pruitt's side and pulled him to cover.

Pruitt was close to passing out. "Bad guys in that house," he mumbled. "We got people down inside."

Kasal grabbed the three nearest Marines and ran forward to the courtyard wall, where the squad leader, Corporal Robert Mitchell, was crouching with five more Marines. Mitchell led them forward, and they stacked along the wall outside the door. Mitchell was in charge. Kasal considered himself just another Marine pitching in. Taking no fire, they tumbled through the doorway.

It was a new house, with clean beige drywall and a light, brown-speckled concrete floor covered with cement dust and swaths of bright red blood. Inside the doorway Kasal saw two dead Iraqis.

Sanchez and Rodriguez were yelling for a corpsman. "Get Doc in here!" they yelled. "Carlisle's bleeding out!"

The insurgents knew the Marines had to move across the main room to get their casualties out, and from the catwalk they had an ideal field of fire. Joining Mitchell inside the house were 1/Sgt Kasal, PFC

Nicoll, and Lance Corporal Morgan McCowan. For Kasal and Nicoll, this was their second day fighting side by side. After four years of service, Nicoll was still a PFC, repeatedly busted by Kasal. In a battle of wills, Kasal had called PFC Nicoll into his office nine times for fighting, drinking, and tardiness.

Nicoll's irreverence was legendary. On the eve of the battle for Fallujah, the battalion commander, Lieutenant Colonel Willie Buhl, gave him the microphone to motivate nine hundred Marines with his "I AM PFC NICOLL!" speech, a parody of Mel Gibson's "I am William Wallace!" exhortation in the movie **Braveheart**.

"Nicoll, you're with me," Kasal said. "Cover my back."

The firing had died down. Mitchell, a school-trained medic, decided not to hesitate. "I'll go across," he said. "You all cover me."

Mitchell ran across the main room in a dead sprint to reach Sanchez, attracting only a few scattered shots. Kasal and Nicoll stepped into the main room, staying close to the wall. Kasal looked at the stairs to his right leading to the second floor. Midway up it looked like someone had chopped a peephole a foot wide out of the cement wall. He next noticed a small room to the left of the room Mitchell had entered.

"Anyone been in that room to the left?" he shouted.

When no one answered, Kasal grabbed two Marines behind him.

"Cover that mousehole and the ladder well," he said. "Nicoll, we'll clear that room to the left."

Kasal kicked open the door and thrust the barrel of his rifle forward, sweeping or "pieing" the room from right to left, ending his two-second scan with his eyes locked on the muzzle of an AK pointed at his nose. The insurgent had been hiding inside the door next to the light switch.

Instead of shooting right away, he yelled in Arabic, then fired. In that instant the shocked first sergeant had jumped a foot back, and the AK rounds streaked by, hitting the wall. Kasal stuck his rifle barrel over the top of the AK barrel and pulled the trigger, sending ten bullets into the man's chest. The thickset man, dressed in a khaki shirt with a black chest rig holding a row of AK magazines, slowly slumped to the floor. Kasal pushed back the insurgent's sand-colored helmet and, not wanting to be killed by a dying man, shot him twice more in the head.

Without looking behind him, Kasal shouted over his shoulder, "Cover that ladder well!" and stepped forward to look around the small bathroom a second time. As he did so, bullets hit the wall around him, and he felt like someone had hit his legs with a sledgehammer. He fell into the doorway and was hammered again. He started to crawl around the corner, then remembered Nicoll was in the open behind him.

Lying on his side, Kasal looked back and saw Nicoll propped against a wall. Nicoll jerked and winced as the bullets hit him, shoving his hand under his armored vest. When he pulled it out, it was covered with blood. Lying on his stomach, Kasal reached up and grabbed Nicoll by the sleeve, pulling him down.

As he did so, he felt a baseball bat hit him across the ass, and he knew he had been shot again.

The insurgents had held their fire, then sprung their ambush. The firing went on and on; Kasal estimated it continued for thirty seconds. Why had those Marines taken their eyes off that damn mousehole, he wondered.

Kasal pulled Nicoll to his left into the room. He propped Nicoll's shattered left leg on his stomach, trying to tie a pressure bandage as a tourniquet. His hands were sticky with blood, and he kept fumbling with the tourniquet, worrying that Nicoll was going to bleed to death due to his clumsiness. He heard a thump to his right and turned his head to see a pineapple grenade lying just out of reach. He rolled left on top of Nicoll and bear-hugged him as the explosion went off. He felt sharp pressure in his legs and buttocks and knew he had been hit again. When his head stopped ringing, he shoved his rifle out the door so the Marines would know which room they were in. He didn't want to be hit by friendly fire, and he knew they would be coming for them.

Down the hall, Mitchell heard Nicoll yell, "I'm hit!" and 1/Sgt Kasal yell, "Get that goddamn cocksucker!"

"Is Nicoll okay?" Mitchell shouted. "Is he going to die?"

Sanchez felt his stomach turn over again. Nicoll was one of his best friends. He couldn't die. This was all wrong. They had to get them out of there.

Mitchell told Sanchez to take care of Carlisle. Without a word he ran out of the room, hugging the wall as he sprinted for the bathroom. A grenade bounced and exploded behind him, and several AKs started firing. One round hit Mitchell's rifle in the chamber. Another ricocheted off of his weapon and tore into his thigh—his third Purple Heart.

He skidded into the bathroom. Kasal lay on his side to let Mitchell attend to Nicoll in the cramped space. As the blood dripped from him, Kasal's blood pressure fell and he drifted in and out of consciousness. Each time he jerked back, he yelled at Nicoll to stay awake. Nicoll was nodding off for minutes at a time, then muttering that he was okay.

"Get him out," Kasal said, "or he'll bleed to death."

Outside 1/Lt Grapes ran up to the house as Pruitt, Eldridge, Weemer, and Farmer were being helped into medevac Humvees. Over a handheld radio Grapes reached Mitchell.

"Find us another way out," Mitchell said, "or to kill those fucks so we can walk out!"

Cpl Wolf, who had bandaged Mitchell's arm in the fight the day before, pushed into the entryway next to Grapes and started shouting to Mitchell: "I got to get over there, man! You're my boy! I've gotta come over there!"

Grapes and Wolf circled the house and found no other doors. The five windows had one-inch steel bars covering them.

"Where are they firing from?" Grapes asked Mitchell over the radio.

"There's a ladderwell, and a skylight over the living room. At least one of them is on the roof!"

"All right," Grapes told Wolf. "You get your team

ready to pull them out. I'll put shooters on the roof across the street to suppress those guys. Once I give you the signal, get in there and pull them out."

Wolf agreed. While Wolf put together his rescue team, Grapes led a heavily armed squad onto the roof.

Sergeant Byron W. Norwood, who commanded a Humvee with a .50 caliber, entered the foyer with Wolf to see how he could bring the heavy gun to bear. Formerly a crew member on Col Toolan's humvee, Norwood came from a small town in Texas. His sharp wit had reminded Toolan of New York City–type humor. Norwood poked his head around the doorway just as an insurgent let loose a burst. Rodriguez, guarding the door to the bedroom, saw Norwood peek into the main room and watched as his eyes suddenly grew wide. The bullet hit Norwood in the forehead, killing him instantly. Wolf was hit in the chest by the same burst and fell back unharmed, a bullet lodged in his armor vest.

Seeing the expression on Norwood's face terrified Rodriguez. **I'm gonna be the next one shot,** he thought. Rodriguez asked Sanchez to relieve him in the doorway.

The Quick Reaction Force, a squad from Lieutenant John Jacobs's 2nd Platoon, arrived on the scene. Within seconds Jacobs had his Marines maneuvering to bring fire on the insurgents.

On the nearby roof the Marines with Grapes poured fire toward the skylight. They were at the same height, though, and the bullets were passing over the heads of the insurgents. With the wounded inside, throwing grenades or bringing heavy weapons into play was out of the question. Wolf couldn't push across the main room without better suppression.

Chandler and Severtsgard, trapped in the kitchen, thought they could batter their way through a pad-locked metal panel leading to the entryway. After shooting and hammering at the panel for several min-utes, they pried it open and squeezed through. Wolf laid down suppressing fire, and they staggered through the entryway and out into the courtyard.

Both were bleeding badly. Chandler was howling in pain, his leg twisted in a spiral fracture from hip to foot. Severtsgard slumped down against the courtyard wall, blood pouring from his fractured foot. Lance Corporal Stephen Tatum came to his aid. Tatum, who had the thickest pair of glasses in Kilo Company, offered to remove Severtsgard's torn boot.

"Go to hell, you blind fuck! No way you are work-ing on my foot!" Severtsgard yelled at his friend, get-ting to his feet and limping toward the nearest Humvee.

Grapes and Jacobs knelt by the wall to plan what to do next. Five Marines were trapped inside. Rifle fire wasn't budging the insurgents hiding behind the ce-ment wall on the catwalk above the main room, and Mark 19 fire or hand grenades would injure the trapped Marines.

"Flashbangs! The insurgents will think they're grenades and duck," Grapes said.

Jacobs led his men to the entryway, flipped in two

flashbangs, and rushed in firing. The insurgents immediately returned fire. Stalemate.

Back outside Grapes, Crossan, and Private Justin Boswood crept up to a bedroom window in the back of the house. Grapes and Boswood took turns with a sledgehammer, hammering at the steel bars. Grapes could hear his wounded Marines wailing in pain inside. He could hear Mitchell yelling, "Get us the fuck out of here!" After smashing and smashing, they pried two bars slightly apart. They stripped off their armor and gear and squeezed through. Marines handed their weapons to them.

Boswood pulled a dead insurgent's body out of the doorway, the blood from his skull covering the floor. Grapes slid on his back into the main room, his sights fixed on the skylight above. Boswood knelt over Grapes's chest, covering the stairs.

Grapes, Jacobs, and Sanchez at last had the catwalk in a three-cornered crossfire.

"Ready?" Grapes yelled. "Fire!"

From three angles the Marines fired up at the cross-walk, forcing the insurgents to duck behind the wall.

Lance Corporals Christopher Marquez and Jonathon Schaffer sprinted across the kill zone, grabbed Kasal, and dragged him back to the entryway. Then they ran back and brought out Nicoll. Then Mitchell.

That left Sanchez, Rodriguez, and Carlisle in the back bedroom down the hall. The Marines could either continue running the gauntlet across the main room or get through the bars over the bedroom window. Corporal Richard Gonzalez, a demolitions expert known as the "mad bomber," suggested blowing the bars off the window.

"Are you fucking crazy?" Sergeant Jose Nazario yelled. "You'll fucking kill them! Don't blow it!"

Corporal Eric Jensen came running up with a long chain that was looped around the bars. Jensen hooked the chain to a Humvee and pulled out the bars. Sanchez and Rodriguez put Carlisle on a makeshift stretcher and passed out his limp body.

With all the wounded out of the house, Grapes linked up with Mitchell. "Now we let Gonzalez do his work," Grapes said.

The Marines peppered the house with fire and hooted and hollered as if they were still inside while Gonzalez prepared a twenty-pound satchel charge—sufficient to blow down two houses. Gonzalez crept inside the house and placed the satchel on top of a dead insurgent's body. A few seconds later he ran outside.

"Fifteen seconds!"

They ducked for cover. The house exploded in a huge flash of red, followed by chunks of concrete thudding down as a vast cloud of dust. A pink mist mixed with the dust and gunpowder in the air. Grapes was happy to see it.

The Marines waited several minutes, then moved forward into the dusty rubble. They saw two bodies lying among the slabs. As they drew closer, they noticed one of them move.

"They're still alive!"

An arm flicked limply forward, and a grenade tumbled toward the Marines. They turned and ran for cover. Sanchez saw Grapes and Crossan racing by him. **I'm too slow! I'm fucked!** he thought. The grenade went off, injuring no one.

Seven Marines climbed back up the rubble and fired two hundred rounds into the two insurgents. Among the detritus, 1/Lt Grapes found a woolen winter skullcap with bright colors, the kind worn by fighters in Chechnya. He kicked it into the dirt.

FIVE CORPORALS

AS GRAPES AND THE 3RD PLATOON battled the foreign fighters in the house from hell, other jihadists were burrowing in across southern Fallujah. India Company, just east of Kilo, was running into the same badgerlike resistance. The previous day India had fought for hours at a mosque with a blue-and-white-striped minaret. The mosque was built like a fort, with a dirt market square to its front and a row of one-story drab repair shops on the far side of the square. Ammunition caches inside the shops were cooking off, dust from the tank shells filled the air, and the insurgents were firing from inside positions, with few muzzle flashes showing. It took India Company three hours to smash down the mosque wall, drop the minaret, and storm the mosque, finding ten insurgents dead and five severely wounded. India pushed on in the attack, leaving behind the wounded insurgents.

On the thirteenth, Captain Brett Clark led India on a sweep back toward the mosque, again engaging jihadists in scattered houses. The 1st and 2nd Force Recon companies had sent to the battalions teams trained in Close Quarters Battle. At many hard spots a CQB team was asked to conduct the assault. There was no embarrassment in the asking. The clearing and reclearing was affecting some of the lance corporals, and the CQB Marines were the experts. But the toll on the recon teams was heavy.

When the Marines smashed into one small house, a band of jihadists opened fire; the bullets ripped through a closed door and hit one Marine. A man with a chest rig ran at the Marines as they entered. Though hit repeatedly, he staggered forward and blew himself up, killing Lance Corporal Justin D. McLeese. The Marines dragged out McLeese's body and blew the house apart.

Expecting contact at any minute, the Marines of India Company retraced the route of yesterday's attack. When they reached the mosque where they had fought so bitterly the day before, they entered warily. An embedded television journalist began filming the scene. Lying on the dirt floor were the dead and wounded insurgents from the previous day's fight.

A Marine who had been wounded the day before pointed his rifle at a wounded insurgent. "He's fucking faking he's dead! He's faking!" the Marine yelled, and shot the man in the head.

Blood splattered against the wall as the man's legs twitched.

"Well, he's dead now," another Marine said.

The TV journalist sent the video back to the press pool for worldwide distribution.

———

On the fourteenth, the battalions again searched house by house. North of Highway 10, Battalion 3/5 was continuing with its squeegee tactics. Kilo Company was moving through an upper-class neighborhood of three-story houses landscaped with palm trees, grass, and flowered shrubbery. In one attractive house Lance Corporal George J. Payton climbed up a wide stairway and paused on the landing, then opened the door to his left.

A burst of automatic fire tore into his left leg, practically severing it, and he fell to the ground. Lance Corporal Kip Yeager scrambled forward, firing a full magazine from his M16 into the room. As Lance Corporal Mason Fisher fired over his shoulder, Yeager pulled back Payton, who was dying. A half-dozen Marines crouched around him on the stairs, trying to stanch the bleeding. Fisher threw a grenade into the room, and Yeager heard a **clunk!** as it came back out and bounced down the stairs.

Yeager stooped, caught it on the second bounce, flipped it into the room, waited for the explosion, and then went back in firing. Two insurgents were down on the floor. Another tumbled out of a closet. Yeager shot him. As Lance Corporal Phillip Miska burst into the dust-filled room, an insurgent lying behind the door fumbled for a grenade. With Miska in the line of fire, Yeager leaped on the man, drew his Gurkha knife, and plunged it into the insurgent's neck.

———

In the afternoon of the fourteenth, Battalion 3/5 smashed through the twisted labyrinth of the Jolan souk, whose paved alleyways were lined with hundreds of shops protected by padlocked gratings or roll-down metal shutters that the Marines tore off like the tops of beer cans. Air strikes had split open the sides of buildings, exposing demolished rooms and sagging roofs. Telephone poles lay snapped, with hundreds of sheared lines dangling like the webs of giant crazed spiders. It looked like a savage tornado had roared through the downtown district, smashing everything in its path, pausing capriciously to rip some buildings apart brick by brick before moving on.

In souks throughout the Middle East, centuries-old guilds specializing in leather goods, rugs, and jewelry clustered in different alleys. In the Jolan, LtCol Malay saw the same business tidiness and free-market enterprise, with different goods arranged in different alleys. Some alleys offered AKs, while others sold RPGs, IEDs, or mortars. Some shops stocked small-arms munitions, while the upscale shops specialized in spare parts for heavy-caliber weapons. There was even an alley for antiaircraft guns. In six days the battalion executive officer, Major Todd Desgrosseilliers, had inventoried for destruction more than a hundred thousand weapons and large-caliber shells.

Two hundred meters west of the souk lay the Euphrates and the narrow green trestle bridge dubbed the Brooklyn Bridge. In late afternoon, when Malay walked onto the bridge, the trestles stood etched against a beautiful sunset. It looked like a scene from **The Bridges of Madison County.** After mutilating the Americans last March, the mob had written in white paint an Arabic verse on the north trestle. It read: **Fallujah—Graveyard of the Americans.**

Twenty feet away, on the south trestle in thick black paint, a Marine had printed a reply. It read:

THIS IS FOR THE AMERICANS OF BLACKWATER
MURDERED HERE IN 2004.
SEMPER FIDELIS, 3/5 DARK HORSE
FUCK YOU

LtCol Malay squinted at the hand-scrawled note. "Paint over that last line," he said. "Leave the rest."

Malay knew how his Marines felt. That afternoon they had found a female corpse dumped on a street, arms and legs cut off, entrails eviscerated. A later check determined that it was not Margaret Hassan, the English-born director of CARE who had lived in Iraq for two decades caring for the sick and the infirm. Kidnapped from Baghdad four weeks earlier, she had been shown on television tearfully begging Prime Minister Blair to withdraw the British troops before she was executed. The Marines were unable to identity the mutilated female corpse. Like the hacked-up bodies in the torture house next to the merry-go-round at Jolan Park, the woman was laid to rest in a grave under the name "unknown."

By the afternoon of the fourteenth, the Marines had occupied all of the city, from the railroad station in the north to the one-story dwellings in the south.

———

On the morning of the fifteenth, Battalion 1/3 continued to search in the eastern section. In one sharp firefight inside a house, Sergeant Rafael Peralta was shot in the head and fell to the ground. As the other Marines sought cover in the room, the insurgents lobbed a grenade into their midst. Peralta reached out, grabbed the grenade, and rolled on top of it, smothering the explosion. He was recommended for the Medal of Honor. His valor was a credit to Battalion 1/3, which lost fifty killed in Iraq.

South of Highway 10, the remnants of the insurgents had several more blocks of houses to hide in. LtCol Buhl with Battalion 3/1 and LtCol Brandl with Battalion 1/8 linked up and put four companies abreast to finish the job, using squeegee tactics to search every house.

By mid-morning on November 15, Battalion 1/8 was methodically clearing the last rows of half-finished cement houses in the south. The previous afternoon, Alpha Company had searched a hundred dwellings, finding several "muj" houses with drapes across the windows and blankets and drugs in the center rooms. In one house, a dog lay in the kitchen with a butcher knife in its side, a crude way of stopping its barking.

Alpha had captured about twenty Saudis, Egyptians, and Syrians, and Capt Cunningham warned his platoons to be especially careful; the final diehards had no place to run. The platoons had only a few more blocks to clear before they reached the open fields. It was a poor section, the least attractive land in Fallujah, prone to flooding and plagued by mosquitoes. From the telephone poles dangled only a few wires. A house was lucky to have enough current for a few lights, and cooking was done with propane. Many homes were half finished, with piles of sand and bricks scattered about. None of the roads were paved, and most of the houses were simple cement squares with four or five downstairs rooms and a stairway to the roof, for sleeping in the open in the hot weather. They were built of thick brick and concrete and enclosed by stout walls of cinder block and cement. Heavy metal grates or iron bars covered all the windows. Most houses were laid out with fronts facing on a dirt road, but in some sections there was no order, with houses facing in different directions, some catty-corner to each other and not connected to any road.

Second Platoon was clearing a disorderly section of twenty houses when the Marines came under fire from three sides. The insurgents were shooting from the corners of houses and from windows on the street level. Sgt Pillsbury, who had taken over after Lt Hunt was medevaced with crushed fingers a few days earlier, scarcely had to say a word to get the platoon moving. His three squad leaders had come up through the ranks and been together in the battalion for three years. Within minutes the squads had flanked the insurgents, who fled from the block of houses and took up firing positions behind an earthen berm on the far side of the dirt street. Realizing their sudden good fortune, the entire platoon charged forward, climbed to the roofs of two adjacent houses, and poured fire down on the hapless enemy, quickly killing ten.

When the firing ceased, Pillsbury yelled for them to shift west a block to make room for Bravo Company, which was pinching in from the east. Corporal Eubaldo Lovato signaled to his first squad, and they led off, moving to their right to search the next batch of half-finished brick and cement houses. Corporal Connors was half a block behind them with his third squad when he heard a burst of AK firing, the **crump!** of a grenade, and the yell "Corpsman up!"

He ran through the soft sand and dirt toward the next row of houses. In front of him was a beige one-story house with bars on the three windows in front. The house was wedged between two similar cement homes, with scarcely enough room for a man to squeeze between one house and the next. Two Marines were dragging a third out of the beige house. None appeared to be injured.

"Let me go!"

"Shut up, Doc. You're not going back in."

Cpl Lovato had a firm grip on the web gear of Corpsman Julian Mask.

"Desiato is down. Those fuckers kept shooting him," Lovato said, spitting out the foul-tasting black grime from the Composition B powder of a grenade. "There is a serious amount of guys in that room."

"He's down hard," Corporal Lonnie Longenecker said. "He's gone."

LCpl Desiato, who had been in Connors's squad for a year, had been assigned to guard the gear at the base when the battalion left for the Fallujah fight. He had begged Connors to get him into the action.

"I enlisted to fight, not to watch gear," Desiato said.

Connors had finagled Desiato a slot in Lovato's squad. Now he was down, and Connors felt responsible. He looked at the house. There was a large barred window to the right where the main room would be, a small entry door, and a smaller barred window to the left. There were not more than three or four rooms, no second story, and no apparent fields of fire for a defender.

"I'm checking it out," he said.

At twenty-one, Connors was the most experienced squad leader. Captain Cunningham, while he had been short of officers and senior NCOs back in the States, had made him the acting platoon commander for several weeks. Connors had been in eleven gunfights inside houses.

He ran to the doorway and peeked in. Inside, the floor was hard-packed dirt, and there were no interior doors, no fixtures, and no furniture. It was an empty

shell of bricks and mortar with the smell of fresh construction, months away from completion. To his right,
the main room was empty. To his left, a dirt corridor
led past a room and through an open door to a back
bedroom. Lying against the bedroom wall in plain
sight was Desiato's body.

With Longenecker, his fire team leader, one step
behind him, Desiato had stepped into that small, dark
room, swung his rifle to the left, and was slammed up
against the wall by a hail of bullets. He slid down the
wall, face and torso toward the assailants who were
still firing. Bullets continued to strike him in the face,
the armored vest, and the legs. The bullets had pinned
his body against the wall, the SAW lying by his side.

Connors could plainly see Desiato's wounds and
knew he was dead.

LCpl Brown entered and stood behind Connors,
peering over his shoulder.

"Before we do a thing," Connors said, "we have to
be sure he's dead. Can you confirm he's dead?"

Brown looked at the body lying in the kill zone a
few feet away, the wounds all too clear.

"He's dead," Brown said.

"All right," Connors said, "let's get him out of there."

Desiato was so close, lying just inside the room. The
insurgents hadn't said a word or made a sound. With
a quick lunge Connors could grab his web gear, give a
tug, and have the body back in the corridor. He eased
his shoulder into the foyer.

A hail of AK fire ripped past his face as he flung his
body back.

"SAW! Give me a SAW!" Connors screamed.

He turned back into the foyer, letting fly two hundred rounds down the corridor into the back room. He waited, the barrel smoking. No sounds, no return fire.

"Get out," he said over his shoulder, spooning a grenade.

He took out the pin and let the spoon spin loose. He milked the grenade for the count of **one!**, pulled his arm back for an underhand lob, looked down the corridor, and locked eyes with a man with wild black hair and a full beard, his arm also back. The two grenades sailed past each other as Connors shouted "Grenade!" and pushed Brown behind him into the room to his left. They went down in a tangle as both grenades went off, filling Connors's ears with that ringing sensation, mouth instantly dry, teeth black and grimy, an acrid and burning taste in his mouth. The dirt and dust particles filled the room, blocking out all sight. The two Marines got to their knees and staggered out the foyer door to their left.

In the courtyard, Cpl Connors washed out his mouth and wished he could brush his teeth, now filthy with gunpowder. Corporal Camillio Aragon saw a man crawling along the roof and brought him down with one burst. Connors squiggled sideways down the alley behind the house to a small window, stuck his rifle through bars, and got off a long burst, raking the room. Two or three AKs blazed back, and Connors crabbed out of the alley before they could get to the window and shoot down at him.

"It's a fucking Nazi pillbox," he said. "Those haj fucks are gonna die."

He grabbed a one-pound stick of C-4, shoved in a ten-second fuse, and sneaked back to the front door, covered by Lovato. He popped smoke on the time fuse, fired a few rounds from his 9mm pistol, threw the C-4 down the corridor, and ran into the courtyard to his right. With Lovato and two other Marines, he took cover under the overhang of the adjacent house, about thirty feet away. The C-4 blew, but before they could react, an AK muzzle poked out of a hole in the roof next to their heads. Firing blindly, their attacker sprayed the wall a few feet above their heads.

Connors pulled another grenade from his web gear and lobbed it into the hole. It exploded, and a foot encased in a sneaker flew by them.

"All fucking right," Connors said.

The rest of the platoon had pulled back to a large house about thirty feet to their right, and they were the only Marines in the open. Soon they were taking fire from two directions, poor shooters in houses not twenty feet away, but steadily improving. Spurts of dirt were continuously erupting in the open courtyard separating them from the large house.

"I'll get some more grenades," Lovato said, running across the courtyard.

Connors watched the bullets striking behind his friend's feet and thought, **Boy, if he sees those, he'll never come back.** Lovato collected grenades from the other Marines, who were firing wherever they thought the insurgents were hiding, and popped back out the door. This time he did see the dirt puffs around him and dove into a trench next to the large building.

"You're screwed, Connors!" Lovato yelled. "I can't get the grenades to you."

"They have pins in them, for God's sake. Pitch them over!" Connors yelled. "How many do you have?"

"Oh. I forgot. I have three. I'll throw you two."

"What do you need one for?"

"You don't like it, go get your own."

Lovato threw over two grenades, and Connors scooped them up. With the Marines in the house providing heavy fire, Connors and his small group threw their grenades and dashed safely across the courtyard.

Inside the house, SSgt Pillsbury listened to their report.

"We need to get him back," Connors said.

"I'll take care of those assholes sniping at you," Pillsbury said. "You know the situation. You get Desiato."

Connors looked around. Everybody was edging forward. He whispered to Pillsbury: "All those grenades, C-four. I don't want the young guys seeing Desiato when this is over. Just the squad leaders."

"Agreed. The corporals go with Connors," Pillsbury said. "The rest of you fall in on me. I'll assign shooting posts."

Corporals Lovato, Aragon, Donaghy, and Longenecker slipped out of the door behind Connors, moving by hand and arm signals, the roar of the M16s behind them deafening. Aragon slipped first back into the beige house and quickly ducked back out.

"Shit, the body's gone," he said. "They've taken Desiato."

Forty minutes had gone by since they had last been inside the house, plenty of time for the defenders to slip down a back alley or tunnel.

Longenecker ducked inside for a second look and came back out.

"We're fucked," he said. "Shit, shit, shit."

It was their worst fear: a repeat of Mogadishu, the body of an American soldier stripped naked and dragged through the streets. Connors felt like vomiting. He called Pillsbury over his handheld, knowing Generals Sattler and Natonski would stop the whole operation and rip Fallujah apart brick by brick, looking for Desiato.

Pillsbury was aghast. "Check again, for God's sake."

Corporal Brad Donaghy went in for the third time, creeping farther down the corridor for a better look into the back bedroom. The others pressed behind him.

Donaghy backed up a few feet. "I see Desiato," he murmured. "They've pulled him back to sucker us in. They've crossed his legs and put his arms at his sides. I don't know whether they're jerking with us or showing him respect."

Just then an insurgent ran forward into the back room a few feet, fired a burst of AK rounds at an angle down the corridor, and leaped back before the Marines could return fire. Aragon and Longenecker pitched grenades into the room, and the firing stopped.

"Wasn't Desiato a SAW gunner?" Donaghy said. "Well, I didn't see any SAW."

A SAW fired so fast it could cut a man in two.

"We gotta make sure they're down," Connors said, sidestepping toward the open bedroom door. Aragon drew his 9mm and followed on Connors's shoulder. At the edge of the doorway Connors reached down and picked up a piece of cement.

"I'll throw this in there and see if they shoot," he said.

He threw the rock and nothing happened.

"I'll shoot," Aragon said, reaching over Connors's shoulder and squeezing the trigger to his pistol.

Nothing happened. Aragon ejected a round, recocked, and reached around to shoot again. **Blaaam.** The SAW spewed two hundred rounds back at their faces. Connors and Aragon clung to each other and tried to push their heads inside the wall. The stream of bullets, looking like a long red rod of fire, flew by, burning Aragon's cheek. Connors could feel the hot wind, and chips from the cement wall stung his face.

They both tumbled back along the corridor to the opening to the next-door room, bumping into Lovato, who was furiously pulling the pin on a grenade.

"Frag out!" Lovato yelled.

The grenade struck the doorway and bounced back, hitting Connors on his foot. Connors launched himself into the room, the grenade exploding while he was in the air. He landed hard, the wind knocked out of him, groggy, unable to breathe or see for a few seconds. He tried his arms and legs, then wiggled his hands and toes. All were attached and working. He lay alone in the room, keeping his pistol trained on the doorway, worried that the insurgents next door would rush in. After a while he could hear the voices in his radio ear clip.

"Connors, Connors! My God, I think I killed him!" Lovato was yelling. "Answer me, for God's sake, answer me!"

"Yeah, yeah, yeah, I'm fine," Connors said over the radio, "but get me the fuck out of this room right now!"

Longenecker threw covering fire down the right-hand side of the corridor as Connors crawled down the left side. After he fired three rounds, Longenecker stopped shooting.

"I'll supply all the fucking rounds you'll ever need!" Connors screamed.

Longenecker resumed firing, and Connors stumbled out into the bright sunlight of the courtyard.

Aragon poked around in the garbage and pulled out a broken mirror. Smashing off a corner, he taped it to a stick. "We'll poke it around a corner and see where they are," he said.

Connors and Aragon went back down the corridor to try their invention. It fell apart on the first try. So they each threw another grenade into the quiet bedroom and backed out of the corridor.

"Let's check with the staff sergeant," Connors said. "We don't have enough firepower."

Once inside the large house, the five corporals

became uncomfortable from all the stares from their Marines. Aragon asked for a SMAW, and they went up on the roof. The sniper fire had ceased, and Aragon drew aim on the back part of the bedroom, fifty feet away across the courtyard. The rocket struck a little to the left, gouging out a corner of the house but not creating a line of sight into the bedroom. The pillbox remained intact.

Pillsbury called for tank support, and the corporals went down to keep careful watch, determined that Desiato's body was going home and nowhere else. When the tank rolled up with the hatches shut, the gunners sprayed the walls and windows with .50 caliber, then backed into the front of the house, trying to collapse it.

Connors ran forward and banged on the side of the tank with his pistol. When the hatch opened, he vigorously shook his head no—they weren't going to bury Desiato. He couldn't make himself heard over the tank engine, so in pantomine he showed that he wanted the main gun to fire where he directed. He then calculated the angles, pointed his pistol at the front of the house, and fired two bullets, one high and one low, to the left of the doorway. The tanker nodded and backed off, while the five corporals took cover.

BAANG! The first jarring round slammed through the high side of the house exactly where Connors had shot. **BAANG!** Again, dead on, this time through the lower side. The pillbox was breached. The five Marines ran up, three to the main door, one to each hole, rifles aimed in. As the dust settled, through both holes they could see into the back bedroom. Donaghy saw movement, yelled **Oogaf!** (Stop!), and put one round in a man's head. Having moved down the corridor, Longenecker peeked around the corner as an insurgent darted out to fire. Longenecker dropped to one knee and put three rounds into the man's chest. Connors, Aragon, and Lovato rushed forward and flooded the room, firing into every corner, emptying magazines into every crumpled figure they could see.

Through the acrid smoke they counted six insurgents sprawled inside the tiny room, one flattened against the back wall under the window, three sagging along the back wall, and two lying on top of one another in a corner. All wore dark shirts and pants and sneakers. They had backpacks, AK magazine vests, money, binoculars, grenades, AKs, and a Dragunov sniper rifle with a telescope. The oldest—the one with the thick black beard who had thrown the grenade at Connors—looked to be in his late forties. The others were in their twenties or late teens, except for the youngest. He was about twelve or thirteen.

The five corporals—in Homer's words, **deadly men in the strong encounters**—had finished their mission. They took a stretcher, covered LCpl Desiato with blankets, and carried the body from the pillbox back to the platoon position to await transportation to Massachusetts.

———

That afternoon the television networks showed the video of the Marine shooting the wounded insurgent inside the mosque. Al Jazeera played the clip every hour. The terrorists had provided a video of the execution of Margaret Hassan, but Al Jazeera refused to air it, knowing that would provoke outrage against the insurgents. Instead, Al Jazeera posted side by side a photo of Hassan and a picture of the Marine aiming his rifle, suggesting they were the twin sides of terror.

———

Zarqawi and his terrorists had used Fallujah as their sanctuary for six months. The man was the face of evil, cunning and calculating. His suicide bombings had driven the United Nations from Iraq, slaughtered hundreds of Shiites, killed dozens of Americans, and inspired extremists to follow his example. Several times the special forces thought they had him trapped, but he continued to escape.

On November 16, a kilometer east of where Connors had fought, the armored battalion 2-2 had trapped two dozen insurgents in a large walled compound. When the insurgents had held out despite repeated poundings from the Abrams tanks, LtCol Newell, the 2-2 commander, called in air strikes, reducing the complex building by building.

Amid the smoldering wreckage, Newell's soldiers found underground tunnels, shattered body parts, computers, passports, and letters from Zarqawi. An Arabic sign on one wall read "Al Qaeda Organization." Inside a factory for making bombs, a Ford Explorer rigged with explosives sat on the assembly line.

The demolishment of the Zarqawi complex signaled the termination of major combat inside the city. Zarqawi confirmed the defeat by posting an audiotape on the Internet, condemning the Sunni clerical establishment for abandoning his cause in Fallujah.

"You have let us down in the darkest circumstances and handed us over to the enemy," he said.

While his base of operations had been eliminated, Zarqawi himself remained at large.

———

The battle began on November 7, and the Iraqi government declared the city secured on November 13. But as Malay and the other battalions applied squeegee tactics to a larger and larger area, American casualties continued for weeks.

The rationale for stopping the attack in April was a perception that the damage being done was too great. In the month of April, 150 air strikes had destroyed 75 to 100 buildings. In November the damage was vastly greater. There were 540 air strikes and 14,000 artillery and mortar shells fired, as well as 2,500 tank main gun rounds. Eighteen thousand of Fallujah's 39,000 buildings were damaged or destroyed. In the November attack 70 Americans were killed and 609 wounded.

During the twenty-month struggle for Fallujah, 151 Americans had died and more than a thousand were wounded.

In late November a high-ranking American general

from Baghdad drove through the city, looking carefully to the left and to the right. After several minutes
he told the driver to stop. He got out and looked up
and down the devastated street, at the drooping telephone poles, gutted storefronts, heaps of concrete,
twisted skeletons of burnt-out cars, demolished roofs,
and sagging walls.

"Holy shit," he said.

BY INCHES, NOT YARDS

January to May 2005

IN JANUARY 2005 THE IRAQIS WENT to the polls to elect a National Assembly charged with forming a government and writing a constitution. Over 60 percent of the eligible voters nationwide went to the polls, an impressive turnout and a significant success for the supporters of democracy. In the Sunni areas, though, the turnout was less than 8 percent. Sunni leaders and clerics urged a boycott that was obeyed.

The residents slowly returned to a devastated Fallujah. Marines and Iraqi soldiers patrolled the streets and the periphery. Iraqi males of military age were fingerprinted, given retina scans, and issued identification cards. The few vehicles allowed in were rigorously searched. There were scant instances of IEDs or gunfire. Fallujah was the safest town in Iraq, albeit the most heavily guarded. Jobs were scarce, as was potable water and electricity. Fallujah was resolved by locking down the city behind barbed wire—not a model for other cities.

In Ramadi, the situation was unchanged from the summer. Battalion 2/4 had been replaced by Battalion 2/5. "Progress is going to be gained by inches, not yards," the battalion commander, Lieutenant Colonel Randy Newman, said.

In Ramadi there was no identifiable fundamentalist leader like Janabi. Instead, a loose collection of insurgent gangs cajoled and intimidated, controlling the marketplace, the back streets, and the behavior of the people. In response to threats, the entire police force had walked off the job before the January elections. Scarcely anyone voted. In Ramadi, in the third year of the insurgency, it was still predominantly the Americans against the Sunni insurgents operating inside a Sunni city.

As for Fallujah, by the spring of 2005 it had reverted to a non-descript industrial city with no distinguishing characteristics. The insurgency inside the city had been quashed, but at a great price.

The insurgency in Iraq as a whole, however, had not been defeated. Sunni leadership was unrepentant about the past repression of Shiites and unreconciled to being a numerical minority in a democracy. On April 26, 2005, one year after Zembiec's fierce house-to-house fight at the Jolan cemetery, Gen Myers held a press conference at the Pentagon: "Their [the insurgents'] capability is about where it was a year ago," he said.

The American forces had held the line against the insurgents, but only the Iraqis themselves could quell the insurrection. The two Iraqi battalions in the November battle in Fallujah had acquitted themselves well, and their American advisers were proud. They were bothered, though, that the Iraqi soldiers going on leave changed into civilian clothes and hitched rides in buses and cars. None dared wear a uniform off duty. The insurgents had lost their Sunni sanctuary in Fallujah, but they hadn't lost their ability to intimidate.

The insurgency would be finished when an Iraqi soldier in uniform boarded a bus, got off at his local market, and walked home.

NO TRUE GLORY

AFTER THE BATTLE IN THE HOUSE from hell, Sgt Byron Norwood's body was returned to the small town of Pflugerville, Texas. Col Toolan delivered the eulogy at the funeral. Later the Norwoods wrote a letter to President Bush expressing Byron's pride in serving his country. The president invited them to attend the State of the Union address, during which he singled them out for thanks. The twenty-month battle for Fallujah had reached from the house from hell to the White House.

The singular lesson from Fallujah is clear: when you send our soldiers into battle, let them finish the fight. Ordering the Marines to attack, then calling them off, then dithering, then sending them back in constituted a flawed set of strategic decisions. American soldiers are not political bargaining chips. They fight for one another, for winning the battle, and for their country's cause.

There were two separate chains of command in Iraq. Ambassador Bremer had authority for determining the country's policy and the budget, but he did not direct the operations of the American military. General Abizaid had responsibility for security, but he did not direct the development of the Iraqi force to replace the American military. This separation of authority from responsibility constituted a grave systemic flaw.

The responsibility for making critical decisions concerning Fallujah bounced back and forth between the military and the civilians. After the mutilation of the four contractors in Fallujah in April 2004, the White House and high officials reacted emotionally by ordering a full attack on the city. Gen Abizaid was key in making that decision, with Bremer in support. When Iraqi officials reacted with equal emotion against it, Bremer recommended to the White House a cease-fire rather than risk the resignation of Iraqi officials. The Marine option was to finish the battle rather than risk turning Fallujah into an enemy sanctuary. Abizaid concurred with Bremer, not with the Marines. With both field commanders (Bremer and Abizaid) in agreement, the Marine option was closed out and was not presented to President Bush.

As the unilateral cease-fire dragged on, the stream of advice flowing into the White House from multiple sources—Abizaid, Bremer, Sanchez, Blackwill, Blair, and others—resulted in countermands and caused confusion down the ranks. In late April, with Abizaid and Bremer unwilling to seize the city, the Marines turned it over to the Fallujah Brigade. That political decision should have involved the civilian diplomats, but the military chain of command excluded them.

In war, authority and responsibility should reside in the same organization. Iraq required one unified civilian-military staff reporting to a single commander who would be held responsible for all key decisions.

Our military lacked clarity of mission. Some American divisions were pursuing offensive operations, while others were trying to invigorate municipal services and select Iraqi leaders. In July 2003 CentCom announced it was fighting an insurgency. Yet a year was wasted during which American forces could have trained and selected Iraqi military leaders. The dissolution of the Iraqi Army and the failure to develop quickly a replacement security force were the principal shortfalls attendant to the liberation of Iraq.

For these lapses, the generals were as responsible as the civilians. The CPA had the authority to develop the security force—and CentCom had firmly supported the creation of the CPA. When Bremer dissolved the Iraqi military, the Central Command did not object. While having the authority to create a new army, the hastily assembled CPA staff lacked the expertise to do so. The CPA, though, did have diplomats whose negotiating skills were essential to developing a new Iraqi government. The separate military and civilian staffs needed to be pulled together.

The high command, both civilian and military, interfered too much in Fallujah and knew too little. Twice Abizaid overruled his own field commanders, by first ordering them to attack and then ordering them to stop a week later. The televideo was used too often as a substitute for written staff work, while those with critical information, like the division commander Mattis, were not included in those conferences—despite the new technologies. The solipsism that too frequently infects high commands has no place on a battlefield.

Left alone, Conway and Mattis would have continued the attack in April. Had they attacked fully, the outcome in Fallujah would have resembled that in Ramadi: Americans in control of the highways and insurgents in control of the marketplaces, with Toolan and Suleiman working together. Such an outcome, while inconclusive, would have been preferable to Zarqawi developing a bomb factory and exporting mass murderers, thus provoking a second assault in November with increased casualties for all parties.

Whether Fallujah could have been coaxed down a path that avoided a tough fight, either in April or in November, is problematical. In the summer of 2003 the 3rd Infantry Division emphasized economic growth and political inclusion. The money that was available for such goals, however, was a pittance. In the fall of 2003 and the winter of 2004, the 82nd Airborne Division was more prone than the 3rd ID had been to mount military operations. As firefights increased, antagonism spread among the city's youth, adding to the number of insurgents. American foot patrols became more dangerous, while the volume of fire from Bradleys and Humvees created more resentment and more recruits.

Both approaches—infusing money and staging raids—were entirely American. Indigenous leaders were missing. In Fallujah the Americans were on their own.

An insurgency cannot be won by an occupying force alone. Unlike the Germans of 1945, many Sunni leaders in 2004 had not surrendered psychologically. Janabi, Ghazi, Suleiman, and others all sat at the table with the Americans. Some of them were actually the enemy. But as foreigners, the Americans could not determine which sheikhs and imams believed in the new Iraq and had the power to lead, and which did not. Sorting out who was committed to the new Iraq was the duty of the Iraqi officials who stayed in Baghdad. They ignored Fallujah until the April 2004 battle began; then they rushed to save insurgents like Janabi, who were implacably determined to destroy the new Iraq.

The American high command imprudently commenced the April assault against Fallujah without consulting with Iraqi officials or international allies. The Iraqi officials responded by publicly denouncing the United States—a self-defeating indulgence that encouraged the insurgents. These feckless officials were stampeded by Al Jazeera, whose swift employment of digital images opened a new chapter in the book on information warfare and propaganda. Al Jazeera's repeated assertion of horrendous civilian casualties, buttressed by selected pictures, evoked sympathy and anger in Iraq and worldwide. British generals complained to Prime Minister Blair about American "heavy-handed tactics," and President Bush was concerned about what seemed to be a startling number of casualties.

Every battle now has a global audience. The April 2004 siege of Fallujah was lost on the playing fields of digital technology. As LtGen Conway put it, "Al Jazeera kicked our butts."

The sympathy of the Arab press toward the insurgents, no matter how murderous, reflected the widespread resentment in the Islamic world of America and the West. Equally disturbing were the incitements by the Sunni clerics, who in April whipped up an emotional jihad that sent many youths to their deaths with no political objective. The clerics gained power by urging the easily led to rush into the streets, shoot, and die.

Through the Sunni clerics, the insurgents hijacked Islam, wrapping themselves in the religious banner of attacking the infidel occupier. As long as American soldiers, who believed they were the liberators, had to search houses and seize heads of households, resentment against them as occupiers grew. The sooner the Iraqi forces stood on their own, the better for all concerned. But Iraqi officials maintained a hands-off policy toward the Sunni clerics, even those who preached sedition.

The Fallujah Brigade, formed in May 2004, was an effort to coax the foot soldiers of the insurgency away from the hard-core leaders. The hope was that by restoring authority of former Baathists and generals, the residents of Fallujah would see that they had a stake in the new Iraq. The effort failed because in the year since the fall of Saddam a new set of insurgent leaders had come to taste power. None were willing to obey the old generals anymore.

The insurgents considered the Marine withdrawal from Fallujah to be proof of their victory. The American-nuanced strategies of offering money for development and mounting raids to nab insurgent leaders were based on a misdiagnosis of the metastasizing rebellion. Suleiman was the last, best hope for Fallujah, and the insurgents tortured him to death. The only way to remove Zarqawi, Hadid, and Janabi from Fallujah would be to use the gun.

In twenty-first-century conflicts the infantry still has the most dangerous job. Marines in Fallujah attacked room by room, as they had done in Hue City, Vietnam, thirty-six years earlier. But the Pentagon had not equipped the infantry to the extent that their missions demanded. The U.S. military has more combat aircraft and pilots than infantry squads. The infantry squad deserves to be funded as a weapon system every bit as precious as an aircraft and its pilots.

Making war is the act of killing until the opposition accepts terms of surrender rather than suffer more destruction. The ferocity of the November assault on Fallujah shook the leaders in other Sunni cities. Fearing their own city would be next, the elders in Ramadi promised that they would at long last assert control.

Their resolve, however, quickly dissipated, and by the spring of 2005 they were once again standing on the sidelines while the Americans did the fighting.

Two years after the fall of Baghdad, Gen Abizaid said that "building the Iraqi security forces is a phenomenal success." Yet American soldiers were still fighting on the front lines.

The most effective weapon wielded by the insurgents was intimidation. The families of every policeman and soldier were potential hostages. The Sunni cities provided the haven for the insurgents because by and large the Sunnis resented and feared Shiite majority control. The insurgents, though, lacked a political vision to sustain popular support. Eventually they will be ground down by the Baghdad government's huge advantage in resources and by the promise of a progressive future.

The Western press covered incidents of misconduct more fully than the multiple instances of bravery such as that of Sgt Norwood. The stupid, criminal acts at Abu Ghraib prison cast a shadow over the decency of hundreds of thousands of other soldiers. The shooting of a wounded insurgent inside a mosque in November emerged as the most televised event in the battle for Fallujah because, like the Abu Ghraib story, it smacked of misconduct. Yet the Western press paid scant attention to the subsequent investigation that cleared the Marine or to the courage of a Jesse Grapes or a Timothy Connors.

The Western press strived for neutrality, torn between disapproval of the invasion of Iraq and recognition that a democratic Iraq bolstered the security of the West. In World War II the Western press—believing in its cause—had extolled the Greatest Generation of Americans. The warriors who fought in Iraq would not be called the Greatest Generation, because America was divided about the cause for which they were dying. The focus of the press was upon their individual deaths as tragedies.

This was an incomplete portrayal. The fierce fighting at Fallujah attested to the stalwart nature of the American soldier. In **The Iliad** a warrior in the front ranks turned to his companion and said, "Let us win glory for ourselves, or yield it to others." For Greek warriors, there was no true glory if they were not remembered afterward in poem or in song. There will be no true glory for our soldiers in Iraq until they are recognized not as victims, but as aggressive warriors. Stories of their bravery deserved to be recorded and read by the next generation. Unsung, the noblest deed will die.

WHERE ARE THEY NOW?

—

Prime Minister Allawi—Lost his post as prime minister in the 2005 elections but remained the leader of an important secular political party.

Ambassador Bremer—Returned to civilian life as a successful businessman.

Cpl Connors—Resigned from the Marine Corps and went to college. He presented the parents of LCpl Desiato with a poem and a memento from the squad.

LtGen Conway—Was promoted to the post of J-3 operations officer in the Office of the Joint Chiefs of Staff.

LtCol Drinkwine—Took his battalion to Afghanistan, then returned to Fort Bragg, North Carolina.

LCpl Gomez—Recovered from his wounds in the fight at the Jolan graveyard and is serving at Camp Pendleton.

Lt Grapes—Resigned his commission, after the fight in the house from hell, with plans to become a lay missionary for the Catholic Church.

Sheikh Ghazi—Is living in Syria; offered to meet with Americans to discuss future cooperation.

Hadid—Zarqawi reported the "martyrdom" of his psychotic lieutenant in Fallujah, but no body was identified. His description matched that of the bearded leader Cpl Connors killed in the fight to recover LCpl Desiato's body.

Hassani—After lobbying successfully for the April cease-fire in Fallujah, he quit the Sunni Islamic Party when it refused to participate in elections. As a prominent Sunni moderate, he was elected Speaker of the National Assembly.

SgtMaj Howell—Returned to Iraq in mid-2005 as a senior adviser, on his third tour.

Mufti Jamal—Disappeared in July; was replaced as mufti in Fallujah by a cousin of Janabi who is careful and correct in his dealings with the Americans.

Janabi—Gave a press interview in January 2005, wearing a suicide vest and swearing he would never be taken alive. Is rumored to be operating in Ramadi. A

$50,000 reward was posted for his apprehension or elimination.

Col Latif—Is working part-time with old friend MajGen Shawany, the director of Iraqi intelligence.

MajGen Mattis—Was promoted to lieutenant general; directs the Marine Corps Combat Development Command in Quantico, Vir-ginia.

LtCol McCoy—Was promoted to colonel and wrote a book on leadership in combat, entitled **The Art of Command**.

Ra'ad Hussein—The former mayor of Fallujah was released from prison in April 2004, swearing his enemies had set him up. Went to work for LtCol Wesley in April 2005.

LtCol Suleiman—The commander of the Iraqi battalion in Fallujah is buried in his hometown of Haditha. The Marines painted his portrait on a concrete barrier at the eastern entrance to Fallujah, inscribed with the Arabic words **Hero of Iraq.** Seven months after his torture and death, six bodies were found outside Fallujah. Suleiman's tribe had taken revenge.

Col Toolan—Assumed the post of director of the Command and Staff School in Quantico, Virginia.

LtCol Wesley—After serving with the 3rd Infantry Division in Fallujah in the summer of 2003, he returned to Iraq in 2005 as a battalion commander.

Zarqawi—Is the object of an intense manhunt.

———

In early fall, as the 1st Marine Division prepared to attack Fallujah for the second time, a new pickup truck pulled out from the division's home base at Camp Pendleton and headed across the desert toward Illinois. Lance Corporal Aaron Gordon was on his way to visit Toby Gray's mother, as he had promised when Gray's body was carried down from the tower at the railroad station in Fallujah during the fight in April.

Somewhere along Interstate 10 he passed MajGen Mattis, who had a longer list than Gordon's. It took Mattis weeks to drive across country, visiting the families of the fallen.

Resolute men deserve resolute leaders.

ORDER OF BATTLE FOR OPERATION PHANTOM FURY

REGIMENTAL COMBAT TEAM 1

Btry M, 4th Bn, 14th Mar (Firing Btry)
Co B (-) (REIN), 2d CEB, 2d MARDIV
Co A (-), MP, 4th FSSG
Co D (REIN), AAV, 2d AA Bn, 2d MARDIV
Co C (REIN), 2d Tank Bn, 2d MARDIV
AT (TOW) Platoon (-), 23rd Marines, 4th
    MARDIV
Det, 940, Co B, 9th PSYOP Bn
4th Civil Affairs Team, 4th Civil Affairs Group
Platoon from 1st Force Reconnaissance Company
Shock Trauma Platoon (-)(REIN), 1st Force Service
    Support Group
Explosive Ordnance Detachment, 1st FSSG
Co B (-), 1st Bn/4th Marines (REIN)

3 Bn/1st Marines
H&S Co (REIN)
Det 2d Intel Bn
Det Comm Co, HQ Bn, 2d MARDIV
Det, HQ Btry, 11th Marines
Co I, K, L, Wpns Co
Truck Platoon (Prov), 2d Bn, 14th Marines
1st Platoon, Co C, 4th Combat Engineer Bn
Co D, 1st Specialized Special Forces Bn (Iraqi)

3 Bn/5th Marines
H&S Co (REIN)
Det 2d Intel Bn
Det Comm Co, HQ Bn, 2d MARDIV
Det, HQ Btry, 11th Marines
Co I, K, L, Wpns Co
3rd Platoon (-), Truck Co, HQ Bn, 4th MARDIV
2nd Platoon, Co A, 2nd Combat Engineer Bn, 2d
　MARDIV
Co B, 1st Specialized Special Forces Bn (Iraqi)

TF 2nd Bn, 7th Cavalry (ARMY)
A & B Co, 2-7 CAV (Infantry)
C Co, 3-8 CAV (Armored)

Task Force LAR
HQ Co (-) (REIN), 3d LAR Bn
Co C, 3rd LAR
Co B, 1st Bn (REIN)/23rd Marines
36th Commando Bn (-) (Iraqi)

Other Iraqi Units w/RCT 1
ICTF (Iraqi Counterterrorism Force)
lst Bn 1st Brigade Iraqi Intervention Force
4th Bn 1st Brigade Iraqi Intervention Force

REGIMENTAL COMBAT TEAM 7

Co C (-), 2nd Combat Engineer Battalion
Co B (-), MP, 4th FSSG
2nd Force Reconnaissance Co (-)
44th Engineer Bn, 2nd Brigade, 2nd Infantry
    Division (Army)
Co C (REIN), 2nd AA Bn

1st Bn (REIN)/8th Marines
H&S Co (REIN)
Det, 2nd Intel Bn, II MEF (HET)
Det Comm Co, HQ Bn, 2nd MARDIV
Det HQ Battery, 11th Marines
Co A,B,C
Weapons Co
1st Platoon, Truck Co, HQ Bn, 2nd MARDIV
1st Platoon, Co C, 2nd Combat Engineer Bn, 2nd
    MARDIV
2nd Bn, 1st Brigade, Iraqi Intervention Force
Emergency Response Unit (Iraqi–Ministry of
    Interior)

Battalion Landing Team (1/3) (from 31st MEU)

1st Bn/3rd Marines (REIN)

H&S Co, Co A,B,C, Weapons Co

2nd Platoon, Co C, 3rd AAV Bn

Combat Engineer Co (-), Combat Assault Bn, 3rd Marine Division

C Battery, 1st Bn/12th Marines

Co A (-), 1st LAR

Co C (-) (REIN), 2nd AAV Bn

Co A (-) (REIN), 2nd Tank Bn

Co C (-), 2nd Combat Engineer Bn

5th Bn, 3rd Brigade, Iraqi Intervention Force

TF 2-2 In (-) (ARMY)

6th Bn, 3rd Brigade, Iraqi Intervention Force

2nd Brigade (-) (REIN), 1st Cavalry Division "Black Jack Brigade" (ARMY)

TF 1-5 Infantry (Stryker)

TF 1-5 Cavalry

759th Composite MP Bn (ARMY)

2nd Recon Bn

Co A (REIN), 2nd LAR, 2nd MARDIV

NOTES

p. ix   *The Iliad* . . . trans. Richard Lattimore, University of Chicago Press, 1961, (book 12, 11. 322–28).

PROLOGUE

p. 4   **Blackwater Security** . . . Connie Mabin, "Slain Contractors Included 3 Veterans," Associated Press, April 2, 2004.

p. 6   **the resistance** . . . Jeffrey Gettleman, "4 from US Killed; Mob Drags Bodies," **New York Times,** April 1, 2004, p. A1.

p. 8   **like the fog** . . . Jeffrey Gettleman, "Mix of Pride and Shame Follows Killings and Mutilation by Iraqis," **New York Times,** April 2, 2004, p. 1.

p. 8   **kill them** . . . E-mail to author, March 31, 2004.

p. 10   furious. . . . Dr. Juan R. I. Cole, www.juan-cole.com, July 2, 2004.

p. 10   unpunished . . . Sewell Chan and Karl Vick, "US Vows to Find Civilians' Killers," **Washington Post,** April 2, 2004, p. A1.

p. 11   overwhelming . . . Ibid.

p. 12   immediately . . . Los Angeles Times, October 4, 2004, p. A1.

p. 12   go get those responsible . . . David Ignatius, "Making Do in Iraq," **Washington Post,** June 22, 2004, p. A17.

p. 12   not told . . . Los Angeles Times, October 4, 2004, p. A1.

CHAPTER 1

p. 17   nearby roof . . . Ian Fisher, "US Force Said to Kill 15 Iraqis," **New York Times,** April 30, 2003, p. 1.

p. 17   to cover the story . . . Edmund Blair of Reuters, Ellen Knickmeyer of AP, Ian Fisher of the **New York Times,** Rajiv Chandrasekaran of the **Washington Post,** Michael Sackman of the **Los Angeles Times,** Phil Reeves of the **Independent** (U.K.), and Dan Murphy of the **Christian Science Monitor.**

p. 17   shooting in the air . . . Elizabeth Warnock Fernea, **Guests of the Sheik: An Ethnography of an Iraqi Village** (New York: Anchor Books, 1969).

p. 17   under attack . . . Rajiv Chandrasekaran and Scott Wilson, "Iraqi City Simmers with New Attack," **Washington Post,** May 2, 2003, p. 21.

p. 17   the next day . . . Scott Wilson, "U.S. Forces Kill Two During Iraqi Demonstration: Some Baath Party Loyalists May Be Provoking U.S. Soldiers," **Washington Post** Foreign Service, April 30, 2003.

p. 20   flowing in from Saudi Arabia . . . Stephen Schwartz, "Saudi Mischief in Fallujah," the **Weekly Standard,** June 16, 2004, p. 1.

p. 20   redeem you, O Islam . . . Michael S. Doran, "Intimate Enemies," **Washington Post,** February 18, 2004, p. A19.

p. 21   betrayed the ruling caliph . . . Ibid.

p. 21   we'll kick you out . . . Chandrasekaran and Wilson, "Iraqi City Simmers with New Attack." **Washington Post,** May 2, 2003, p. A21.

p. 22   3rd Infantry Division . . . John Hendren, "Fallouja Was Not the Prize Brigade Expected," **Los Angeles Times,** June 3, 2003.

p. 22   ask for candy . . . Douglas Birch, "Rebellious City in Iraq Poses Stern Test of American Resolve," **Baltimore Sun,** June 12, 2003.

p. 22   kebab restaurant. . . . Rajiv Chandrasekaran, "Iraq's Barbed Realities," **Washington Post,** October 17, 2004, p. B1.

p. 23   local security forces . . . 2nd Brigade, 3rd ID Campaign Plan Brief, undated.

p. 24   routine patrol vehicle . . . Alissa J. Rubin, "U.S. Conducts Wide-Ranging Sweeps in Iraq," **Los Angeles Times,** June 16, 2003, p. l.

p. 24   a soldier asked . . . Daniel Williams and Rajiv Chandrasekaran, "U.S. Troops Frustrated with Role in Iraq," **Washington Post,** June 20, 2003, p. 1.

p. 24 dropped a bomb ... Jim Krane and Colleen Slevin, "Explosion at Mosque Kills Five Iraqis," **New York Times,** July 1, 2003.

p. 25 checkpoints ... Rajiv Chandrasekaran, "In Iraqi City, A New Battle Plan," **Washington Post,** July 29, 2003, p. A1.

p. 26 water-pumping station ... Ibid.

p. 26 American fatalities ... LtGen James Conway, USMC, Defense Department Briefing, the Pentagon, May 5, 2004.

p. 27 through western Fallujah ... Ron Martz, "Volatile Fallujah 'a Little More Stable,' " **Atlanta Journal-Constitution,** July 21, 2003.

p. 27 freedom of movement ... Ibid.

p. 27 hostile place ... Chandrasekaran, "In Iraqi City, a New Battle Plan," p. A1.

CHAPTER 2

p. 30 to be one line of authority ... General Tommy Franks, **American Soldier,** New York: ReganBooks, 2004, p. 295.

p. 30 Johnson had shifted ... Howard B. Schaffer, **Ellsworth Bunker** (Chapel Hill: University of North Carolina Press, 2003), p. 188.

p. 30 pacification programs ... Edward P. Metzner, **More Than a Soldier's War: Pacification in Vietnam** (College Station: Texas A&M University Press, 1995), pp. 156 and 192.

p. 30 his deputy CentCom commander for reconstruction ... Franks, op. cit., p. 532.

p. 31 **more political clout and money from the White House** . . . Franks, op. cit., p. 531.

p. 32 **classical guerrilla-type campaign** . . . Vernon Loeb, " 'Guerrilla' War Acknowledged," **Washington Post**, July 17, 2003, p. 1.

p. 34 **banana republic** . . . Ariana Eunjung Cha, "Flaws Showing in New Iraqi Forces: Pace of Police Recruiting Leads to Shortcuts," **Washington Post**, December 3, 2003, p. A1.

CHAPTER 3

p. 39 **82nd Airborne Division returned** . . . When the 3rd ID headed home, the 3rd Armored Cavalry Regiment sent in a small contingent to provide temporary overwatch of Fallujah for a few weeks. During that time, another American soldier was killed by an IED.

p. 41 **inside the city** . . . Anthony Shadid, "2 U.S. Soldiers Killed by Mines on Iraqi Roads," **Washington Post**, August 28, 2003, p. 14.

p. 42 **six-month-old American occupation** . . . Rajiv Chandrasekaran, "A Burst of Gunfire, Then a 'Hail,' " **Washington Post**, October 14, 2003, p. 1.

p. 42 **three IEDs** . . . Brian Bennett, "Into the Danger Zone," **Time**, October 13, 2003, p. 48.

p. 43 **same kind of regime** . . . Tini Tran, "General: 3 to 6 GIs Dying in Iraq a Week," Associated Press, October 2, 2003.

p. 43 **God is great** . . . Bennett, "Into the Danger Zone," p. 48.

p. 48   seven   paratroopers   wounded . . . David
Lamb and Tyler Marshall, "In 2nd Ambush on Iraqi
Road in 2 Days, 1 U.S. Soldier Dies," **Los Angeles
Times,** October 21, 2003.

p. 50   government jobs . . . Charles Clover, "Falluja's
Message of Hate for US Troops," **Financial Times,**
January 12, 2004, p. 6.

p. 50   the problems here . . . Rajiv Chandrasekaran
and Vernon Loeb, " 'The Battlefield for All Iraq,' "
Washington Post, November 4, 2003.

p. 50   increased activities . . . Ibid.

p. 51   power generators . . . Dexter Filkins, "In Die-
Hard City, G.I.'s Are Enemy," **New York Times,**
November 4, 2003, p. 1.

p. 51   stop the violence . . . Susan Sachs, "Law and
Order: Iraqi Tribes, Asked to Help G.I.'s, Say They
Can't," **New York Times,** November 11, 2003,
p. A1.

p. 51   sheikhs   had   power . . . Associated Press,
"Violent Fallujah Becomes Quiet," November 22,
2003.

p. 51   control their tribes . . . Associated Press, "In
Iraq, Treading Carefully While Fighting Insurgency,"
Baltimore Sun, November 16, 2003.

p. 52   schoolteacher in Fallujah . . . Susan Sachs,
"Tribes in Falluja Where G.I.'s Seek Help Say They
Can't," **New York Times,** November 11, 2003,
p. A10.

p. 52   thousand-pound bombs . . . "US Jet Bombs
Insurgents after Fallujah Attacks," **"PA" News,**
November 9, 2003.

p. 52 **combination of all three** ... Green Left Weekly, November 12, 2003.

p. 52 **crush a walnut** ... Alissa J. Rubin and Patrick J. McDonnell, "U.S. Gunships Target Insurgents in Iraq amid Copter Crash Inquiry," Los Angeles Times, November 19, 2003.

p. 54 **Mahadaai** ... Alan Sipress, "US. Presses Counteroffensive, But Insurgents Strike Again," Washington Post, December 5, 2003, p. 21.

p. 54 **release several women** ... Associated Press, "In Iraq, Treading Carefully While Fighting Insurgency," Baltimore Sun, November 16, 2003.

p. 54 **attacks by explosive devices** ... Patrick J. McDonnell, "Town Preoccupies the Occupation," Los Angeles Times, November 17, 2003, p. 1.

p. 55 **Iraqi was killed** ... CentCom News Release, December 16, 2003.

p. 55 **to fight now** ... Tracy Wilkinson, "Bombs Kill 2 American Soldiers, 2 Iraqi Youths," Los Angeles Times, December 29, 2003.

p. 55 **fire at them** ... Charles Clover, "Falluja's Message of Hate for US Troops," Financial Times, January 12, 2004, p. 6.

p. 56 **you die** ... Tracy Wilkinson, "Bombs Kill 2 American Soldiers, 2 Iraqi Youths," Los Angeles Times, December 29, 2003.

CHAPTER 4

p. 57 **50 percent** ... Washington Post Opinion Polling, About.com, February 15, 2005.

p. 59 their lives . . . Michael M. Phillips, "Before Heading to Iraq, Marines Learn People Skills," **Wall Street Journal**, January 6, 2004, p. 1.

p. 59 with an assessment team . . . Author was a member of the Eikenberry team.

p. 60 external borders . . . "U.S. to Unveil Plans for New Iraqi Army," **New York Times**, June 23, 2003.

p. 60 Guard soldier . . . OSD Unclassified Working Paper, November 11, 2003.

p. 60 Wolfowitz said . . . House Armed Services Committee Hearing, June 22, 2004.

p. 61 noneffective . . . Author interviews in Ramadi and Fallujah with the 82nd, January 16–20, 2004.

p. 61 a thousand officers . . . Commander's Conference Report, Al Anbar Governance Coordinator, November 4, 2003.

p. 62 he said . . . "Commander: 'Not Enough Hate' for Iraqi Civil War," CNN, June 30, 2004.

p. 62 the bottlenecks . . . At a hearing on September 17, 2004, for instance, Senator Chuck Hagel (R–Nebraska) pointed out that of $4.2 billion authorized for water and sewage works, $16 million had been spent; of $367 million set aside for specific military items, $7 million had been spent; and of $3 billion authorized for law, order, and justice programs, $167 million had been spent.

p. 63 should have . . . CSPAN, House Foreign Operations Subcommittee Hearing, September 24, 2004.

p. 65   two French citizens . . . Craig S. Smith, "2 French Citizens Are Killed by Gunmen on Iraqi Road," **New York Times,** January 7, 2004.

p. 65   around the city . . . Patrick Rucker, "Copter Crew Used to Saving Lives," **Chicago Tribune,** January 28, 2004.

p. 65   second shoot-down . . . Daniel Williams and Alan Sipress, "Helicopter Crash in Iraq Kills Nine U.S. Soldiers," **Washington Post,** January 9, 2004, p.12.

p. 65   the Fallujah area . . . Charles Clover, "Falluja's Message of Hate for US Troops," **Financial Times,** January 12, 2004, p. 6.

p. 67   at your throat . . . Karl Zinsmeister, **Dawn over Baghdad** (San Francisco: Encounter Books, 2004), p. 152.

p. 67   guerrilla war . . . Don Van Natta, "Who Is Abu Musab al-Zarqawi?," **New York Times,** October 10, 2004, p. 4-1.

p. 67   blood on a wall . . . Hannah Allam and Tom Pennington, "Troops Battle to Rid Town of Suspected Cell," **Philadelphia Inquirer,** January 23, 2004.

p. 68   we get killed . . . Ibid.

p. 68   in tactics . . . Interviews with the 82nd, Fort Bragg, North Carolina, February 2–3, 2005.

p. 69   firefights . . . Interviews with commanders in Fallujah, January 14–15, 2004.

p. 69   grow back stronger . . . CBS 60 Minutes, "On Patrol in the Sunni Triangle," February 8, 2004.

p. 69 **to be removed** . . . Anthony Shadid, "In New Iraq, Sunnis Fear a Grim Future," **Washington Post,** December 22, 2003, p. 1.

CHAPTER 5

p. 72 **their future** . . . "Fallujah Raids Administer Severe Jolt to US Transition Plan," DEBKA**file,** February 14, 2004.

p. 72 **promptly canceled** . . . Combined Dispatches, "Iraqi Rebels Strike During Abizaid Visit," **Washington Post,** February 13, 2004, p. 1.

p. 73 **death to collaborators** . . . Mariam Fain, "21 Killed, Prisoners Freed in Iraqi Raid," washingtonpost.com, February 14, 2004.

p. 73 **would be well** . . . Jim Michaels, "In an Iraqi Hot Spot, New Iraqi Police Chief Takes the Heat," **USA Today,** February 10, 2004, p. 1.

p. 74 **twenty-three policemen** . . . Rowan Scarborough, "Inside Job Suspected in Iraq Attacks," **Washington Times,** February 17, 2004, p. 1.

p. 76 **charges of conspiracy** . . . Tom Lasseter, "U.S. Detains Mayor After Deadly Attack," **Miami Herald,** February 17, 2004.

p. 76 **Anbar Provincial Council** . . . Dexter Filkins, " 'Liberty or Death' Is a Grim Option for the Local Councils," **New York Times,** February 15, 2004, p. 10.

p. 79 **pick up a gun** . . . " 'This place is crazy'—In Fallujah, it's not if you get shot at, but when," March 3, 2004, www.hodierne.com/iraq2.

p. 79 **division** . . . The U.S. Army had four divisions with two-star commanders reporting to the three-star JTF. The Marines were sending an experienced three-star (Conway) who would report to the JTF.

p. 81 **a man's neck** . . . Ron Harris, "Commander Calls Fallujah Most Difficult Area," **St. Louis Post-Dispatch,** April 1, 2004, p. 1.

p. 81 **the armed resistance** . . . Carl E. Mundy III, "Spare the Rod, Save the Nation," **Washington Post,** December 30, 2003, p. A23.

p. 82 **as amicably** . . . Thomas E. Ricks, "Marines to Offer New Tactics in Iraq," washingtonpost.com, January 7, 2004, p. A1.

p. 82 **fired upon** . . . Steven Komarow, "Favored by Saddam, Fallujah Seething Since His Fall," **USA Today,** April 2, 2004, p. 4.

p. 83 **attack us** . . . Army Major General Charles H. Swannack, Jr., "82nd Airborne Division Commanding General's Briefing from Iraq," U.S. Department of Defense News Transcript, March 10, 2004.

p. 84 **bloodied** . . . Darrin Mortenson, "Army Commander Says Marines Face Challenge in Quieting Iraqi Town," **North County Times,** March 25, 2004.

CHAPTER 6

p. 89 **to the States** . . . Karl Vick and Sewell Chan, "10 Iraqis Are Killed in Spasm of Attacks," **Washington Post,** March 19, 2004, p. 15; Capt Zembiec, several interviews by author, Fallujah, April, May, and July 2004.

p. 89   near the city . . . Edmund Sanders, "3 Iraqis Killed, 4 U.S. Troops Wounded in Separate Attacks," **Los Angeles Times,** March 25, 2004.

p. 89   twenty-six the number of attacks . . . Eric Schmitt, "The Siege of Fallujah, A Test in a Tinderbox," **New York Times,** April 28, 2004, p. 1.

p. 89   made safe . . . LtGen Conway, interviewed by author, Fallujah, July 24, 2004.

p. 90   kites flying . . . Battalion 2/1 After Action Report, March 26, 2004.

p. 91   in the head . . . Dexter Filkins, "Up to 16 Die in Gun Battles in Sunni Areas of Iraq," **New York Times,** March 27, 2004, p. 1.

p. 91   seeking revenge . . . Ibid.

p. 93   mess with the people of Fallujah?" the mob chanted . . . Sewell Chan, "Descent into Carnage in a Hostile City," **Washington Post,** April 1, 2004, p. A1.

p. 93   turned the corner . . . John F. Burns, "Reminder of Mogadishu: Acts of Hatred, Hints of Doubt," **New York Times,** April 1, 2004, p. A1.

p. 94   see this . . . Jeffrey Gettleman and John F. Burns, "5 G.I.'s and 4 Contractors Are Killed in Separate Attacks," March 31, 2004.

p. 94   aggressive . . . Paul McGeough, "Fallujah Braces for US Reprisal," theage.com, April 3, 2004.

p. 95   overwhelming . . . 119 JTF-7 Press Conference, April 1, 2004.

p. 97 *Hawza*... Charles Snow, "The Political Scene," **Middle East Review** 47, April 12, 2004.

p. 97 **top aide**... Larry Diamond, "What Went Wrong in Iraq," **Foreign Affairs**, September 2004, p. 40.

p. 98 **Terrorize your enemy**... John F. Burns, "The Struggle for Iraq; Uprising," **New York Times**, April 5, 2004, p. 1.

p. 98 **Kut**... David Stokes, "Al-Kut, Iraq: After-Battle Report," **Middle East Quarterly,** January 10, 2005.

p. 98 **Najaf**... Senator Joseph Biden, interview by CBS, "Battles Sweeping Iraq," April 7, 2004.

CHAPTER 7

p. 103 **northwestern outskirts of Fallujah**... Darrin Mortenson, "Marines Launch Major Offensive in Fallujah," **North County Times,** April 4, 2004.

p. 103 **local sheikh**... Tony Perry and Edmund Sanders, "Fallouja Residents Brace for Assault by Marines," **Los Angeles Times,** April 6, 2004.

p. 104 **Tyler Fey**... Darrin Mortenson, "Wrap-up of Falluja Battle," **North County Times,** June 6, 2004.

p. 116 **104 had mutinied**... David H. Hackworth, "The Combat Task," www.couplescompany.com, May 1, 2004.

p. 116 **not coming to Fallujah**... At real risk to

themselves, the Iraqi officers had protected the advisers from the mob on the road, yet they wouldn't lead their soldiers. Unlike the case in the American military, the officers, not the sergeants, formed the backbone of the Iraqi Army. The sergeants were followers, not organizers. Without the officers, the system stopped.

"It's a peasant army," Lane said. "A whole company responds to one officer. If he's weak, a hundred men are out of the fight. The officers are intelligent enough, but they lack initiative. It's a mystery to me what will make them fight consistently."

It is in the Euro-American tradition to press battle to its bloody conclusion. Unlike the case in other cultures, in the West battle is not a matter of posturing. Frequently it is not an extension of politics, where compromise is expected. Battles are fought to the death. Historians trace this attribute and the martial ascendancy of the West to Alexander the Great at the 482 B.C. Battle of Gaugamela, 150 miles north of Fallujah, where he defeated the Persians. And among countries of the West, none has suffered the stupendous casualty rate of the American Civil War, when one in four soldiers, Union and Confederate, died. Added to that tradition, the American Marine was trained as a shock troop and steeped in the traditions of World War II, when Marines crawled over the bodies of their fallen comrades on island after island to wipe out the Japanese defenders. The net result was that nothing in their psyches prepared American

Marines for soldiers who walked off the job, as if they were union members going on strike.

The Marines had encountered no such mutiny in prior wars. The Vietnamese soldiers had stuck like glue alongside their advisers, and the Combined Action Platoons, which sent Marine squads into villages to fight alongside Vietnamese farmers, had been a singular success. In the war before that, South Korean soldiers had considered it an honor to fight alongside Americans. Indeed, since the beginning of the twentieth century the Marines had been raising and training constabularies. Fish swam, birds flew, and soldiers fought—that was the law of nature. Mutinies simply did not happen.

CHAPTER 8

p. 118 $700,000 . . . Yaroslav Trofimov, "To Find Peace in the Sunni Triangle, Talk to the Sheikhs," **Wall Street Journal**, November 5, 2003, p. 1.

p. 118   sheikh system . . . Mines too was careful not to offend the sheikhs and, to build support, awarded contracts that didn't always go to the lowest bidder. He referred to the Baathist Sunnis as "cornered tigers."

"The coalition is not just an occupying power," Mines wrote to his superiors. "It is a power involved in disempowering the Sunnis, first through military occupation and ultimately by leaving the Sunnis subordinated to the Shiites in the new Iraq."

p. 139   ten separate firefights . . . These include both Chapters 8 and 10. The firefights were: Joker 3-1 at grid 432 993; Rainmaker at 432 994; west of the cemetery, Joker 3-3 and 3-2 at 425 995; Joker 1-1 and 1-2 and Terminator at 434 999; Reaper at 434 994; Bastard Forward at 535 993; Bastard 3 at 434 991; Joker 6 near the stadium at 438 990; Joker 1-3 and Joker 4 at 450 989; Porky 1, 6, and 3-3 south of the fish hook two kilometers east of the stadium at 468 038; and Head Hunter 2 three kilometers north of the stadium at 448 025.

CHAPTER 9

p. 143   gingerly . . . Douglas Jehl, "U.S. Says It Will Move Gingerly Against Sadr," **New York Times,** April 7, 2004, p. 9.

p. 144   miles per day . . . Major Martha G. Granger, "The 1st AD in Operation Iraqi Freedom," **Military Review,** Nov–Dec 2004.

p. 144   situation worsened . . . David E. Sanger and Douglas Jehl, "The Struggle for Iraq: War Policy; Generals in Iraq Consider Options for More Troops," **New York Times,** April 6, 2004, p. A1.

p. 145   more trusted . . . Anthony Shadid, "Iraqi Council Halts Arab TV Network's News Broadcasts," **Washington Post,** November 24, 2003.

p. 145   channel called Al Iraqiya . . . Alan Sipress, "For Many Iraqis, U.S.-Backed TV Echoes the Voice of Its Sponsor," **Washington Post,** January 8, 2004, p. 15.

p. 145   closure of offices . . . Isabel Hilton, "Al-Jazeera: And now, the other news preferred Jazeera," **New York Times Book Review,** March 6, 2005.

p. 145   suspension of the network . . . Shadid, "Iraqi Council Halts Arab TV Network's News Broadcasts."

p. 146   crew . . . Aljazeera online, "Aljazeera News Crew Inside the Town," April 8, 2004.

p. 146   the Israelis . . . Barbara Slavin, "Mosque Strike Seen Stoking Rage," **USA Today,** April 8, 2004, p. 1.

p. 146   for Fallujah . . . Karl Vick, "Shiites Rally to Sunni 'Brothers,' " **Washington Post,** April 9, 2004, p.1.

p. 146   for rebelling . . . Rajiv Chandrasekaran, "Anti-U.S. Uprising Widens in Iraq; Marines Push Deeper Into Fallujah," **Washington Post,** April 8, 2004, p.1.

p. 146   across the city . . . Pamela Constable, "Marines Fight for Control of Fallujah, Inch by Inch," washingtonpost.com, April 7, 2004.

p. 146   rallying point . . . Edward Wong, "Battle for Fallujah Rouses the Anger of Iraqis Weary of the US Occupation," **New York Times,** April 22, 2005, p. A14

p. 147   infidel occupiers . . . Karl Vick and Anthony Shadid, "Fallujah Gains Mythic Air," **Washington Post,** April 13, 2004, p. A1.

p. 147   175,000 stories . . . As of October 17, 2004, the count on Google was 713,000 stories about Fallujah.

p. 148   initial impressions . . . Peter Braestrup, **Big Story: How the American Press and Television Reported and Interpreted the Crisis in Tet 1968 in Vietnam and Washington** (Novalo, Calif.: Presidio, 1994), p. 517.

p. 149   is lying . . . BrigGen John Kelly, 1st MarDiv headquarters, May 9, 2004.

CHAPTER 11

p. 178   morning of April 7 . . . Battalion 1/5 began the day by launching a raid across Highway 10. After studying a detailed overhead photo, an informant had pointed out the home of Qhalil Hawadi, an entrepreneur who sold rockets and mortars at bargain prices. First Lieutenant Josh Glover of Weapons Company—call sign Red Cloud— jotted down the ten-digit GPS coordinates, which would place him within ten meters of Target 204. At two in the morning, Glover pushed north across Route Michigan with a platoon mounted in four trucks. Racing up to the designated building, the platoon blew the locks on the courtyard gate, smashed in the front door, and burst into an empty store. Emerging sheepishly, Glover knocked on next door, politely inquiring through a translator about Hawadi's whereabouts. A woman pointed to a nearby house, and again Glover knocked. A portly man in a white dishdasha answered, protesting that he was a car salesman. A quick search turned up several documents identifying him as Hawadi, and

Glover drove with the prisoner back across Michigan before dawn with no shots fired.

Alpha and Bravo were working their way west toward 873 Easting or Phase Line Violet, a wide street two kilometers inside the city that ran perpendicular to Route Michigan. As Bravo Company approached Violet from the east, the volume of fire picked up. Glover's platoon, Red Cloud, was mounted in two highback Humvees and four gun trucks, two Humvees with .50 cals and two with Mark 19s. When Red Cloud headed south on Violet to provide fire support for the infantry approaching from the east, they ran into a hornet's nest of bullets and RPGs. Oil barrels were scattered at intervals on the west side of Violet as target reference points, and each time the Humvees passed a barrel, there would be a flurry of fire from nearby alleys and cross streets. Twenty minutes into the fight the front ends of the four gun trucks had been peppered, yet no Marine was seriously hit. A heavy slug had punched a hole the size of a silver dollar in the windshield of Glover's command vehicle, inches from the head of Lance Corporal Charles Williams, who shrugged and grinned. The lead gun truck had ripped through 1,100 rounds of .50 cal, and the next truck in line had fired 800 rounds of 7.62 ammo. The radiators on both trucks were steaming and leaking from numerous hits, and Gunnery Sergeant William Paulino had them hauled off the street and into an alleyway.

They were still taking RPGs from a house at an

intersection two hundred meters to the south. Glover called up a tank, designated the house by its color—gray with a blue air conditioner—and pulled his platoon into a side alley while the tank's main gun blew in the side of the house, piece by piece.

p. 181   accurately reported . . . Tony Perry and Edmund Sanders, "The World; U.S. Bombs Mosque in Fallouja; Military Says Site Was Used to Launch Strikes; Troops' Tours May Be Extended," **Los Angeles Times,** April 8, 2004, p. 1.

p. 181   Marine losses . . . Jeffrey Gettleman and Douglas Jehl, "Up to 12 Marines Die in Raid on Their Base as Fierce Fighting Spreads to 6 Iraqi Cities," **New York Times,** April 7, 2004, p. A1.

p. 181   fights were raging in Ramadi . . . Not wanting the insurgents to think they had free rein, Kennedy ordered Golf Company to send a combat patrol downtown. It was mid-morning when First Lieutenant Eric Quist and 2nd Platoon reached the market, which was almost empty. With machine guns mounted on four Humvees in support, the dismounted platoon then walked south across Michigan to the cemetery where Hesselbeck had fought the day before. Men were flocking early to the mosques, children were being shooed inside, and shop owners were pulling down their metal storefront shutters and hastening away. The store owners told Quist, who had no interpreter, that it was time for "lunch."

"Okay," PFC Abbit said to his platoon leader, "here we go."

Within minutes, fighting erupted—a repeat of the day before. Quist's squads were hit from all sides and dodged inside courtyards, climbing onto the roofs to form three strongholds. No ordinary civilian traffic was moving in the midst of this firestorm, but ambulances and police cars were zipping around and the Marines saw them dropping off fighters as well as picking up the wounded and the dead. From a rooftop, Quist watched men ducking out the back gate of a small mosque three blocks away. When LCpl Cantu was hit by shrapnel from an RPG, Quist called for the Quick Reaction Forces and a medevac. Dobb's platoon from Weapons Company, a platoon from Fox, and a platoon from Golf, accompanied by Bronzi, responded. PFC Marby, a quiet, highly respected Marine who never complained, was walking around a corner when hit three times in the chest by machine-gun bullets. Lieutenant Dobb's platoon fought through two ambushes, picked up the wounded, and evacuated them to Hurricane Point. Cantu pulled through, but Marby died.

Bronzi led them, as he had the prior day, east to west, along the same streets. Once more, the four-lane width of Easy Street was swept with grazing fire, and Fox Company took seven wounded, the intensity of the fight easing only when Dobb brought up a mounted .50 cal and hammered the houses Fox pointed at. Quist came up, spotted the flicker of a machine gun, grabbed an AT-4 rocket, and fired. The rocket team muttered about "Corporal Quist," upset they hadn't seen the machine gun. Quist handed over the rocket launcher. There would be more targets. Cars were dropping off gunmen a few blocks away, while the orange and white taxis drove across alleyways, men firing out the windows.

The Marines were quicker than they had been the prior day to employ the Mark 19 to dislodge shooters on rooftops, and the insurgents weren't as tenacious. Bronzi led the force south down Easy Street to the soccer stadium, repeating in reverse his fight of the day before. Separate fire teams cleared any house suspected of harboring rebels. It was tedious, unrewarding work. Almost always the fleeter Iraqis had escaped out the back, sometimes leaving behind a few dead. No rebel group stayed behind to fight to the death, and firefights inside a house were rare. Near the stadium a flurry of RPG rockets from a roof hit an electric transmission box, setting off a spectacular shower of hissing red sparks. Bronzi took the handset from his radio operator, Corporal Jesse W. Gonzalez, to warn the Humvees to stay away. An insurgent ran into the street, his AK pointed at the unsuspecting company commander. Gonzalez fired a long burst as a startled Bronzi flinched, then looked behind him.

"Gonzo, you fucking blew that guy's head off," Bronzi said.

Within minutes he and Lt Stevens had led Mobile Assault Platoon 2 in seven Humvees through the city, heading north up Route Apple, a narrow, paved rural road, clogged with traffic and flanked in close by rows of cement courtyard walls and scruffy little shops. Farther off the road stretched a series of open fields separated by deep irrigation ditches.

Inside the city at the stadium Bronzi with the 3rd and 4th Platoons had one final stiff fight. The insurgent fire was inaccurate but heavy, and he had to shelter his vehicles. With one machine gun spotted three blocks to his south and another to the east, he called to the Cobras hovering overhead to strafe the building.

"There are no friendlies south of the ninety-nine grid line," he said. "I'll talk you on."

"Negative," the pilot said. "We need an eight-digit grid and a mark on target."

Bronzi said he could see the house, but the pilot refused to fire. The Rules of Engagement protected civilians as much as Marines. Exasperated, Bronzi sent a squad backed by a Humvee with a Mark 19 in each direction to silence the guns. When the gunners saw the Marines closing on them, they ceased fire and pulled out, leaving the Marines in charge of the critical downtown thirteen square kilometers, extending from the Government Center east to the stadium. Joker had lost one Marine killed and eight wounded. They had apprehended about thirty males and were tired of estimating how many they had killed.

In the street fighting, most of the riflemen could remember most of the Iraqis they hit and saw go down, but at the end of the day not too many cared. The first day, if the platoon hadn't lost anyone, stories were swapped. **Did you see that dude I hit in the head? He was all messed up.** The second day (April 7) there were many fewer stories. Far removed from the press assembled in Fallujah, shooting insurgents in Ramadi was becoming routine.

p. 182 support . . . Alan Cowell, Clifford J. Levy, Richard Bernstein, Emma Daly, Eric E. Arvedlund, and Joel Brinkley, "The Struggle for Iraq: Overseas; Turmoil in Iraq Jangles Nerves in Allied Capitals, and Bush Works to Shore Up Support," **New York Times,** April 8, 2004, p. A7.

p. 182 had objected . . . Patrick E. Tyler, "The Struggle for Iraq: Allies; Blair to Visit Bush Next Week for Talks Dominated by Iraq," **New York Times,** April 6, 2004, p. A13.

p. 182 high-handedness . . . Alex Russell, "Britain and US 'Divided on Iraq Policy,' " **London Daily Telegraph,** April 14, 2004, p. 1.

p. 183 this insurgency . . . Tony Perry and Nicholas Riccardi, "The World; Thousands in Fallouja Flee; Council Totters; A Cease-fire in the City Crumbles After Less Than Two Hours. Five More U.S. Troops Die in Iraq in the Coalition's Deadliest Week Since Hussein's Ouster," **Los Angeles Times,** April 10, 2004, p. A1.

p. 183 Krepinevich . . . Tom Squitieri, "Fear of Losing Control Drives Assault," **USA Today,** April 7, 2004, p. 10.

p. 183   mob reaction . . . Ibid.

p. 184   dealing directly . . . Tony Perry and Edmund Sanders, "The World; U.S. Bombs Mosque in Fallouja; Military Says Site Was Used to Launch Strikes; Troops' Tours May Be Extended," **Los Angeles Times,** April 8, 2004, p. 1.

p. 185   engaged to the daughter of King Abdullah . . . Jim Hoagland, "Obsessed with Iran," **Washington Post,** May 28, 2004, p. A23.

p. 186   threatened to quit . . . Tony Perry and Nicholas Riccardi, "The World; Thousands in Fallouja Flee; Council Totters," **Los Angeles Times,** April 10, 2004, p. A1.

p. 187   suicide vests . . . 1st MarDiv Press Release #04-99, April 8, 2004.

p. 188   explosives discovered . . . Darrin Mortenson, "Marines Deploy Heavy Firepower in Fallujah," **North County Times,** April 9, 2004.

p. 189   finish the fight . . . Briefing to Deputy Secretary of Defense at MEF HQ, June 19, 2004.

p. 189   fighting well . . . Sergeant First Class Pinkham, interview by author, 1st MarDiv HQ, April 14, 2004.

p. 189   Iraqi desertions . . . Channel News Asia broadcast summary, June 30, 2004.

p. 189   had deserted . . . Ibid.

p. 190   chain of command . . . Interview on NBC Meet the Press, September 26, 2004.

p. 191   quit . . . John F. Burns, "The Struggle for Iraq: Insurgency: Fighting Halts Briefly in Fallujah;

U.S. Convoy Hit Near Baghdad," **New York Times,** April 10, 2004, p. A1.

p. 191 illegal . . . Michael Rubin, "Losing the Shia," **Middle East Quarterly** [online], August 19, 2004.

p. 192 wounded . . . Aljazeera.net., "Doctor Reveals Falluja's Toll," April 9, 2004.

p. 192 one big Fallujah . . . Alissa J. Rubin and Doyle McManus, "Why America Has Waged a Losing Battle on Fallouja," **Los Angeles Times,** October 24, 2004, p. 1.

p. 193 *Los Angeles Times . . .* Ibid.

p. 194 9/11 Commission . . . David E. Sanger, "Threats and Responses: News Analysis; Sticking to Their Scripts," **New York Times,** April 9, 2004, p. A1.

p. 194 CPA announcement . . . globalsecurity.org, June 14, 2004.

p. 194 objectives . . . Eric Schmitt, "Marines Battle Insurgents in Streets of Falluja," **New York Times,** April 9, 2004.

p. 196 weeks ahead . . . www.presidency.ucsb.edu, April 10, 2004.

p. 197 aghast . . . Nicholas Riccardi and Tony Perry, "The World; Iraqi Leaders, Insurgents Have Hope for Cease-Fire," **Los Angeles Times,** April 11, 2004, p. A 1.

p. 197 Governing Council . . . Ibid.

p. 197 unacceptable . . . Rowan Scarborough, "Iraqi Politicians Called Obstacle to U.S. Force," **Washington Times,** April 15, 2004, p.1

CHAPTER 13

p. 221   36th Iraqi National Guard Battalion . . . Tony Perry, "At Least One Iraqi Battalion Is Ready to Help U.S.," **Los Angeles Times,** April 13, 2004.

p. 221   from the city . . . Christine Hauser, "Iraqi Claims U.S. and Falluja Foes Agree to a Deal," **New York Times,** April 11, 2004, p. 1.

CHAPTER 14

p. 231   inexcusable . . . Peter Johnson, "U.S. Says Al-Jazeera Putting Troops at Risk," **USA Today,** April 19, 2004, p. 4D.

p. 232   for ambush . . . Patrick Graham, "Beyond Fallujah," **Harper's Magazine,** June 2004, p. 37.

p. 232   northeast of Fallujah . . . Jeffrey Gettleman, "Marines Use Low-Tech Skill to Kill 100 in Urban Battle," **New York Times,** April 15, 2004, p. 1.

p. 238   Glover . . . This section about Red Cloud is drawn from interviews in April 2004 at Fallujah with LtCol Byrne, Maj Farnum, Lt Glover and his platoon, and later discussions with Farnum. See also "1/5 Laydown: Battalion Summary of Actions" (April 14, 2004) and April 14, 2004, report from 81 Mortar Platoon Commander to CO, 1/5.

p. 240   picnic . . . E-mail from Lance Corporal Victor Didra, "WhiskeyD," March 4, 2005.

p. 243   to their fifties . . . "Marines Fight for Life in Lion's Den," www.spacewar.com, April 16, 2004.

p. 243   the   Marines... Pamela   Constable,   "A Wrong Turn, Chaos and a Rescue," **Washington Post,** April 15, 2004, p. 20.

CHAPTER 15

p. 252   represented the CPA... Tony Perry, "Firing Up New Weapon in Fallouja: The Bulldozer," **Los Angeles Times,** April 15, 2004.

p. 252   finish   the   job... Willis   Witter,   "Iraqi Snipers Work in Teams to Hit Marines," **Washington Times,** April 12, 2004, p. 1.

p. 252   Marines were dying... Sewell Chan and Pamela Constable, "Attacks Test Truce in Fallujah," **Washington Post,** April 15, 2004, p. 22.

p. 253   for long... Ibid.

p. 255   attacking   our   Marines... Sewell   Chan, "General Calls Insurgency in Iraq a Sign of U.S. Success," **Washington Post,** April 16, 2004, p. A10.

p. 257   civilians dead... John Daniszewski, "Britain Seen Backing US Request on Troops," **Boston Globe,** October 19, 2004, p. A16.

p. 257   weapons unsuited... Letter to the Editor, "Sir Graham Boyce and 51 Others," **Guardian,** April 27, 2004.

p. 257   heavy-handed... AP Online, "00:29," April 17, 2004.

p. 257   redouble our efforts... Associated Press, "U.K. Paper Publishes Alleged Iraq Memo," May 23, 2004.

p. 258 **fact of life . . .** Michael Evans, "Army Chief Admits Friction with US Commanders," **Times** (London), April 21, 2004, p. 1.

p. 258 **important** **work . . .** President George Bush and Prime Minister Tony Blair, "Bush, Blair Discuss Sharon Plan; Future of Iraq in Press Conference," Office of the Press Secretary, April 16, 2004.

CHAPTER 16

p. 272 **plans . . .** The plans for each attack by Task Force Ripper were actually as extensive as the preflight checklist for the pilot of a 747 aircraft. "Assume everyone you question is lying to you. Believe no one," Stuka said. "Whenever you can, use the tanks against hard points. Inside the town, if you can't see your adjacent units, employ indirect fires only as a last resort."

Before leaving on the operation, the battalion chaplain, Lieutenant Mike Foskett, held a brief service attended by about fifteen Marines.

"Most Marines aren't regular church-goers. They all come, though, for the memorial service when we lose a Marine," Foskett said. "Marines are functional atheists who believe in God. They pray, but they pick which rules to follow. Religion is based on relations—whether I can relate to them—rather than on doctrine. The word **fuck** is an adjective, noun, verb, and burp. After two years in the battalion, I catch myself using it. Hey, what kind of minister would I be if I didn't relate to my flock?"

p. 275   main highway . . . Separate from Task Force Ripper, Mattis had sent his assistant division commander, Brigadier General John Kelly, to command a force opening the highway south of Baghdad. While driving to the link-up location, Kelly's command group of twenty Marines was ambushed. After an IED disabled the lead Humvee, Kelly's other vehicles had to remain in the kill zone to extract the wounded. The insurgents were firing from a berm about 200 meters away, and PFC Chance Phelps stood in the turret of a Humvee, laying down suppressive fire with a 240 Golf machine gun until a bullet struck him in the eye, killing him instantly. (LtCol M. R. Strobl USMC wrote a moving story about bringing PFC Phelps home.)

With a vehicle destroyed, the group fought their way out on foot, with Kelly refusing to divert air support from another battle to cover his movement. "We'll handle this," he said.

He reached the highway just as a National Guard supply convoy, fleeing from an ambush, raced into the Marine cantonment. Kelly had to act as a traffic cop as the Marines drove out to attack the ambushers while the supply drivers were driving inside the gates to escape the ambushers. The captain in charge of the convoy nervously explained that her drivers had never been in Iraq, let alone in combat. Kelly angrily thought of some dispatcher sitting in air-conditioned comfort in Kuwait casually sending them north as if they would be driving from Los Angeles to San Francisco. It was insane to send them alone up a highway that passed near Fallujah. To settle their nerves, he let them stay another day before proceeding to Baghdad, escorted by a Marine rifle platoon.

p. 275   pulled back . . . There were three key American maneuvers on the battlefield in mid-April. The first was the battle for Ramadi, provoked by the insurgents. The second was the dispatch by LtGen Sanchez, with the enthusiastic support of Bremer, of the 1st Armored Division to hound and corral Sadr's militia. MajGen Dempsey's soldiers prevented a chaotic situation from spinning out of control among the Shiites. The second action was the decision by Mattis to sweep the area west of Baghdad. By moving fast and in force, Task Force Ripper under Col Tucker reopened the highways from Fallujah to Baghdad and clamped a lid on the spontaneous uprising sweeping like a prairie fire toward Baghdad. While they lacked sustaining logistics and command and control, they had enthusiasm, manpower, mobility (via pickups and cars), popular support, and momentum. Task Force Ripper stopped the Sunni insurgents from rolling into Baghdad from the west while Sadr's militia was battling in the streets to the east. For a few weeks they hovered close to the tipping point where the Sunni population, latently sympathetic, could have poured onto the streets and highways, changing the dynamics of the conflict. Militarily, it was a near miss for the insurgents.

Conversely, Fallujah was a military diversion for the insurgents even as it emerged as a political rallying point. By rushing inside Fallujah, insurgent fighters diverted themselves from the high-payoff strategy of squeezing and discombobulating Baghdad. While the momentum of the Sunni insurgency was checked on the military chessboard, the rebel stronghold inside Fallujah remained intact as political maneuvers prevented the Marines from applying force.

CHAPTER 17

p. 278   sandbags . . . Darrin Mortenson, "Troops Take Over Houses of Fleeing Fallujah Residents," **North County Times,** April 15, 2004.

p. 279   sharia . . . Bernard Lewis, **The Crisis of Islam** (New York: Random House, 2003), pp. 10, 31.

p. 282   day by day . . . Jeffrey Gettleman, "Marines in Falluja Still Face and Return Relentless Fire," **New York Times,** April 14, 2004.

p. 282   British   journalist . . . Patrick   Graham, "Falluja in Their Sights," **Guardian,** October 21, 2004.

p. 285   eighty-two buildings . . . RCT 1 Ops Center, "Air Officer Computer Records of Air Strikes," July 22, 2004.

p. 285   storyline . . . Stephen Farrell, "Fleeing Family Films Scenes from City Racked by Violence," **Times** (London), April 13, 2004.

p. 286 resolve the siege . . . UN Situation Report 199FAB, April 19–25, 2004.

p. 286 broken weapons . . . Rajiv Chandrasekaran and Karl Vick, "Marines Say Time Running Short in Fallujah," **Washington Post,** April 23, 2004, p. 10.

p. 286 weapons . . . Rajiv Chandrasekaran and Pamela Constable, "Deal Struck on Fallujah Attacks," **Washington Post,** April 20, 2004, p. 1.

p. 289 days, not weeks, away . . . Rajiv Chandrasekaran and Karl Vick, "Marines Say Time Running Short in Fallujah," **Washington Post,** April 23, 2004, p. 10.

p. 289 siege . . . Eric Schmitt, "U.S. General at Falluja Warns a Full Attack Could Come Soon," **New York Times,** April 22, 2004, p. A15.

p. 289 notice . . . UN Situation Report 199FAB, L. Paul Bremer Speech of April 23, 2004.

p. 290 army of occupation . . . Associated Press, April 26, 2004.

CHAPTER 18

p. 297 give them support . . . ABC Television, Presidential Debate, September 30, 2004.

p. 297 Fallujah is returning to normal . . . Jason Keyser, "U.S. Forces Continue to Battle Insurgents," Associated Press, April 23, 2004, p. 26.

p. 297 Thirty-two . . . Nicholas Riccardi, "A Peacemaker Runs the Gauntlet in Fallouja," **Los Angeles Times,** April 16, 2004.

p. 297 **Marines had died . . .** Between April 1 and 24 six Marines had been killed in Fallujah in 2/1; five in 1/5 plus one attached AAV; and three in 3/4. Source: RCT 1 April Casualty Roll-up.

p. 297 **hand-wringing . . .** Bob Woodward, **Plan of Attack,** (New York: Simon & Schuster, 2004), p. 178.

p. 298 **relations impact . . .** Alissa J. Rubin and Doyle McManus, "Why America Has Waged a Losing Battle on Fallouja," **Los Angeles Times,** October 24, 2004.

p. 298 **hostilities could resume shortly . . .** L. Paul Bremer III, Televised Address, Baghdad, April 23, 2004.

p. 298 **cautioned that widespread uprisings . . .** David E. Sanger and Thom Shanker, "Bush's Decision on Possible Attack on Falluja Seems Near," **New York Times,** April 24, 2004, p. A1.

p. 298 **antibody in their culture. . . .** Michael R. Gordon, "Debate Lingering on Decision to Dissolve the Iraqi Military," **New York Times,** October 21, 2004.

p. 299 **damage to the city . . .** John Kifner and John F. Burns, "Inside Falluja, a Cease-Fire in Name Only," **New York Times,** April 26, 2004, p. A1.

p. 299 **Arab TV crews . . .** Jim Hoagland, "On Tiptoe in Iraq," washingtonpost.com, July 25, 2004.

p. 299 **three hundred . . .** Stu Jones, 1st MarDiv headquarters, May 9, 2004.

p. 300 **joint patrols . . .** Richard W. Stevenson and David E. Sanger, "For Bush, Same Goal in Iraq, New Tactics," **New York Times,** May 2, 2004.

p. 302   350 Iraqi . . . Tony Perry, "Insurgents Spark a Fierce Battle in Fallouja," **Los Angeles Times,** April 22, 2004, p. 6.

p. 307   crime was rampant . . . Stu Jones, 1st Mar-Div headquarters, May 9, 2004.

p. 309   the minimum casualties possible . . . David Sanger and Thom Shanker, "Bush's Decision on Possible Attack on Falluja Seems Near," **New York Times,** April 25, 2004.

p. 310   banana trees . . . Jeffrey Gettleman, "The Baathification of Fallujah," **New York Times Magazine,** June 20, 2004, p. 51.

p. 310   demonstrates a level of leadership . . . LtGen Conway, Press Conference at the MEF, May 1, 2004.

CHAPTER 19

p. 335   insurgents understand is violence . . . Tony Perry and Rick Loomis, "Mosque Targeted in Fallouja Fighting," **Los Angeles Times,** April 27, 2004, p. 1.

CHAPTER 20

p. 336   Marines sitting in a cordon . . . LtGen Conway, interview by author, MEF headquarters outside Fallujah, July 24, 2004.

p. 237   someone who can . . . LtGen Conway, Press Conference, Camp Fallujah, May 1, 2004.

p. 338   everything ... John F. Burns, "U.S. Pummels Rebel Positions as Fierce Clash Shakes Falluja," New York Times, April 28, 2004.

p. 338   occupation ... Louis Meixler, "Iraq's Council Chief: U.S. Is at Fault," Philadelphia Inquirer, April 27, 2004.

p. 338   not delivered ... Rajiv Chandrasekaran and Sewell Chan, "Warplanes Pound Sections of Fallujah," Washington Post, April 29, 2004, p. 1.

p. 340   three dozen laser-guided bombs ... Eric Schmitt and Thom Shanker, "A Full Range of Technology Is Applied to Bomb Falluja," New York Times, April 30, 2004, p. A1.

p. 342   was furious ... Alissa J. Rubin and Doyle McManus, "Why America Has Waged a Losing Battle on Fallouja," Los Angeles Times, October 24, 2004.

p. 343   majority ... Michael Rabin, "Losing the Shia," Middle East Quarterly, August 19, 2003.

p. 343   calling the agreement "appeasement" ... Rubin and McManus, "Why America Has Waged a Losing Battle on Fallouja."

p. 344   press and political attention ... CBS 60 Minutes, April 28, 2004.

p. 344   injustices ... James Risen, "G.I.'s Are Accused of Abusing Iraqi Captives," New York Times, April 29, 2004.

p. 345   knowing nothing ... Rajiv Chandrasekaran, "Deal Brings Old Uniforms Back in Style," Washington Post, May 7, 2004, p. A1.

p. 345   poisonous ... Rajiv Chandrasekaran, "Mistakes Loom Large as Handover Nears,"**Washington Post,** June 20, 2004, p. A1.

p. 346   there's a disconnect ... Rajiv Chandrasekaran, "Marines Plan Handoff to Militia in Falluja," **Washington Post,** April 30, 2004, p. 1.

p. 346   Ad hoc ... Rajiv Chandrasekaran, "Deal Brings Old Uniforms Back in Style," **Washington Post,** May 7, 2004, p. A1.

p. 346   Latif as "conversations going on" ... Tony Perry, Jeffrey Fleishman, and Patrick J. McDonnell, "Fallouja Pullout May Be in Works," **Los Angeles Times,** April 30, 2004, p. 1.

p. 347   from Baghdad to the Beltway ... LtGen Conway, Press Conference, MEF headquarters, May 1, 2004.

p. 347   Fox News ... Gen Myers, interview by Chris Wallace, May 2, 2004, Fox News.

p. 347   a strong fight in there ... Katarina Kratovac, "Marines Hand Over Falluja to Iraqis," **Star and Stripes,** Mideast ed., May 2, 2004, p. 3.

p. 348   here to free them ... John Kifner, "The Marines Enter Falluja, With Peace Their Aim," **New York Times,** May 11, 2004, p. A12.

p. 348   They know the populace ... John Kifner and Ian Fisher, "U.S. Weighs Falluja Pullback, Leaving Patrols to Iraq Troops," **New York Times,** April 30, 2004, p. 1.

p. 348   grated ... Alissa J. Rubin and Doyle McManus, "**Why America Has Waged a Losing Battle on Fallouja,**" **Los Angeles Times,** October 24, 2004, p. A1.

p. 348   went in . . . Agence France-Presse, "Some Marines Angry over Deal to Pull Out of Fallujah," Patrick Moser, April 30, 2004.

p. 348   killed . . . Ibid.

p. 349   parts of the conversation . . . LtGen Conway, Press Conference, MEF headquarters, May 1, 2004.

p. 350   just verbal orders. . . . Ibid.

p. 350   catch up . . . Wallace interview, Fox News, May 2, 2004

p. 350   Blackwater atrocities . . . Myers interview, May 2, 2004.

p. 350   succeeded . . . Rajiv Chandrasekaran, "Fallujah Rejoices Amid US Pullback," **Washington Post**, May 2, 2004, p. 1.

p. 350   have not flinched . . . John Kifner, "On or Off? Odd US. Alliance with an Ex-Hussein General," **New York Times**, May 3, 2004.

p. 351   many of these men . . . Jeffrey Gettleman, "The Re-Baathification of Falluja," **New York Times Sunday Magazine**, June 20, 2004, p. 55.

p. 351   their city . . . Interview by author, MEF headquarters, July 24, 2004.

CHAPTER 21

p. 359   music blared . . . Dah Jamali, "Falluja Rebels, Residents Celebrate Victory over US Marines," **New Standard**, June 15, 2004.

p. 360   everyone was a mujahedeen . . . Christine Hauser and John Kifner, "Falluja District Begins to

Relax as Iraqi Force Patrols the Streets," **New York Times,** May 10, 2004.

p. 360   out of politics . . . Dexter Filkins, "Falluja Pullout Left Haven of Insurgents, Officials Say," **New York Times,** July 8, 2004, p. 1.

p. 360   shared responsibility . . . President Bush speech at Army War College, May 24, 2004.

p. 361   approval rating . . . Washington Post Web, about.com, May 15, 2004.

p. 361   highest monthly total . . . http:// icasualties.org/oif/, April 2004.

p. 361   clearly saved a lot of lives . . . Thom Shanker, "U.S. Shifts Focus in Iraq to Aiding New Government," **New York Times,** June 1, 2004.

p. 361   mantra . . . Tony Perry, Patrick J. McDonnell, and Alissa J. Rubin, "Deadly April Battle Became a Turning Point for Fallouja," **Los Angeles Times,** May 17, 2004, p. 1.

p. 362   150 air strikes . . . RCT 1 air officer computer records, RCT 1 ops center, May 7, 2004.

p. 362   between 35,000 and 45,000 civilians . . . Rachel Jordan, "Dresden: An Allied Air Raid with Axis Tactics," **Stones from the River,** at meredith.edu, October 23, 2004.

p. 363   posted a video . . . BBC News, "Zarqawi Beheaded US Man," May 13, 2004.

p. 363   bloody torso . . . See Nicholas Berg, Wikipedia. org.

p. 364   outsiders . . . Press conference at the Falluja Liaison Center, May 20, 2004.

p. 364   murderous bastards . . . Ibid.

p. 364 **more defeats** . . . Testimony before Congress, May 21, 2004, quoted in **Project for the New American Century,** May 24, 2004.

p. 364 **reporters** . . . Daniel Williams, "Reporting Under the Gun in an Ambush Zone," **Washington Post** Foreign Service, June 8, 2004, p. C1.

p. 365 **joined them** . . . Daniel Williams, "Despite Agreement, Insurgents Rule Fallujah," **Washington Post** Foreign Service, June 7, 2004, p. A15.

p. 365 **mess with** . . . Laura King, "Insurgents and Islam Now Rulers of Fallouja," **Los Angeles Times,** June 13, 2004.

p. 365 **sharia** . . . Ibid.

p. 365 **haircuts** . . . Associated Press, "Hardline Islamic Leaders Assert Power in Falluja," May 26, 2004.

p. 366 **latest haul** . . . Major David Bellon, e-mail to author, September 18, 2004.

p. 366 **trickled into** . . . Fooad Al Sheikhly and Jeffrey Gettleman, "Iraqi Official Says U.S. Raid Aimed to Kill Foreign Rebels," **New York Times,** June 21, 2004, p. A9.

p. 366 **liberated city** . . . Dahr Jamail, "Falluja, Pacified," **New Standard,** June 3, 2004.

p. 366 **for ransom** . . . Sameer N. Yacoub, "Fallujah Police Accused of Giving Up Shiite Truckers to Sunni Executioners," CNN NEWS, June 15, 2004.

p. 366 **disemboweled** . . . Hannah Allam, "Extremism Sweeping Iraq Among Sunni, Shiite Muslims Alike," azcentral.com, June 15, 2004.

p. 366 communards . . . Alistair Horne, **Seven Ages of Paris** (New York: Vintage Books, 2004), p. 262.

p. 367 Zarqawi . . . Edward Worg and James Glanz, "South Korean Worker Is Beheaded by Iraqi Terrorists," **New York Times,** June 23, 2004, p. A11.

p. 367 Sun-il . . . See Kim Sun-il, Wikipedia.org.

p. 367 supposition . . . Daniel Williams, "Despite Agreement, Insurgents Rule Fallujah," **Washington Post,** June 7, 2004.

p. 368 thirty bombings . . . Michael Rubin, "The Fallujah Problem: A Job That Needs Doing," **National Review,** June 25, 2004.

p. 368 against safe houses . . . Associated Press, "Large Explosions Rock Falluja," June 22, 2004.

p. 368 executing fourteen . . . Borzou Daragahi, "Fallujah Ruled Taliban-style: Liquor, Pop Music Banned by Militants Who Are Taking Control of Iraqi City," **Pittsburgh Post-Gazette,** June 24, 2004.

CHAPTER 22

p. 375 faint heartbeat . . . Damien McElroy, "New Iraqi Police Fight US Troops Who Trained Them," **Daily Telegraph,** June 27, 2004.

p. 375 all-day battle . . . Edward Cody, "Scores Killed as Insurgents Launch Attacks Across Iraq," **Washington Post,** June 24, 2004.

p. 375 bombs . . . Naseer Al-Nahr, Al Jazeera, July 7, 2004.

p. 376   right direction... Dexter Filkins, "Fallujah Pullout Left Haven of Insurgents, Officials Say," New York Times, July 8, 2004, p. A1.

p. 376   worst place... CNN, **CNN Presents: Countdown to Handover of Iraq**, June 27, 2004, transcript.

p. 376   vipers... **Los Angeles Times,** October 24, 2004.

p. 376   fiefdoms... Ghaith Abdul-Ahad, "Fallujah Is Calm by the Time I Arrive," **Weekend Australian,** July 3, 2004.

p. 376   new jihadists... Michael Ware, "Meet the New Jihad," **Time,** June 27, 2004.

p. 377   incubator... Edward Cody, "Sunni Resistance to US Presence Hardens," **Washington Post,** July 7, 2004, p. A1.

p. 377   massive force... Jack Fairweather reporting from Baghdad for the **Telegraph** (UK), July 3, 2004.

p. 377   electrician... Hamza Hendawi, "Insurgent-held Fallujah Was Under Sway of Local Electrician and Mosque Imam," Associated Press, November 24, 2004.

p. 377   upscale compound... Anthony Shadid, "Sunni Cleric Says Fallujah Attracted Hundreds of Recruits," **Washington Post,** December 12, 2004, p. A32.

p. 377   Zarqawi took him... Charles Crain, "Iraqi Leader Authorizes U.S. Strike in Fallujah," USA Today, July 19, 2004, p. 6.

p. 378   Islamic Emirate... Pepe Escobar, "The

Islamic Emirate of Fallujah," **Asia Times,** July 16 and 31, 2004.

p. 380   under way . . . James Glanz and Erik Eckholm, "Reality Intrudes on Promises of Rebuilding Iraq," **New York Times,** June 30, 2004, p. A1.

p. 380   four thousand . . . Rajiv Chandrasekaran, "Demise of Iraqi Units Symbolic of U.S. Errors," **Washington Post,** September 25, 2004, p. A1.

p. 381   Decisions about Fallujah . . . Gregg Zoroya, "If Ramadi Falls, 'Province Goes to Hell,' " **USA Today,** July 11, 2004, pp. 31, 1A.

p. 382   31 killed . . . Ibid.

p. 382   284 wounded . . . Lawrence W. Korb and Nigel Holmes, "Two Years and Counting," **New York Times,** March 20, 2005, p A13.

Overall, the Marines comprised 20 percent of the American personnel in Iraq and had suffered 30 percent of the fatalities. Contrary to the myth that the poor, the minorities, and the uneducated do the fighting for America, 95 percent of the fallen had graduated from high school, 75 percent were white, 11 percent Hispanic, and 9 percent African American—numbers that roughly reflect the population as a whole.

p. 383   scared away . . . Gideon Long, "Iraq's Road to Reconstruction Studded with Potholes," Reuters, February 23, 2005.

p. 383   any alarm . . . Pamela Hess, "Ramadi Posts Seen as 'Symbol of Occupation,' " United Press International, August 19, 2004.

p. 384 Al Jazeera's office ... Hassan M. Fattah, "The Arab Media Decide to Focus Coverage on the Voting, Not the Violence," **New York Times,** January 30, 2005, p. A14.

p. 384 police station in Najaf ... Headquarters United States Central Command, August 5, 2004. Release Number 04-08-19.

p. 385 negotiate ... John F. Burns and Sabrina Tavernise, "Iraqi Government Gives Sadr a Final Chance to End Uprising," **New York Times,** August 19, 2004.

p. 387 stolen police cars ... "Najaf Unrest," **Los Angeles Times,** October 2004.

p. 389 pulverized corpse ... Major Bellon, e-mail to author, August 17, 2004.

p. 389 head ... John F. Burns and Erik Eckholm, "In Western Iraq, Fundamentalists Hold U.S. at Bay," **New York Times,** August 29, 2004, p. A1.

p. 390 terror had spawned ... John F. Burns and Erik Eckholm, "In Western Iraq, Fundamentalists Hold U.S. at Bay," **New York Times,** August 29, 2004, p. A1.

p. 390 years to come ... Pamela Hess, "Marines Disband Fallujah Forces," United Press International, August 14, 2004.

p. 390 dealt with accordingly ... Major Bellon, e-mail to author, August 26, 2004.

p. 390 inside the city ... Pamela Hess, "Fallujans May Be Invited into Iraqi Army," United Press International, August 15, 2004.

CHAPTER 23

p. 393 country . . . Craig Whitlock, "Iraqi Soccer Team Pitched Aside by Paraguay in Semis," **Washington Post,** August 25, 2004, p. D1.

p. 394 best people . . . Grant Wahl, "Iraqi Soccer Players Angered by Bush Campaign Ads," **Sports Illustrated,** August 19, 2004.

p. 394 twelve thousand trained . . . Rajiv Chandrasekaran, "Demise of Iraqi Units Symbolic of US Errors," **Washington Post,** September 25, 2004, p. A1.

p. 394 to $6.6 billion . . . David S. Cloud and Greg Jaffe, "US Diplomat Wants More Funds for Iraqi Security," **Wall Street Journal,** August 30, 2004, p. A1.

p. 395 dismembered . . . Rajiv Chandrasekaran, "Allawi Holds Meetings with Insurgents," **Washington Post,** August 30, 2004, p. A1.

p. 399 from scratch . . . Chandrasekaran, "Demise of Iraqi Units Symbolic of U.S. Errors," **Washington Post.**

p. 400 for nothing . . . Stephanie Barry, sbarry@repub.com, September 5, 2004.

p. 400 Jerry L. Durrant . . . Alissa J. Rubin, "Ineffective Iraqi Force in Falluja Disbanded," **Los Angeles Times,** September 11, 2004, p. A1.

p. 400 Rumsfeld . . . Alissa Rubin and Doyle McManus, "Why America Has Waged a Losing Battle on Fallujah," **Los Angeles Times,** October 24, 2004, p. 1.

p. 400 Myers...Press Conference, Pentagon, September 28, 2004.

p. 400 police...Stephen Farrell, "Allawi Lays Down His Law," **Australian**, September 14, 2004, p. 1.

p. 400 CPA did...Ibid.

p. 401 Marine side...UPI, "Only Four in Fallujah Brigade Join US Side," October 11, 2004.

p. 402 cancer of Fallujah...Dexter Filkins, "U.S. Plans Year-End Drive to Take Iraqi Rebel Areas," **New York Times,** September 19, 2004.

p. 404 voted ten to two...Karl Vick, "Fallujah Group Comes to Table," **Washington Post,** October 7, 2004, p. A14.

p. 404 over Zarqawi...F. J. Bing West, "This Time a Fight to the Finish?" **Los Angeles Times,** October 17, 2004.

p. 405 suicide bomber...Associated Press, October 30, 2004.

CHAPTER 24

p. 409 drifting...Beth Gardiner, Associated Press, "Iraq Won't Allow Falluja to Remain Under Insurgent Control," September 30, 2004.

p. 412 martyrs...Bernard Lewis, **What Went Wrong?** (Phoenix Books, 2002), p. 10.

p. 416 playing favorites...The collegial cooperation between the army and Marines, which seemed so normal, had taken a century to achieve. In World War I, concerned that the Marines might emerge as a second army, the revered Army General "Black Jack" Pershing refused to permit Marine units to fight together as a unified division. As World War II drew to a close, relations between the army and Marines in the battle on Okinawa were so bitter that General George C. Marshall pledged that army soldiers would never again fight under a Marine general. In Vietnam the overall commander, General William C. Westmoreland, reported to Washington that he distrusted Marine operations, and his successor, General Creighton Abrams, refused to accept a Marine general as his deputy, accusing the Marines of "inertia" and "pedestrian tactics." See Lewis Sorley, **Thunderbolt: General Creighton Abrams and the Army of His Times** (New York: Simon & Schuster, 1992), pp. 208–209, 390–391.

Vietnam rocked both services to their core, as disgruntled draftees threatened established traditions and discipline. Both services rallied and by the mid-1980s had forged stronger organizations and new war-fighting concepts. In NATO Europe the army championed an Air-Land Doctrine for coordinating massive volumes of firepower to destroy the massive Soviet Army. The Marines, reacting against the search-and-destroy tactics of Vietnam, developed a Maneuver Warfare doctrine that relied upon speed to seize objectives along the world's littorals. Army and Marine officers met to exchange ideas, while Congress passed the Goldwater-Nichols Bill, which transferred power from the Joint Chiefs of Staff to the theater commanders.

The result was that in the first Gulf War in 1991, the CentCom commander, General Norman Schwarzkopf, praised the Marines for the speed of their two-division attack, carried out according to Maneuver Warfare principles. And in April 2003, the march of the 1st Marine Division to Baghdad proceeded with remarkable speed, again applying Maneuver Warfare.

But while the two Gulf Wars (1991 and 2003) erased mutual suspicions between the two services and proved the soundness of joint planning at the high level, each service fought as a separate entity at the division level. During the attack on Baghdad in 2003 the 1st Marine Division, the 82nd Airborne Division, and the 3rd Infantry Division fought in their own individual battle spaces.

In the August battle in Najaf and the November battle for Fallujah, the operational cooperation between the two services reached a new zenith: Marine and army battalions fought side by side.

p. 416   politicized . . . Patrick Cockburn, "Falluja: The Homecoming and the Homeless," **Independent,** December 11, 2004.

p. 416   battalions . . . Order of Battle for Operation Phantom Fury.

p. 419   UAVs . . . Eric Schmitt, "Remotely Controlled Aircraft Crowd Dangerous Iraqi and Afghan Skies," **New York Times,** April 5, 2005, p. A9.

CHAPTER 25

p. 430 surged forward and swept south . . . On the west end of the city Battalion 3/5 led off. At the same time, one kilometer to the east, the tanks and Bradleys of Task Force 2-7 charged south from the railroad station, followed by Battalion 3/1. After relieving pressure on a team from 2nd Force Recon Company, already fighting in the city, 2-7 headed toward Jolan Park. Farther to the east Regimental Combat Team 7 sent an army armored battalion (2-2) through the berm, headed for Highway 10, followed by two Marine infantry battalions (1/8 and 1/3) advancing roughly abreast.

p. 438 wiping . . . Malay's wiper was his three rifle companies advancing abreast, with his executive officer, Major Todd Desgrosseilliers, moving behind the companies with huge D-9 bulldozers to crush shooters trapped in bypassed buildings and engineers to blow the monstrous munitions caches. "We're the old Green Bay Packers sweep," Major Robert Piddock, the operations officer, said. "The opposition knows we're coming, and there's not a damn thing they can do to stop us."

CHAPTER 26

p. 445 Battalion 1/8 . . . "The magnificent bastards" is a sobriquet from its past. At Tarawa in 1944 eight hundred Marines waded across a thousand yards of reef covered by Japanese machine guns; 450 men made it to the beach. See William Manchester, **Goodbye, Darkness: A Memoir of the Pacific War** (Boston: Little, Brown & Co., 1979), p. 239.

p. 449   Marine Corps ROTC . . . The correct technical term is "Navy ROTC with a Marine Corps option," because the U.S. Navy and the U.S. Marine Corps are separate branches of the Department of the Navy. The U.S. Marine Corps is the senior branch, organized by an act of Congress on November 10, 1775.

CHAPTER 28

p. 491   journalist . . . Kevin Sites, "Open Letter to 3/1 Marines," November 17, 2004, www.kevinsites .net.

p. 508   body   parts . . . Jackie Spinner, "Military Believes Zarqawi Headquarters Found," **Washington Post,** November 18, 2004, p. A1.

p. 508   letters from Zarqawi . . . Robert F. Worth and Edward Wong, "House in Fallujah Seems to Have Been Base for Jordanian Terrorist," **New York Times,** November 18, 2004, p. A1.

p. 508   Ford Explorer . . . Jackie Spinner, op. cit., p. 1

p. 509   Zarqawi complex . . . Rowan Scarborough, "U.S. Declares Insurgency 'Broken,'" **Washington Times,** November 19, 2004, p. A1.

p. 509   handed us over . . . John F. Burns, "Tape Condemns Sunni Muslim Clerics," **New York Times,** November 25, 2004, p. A1.

p. 509   75 to 100 buildings . . . Data provided by RCT 1 air officers in ops center at Camp Fallujah, July 28, 2004.

p. 509   main gun rounds . . . Ordnance data provided by division ops center air officers and MEF Lessons Learned team at Camp Fallujah, November 28, 2004.

p. 509   buildings were damaged . . . Ann Scott Tyson, "Increased Security in Fallujah Slows Down Efforts to Rebuild," **Washington Post,** April 19, 2005, p. A15.

p. 509   wounded . . . MEF statistics for Operation Dawn, provided to author on March 21, 2005.

EPILOGUE

p. 511   inches . . . Tony Perry, "Polls Stand Empty in Sunni Stronghold," **Los Angeles Times,** January 31, 2005, p. A1.

p. 512   a year ago . . . Gen Myers, Press Conference, Pentagon, April 26, 2005.

BIBLIOGRAPHY

Abdullah, Thabit, A. J. **A Short History of Iraq: From 636 to the Present.** London: Pearson Longman, 2003.

Atkinson, Rick. **In the Company of Soldiers: A Chronicle of Combat.** New York: Henry Holt & Co., 2004.

Bell, Gertrude. **The Desert and the Sown: The Syrian Adventures of the Female Lawrence of Arabia.** New York: Cooper Square Press, 2001.

Braestrup, Peter. **Big Story: How the American Press and Television Reported and Interpreted the Crisis in Tet 1968 in Vietnam and Washington.** Novato, Calif.: Presidio, 1994.

Bronzi, C. J. **CAAT Concepts.** BLT 2/2, 1998.

Colby, William. **Lost Victory: A Firsthand Account of America's Sixteen-Year Involvement in Vietnam.** Chicago: Contemporary Books, 1989.

DeForest, Orrin, and David Chanoff. **Slow Burn: The Rise and Bitter Fall of American Intelligence in Vietnam.** New York: Simon & Schuster, 1990.

Donovan, David. **Once a Warrior King: Memories of an Officer in Vietnam.** New York: McGraw-Hill, 1985.

Farouk-Sluglett, Marion, and Peter Sluglett. **Iraq Since 1958: From Revolution to Dictatorship.** New York: I.B. Tauris, 2003.

Fernea, Elizabeth Warnock. **Guests of the Sheik: An Ethnography of an Iraqi Village.** New York: Anchor Books, 1969.

Franks, General Tommy with Malcolm McConnell. **American Soldier.** New York: ReganBooks, 2004.

Hiro, Dilip. **The Longest War: The Iran-Iraq Military Conflict.** New York: Routledge, 1991.

Hunt, Richard A. **Pacification: The American Struggle for Vietnam's Hearts and Minds.** San Francisco: Westview Press, 1995.

Kaplan, Robert D. **Imperial Grunts: The American Military on the Ground.** New York: Simon & Schuster, 2005.

Keegan, John. **The Iraq War.** New York: Alfred A. Knopf, 2004.

Lewis, Bernard. **The Assassins: A Radical Sect in Islam.** London: Phoenix, 2004.

———. **The Crisis of Islam: Holy War and Unholy Terror.** New York: Random House, 2004.

Makiya, Kanan. **Cruelty and Silence: War Tyranny, Uprising, and the Arab World.** New York: W. W. Norton & Co., 1993.

————. **Republic of Fear: The Politics of Modern Iraq.** Los Angeles: University of California Press, 1998.

Manchester, William. **Goodbye, Darkness: A Memoir of the Pacific War.** Boston: Little, Brown & Co., 1979.

Metzner, Edward P. **More Than a Soldier's War: Pacification in Vietnam.** College Station: Texas A&M University Press, 1995.

Oberdorfer, Don. **TET! The Turning Point in the Vietnam War.** Baltimore: Johns Hopkins University Press, 1971.

Pax, Salam. **The Clandestine Diary of an Ordinary Iraqi.** New York: Grove Press, 2003.

Peterson, Michael E. **The Combined Action Platoons: The U.S. Marines' Other War in Vietnam.** New York: Praeger, 1989.

Roux, Georges. **Ancient Iraq.** London: Penguin Books, 1992.

Sasson, Jean. **Mayada, Daughter of Iraq: One Woman's Survival Under Saddam Hussein.** New York: Dutton, 2003.

Shulimson, Jack. **U.S. Marines in Vietnam 1968.** Washington: History and Museums Division, U.S. Marine Corps, 1997.

Souza, Corinne. **Baghdad's Spy: A Personal Memoir of Espionage and Intrigue from Iraq to London.** London: Mainstream, 2003.

Tripp, Charles. **A History of Iraq.** Cambridge, U.K.: Cambridge University Press, 2002.

U.S. Marine Corps Small Wars Manual. Washington: U.S. Government Printing Office, 1940.

Valentine, Douglas. **The Phoenix Program.** Lincoln, Neb.: Backinprint.com, 1990.

Wallach, Janet. **Desert Queen.** New York: Anchor Books, 1999.

Woodward, Bob. **Bush at War.** New York: Simon & Schuster, 2002.

————. **Plan of Attack.** New York: Simon & Schuster, 2004.

Zinsmeister, Karl. **Boots on the Ground: A Month with the 82nd Airborne in the Battle for Iraq.** New York: Truman Talley Books, St. Martin's Press, 2003.

————. **Dawn over Baghdad: How the U.S. Military Is Using Bullets and Ballots to Remake Iraq.** San Francisco: Encounter Books, 2004.

Zucchino, David. **Thunder Run: The Armored Strike to Capture Baghdad.** New York: Atlantic Monthly Press, 2004.

ACKNOWLEDGMENTS

FROM THE TIME SADDAM FELL IN April 2003
through the Iraqi election in January 2005, twenty
American and four Iraqi battalions battled in and
around Fallujah. In preparing this book, I made five
trips to that city, spending about five months with
many of the battalions. Over the course of sixteen
months, I interviewed or observed at close hand on
operations more than seven hundred soldiers and
Marines in the Fallujah area. Many interviews extended over weeks, and the Internet was a tremendous tool for checking back about firefights and
battles. As word spread, I received a steady stream of
e-mails from soldiers and Marines, some poignant,
some hilarious, and all filled with that cocky grunt
spirit that pervades American infantry battalions.

Regrettably, sheer space and the demands of narra-
tive coherence made it impossible to include many of

the stories or to write of every unit. Mr. John Ripley and the Marine Corps Historical Division are hard at work writing the definitive accounts of Najaf and Fallujah, to include all units in those battles.

Mr. John Flicker of Bantam Books performed an absolutely superb job as editor. A former scout team leader in the 82nd Airborne with a strong work ethic, Flicker worked tirelessly to trim and shape this book. My agent, Dan Mandel, provided, per usual, sage advice.

And special thanks are due to Janet Biehl for the careful copyediting and to Betsy Regan for constant encouragement and valued critiques of the draft manuscript.

WITH APPRECIATION

LtCol Abbas
Col Mohamed
LtCol Abas
LCpl Christopher Abeita
Lt Bryan Abell
Mr Khalid Aboud
1/Lt Elliot Ackerman
LCpl Thomas Adametz
LtCol John Adams
Maj Adham
Mr Ahmed
Capt Hamed Alaysh
LCpl Merardo Alcaraz
HM2 Philip Alexanian
Col Saad Al-Harbia
LtCol Muhamed Ali
   Hussein
LtCol Almaleky
Capt Steven Alvarez
Cpl Steven Andaluz
Mr Gary Anderson
LCpl Jeremiah Anderson
LCpl Eduardo Arias
Lt Douglas Arugman
LCpl Patrick Ashby
Mr Frank Atkins
Sgt Juan Avalos
Capt Mark Baaden
Capt John Bailey

Capt Timothy Bairstow
Mr. William Bajr
Col Gil Baldwin
Col Tom Baltazar
1/Lt David Bam
Capt Banning
Col Jesse Barker
Maj Bartlett
Capt Paul J. Batty
Lt Glen Bayliss
LCpl Steven Beasley
LCpl Craig Bell
SgtMaj Wayne R. Bell
Major David Bellon
LCpl Omar Beltran
SgtMaj Michael D. Berg
Capt Theodore
   Bethay II
2/Lt Joshua Biggers
Sgt Brian Bishop
Cpt Ed Bitanga II
Amb Robert Blackwill
Mr Josh Boehm
SgtMaj James Booker
Mr Max Boot
Sgt Sean Bourier
CWO Roy Bourne
Maj Russell Boyce
Pfc Bernard Boykin

1/Sgt David L. Bradford
1/Lt Barret Bradstreet
Capt Bragg
SSgt Jason Branch
LtCol Gary Brandl
Amb L. Paul Bremer
Capt Brickheiser
LtCol George Bristol
Sgt Justin Britt
1/Sgt Matthew
   Broadshire
1/Lt Casey Brock
SSgt Jon Brodin
Capt Christopher Bronzi
CWO Robert Brooks
Capt Greg T. Brown
Lt Colin Browning
Pvt Jason Bruseno
Col Arthur Buck
LtCol Nicholas
   Buckerwicz
LtCol Willie Buhl
Lt Joshua Burgess
Gov Kareem Burgis
Pfc Daniel Burkart
Capt Michael Butler
LtCol Brennan T. Byrne
Maj Caja
Lt JD Campbell
Sgt Ronald Campbell
SSgt Trevor Candelin

Sgt Timothy Canfield
Sgt Phillip Cantrell
Sgt Miguel Cantu
LtCol Dominic
   Caracclio
Capt Ted Card
Cpl Raymond Carroll
SgtMaj Randall Carter
Gen George W. Casey
Cpl Jonathan Cashman
Cpl Matthew Casler
Gunny Ishmael Castillo
CWO Caudall
1/Lt Nathan Chandler
LCpl Marcos Cherry
Maj Chessani
Sgt Jason Chilson
CWO Albert
   Christianson
Capt Brett Clark
HM3 Adam Clayton
Maj Joseph R. Clearfield
Cpl James Click
Col Nick Clissett
Sgt Damien Coan
Cpl Michael Cochran
1/Lt Thomas Cogan IV
Dr. Eliot Cohen
CWO Bernard Coleman
SSgt Patrick Coleman
CWO Chuck Colleton

Sgt Christopher
  Collette
Maj Kevin Collins
Capt Ben Connable
Col Buck Connor
Cpl Timothy Connors
Cpl Thomas Conroy
LtGen James Conway
SPC Neal Cooper
LCpl Bryan Costello
LCpl Ty Cotton
CWO Gene Coughlin
Capt Kevin Coughlin
CWO Crandall
Sgt Sean Crane
Dr Colin Crickard
CWO Anthony
  Crutcher
Cpl Jose Cruz
Gunny James Cully
Capt Aaron M.
  Cunningham
Maj Hugh Curtright
Cpl Jonathan Cushman
Capt Phil Cushman
Sgt Timothy Cyparski
LCpl Robert Daniels
1/Lt Matt Danner
Capt Jesse Davidson
Maj Chris Davis
1/Lt Ben Deda

Capt Jason Deel
LCpl Vincent Degani
1/Sgt Patrick I.
  DeHerrera
Capt Michael
  DelPalazzo
Capt Vincent Delpedio
HM3 Tyronne Dennis
Mr Robert Derocher
Maj Todd
  Desgrosseilliers
Fr William Devine
Maj Mark DeVito
1/Lt Ben Diaz
LtCol Victor Didra
Col Thomas Dietrich
1/Lt Frank Dillbeck
Maj Christopher Dixon
1/Lt David Dobb
LtCol Dan Donohue
SSgt Michael Drake
LtCol Brian Drinkwine
SPC Khaled Dudin
1/Lt Ian Duncan
BG Joseph Dunford
HM3 Jason R. Duty
1/Lt Anthony Eanarelli
CWO Ebrey
Capt Jamie Edge
Cpl Eric Egging
MajGen Karl Eikenberry

1/Sgt Andreas Elesky
Dr Ashraf Ellassal
LtCol Elliott
Maj Kyle Ellison
Sheik Favah Ensabah
SSgt Antwan Epstar
Cpt Bret Erwin
Capt Bryant Esteves
Lt Ziad Fakhoury
1/Sgt Steven Fantan
SSgt Johnny Faradjian
Maj Peter Farnum
Maj Mike Fenzel
SSgt David Fergusen
Cpl Cameron Ferguson
Cpl Juan Fernandez
LCpl Derek Fetterolf
LCpl Mason Fisher
Mr John Flicker
LCpl John Paul Flores
Maj Foay
Sgt Jennifer Forman
CWO Stanley Foster
SgtMaj Philip Freed
Lt Kevin Frost
1/Sgt Derek Fry
Sgt Terry Fullerton
Sgt Timothy Funke
1/Lt David Funkhouser
Capt Mike Gaines
LCpl Josh Galbreath

SSgt Andrew Garcia
Capt Jer Garcia
Capt Ken Gardner
LCpl Zac Garland
Cpl Daniel Gattoni
Capt Robert George
Sgt David Gettemeir
1/Lt Brian Gibbons
Maj Greg Gillette
Maj Brian Gilman
LCpl Brian Gilmore
LCpl Steven Gips
1/Lt Joshua Glover
LCpl Graham Golden
LCpl Carlos Gomez
LCpl Aaron Gordon
Capt Brad Gordon
Capt Kurt Gordon
Mr Michael Gordon
Sgt Jonathan Graham
Lt Jesse Grapes
LCpl Toby Gray
Capt Greely
Sgt Michael Green
Cpl Stuart Greenfield
SSgt Willie Gresham
Lt Col Michael Groen
1/Lt Jon Gross
1/Sgt Gerardo Gueta
Sgt Jose Guillen
LCpl Carl Gulevian

Sgt Carlos Gutierrez
Maj Dave Habbrill
Gunny Matthew
  Hackett
Capt Abu Hadi
MstSgt Daniel Hakala
SSgt Clint Hale
Pfc Deryk Hallel
1/Sgt Hamid
Capt William Handricks
LCpl Chris Hankins
Mr Youness Hansali
SSgt Jeffrey Harper
Maj David Harrill
Capt Dom Harris
CWO Richard Harris
LtCol Scott Hartsell
Cpl James Harwin
SSgt Hussein Hassan
  Lafta
LtCol Hatim Jassim
LtCol Muhamed Hatim
LCpl Robert Haviland
LCpl Chris Hawkins
LCpl Nathan Haynie
Cpl Mandwell Hearn
Capt Brian G.
  Heatherman
BG Dennis J. Hejuk
1/Lt John Helfinstine
Cpl Brain Hemmelgarn

Capt William Hendricks
Col Pat Henry
LCpl Richardo
  Hernandez
1/Lt John Hessner
LCpl Michael Hibbert
Sgt Jack Hightower
Cpl Caleb Hocking
Maj Ronald P. Holden
LCpl Lane Holmes
Sgt Allen Holt
1/Lt Jake Hoo
LtCol Hooks
SgtMaj David Howell
LCpl George Hruby
LtCol Ken Hubbard
HM3 Herman Huerta
Col Frank Hull
Mr Hussein
Maj Hussey
1/Lt Joe Iams
Maj Muhamed Ibrahim
1/Lt Joel Imans
1/Lt Zachary Iscol
Mr Jamal Jaafar
LtCol Jabar
Maj Lance Jackola
SSgt Jonathan D.
  Jackson
LtCol Richard Jackson
Cpl Samuel Jackson

Mr. Gilbert Jacob
Lt John Jacobs
Chief Muhammad
 Jaddan
Sgt Jason James
2/Lt Joshua Jamison
Capt Joseph Jasper
CWO Winston Jaugan
Mr Nate Jensen
Capt Timothy Jent
SSgt PJ Jerka
1/Lt Oscar Jimenez
Fhaer Al Joher
Lt Robert L. Johnessee
Capt Shannon Johnson
Cpl Joseph Johnston
GNY Daniel Jonas
2/Lt Gregory Jones
Mr Stuart Jones
LCpl Ronald E. Jones Jr.
Sgt Jesse Jordon
LCpl Jose Juarez
1/Lt Razied Zouad
 Kadem
Capt Stephen Kahn
Maj Larry Kaifesh
1/Lt Stephen Karabin
1/Sgt Brad Kasal
Capt Kasprzy
SSgt Christopher Kelly
Capt John Kelly

BG John F. Kelly
LtCol Paul Kennedy
LCpl Ryan Kennelly
LCpl Jesse Kettner
LtCol Gyles Keyser
Sgt Raphip Khadim
Capt Saleem Khan
Mr John Kifner
1/Sgt Klecko
CWO Kline
1/1/1/Lt Eric Knapp
Cpl Richard Koci
SSgt Sean Kohlmeyer
BG Richard S. Kramlich
LtCol James G. Kyser
SFC Michael Lahoda
CSM Bryant C. Lambert
Maj David Lane
LCpl Daniel Laskowski
Col James Lasswell
LtGen Muhamed Latif
Maj Byron Lawson
1/Lt Matthew Leclair
1/Lt Andrew Lee
1/Lt David Lee
LtCol Michael J. Lee
Maj Leonard
LtCol Clarke Lethin
LCpl Daniel Ligon
1/Lt James Lindler
HN Benjamin Liotta

SSgt Jeremy Lirette
Sgt Deverson Lochard
Maj Mark Lombardo
Sgt Manuel Lopez
1/Sgt Richard Lopez
Sgt Todd Luginbuhl
LCpl Ricardo Lulves
Capt Tony Lumpkin
Mr William Luti
MSgt Lynch
Maj TJ MacDonald
Cpl Chris MacIntosh
1/Sgt Alphonso Mack
Sgt Jose Magana
Sgt Lawrence Magnani
2/Lt Joseph Maher
1/Lt Majil
LtCol Pat Malay
LCpl Nicholas
  Maldonado
Mr Dan Mandel
Cpl Chris Mandia
Col Mike Manske
LCpl Gabriel Manzo
Cpl David Marksberry
SSgt Peter Marrufo
Col Nick Marshall
1/Lt Carl Martinez
HM2 Early Matthew
MajGen James Mattis
LtCol John Mayer

Mr Dobie McArthur
SSgt Dennis McCarthy
Cpl Matt McCauley
LtCol Bryan P. McCoy
CWO Randall
  McCrumb
CWO Paul McElearney
Maj Brandon McGowan
1/Lt Douglas McGowan
LCpl Jordan McGuire
Cpl Jared McKenzie
SSgt Johnny McKnight
Cpl Sean McLane
Mr. Doyle McManus
LtCol Colin McNiece
Capt Andrew McNulty
LCpl James McQuoid
Mr Ron Meese
Lt Robert Merrillo
Sgt Abdul Merulik
Cpl Darrell Justin Mesa
Sgt Cantu Miguel
Maj Andrew Milburn
1/Sgt Alan Miller
Maj Fred Miller
Sgt Jeremy Miller
Mr Keith Mines
LtCol Hector Mirabile
CWO Carl Mirarchi
Cpl Stosh Modrow
Sgt Winston Molina

LtCol Steve Moniz
SSgt Colin Moore
Capt Jeff Moore
Capt Roy Moore
Col Tracy Moore
Cpl Albert Morales
SSgt Moreno
SSgt Samuel Mortimer
Cpl Christopher Moss-
  Warrington
HM2 Victor Moyer
Lt Michael Mroszczak
Col Jim Mulvenna
Capt Brian Mulvihill
SSgt Pete Munefo
Capt Mark Murphy
Mr Arthur Murphy
LCpl Kenneth Myhre
LCpl Alexander Navarro
Sgt John Neary
Capt Arturo Neely
Maj Brian Neil
Cpl William Nelson
LtCol John Neumann
LtCol Pete Newell
LCol Randy Newman
LCpl Roland Newton
LCpl Millton Nieto
1/Lt Nofan
1/Lt James Nolan
Maj Jasim Nooman

Maj Kevin Norton
1/Lt Knox Nunally
Sgt Shane Nylin
LtCol Dan O'Donohue
SSgt John O'Keefe
Cpl Matthew O'Brien
LtCol Gregg P. Olson
LCpl David Omalia
PFC Garrett Opper
LCpl Darius Ortiz
Sgt Hector Osorio
LtGen Jeffrey W. Oster
Maj Soutsana Ounkham
Lt Jerry Parchman
1/Sgt Roger Parker
Sgt Thomas Parks
LCpl Tacoma Parris
1/Lt Wes Pass
CWO William Paulino
LCpl Michael Payne
Mr Tony Perry
LtGen Dave Petraeus
Maj Andrew Petrucci
1/Lt John Pettinelli
Maj Robert Piddock
Maj John Piedmont
Chaplin Stephen Pike
SSgt Richard Pillsbury
MSgt Pinkham
LCpl Andrew Pizzutelli
Cpl Ethan Place

Sgt Abelardo Planas
SgtMaj Dave Plaster
LCpl Ben Poester
MSgt Rashed Qawasimi
Cpl Shane Quarino
LCpl Kevin Quihuis
1/Lt Erik Quist
Capt Mou Racid
LtCol James Rainey
Cpl Jose Ramirez
Gunny Eduardo Ramos
LtCol Michael Ramos
Capt George Ramsey
Maj Kelly Ramshur
Sgt Jeremiah Randle
CWO Tracy Reddish
Ms Elizabeth Regan
LtCol Austin E.
    Renforth
LCpl Nicholas Renkosik
SSgt Joseph Reno
SSgt Joseph Repazzo
SgtMaj Rudy Resto
LCpl Robert Reynolds
Capt Brad Richardson
Maj Brian Richardson
LCpl Robert Robinson
SSgt Larry Robles
Sgt Randall Rockman
SSgt Damien Rodriguez
SSgt George Rogers

Sgt Jesus Romero
Capt Sam Rosales
Capt Kelly D. Royer
Secy Donald R.
    Rumsfeld
LCpl Jon Rymes
Col Saadd
1/Lt Sabah
LCpl Jonathan
    Salisibarra
Sgt Roneil Sampson
Sgt Alberto Sanchez
Capt Dennis Sanchez
Capt Douglas Sanders
SSgt Daniel Santiago
1st Sgt Jose Santiago
Sgt Romeo Santiago
LtGen John F. Sattler
LCpl Jeremy Saucier
Capt Morgan Savage
Maj Thomas Savage
Capt Walker Savage
1/Lt Sean Schickel
Ssgt Blaine Schlagetoer
Dr James R. Schlesinger
HM3 Brandon Schwartz
CWO Justin Scott
1/Lt Rob Scott
Lt Matthew Seekers
SSgt Scott Sherman
Capt Don Shove

Col Michael Shupp
1/Lt Brian Sitko
Capt Mike Skaggs
1/Sgt William Skiles
LtCol Phil Skuta
Cpl Garrett Slawatych
LCpl John Sleight
MSgt Smallberg
Capt David Smay
CWO Ben H. Smith
Cpl Eric Smith
LCpl Ian Smith
Capt Jason E. Smith
1/Lt Rob Smith
Col Jefforey Smith
1/Lt Carter Smyth
Capt Rich Snead
1/Lt Jason Snyder
Capt Blair Sokol
MajGen Jasem Soleh
Capt Terry Sommer
Dr Kenneth Son
1/Lt John Soto
Cpl Ted Stanton
1/Lt John Stephens
SSgt James Stevens
1/Lt Stiko
Capt Kyle Stoddard
Pfc Sean Stokes
SSgt Michael Stout
Mr Ian Strachan

Mr Chris Straub
LtCdr Joseph Stricklin
HM2 John L. Strough
LtCol Stuka
Maj Michael Styskal
LtCol Suleiman
Capt Ed Sullivan
Maj Anthony Swann
LtCol Rory E.
   Talkington
1/Sgt Harrison Tanksley
Fr Conrad Targonski
Maj Michael Targos
SSgt Francisco Tataje
Sgt Guy Tchoumba
Dr Ali Thamir
Lt Steven Thomas
Mr Jim Thomas
1/Lt John Thomas
Maj Geoffrey Thome
1/Lt Steve Thompson
Cpl Samuel Topara
Col John Toolan
Capt Wyath Towle
Cpl Brandon Traub
Sgt Daniel Tremore
LCpl Joe Trotter
Col Craig Tucker
BG Turham
PFC Todd Tviede
Maj Unkum

LCpl Aaron Ustin
1/Lt Vincent Valdes
LCpl Rafael Valencia
Sgt Jose Vasquez
Capt William Vaughan
Maj Jorge Velasquez
SSgt Marwin Vest
Cpl Vesterman
1/Lt Bill Vesterman
SSgt Anthony Villa
LCpl Robert Villalobos
2/Lt Ben P. Wagner
1/Lt Curtis Walker
Cpt Jason Walker
Maj Timothy Walker
HM Everett Watt
Mr Matt Waxman
SSgt Travis Wease
Capt Rob Weiler
Cpl Stanley Weingart
1/Lt Lucas Wells
Maj Douglas Welt
LtCol Eric Wesley
Capt Owen West
Capt Brad Weston
LCpl Andrew White
CWO Stuart White

SSgt Roy Whitener
LCpl Andrew Wike
LCpl Charles Williams
Sgt Michael Williams
Cpl Joseph Willis
LtCol Dan Wilson
LCpl Daniel Wilson
Gunny David Wilson
Gunny Robert Wilson
1/Sgt Curtis Winfree
Maj Mark Winn
Dr Paul D. Wolfowitz
SPC Annette Wood
CWO Mark J.
   Woodward
Maj Michael Wyley
LCpl Kip Yeager
Cpl Michael Yerena
1/Lt Robert Croft
   Young
Mr Azad Yousef
Sgt Jarid Zabaldo
Maj Michael Zacchea
Capt Douglas Zembiec
Capt Auda Ziboun
CWO Jerry Zimmerman
HM3 Michael Zobec

ABOUT THE AUTHOR

———

F. J. BING WEST is the author of the award-winning **The March Up: Taking Baghdad with the United States Marine Corps** (Bantam, 2003). **The March Up** was chosen by the U.S. Marine Corps Heritage Foundation for the General Greene Award for Nonfiction in 2004 and also won the Colby Award for Military History. West also wrote the Vietnam classic, **The Village,** about a Marine squad that lived in a village for 485 days. **No True Glory** is based on six extended trips to Iraq and hundreds of interviews. Universal Studios has purchased the film rights to the book. West and his son Owen, also a Marine, are writing the screenplay. His articles have appeared in **Slate,** the **Los Angeles Times,** the **New York Times,** and the **Wall Street Journal.**

A graduate of Georgetown and Princeton universities, West served in the Marine infantry in Vietnam and as Assistant Secretary of Defense for International Security Affairs in the Reagan administration. He is a member of the Council on Foreign Relations and St. Crispin's Order of the Infantry. He appears regularly on **The News Hour** and Fox News. West lives in Newport, RI. Visit his Web site at www.westwrite.com.

INDEX